Social and Cognitive Treatment of Children and Adolescents

Practical Strategies for Problem Behaviors

Richard P. Barth

Social and Cognitive Treatment of Children and Adolescents

Jossey-Bass Publishers

San Francisco   •   London   •   1986

SOCIAL AND COGNITIVE TREATMENT OF CHILDREN AND ADOLESCENTS
Practical Strategies for Problem Behaviors
   by Richard P. Barth

Copyright © 1986 by: Jossey-Bass Inc., Publishers
                     433 California Street
                     San Francisco, California 94104
                               &
                     Jossey-Bass Limited
                     28 Banner Street
                     London EC1Y 8QE

Library of Congress Cataloging in Publication Data

Barth, Richard P. (date)
   Social and cognitive treatment of children and
adolescents.

   (The Jossey Bass social and behavioral science series)
   Bibliography: p. 443
   Includes index.
   1. Social work with children—United States.
2. Social work with youth—United States.   3. Problem
children—Counseling of—United States.   I. Title.
II. Series.
HV741.B3   1986   362.7′4′0973   85-45899
ISBN 0-87589-675-8

The individually tailored rating scale for assessing anger that
appears in Chapter Six is adapted by permission from A.
Spirito, A. J. Finch, Jr., T. L. Smith, and W. H. Cooley,
"Stress Inoculation for Anger and Anxiety Control: A Case
Study with an Emotionally Disturbed Boy." *Journal of Clinical
Child Psychology*, 1981, *10*, Table 1.

Manufactured in the United States of America

The paper in this book meets the guidelines for
permanence and durability of the Committee on
Production Guidelines for Book Longevity of the
Council on Library Resources.

JACKET DESIGN BY WILLI BAUM

FIRST EDITION

Code 8606

The Jossey-Bass
Social and Behavioral Science Series

To my mother and father,
Gary and Marilyn Piccione,
with limitless affection,
appreciation, and admiration

Preface

Children and youth, their friends, siblings, and schoolmates are the central characters of this book. Parents, teachers, social workers, and counselors fill the supporting roles. The setting is the realm of children and parents: the home, family, school, neighborhood, workplace, clinic, and treatment center. The drama arises from changes in the lives of the central characters and in their settings. The tale is cheerful during moments of harmony and togetherness but dreary when the characters are troubled and each struggles privately in his or her own setting. This book was written to improve the ending of the story for children and youth.

For nearly a century, social workers, psychologists, psychiatrists, and educators have endeavored to help troubled children, youth, and their families in various settings. More recently, child-helping professionals began to emphasize research-based practice and to stress the accountability of practitioners' helping efforts. This emphasis has evolved from educators' and practitioners' growing recognition that traditional ways of working with children and youth have too often been ineffective. Through these efforts, practitioner-researchers in social work, education, psychiatry, and psychology are amassing and testing new techniques for helping children and youth that draw on research about social and cognitive contributors to normative and problem behavior. These emerging social and cognitive methods promise to increase practitioners' ability to ameliorate problems of impulsivity, aggressiveness, school phobia and nonattendance, depression, suicide, and stealing, to name only a few. These methods rely on the same data-based approach used by an earlier generation of behavior modifiers, but also include treatment strategies capitalizing on children's cognitive styles and the importance of their social contexts. These techniques should help reverse practitioners' frustration and the negative reviews of outcome studies on treatment of children. This book concerns these techniques and their use in community settings.

I have endeavored to provide readers with practical and clear guidance for using new social and cognitive methods on behalf of children. The relevance of these techniques will be apparent to professionals who provide group care, family therapy, child therapy, school-based services, and consultation to other professionals and nonprofessionals. Professionals who work with seriously troubled children—including psychologists, regular and special educators, social workers, marriage and family counselors, group care providers, speech therapists, guidance counselors, and psychiatrists—will find treatment strategies that expand their current repertoires.

In writing this book, I drew on the strengths of social work, psychology, and education. I borrowed with admiration and gratitude from social work's traditional reverence for the social context of helping, its appreciation for the range of formal and informal services that may contribute to helping efforts, and its commitment to clients with the most complex problems and the fewest resources. I enlisted psychology's tradition of carefully articulating the treatment elements, of researching the outcomes, and of developing strategies for clinical evaluation. My years as a special educator taught me that change comes slowly but surely if you have certain goals, a research-based interventive plan, and perseverance. Certainly, social workers, psychologists, and educators are coming increasingly to integrate each other's traditions. I will cite many examples of this integration in the text. Yet even more effort to blend these perspectives is warranted. With *Social and Cognitive Treatment of Children and Adolescents*, I hope to bring professionals from these disciplines and others closer to an understanding of a complex but describable model for helping children.

Three stanchions support the social and cognitive methods described in this book. The first is social learning theory. The methods herein described rely on the concept, articulated by Albert Bandura (1977), that our behavior is strongly influenced by our belief that we can achieve and that we will be rewarded for so doing. The second stanchion supporting these methods is that social learning occurs in a social or institutional context, or "social ecology." A child's success is limited by the ability of the social ecology to promote that success. (Whereas "cognitive-behavioral" is an increasingly recognized practice orientation and term, both the practice and term fail to fully acknowledge the significance of the broader social context on the child's learning.) The third stanchion—that interventions will best succeed when they promote the ability of caregivers and other social-network members to become child helpers—is aligned with the social learning and social ecology pillars. If we believe in the importance of social learning and in the influence of the social ecology, we must commit ourselves to practices that give professionals the responsibility for enlisting the support of people of any age who can provide longer-lasting resources for the child.

Overview of the Contents

This book has two major parts. Part One provides background on the practice of the social-cognitive approach, and Part Two demonstrates the use of this approach with a range of problems affecting children and youth. The text attempts to reduce, synthesize, and make readily understandable materials from a broad range of sources. Extended case vignettes aid the reader in understanding the assessment, treatment, and evaluation procedures. Uses of social and cognitive methods are illustrated for school-age children and adolescents.

In Part One, Chapter One reviews various influences on the behavior of children and their caregivers. Chapter Two considers the process of assessing children and their environments.

Because practitioners rarely have sufficient time to conduct adequate assessments, they need guidelines and techniques that are
efficient and that do not leave them with that gnawing sense
that their assessment took precious time but made little difference
to the planning and delivery of their intervention. Although the
chapters in Part Two will provide specifics on assessing individual problems, the framework provided in Chapter Two offers
a key to assessing all the problems addressed in this book, as
well as those not considered here but that practitioners will
nonetheless confront. Chapter Three does the same for intervention strategies. The task-centered approach to building the competencies of children, youth, and their caregivers is described,
and the intervention process from engagement to changing behavior to referral or termination is articulated. Chapter Four
reviews strategies for involving parents, teachers, group home
counselors, siblings, and peers. Children's problems stem from
their relationships with their environments. Interventions must
include the other members of the environment if they are to
make lasting changes in a child's behavior. This chapter eval-
uates approaches to improving the collaboration between practitioners and the adults and youth who comprise a child's world.
Chapter Five presents the specifics of cognitive and social intervention strategies. Although much of working with children and
youth involves the coordination of services rather than direct
intervention, the time comes when the buck stops on a professional or nonprofessional caregiver's desk and he or she must
work to improve a child's accommodation to the environment.
This chapter frames well-tested procedures for accomplishing
that. Later chapters further illustrate these social and cognitive
techniques.

The problems addressed in Part Two are among those
that most plague practitioners working with children in community settings. Some, such as suicide, running away, firesetting, and stealing, are rarely discussed in books on treatment
of children and youth even though they are common reasons
for removing children from their homes and placing them in
personally and financially costly settings. Other problems, such
as aggression and nonattendance, are more commonly found

in troubled children and are more often discussed in books on child treatment. These discussions, however, are seldom accompanied by a rigorous look at which interventions have proven most effective. Underachievement is another common problem—one that often precedes or accompanies other problems—but one given little attention in practice literature other than the special education literature. (Eating disorders, enuresis, and encopresis, which are also amenable to social and cognitive approaches, were not included in the text for fear of overwhelming the reader's time and budget.) The final chapter provides strategies that readers may use in their efforts to begin applying these techniques despite the shortage of supervisors and peers who are skilled in their use.

Acknowledgments

I am thankful for the many kinds of assistance I have received from a few key contributors to this book. Harry Specht, dean of the School of Social Welfare at the University of California at Berkeley, and my colleagues there have helped with their successful efforts to make the School of Social Welfare an enjoyable place to learn and work. Sharon Ikami has prepared this manuscript and completed numerous other tasks with such efficiency and good cheer that I have had no excuses for not rewriting as much and as often as the book required. Jordana Ash, Mary Berry, Christine Frazita, Serena Jones, and Vicki and Shari Keller were excellent research assistants. My collaborations with Jim Whittaker, Francine Sohn, Robert Schilling, Steven Paul Schinke, William Haven, Lewayne Gilchrist, Eileen Gambrill, and Betty Blythe, among many fine colleagues, provided ideas that I drew on often in my writing. David Kurtz and Dennis Moore took time from busy schedules to provide detailed and constructive critiques of an earlier draft. My students have given me impetus to clearly describe the practices of child helpers. My brothers Gary Barth and Paul Piccione provided much encouragement and listened and responded carefully to my concerns. Alan Chai, Karen Courington, Charles Horstman, and Deirdre McGuire have provided friendship across years, settings, and my disappearances into the nether world of writing. To Nancy Sharp Dickinson I am also deeply grateful. Authoring a book consumes much time and inspires many second and third thoughts. She has listened to them often and, equally important, has diverted me from them. I am thankful for her faith in me and in this book.

Berkeley, California   Richard P. Barth
January 1986

Contents

The Author

Richard P. Barth is an assistant professor at the University of California at Berkeley and chairman of the School Social Work Program. He holds an A.B. degree in psychology from Brown University and an M.S.W. degree and D.S.W. degree from the University of California at Berkeley. In his present position he teaches direct practice with individuals, groups, and families; child welfare practices and programs; school social work practice; and treatment of problems of children and youth. Barth was previously on the faculty of the University of Washington where he coordinated a multiyear project to design, deliver, and evaluate mental health services for adolescent mothers. He is book review editor for the journal *Children and Youth Services Review*.

Barth's previous and current practice with children and youth includes teaching autistic children manual and oral communication, training learning disabled adolescents in social skills, providing educational counseling and psychotherapy for learning disabled youth, teaching special education classes, consulting with families in a group home for adolescents, performing social work in juvenile hall, conducting family therapy with young mentally ill adults, and leading sexuality groups for adolescents at risk of unwanted parenthood. Barth has conducted workshops on adolescent pregnancy prevention, self-control training for youth, parent-adolescent communication, and behavioral management techniques for working with juvenile offenders and youth in day treatment programs. He currently consults with child welfare services, day treatment programs, and a residential care program.

Barth has published more than forty journal articles and book chapters concerned with his practice. Among the journals in which he has published are *Social Work, Journal of Counseling Psychology, Review of Educational Research, Child Welfare, Children and Youth Services Review, Child Abuse and Neglect,* and *Social Work in Education.* These writings deal with providing social supports in adolescence, improving school performance and attendance, coping with teenage parenthood, promoting successful independent living for adolescents leaving foster care, facilitating older child adoptions, collaborating between schools and child welfare services, helping families of the mentally retarded, teaching anger control to abusive and neglecting families, collecting competent evidence on behalf of children, and implementing case management services.

Social and Cognitive Treatment of Children and Adolescents

Practical Strategies for Problem Behaviors

A Framework
for Effective Practice
with Children
and Adolescents

The chapters in Part One describe and illustrate the principles of social and cognitive treatment of children and adolescents. These principles come alive with case examples; a description of the processes of assessment and intervention; strategies for improving outcomes by giving clients choices about the goals and means of treatment; discussion of strategies for enlisting the support of other professionals, of caregivers, and of family members; and presentations of the specifics of social and cognitive techniques for changing behavior. These chapters also outline the entire process of treatment and discuss the benefits of ongoing collaboration with other professionals and caregivers—an essential element for practitioners treating children with serious problems in community settings.

1

Understanding
Children's Development
and Social Context

Concerned caregivers and child helpers have long called on their creativity to invent and implement strategies to help troubled children and youth and their families get out of trouble and stay out of trouble. Recent research shows that some of these inventions are demonstrably effective but that others contribute little help to child and family welfare that time alone would not have given. Now, building on more than two decades of practice and research, clinicians are drawing on the power of social and cognitive methods. These emerging methods promise to increase practitioners' abilities to ameliorate thorny problems that have long tormented school teachers, probation officers, group- and foster-home parents, child therapists, and other concerned caregivers. By improving outcomes for children, these techniques should help reverse the frustrations of practitioners and the fortunes of children and youth.

Although scholarly review articles and book chapters are chronicling the effectiveness of these methods, the availability of practical information about social and cognitive strategies for helping children is limited. As it stands, review and research articles too rarely provide adequate descriptions of techniques for promoting social and cognitive change or of applications of these techniques in community settings. Practice books, on the other hand, are too rarely guided by research. A recent review of textbooks about techniques for working with children in special education and social-work settings revealed that out of 1,252 citations, only 44 (3 percent) were citations of studies of the effectiveness of these techniques (Leviton and Cook, 1983).

The methods discussed here are among those that have been evaluated as useful by practice-researchers. This book is one of a growing number employing the same criteria (see, for example, Gambrill, 1983; Schinke, 1981). The choice of the nomenclature *social and cognitive* to describe these methods is less common. *Cognitive-behavioral* or *empirically based* are more common terms, but these are less precise descriptions of the methods and approaches discussed here. *Social* refers here to several key helping phenomena. The first is the social interactions that professional child helpers engage in with caregivers and children. The second is the teaching of social skills that may be needed to help caregivers and children obtain the rewards they deserve and want from their social milieu. In this book more than in those with a cognitive-behavioral perspective, *social* also indicates the significance of the social environment or *ecology* (Bronfenbrenner, 1979) of the child. *Social* communicates the importance of nonprofessionals in the world of children and their families and of the formal and informal social services on which families often rely. *Social* also reminds readers that when interventions involve members of a child's present and future social ecologies, the effects are more likely to last. And just as *social* has a broader significance than *behavioral*, so social interventions may have a broader effect than do behavioral interventions.

Growing evidence indicates that helping children develop more effective cognitive strategies adds power to already well-established social and behavioral strategies (Kendall, 1984). *Cognitive* refers to several elements of thought necessary for competent performance by children, caregivers, and professionals. Cognitive skills enable people to know, to feel, to motivate themselves, and to solve problems. Cognitions certainly include knowledge—the knowledge of resources, of effective parenting strategies, and of problem-solving approaches, for example. Cognitions are also inseparable from emotion and motivation

(Mann and Sabatino, 1985). The feelings of children and their significant others stem from and influence their thoughts. So, too, do cognitions influence social behavior and change as a result of social experiences. Strategies for problem solving are most definitively cognitive and form a key component of the treatment approach presented in this book. Anger-management training, social problem solving, and self-instruction are among the procedures that include cognitive-skill training and that will be described. This book endeavors to clarify ways for troubled children to develop lasting social and cognitive skills that will enable them and those in their worlds to lessen their troubles.

Although committed to describing applications of tested procedures for helping children, this book would leave many community practitioners unsatisfied if it only mentioned methods that have been tested and positively identified as effective for children of a certain age, diagnosis, cultural group, or gender. Effective practice requires reasoned generalization to unique situations, problems, and clients. Thus, some cognitive-skill training procedures and social-network strategies that have not been unequivocally supported by investigators (see Meador and Ollendick, 1984) but that are promising are included in these pages. The risk of forwarding strategies that need more testing is that practitioners will overemphasize them and neglect more conventional and better-documented procedures. This risk should not, however, keep practitioners from pursuing these procedures. Nor should they fall victim to what Kendall (1984) laments as a too common complaint: "I tried it once and it didn't work." Nevertheless, unproven methods should not supplant methods based on proven tenets of social learning theory and practice.

Child Helpers

Every member of a child's world has the potential to help or hinder the child's fit with this world. Each person who provides supervision and needed resources—whether parent, teacher, peer, sibling, bus driver, probation officer, social worker, or grandparent—is a potential *child helper*. Professionals and nonprofessionals can serve as child helpers by sharing resources or by improving or maintaining children's fit with their social ecologies. For example, peers who unknowingly provide new ideas, hopes, and examples to their friends and their friends' families are child helpers. Well-intentioned professionals or nonprofessionals who fail to bring new resources to bear on behalf of change remain only *potential* child helpers and caregivers.

Child helpers can serve many purposes. A child helper may coordinate other services to a child and rarely meet with that child, may be a child's therapist and meet with the child regularly, or may be a ward aide who interacts often with a child and receives supervision from another child helper. Child helpers may be called *case managers, child* or *family therapists, consultants,* or *mom* or *dad.* Readers with strong professional identifications need not put those aside but can use this unfamiliar term to remind themselves to ask: Am I considering the range of child-helping roles that I might assume with this child, and am I aware of the range of child-helping roles that other people in this child's life might take? If the term *child helper* encourages a therapist to assume a case-manager role or a case manager to articulate a child-helping role for a day-care provider, then the choice of terms has been well made. (Implications for assuming different roles with a child and family are discussed further in Chapter Four.) The choice of this nomenclature does not reflect any disregard for training or work experience nor any assumption that all child helpers do the same work with the same efficacy. The term *child helper* is intended to remind professionals that they share a common purpose with each other and with members of a child's environment, and furthermore, that they can focus their combined efforts on child helping or, instead, remain only potential child helpers.

Ecological Threats to Children's Welfare

Childhood has been worse (DeMause, 1980). Still, it could be better. A review of studies of the prevalence of maladjustment among children reveals that 11.8 percent of America's children have behavioral symptoms of maladjustment (Gould, Wunsch-Hitzik, and Dohrenwend, 1981). A growing awareness of social, cognitive, and physical contributors to the welfare of children lends promise to hopes for a brighter future for children. Although this increased understanding of the influences on childhood adjustment is promising, it is also burdensome. The more complex the working model of childhood, the more elements that professionals must assess when a problem arises. Full-scale social-ecological models incorporate a complex network of personal, familial, institutional, community, and life-change forces and their interactions. Hess and Howard (1981) argue that all of these major elements play such key roles in children's functioning that they are "never to be overlooked" (p. 501). Child helpers cannot assess and intervene in all social-ecological influences on a child, but a familiarity with ecological models of childhood is crucial, because these models reveal the unmet challenges and incomplete transitions that are often the sources of a child's maladjustment, as well as the resources needed to return a child to a desirable developmental path.

Central to this chapter and this book is a concern with helping children and youth maintain a stable relationship with their caretakers, schools, and communities. Initially, this means helping children stay in their own homes, classrooms, and neighborhoods. Failing that, the goal is to help children adjust to and benefit from effective short-term, part-week, or part-day experiences in respite-care, shelter-care, foster-care, special classroom, or day-treatment settings. Last, this may mean helping children participate in well-delivered residential services and, when children are unable to return to their own homes and communities, adapt to substitute environments. Providing children with minimally restrictive and yet sufficiently instructive environments calls for understanding characteristics of social ecologies that foster the development of childhood competence and that support family change. Social and cognitive behavior that can help children fit into most ecologies will be described as a framework for later discussions of assessment and intervention. Finally, this chapter closes with an overview of competencies that child helpers will find fundamental to their efforts to strengthen the alliance of family, child, and setting.

Transitions and Resources

Moments of child and environmental congruence are often fleeting, because childhood involves so much growth and change. Children's physical development alters their relationship to their surroundings. Siblings, peers, and adults also change, as do schools, neighborhoods, and communities. Almost by definition, change leads to maladjustment. This maladjustment typically is short-lived, but multiple changes may have more enduring effects. Rutter (1979) finds a relationship between the number of stressful changes and the severity of children's behavior problems. The strength of the relationship between children's problems and stress increases as the number of stressful events increases. Children and their families adapt with differing effectiveness to a few stressors, but the effect of stressors on children and their families becomes more similar and debilitating as the amount of stress increases.

One change characterizes all transitions: the change in resources available to members of the social ecology. The resources of the community, neighborhood, and extended family are fundamental to successful child rearing (Cowen, Lotyczewski, and Weissberg, 1984; Sandler, 1979). Isolated children and families are at risk. Simply stated, the more resources a family can muster, the fewer the transitions the family will experience as stressors. These family resources include information, health, morale, maternal sufficiency or aid, personal skills, and examples of competent performance. The more resources a family can draw on, the fewer the stressors and the less the hazard for family members.

Family and Home Transitions. Family forms are many and multiplying. Kellam, Ensminger, and Turner (1977) encountered eighty-four family constellations in their study of Chicago's Woodlawn area. Some families experienced as many as ten constellations. The accidental death of a competent and loving parent is perhaps the most graphic example of a rapid change and loss of family resources. The family is instantaneously deprived of a dependable and unique source of well-being. Remarriage also changes family resources. The change may ultimately increase the family's overall resource level, but the process of integrating a new parent's resources may temporarily reduce the resources available to any individual family member. For example, an older adolescent child who had been acting as an adult in an informal coparenting role may lose this position and its attendant status when his or her parent remarries. This child may subsequently seek to reclaim lost rewards by affiliating with more daring, pseudo-adult friends. Transitions also require families to reallocate and readjust their resources. These efforts may lead to the need for helping services by aggravating children's previous difficulties or generating new problems. Even when family membership is constant, changes in health, income, housing, and family roles create resource shifts and demand adaptation. Awareness of such changes will suggest areas for assessment and intervention.

Disruptions such as the birth of a sibling stretch maternal resources but may provide a counterbalancing opportunity for brothers and sisters to learn by assuming new roles and responsibilities. New stepparents and stepsiblings, foster children, or live-in relatives may not return as much to family resources as they take. During hard economic times, one magnanimous stepparent invited numerous kin to live with him and his wife and stepchildren until his three-bedroom apartment had fourteen residents, including a developmentally disabled sister and two children with special needs. His wife finally left home, seeking consultation. With this author's support, she gained her husband's participation in treatment. This contact provided an additional resource and was followed by an end to the stepfather's drinking and obsessive and expensive lighting of prayer candles, the return of a teenage nephew and his new bride to their mother's home, enrollment of the children with special needs in a special education preschool program, job training for the sister, and marital reunification. In summary, this man's naive effort to serve as a resource for his family and stepfamily led to a disruption of his own family that was finally remedied by professional help. Thus, although transitions may provide opportunities for new resource development, most lead at least temporarily to diminished resources, an "emptying of the family ecosystem," and untoward developmental outcomes (Bronfenbrenner, 1979).

Change in Material Possessions. Social class is a powerful predictor of personal and family problems (see, for example, Dohrenwend and Dohrenwend, 1974; Pelton, 1981). Even though the loss of financial resources is not only a problem for the poor, the adjustment to loss is most difficult for those with the least to lose. The significant loss of financial resources means increased dependence on friends, kin, and social agencies and is usually accompanied by loss of status and rights. Many families only reluctantly discuss the loss of material support. Because of its possible association with family maladjustment, this loss deserves attention, assessment, and assistance.

Changes in Physical Health, Mental Health, and Morale. Fatigue comes packaged with parenthood. Mothers, whether working or not, carry the major responsibility for child rearing and are particularly in need of additional formal and informal resources (Patterson, 1980).

Parents' loss of mental health and morale from marital distress also causes trouble for children (Hetherington, 1979), as does having a parent with a psychological disturbance (Neale and Weintraub, 1975). Children of both types of parents are likely to have school problems (Weintraub, Prinz, and Neale, 1978). Not surprisingly, spousal abuse has similar effects. The children of battered women are prone to display the aggressive behavior they have witnessed at home (Rosenbaum and O'Leary, 1981a). Families are resilient and resourceful but apparently cannot easily withstand the damage and isolation of extreme marital conflict. Assessment of children's needs and intervention in children's behalf too often are sidetracked by overinterest in marital relationships; especially troubled relationships between caregivers need to be addressed, however, during treatment of children.

School and Work. Much of each day for family members is spent at school or at work. In their early years of life and in the early hours of the day, children often spend their time in such out-of-home settings as day-care centers, nursery schools, Head Start programs, Project Follow-Through, breakfast programs, and after-school programs. Economic and social conditions all but require parents to spend a substantial part of each day in out-of-home employment. The mother's employment may have positive effects on family welfare, including improved family relationships stemming from an improved financial condition, opportunities from good child care, and improved maternal self-esteem (Kamerman and Hayes, 1979). Still, home-school-work transitions can tax family time and energy and cause guilt, worry, and strain (Spakes, 1982). Perhaps less likely to cause acute problems—but more central to family adjustment—are the daily transitions from home to school or work.

The transition to school or work is not always cause for celebration. For children reared primarily at home in their first years, the transition to preschool may cause considerable distress for both children and parents (Signell, 1972). School or work is barely tolerable for many children and adults and, like most anxiety-inducing experiences, time away from school or work increases the person's dread and avoidance. For more than a few children and adults, the transition from home to school each day is cause for conflict and even violence (Coltoff and Luks, 1978).

Changes in school or work may follow from job transfers or assignment to new school or class sites. The transition to junior high school is especially disruptive for many children as they simultaneously lose their command of the physical environment, their peer network, and the constancy of a single teacher. One successful program restructured the seventh grade to re-create some aspects of the elementary grades by providing new students with a homeroom teacher who also taught other classes and a cadre of peers who all took the same classes. Students in this setting had better grades, fewer absences, and less distress than their counterparts in schools where children all had different schedules and no single key teacher (Felner, Ginter, and Primavera, 1982).

Job promotions and change can lead to redistribution of family resources and cause new work hours, changes in co-workers and friends, changes in commuting and child-care arrangements, and even moves to different neighborhoods. More unsettling is the loss of work. Unemployment's influence can reach into every aspect of home life and encourage domestic violence, health problems, depression, and family breakup (Liem and Rayman, 1982). The subsequent isolation may tear at the fabric of families' social-support systems and further deplete the resources available to children and youth. In communities with elevated unemployment rates, the loss of informal resources and morale throughout the community also can take its toll on family life. Child helpers without knowledge of job-related resources are at a disadvantage.

Neighborhood and Community. The child and family spend critical moments in the neighborhood and community. This is the turf of childhood (Garbarino, 1982). Although the neighborhood's role in child rearing has lost some significance as family mobility has increased and more private forms of entertainment have become more prevalent, its importance to children and families should not be underestimated. The neighborhood is often the testing ground for family behavior. Parents learn about the appropriateness of their parenting behavior from watching other parents. Children witness other children in other families behaving in different ways than they are permitted to do. Consensual definitions of adjustment and maladjustment are shared: "Danny didn't talk until he was two years old, and my niece didn't talk until she was two-and-a-half years old, so it's too early to start worrying. Just keep talking to him and eventually he'll talk back."

From neighors may come friends, a social network, and social support. Parents need friends. Even acquaintances may contribute some of the benefits of social support, such as assistance in problem solving, provision of additional information and skills, feedback about acceptable behavior, opportunities for emotional acceptance and encouragement, positive confrontation over self-defeating statements or actions, and offers of material aid (Barrera and Ainlay, 1983). Children need their parents' friends as well. Children's adjustment is both directly and indirectly influenced by their parents' friendships and support networks (Cochran and Brassard, 1979).

Families without neighborhood supports risk many problems. The neighborhood's importance may be more critical to the welfare of poor families, because more affluent families can often purchase support, encouragement, and material aid. Social isolation has often been reported to affect child rearing (Presser, 1980). The neighborhood regulates opportunities for social integration and, finally, influences child rearing. Garbarino and his colleagues conducted a series of studies confirming this relationship. To determine whether child-maltreatment rates are predictable by the ecological characteristics of counties, they studied two neighborhoods with similar socioeconomic and demographic characteristics but mildly different child-maltreatment rates (Garbarino, 1976; Garbarino and Sherman, 1980). Interviews with families and community members revealed that the low-risk neighborhood had one-fourth as many members who never engaged in neighborhood exchanges, twice as many children with regular neighborhood playmates, three times the number of children cared for by parents after school, and one-fifth more people reported by mothers as taking an interest in their child's welfare. Overall, the low-risk neighborhood received a far higher rating by mothers as a good place to raise children.

Communities of Interest. Communities are more than geographic entities. Communities may also form around shared values, cultures, or personal characteristics. Religion, ethnicity, gender or sexual orientation, sports, unions, music, and the outdoors each may serve as a community of interest for a family, parent, or youth. Even though the activities evolving from these shared interests may be circumscribed in time and place, their influences may transcend the moments of shared participation. As family difficulties mount, families may withdraw from active involvement in communities of interest. Isolated families may not have any shared community activities or interests. Some families develop difficulties when involvement in a community of interest that provided an essential resource ends. In each case, child helpers may find that members of these organizations have resources to share, and that increased family contact with social, recreational, and ethnic communities can support child-helping efforts.

Unfortunately, all communities of interest are not prosocial. Some threaten adjustment. Deviant cultures may draw parents and their children into antisocial behavior. Cauce, Felner, and Primavera (1982) found that adolescents with high levels of informal social support had lower school attendance and grades. Cultures fostering drug abuse and prostitution among the young may provide the mutual aid functions of other communities of interest with less beneficial results (Barth, 1983). Too much involvement in peer activities, whether the activity is encouraged by the mainstream culture or whether it is renegade, may deprive family members of the incentive to develop or maintain their developmentally corrective contact with school, work, and home.

Some communities of interest have formed in response to family problems. From a recognition of shared problems may come an acceptance of asking for aid. Schools have begun programs for children with alcoholic parents, in part to encourage the children to draw on the resources of other children and families when alcoholic bouts deplete their own families' caregiving abilities. One organization, Toughlove, brings parents of difficult-to-manage teenagers together to gain strength from each other (York and York, 1980). Parents identify their goals for their children and for themselves and call on other members of Toughlove to keep them from abandoning those goals in the face of self-doubt and pressure from their children. Parents Anonymous, perhaps the best known of all family self-help groups, helps parents at risk of abusing their children. Self-help need not be preestablished or large. Child helpers can link two or three people with similar concerns or needs and achieve similar results.

Children's Competencies

Children develop the competencies of living in myriad interactions with many children and a few adults. Through these interactions and especially through relationships arising from them, the social ecology (Bronfenbrenner, 1979) of a child offers its resources. *Social ecologies* are the people, places, times, and contexts in which social interaction occurs. Social ecologies set the limits of development, create the hazards that cause developmental damage, and most central to the child helper's interests, provide helping resources. The social ecology offers the source of and solution to children's problems. A child's social ecology extends from the kitchen table to church school to the county supervisors' meeting to the economic and social conditions that influence the child's life (Bronfenbrenner, 1979). These latter systems have an undeniably great impact on a child's life and warrant the application of child-advocacy skills, but the more immediate concern of the child helper as described in this book is children's social settings.

Each social setting offers children new roles, relationships, and resources. In turn, each setting entails expectations for performance in roles and relationships. Access to resources typically follows the competent execution of those roles. The school child able to talk politely, exercise bladder control, and sit still will have the chance to learn to read. The child who understands sharing is granted the generous learning opportunities of friendship. The youth who manages his or her time well can at the same time get credits toward a diploma as well as supervised work experience. Competent performers in their social ecology get the resources.

The roles and relationships of children and youth are set in the family or home, the day-care center or school, and the neighborhood or community. Even though these roles may overlap (as they do when the child's day care is at an aunt's home), the requirements of each setting indicate a unique pattern of competencies. The concordance between the child's competencies and the requirements of a setting defines the need for adjustment. Similarly, the match between the role expectations and relationships across key settings defines the range of competencies required of a child. Despite growing sensitivity to cultural differences, educational and social services for children have limited capacity to adjust to the idiosyncratic behavior of children and their families. The child helper strives to extract the maximum flexibility from these symptoms and to provide families with new competencies that foster adaptive responses.

Even though each setting makes unique demands on children and youth, the set of responses that will satisfy those demands is not independent. Children, like adults, have cognitive and social styles that lead to consistencies in behavior across inconsistent circumstances. Perhaps also, like adults, about equal parts of a child's behavior are determined by the setting and by personality (Mischel and Peake, 1982). The personalities of adolescents certainly do have substantial influence on their problem behaviors (Jessor and Jessor, 1977). Barker and Schoggen's (1973) pithy observation to the effect that people behave like churchgoers when in church and like fans when in a stadium does not deny that churchgoers and fans sit in rows, sing along when the organist plays, and pass money to the aisle without stealing it. Studies of children's behavior across home and school settings reflect these consistencies and inconsistencies. Several studies find differences between children's home and school performances (see, for example, Bernal, Delfini, North, and Kreutzer, 1976), but more find similarities (see, for example, Harris and Reid, 1981). Children and youth apparently need adequate cross-setting social and cognitive competencies as well as setting-specific competencies.

Social Competencies

A socially competent child engages in social interactions that increase the resources of the child and his or her ecology. A more specific breakdown of social competencies will facilitate the child helper's ability to assess and develop goals for children and youth.

Accepting and Exerting Influence. Children and youth in many settings and roles must accept the efforts of older caregivers to influence them. The cognitive and experiential limitations of young people leave them vulnerable to exploitation, injury, and lost learning opportunities if guidance is not provided and accepted. Accepting the influence of others may involve simply following the social example of a classroom leader (a momentary caregiver by authorization), or it may involve changing antisocial behavior after a court reprimand and penalty. Even acknowledging that the social environment must provide support for this competency and that some forms of influence are more effective than others, children must accept influence in many settings and from many caregivers. *Accepting* influence is not antithetical to *exerting* influence. Children without the ability to exert influence are also disadvantaged. Successful children and youth must not only protect themselves from exploitation but must also regulate peer social interactions (White, 1979), negotiate with parents (Barth, Schinke, and Maxwell, 1985; Robin, 1980), and express learning needs (Weinrott, Corson, and Wilchesky, 1979). Ways to foster the complex set of cognitive and social skills undergirding this competency are described throughout this book.

Increasing Self-Care. Social development calls for the growth from total dependence to mutual interdependence. Competent youth increase their self-care skills as they grow. Self-care skills (such as tying one's own shoelaces) are not necessarily social, but some (such as preventing venereal disease) are very social, and others (such as daytime soiling by school children) involve personal grooming that has social impact. Self-care skills often affect family relationships, as parents with few supports may have to rely on children to care for themselves during nonschool hours. Children who are not able to care for themselves at their parents' level of expectations are particularly vulnerable to parental sanctions and abuse.

Engaging the Company of Others. Children able to engage in reciprocally enjoyable social exchanges will find many resources available at a low personal cost. More at risk are children with difficulty participating in any social interaction. Much research suggests that troubled adults were isolated children and youth. Elementary school children rejected by their peers, for example, have increased likelihood of mental health problems up to thirteen years later (Cowen and others, 1973) and of delinquency (Roff, Sells, and Golden, 1972). Adult ratings of children's social competence carry similar predictive validity (Edelbrock, 1980; Hartup, 1979). Although these findings do not mean that socially isolated children typically become troubled adults, the association supports the belief that the untalkative, anxious, and self-stimulating child loses the learning opportunities and growth that follow social exchanges.

Conflict Resolution. Disagreements about territory, possessions, privileges, and rights are hallmarks of childhood and adolescence. Children who can competently contribute to the resolution of peer and family conflicts are likely to avoid fighting, withdrawing, coercion, and temper tantrums and are more likely to be liked by peers and teachers (Richard and Dodge, 1982; Snyder, 1982). The majority of children and youth find strategies for resolving these conflicts that are socially acceptable and do not lead to serious personal losses. Many young people who find their way to child-helping agencies have limited and unacceptable conflict-resolution strategies. Conflict-resolution skills include cognitive strategies for defining problems and generating and evaluating likely solutions as well as social skills for implementing the problem-solving process. Reciprocal and rewarding social relationships prevent many conflicts from arising (Fischer and Ury, 1981).

When conflicts arise, reliance on the most appropriate conflict resolution yields the speediest and most satisfactory results. Mutual problem-solving and decision-making strategies (further discussed in Chapter Six) show promise for helping children, youth, and their parents identify and implement agreeable solutions (Edelson, 1981; Kifer, Lewis, Green, and Phillips, 1974). Some children seem to resolve their own and other children's conflicts with considerable skill (Snyder, 1982). Unfortunately, naturalistic studies of how they accomplish this have not been done. Research on strategies that adolescent mothers and parents of older children use to cope with conflict suggests that the children and youth with the most diverse conflict-reduction skills manage most successfully (Barth, Schinke, and Maxwell, 1983; Colletta and Gregg, 1981). Children and youth often benefit from knowledge of and practice with alternative conflict-resolution strategies.

Cognitive Competencies

Cognitive skills contributing to competence are as difficult to isolate as social skills. Research suggests that intelligence quotient (IQ) is associated with overall competence (Oden, 1968). Discussion of how to increase IQ is, however, outside the bailiwick of this book. Cognitive competencies that may contribute to prosocial behavior and increase the yield from learning opportunities are of utmost concern to child helpers and include the following.

Interpersonal Problem-Solving Skills. Cognitive skills for solving interpersonal problems have been reported by several researchers to contribute to the adjustment of children and adolescents (see, for example, Gesten and others, 1982; Kendall and Fischler, 1984; Spivack and Shure, 1974). Component cognitive skills inlcude at least these five: (1) identifying that a problem exists, (2) generating alternative solutions, (3) taking the perspective of the other party or parties, (4) determining the consequences of the options that were generated, and (5) evaluating the consequences to choose the best solution. Researchers cannot identify which components or combination of components are most essential for competent problem solving, but there appears to be a modest association between skills in each area and effective role fulfillment.

Self-Management. A child's ability to set the goals and incentives necessary for successful performance seems to be related to successfully negotiating the demands of family, school, and community life. Mastery of self-management procedures per se has not been tested as a predictor of future well-being, but impulsive children may have greater difficulty in multiple settings and across time than their less-impulsive peers (Kogan, 1983; McCord and Sanchez, 1983), and unsuccessful children and youth provided with self-control training have improved their social and school competence (Kendall, 1981).

The self-management process includes many components. According to Karoly (1977), self-management's core components are (1) commitment, (2) goal setting, (3) arousal management, (4) self-monitoring, (5) evaluation, and (6) self-administration of consequences. Each is briefly considered.

Self-management by its nature requires effort and temporary sacrifice, or *commitment*. If it did not, it would simply be known as self-enjoyment. Commitment requires some additional cognitive conditions, such as a preference for the outcomes of the self-managed response over other responses; the personal attribution of responsibility for outcomes, at least in part, to oneself; and the expectation of success through self-management.

Commitment is limited by the opportunities young people perceive themselves to have if they are successful. Commitment is also influenced by social incentives, but it does require certain minimum cognitive conditions. Without some of the aforementioned conditions, the commitment to engage in self-management and achieve additional social incentives is insufficient. Child helpers should also work on program and policy battlefronts to increase the social choices and rewards available to youths.

Goal setting provides children with a guide for performance and cues for self-rewards or consequences. When children set goals, their achievements are greater (Gagne, 1975). Children may initially set goals that are too vague or too low to allow evaluation or to inspire a concerted effort, but they can learn to set higher and clearer standards (Jones and Ollendick, 1980).

Good performance relies on a medium amount of *arousal management*. Overstimulation may result in an inability to concentrate, speak clearly, or control urinary functions; understimulation may undermine initial commitment and keep efforts below the level needed to overcome inertia. Children who can notice and modulate changes in arousal are less likely to overreact to events.

A burgeoning body of research suggests that children and youth who use *self-monitoring* probes can proceed with more care and accomplishment (Kendall, 1981; O'Leary and Dubey, 1979; Pressley, 1979). Self-monitoring is the inner ear of performance, guiding the child down the winding and uneven path to goal attainment. Once a plan has been embraced and performance is under way, competent children and youth can focus on whether or not they are implementing their plans. Depending on the nature of the desired performance, children can monitor their own behaviors by identifying what they are doing; for example, the child may say, "I'm staying calm and not getting mad," "I'm watching what I'm doing," "That's two classes I went to—only three to go," or "I'd better check on what I'm supposed to do again."

Evaluating the success of personal effort involves comparing the actual performance and outcome with the initial performance and outcome goals. Research has shown that self-monitoring coupled with evaluation often helps increase appropriate behavior (see, for example, Sagotsky, Patterson, and Lepper, 1978; Ollendick, 1981). When accurate self-assessments are initially rewarded by child helpers, they help prolong competent behavior even after rewards are discontinued (Wood and Flynn, 1978). Evaluation of performance is closely linked to self-monitoring and addresses the question, "Did I do what I had planned?" This is not the same as evaluation of the outcome itself: "Did I achieve what I wanted?" The distinction is not difficult for child helpers to see, although children and youth may have less acuity.

Self-administration of consequences, or self-reinforcement, may have powerful positive effects (Felixbrod and O'Leary, 1974; Brigham and Stoerzinger, 1976). Self-punishment in the form of response cost (Cautela, 1976; Humphrey, Karoly, and Kirschenbaum, 1978) and negative self-statements (Masters and Santrock, 1976) also contributes to the control of behavior. Nelson and Birkimer (1978) found that self-instruction training without self-reward is less effective in reducing impulsive performance. Children, on the whole, are capable of judiciously administering rewards after reward giving has been modeled by child helpers. Children can also learn from child helpers to recognize when they do not complete their plans or perform up to expectations and to generate coping responses that foster renewed commitment and effort rather than anger.

Academic Skills. Self-management skills provide the fundamentals for academic achievement, but technical cognitive skills are also needed. Chapter Eight further discusses competencies needed to meet such challenges as making sense of written English.

Child Helper Expertise

To successfully apply a range of interventive roles and techniques, practitioners must recognize the constraints and opportunities of the client's culture, community, development, and motivation. The best and the worst intervention will similarly fail without the support of such knowledge.

Client Cultures. Cultural influences on the child and family extend beyond the physical community. Ideas about what actions are acceptable, what motivates behavior, and what solutions are tenable develop over centuries and have influence beyond our awareness. The child helper's difficult goal of improving person-environment fit (Germaine, 1983) is complicated by the necessary question: Who defines the best fit? For instance, the definition of child maltreatment, an example with weighty implications, varies by the cultural origins of the client (for example, whether the client is Samoan, Native American, or Japanese) as well as by the professional training of the child helper (for example, whether the child helper is a police officer, lawyer, or social worker) (Giovannoni and Becerra, 1979). Conflicts about the appropriate environment often arise from opposite ideas about the cultural needs of a developing child. The once-popular placement of Native American children in the culture of the suburbs rested on the assumption that such a culture is the ideal developmental medium for children of all backgrounds. Cultures also shape the meaning of problems and of helping (Snowden, 1982); for example, mental health and child welfare professionals are typically low on the list of desired resources among people from many cultures. Helping relationships among families who are culturally uneasy with child helpers may have to proceed slowly and carefully. Misunderstandings may cause a breakdown in collaboration. At times, misunderstanding can have tragic results. In one case, a Vietnamese father hung himself out of shame when his daughter was taken into shelter care because of suspected physical abuse. The bruises and abrasions on her body were later recognized as the signs of an ancient healing method. The cost of cultural ignorance is rarely so high, but cultural background always deserves consideration.

Child helpers cannot, of course, understand all cultures and cultural phenomena. What, then, must culturally competent child helpers know? They must know when to look for and how to obtain cultural information. Exploration of the child's social ecology can lead to cultural understanding. Contact with members of the neighborhood, school, and family may raise hypotheses about cultural influences. Confirming or disconfirming these hypotheses requires asking members of the ecology about their cultural beliefs:

Child helper: What will little Tom's grandmother say if you reward big Tom for helping with the baby while you rest?

Young mother: She won't say anything to me. She'll make Tom Sr. feel like he's not a man, though, and he'll tell me that he won't do it anymore.

Child helper: What might help?

Young mother: If you tell her that it must be this way she'll listen. She respects doctors.

Child helper: I'm not a medical doctor, you know.

Young mother: Yes, I know—but she doesn't.

Cultural differences between child helpers and clients (or even between members of a client's family) may arise regarding personal, family, and societal roles. Table 1 identifies end-points of the range of several beliefs that may influence a client's receptivity to, and use of, treatments. Even though each belief cannot be assessed prior to the implementation of an interventive plan, providing clients with choices about the desired intervention and continued sensitivity to the influence of differences in beliefs will promote the success of the treatment.

Because beliefs about these issues may differ even within subpopulations and families, the child helper is spared the responsibility of mastering every typical association between ethnic or cultural groups and beliefs. Interviews should ascertain belief systems relevant to the child helper's efforts to improve family functioning.

Consultations regarding culture are indispensable when important decisions arise concerning members of identified ethnic groups. In cases involving substitute care for Native American children, contact with Native American consultants is required by law (National Indian Child Welfare Act, 1978). The idea of cultural consultation is sound and warrants imitation by child helpers working with other population groups, because child-care goals, standards, and practices differ across cultures

Table 1. Culturally Shaped Beliefs.

PERSONAL

Privacy

Taciturn and not eager to share personal or family events.	Ready to describe personal experiences and share family events.

Time

Relaxed and aware of natural rhythms of time.	Very aware of clock-time and punctuality.

Faith

Skepticism about healers or external helping forces.	High regard for healers and strong belief in the power of others.

Physical Contact

Appreciates physical distances and minimal touching.	Accepts or desires physical greetings, guidance, or reassurance.

FAMILY ROLES

Decision Making

Parents should fully govern all family decisions.	Children should have equal opportunity to influence family decisions.

Privileges

Children's privileges should be determined according to their performance.	Children's access to privileges should be independent of their performance.

Physical Punishment

Physical punishment is an important contributor to children's socialization.	Physical punishment violates the rights of children.

Sex Roles

Men and women or boys and girls have different rights and responsibilities.	Men and women or boys and girls have equal rights and responsibilities.

Elders and Kin

Elders and kin are an integral part of family life and child rearing.	Elders and kin are a tangential part of family life and child rearing.

SOCIETAL ROLES

Cultural Integration

Participation in cultural activities is essential to family life.	Assimilation into the mainstream is best for family life.

Community Groups

Social organizations are tangential to family life.	Social organizations offer broad benefit to families and individuals.

Public Institutions

Public institutions and programs threaten family life.	Public institutions and programs supplement family life.

and within cultures. Although child helpers can assess how different a family's child care is from the child care expected in their own cultures, members of the family's own culture often are needed to judge the fit between the family's child care and the expectations of the family's own culture. Congruence with the culture of origin may be the initial goal of intervention so the family can gain the support and benefit of its own community. Only then may the child helper succeed in the more difficult goal of helping clients bridge the gap between the expectations of their culture and those of the mainstream culture.

Environmental Resources. Knowledge of informal and formal resources can facilitate helping efforts. At its most basic, this knowledge includes awareness of national self-help programs such as Al-anon, Parents Anonymous, Toughlove, and the Association of Retarded Citizens; and social, health, and educational programs such as Aid to Families with Dependent Children (AFDC), Achievement Place, Early and Periodic Screening, Diagnosis, and Treatment (EPSDT), Family Services Agency of America, Head Start, regional centers, youth service bureaus, and social security insurance. With the latter group of services, knowledge of eligibility requirements is also crucial. Indigenous resources that address individual community needs—a Young Women's Christian Association (YWCA) summer program, a group for children of alcoholic parents, a crisis-resolution house, or a self-help program for sexually abused children—typically have less certain guidelines and attributes but offer flexibility and responsiveness. Knowing the people who staff these resources facilitates decision making about the likely fit between the resource and a client. For example, a teenager with a drinking problem may be more comfortable attending a more youth-oriented or less religiously oriented chapter of Alcoholics Anonymous (AA) after an introduction to a sponsor the child helper knows and trusts.

Importantly, knowledge of resources should include familiarity with outcome research on available programs. Evaluations of programs with sites across the nation like Project Re-ED and the Teaching Family Model (Achievement Place) are mounting (Hobbs, 1982; Kirigin, Braukman, Atwater, and Wolf, 1982).

Parent-training programs that replicate or extend programs with well-documented outcomes (for example, Fleischman, Horne, and Arthur's [1983] and Szykula, Fleischman, and Shilton's [1982] replications of the Oregon Social Learning Center's success [Patterson, 1982] in Wyoming) warrant some confidence. Alternately, the many unflattering reviews of Parent Effectiveness Training call for cautious referral (Doherty and Ryder, 1980; Rinn and Markle, 1977), as do the evaluations of the program reviewed in the documentary *Scared Straight* (Buckner and Chesney-Lind, 1983; Finckenauer, 1979).

Development. Children's conflicts with their families, schools, and communities and with themselves may be self-limiting. Many children seem to "grow out of" their problems. In fact, their readjustment is probably partly due to changes in the social ecology, in the competencies of the children and their caregivers, and in the children's physical resources through maturation. Both normal and abnormal development involves all of these changes. Changes may occur simultaneously, and some changes may trigger other changes. Researchers have struggled mightily to isolate the contributors to development and, no less, to determine what is normal. While this process goes on, child helpers are left to make decisions with important personal, social, ethical, and financial consequences about which problems require intervention. This treatment attempts only to frame some pivotal developmental issues; additional discussion is available in other texts (see, for example, Brim and Kagan, 1980; Garbarino, 1982; Gardner, 1978).

One key question is: *how does development occur?* Development can be characterized as fluid, reciprocal, unending, and limited by physiology and learning opportunities. Stage theories of development—most prominently Erikson's (1963) and Piaget's (1954)—are slowly giving way to the theory that the developmental process is more flexible than fixed, more incremental than abrupt, more even than uneven (Brim and Kagan, 1980; Clark and Clark, 1977).

Children must have both maturational readiness and learning opportunities for development to occur. A child's attainment of competence is typically as uneven as a child's learning opportunities. Different children may achieve developmental milestones at similar times, and individual children may characteristically be fast or slow at achieving milestones. Age is a measure of time—not development (Harris and Ferrari, 1983). The 2 percent of adults who experience bed-wetting (Oppel, Harper, and Ryder, 1968) are evidence that maturity alone is insufficient for development; a few have physical limitations, but most have never had correct training (Doleys, 1983). Nor does hyperactivity uniformly cease with puberty, as once thought, although its character may change (Hechtman and Weiss, 1983).

Development is reciprocal. Parents and children (and child helpers) learn as they teach and teach as they learn (Bell and Harper, 1977). As Patterson (1976a) writes, parents are "victim and architect" of their children's problems. Children's physical characteristics partly determine parents' initial responses. Sick, premature, autistic, and disorganized infants may innocently trigger awkward and ineffective parenting from otherwise able and affectionate adults. Adults and their children teach each other to be assaultive (Patterson, 1982). Even though this response to problem solving may be learned in the family of origin, parents with no experience as victims of violence can also learn to attack if shown how (Rosenbaum and O'Leary, 1981b). As already discussed, individuals and their ecologies also have a mutually formative relationship. The reciprocal perspective may someday make current unidirectional conceptions of development inconceivable. This would mean an end to such pejorative labels as the "schizophrenegenic mother," the "bad seed," and the "never-amount-to-anything family." Child helpers will find the reciprocal perspective fruitful for understanding the development of children and caregivers and for understanding and resolving impasses in child helping.

Because behavior is a product of ecological, constitutional, and personal characteristics, only the fluidity of these characteristics limits change. Kagan (1978) makes an eloquent, research-anchored case against the "nonsense" of the irreversibility of development. He presents the hypothetical cases of two three-year-olds: one first in a happy and positive home and then removed for a ten-year stint in a violent, cynical, and degrading home; and the other child initially in a negative environment and then shifted for ten years into a benevolent one. Kagan asks the reader to imagine the outcome. It is not a difficult request. Crissey (1977) reports on a forty-year follow-up of her study of differential treatments of children of retarded mothers and children who were themselves initially judged as mentally retarded (Skodak and Skeels, 1949). The differing outcomes for children who start life with serious disadvantages and then enter placements with a range of riches clearly demonstrate the malleability and reversibility of development given corrective environments.

Children continue to develop through adolescence. Puberty brings hormonal changes but does not signal an end to cognitive or physical development. The myth that adolescents are beyond correction keeps child helpers from adequately addressing their needs (Hobbs and Robinson, 1982). This is all but tragic, as this group has many service needs and much growth ahead. With proper techniques, even the cognitive styles of mentally retarded adolescents can be modified (Feuerstein and others, 1981). Adolescents' problems have had a longer time to develop and are often expressed more vigorously than are children's problems, but adolescents have also had more opportunity to learn competencies and can apply their vigor toward change.

Other changes may result from the interaction of physical change and learning. In Gersten and colleagues' (1976) longitudinal look at the stability of problem behaviors, anxiety was not stable until middle adolescence. Not until then was prediction into adulthood reasonably accurate. Treatment of mild disturbances in children in middle latency to early adolescence appears to yield little benefit later on, as shown when these children are compared to those with similar disturbances who are not treated. Other constellations of behavior, such as school nonattendance and aggression, are far more stable under conditions of limited environmental change, as shall be shown in later chapters. These more stable problems seem to have turning points after which intervention may be more difficult. Youth who manifest behavioral disturbances at the point from which stability usually occurs often have been disturbed from their early years.

Another key question regarding development is: *is abnormal only a matter of definition?* Child helpers must grapple with the nasty problems of labeling and diagnosis. Recognizing the impact of the child's ecological framework on behavior only aggravates the difficulty. Labeling the child often seems like blaming the victim. The instability of behavioral disturbances also makes labeling seem villainous and wrong. If behavior is a function of environmental stresses and demands, *situational adjustment disorder* seems the most appropriate label for children's problems. The popularly perceived dangers of labeling, even if supported by less than conclusive evidence (MacMillan, 1982; Reschly and Lamprecht, 1979), also are warnings against diagnosis and classification. In all, these issues certainly call for the child helper to consider carefully Hobbs's (1982) contention that "emotional disturbance is not something in the person, not something a child or adolescent has, not a neurosis or behavior disorder or anything else that does not express an ongoing transactional process. Emotional disturbance is not a symptom of individual pathology, but of a malfunctioning ecosystem" (p. 14).

Still, do not children show consistent and characteristic sets of problem behaviors—based perhaps on underlying physical attributes—that can reliably be identified? Further, might diagnosis and classification *serve* children by providing entree to services, helping their families and caregivers make sense of their problems, guiding child helpers to pertinent treatment literature, and facilitating the development of knowledge? The existence of organic contributors to behavioral disturbances is the best argument for giving children's problems diagnostic labels. For example, autism is a well-defined syndrome with apparent physiological underpinnings (Hauser, DeLong, and Rosman, 1975). Even though autism's expression and its primary and secondary contributors are not identical across children, autism's physical bases make diagnosis possible even in the first three years (Schopler, 1978). This syndrome is clearly not just learned or a simple composite of discrete and independent problems. Hyperactivity also appears to have a physiological component. Hyperactivity commonly begins in infancy (Campbell, Scheifer, Weiss, and Perlman, 1977) and is diagnosable by age two (Chamberlain, 1977).

A common cluster of behaviors is observable for hyperactive children throughout their childhoods (Barkley, 1981). Although the extent of physiological insult and environmental and familial contexts influence the characteristics of hyperactivity, this condition is also the result of much more than labeling biases or detrimental child care.

Knowledge of diagnosis also facilitates the child helper's use of helping services. Categorical labels provide rallying points for parent self-help groups and leverage for obtaining suitable classroom placements or special services via the Education for All Children Act of 1974 and funding for new programs (Clarizio and McCoy, 1983). Thus, pragmatism and practice argue for a careful use of empirically based classifications. Most child helpers have little choice about which classification systems they must apply; choices are made at the point of implementation. Many children currently have no classification or a global classification (Cerreto and Tuma, 1977), several classifications (Gorham and others, 1975), or unsubstantiated classifications (O'Leary and Turkewitz, 1978). These practices should not prevail.

Motivation. Behavior obeys the law of *inertia*, a fundamental property of matter. It does not start or stop unless there is good reason. Child helpers can help provide good reasons for behavior change with actions based on knowledge of motivation. Motivation to act and to maintain action arises from the child's or caregiver's very personal understanding of the available benefits and penalties within the social ecology. Awareness of social and cognitive conditions associated with change helps the child helper perform in every role. The desire for astute matching of social incentives with personal traits may help motivate the child helper to pore over research articles at the university library, motivate the physician's receptionist to arrange a medical evaluation of the child that day, motivate the parent to keep firm limits, and motivate the adolescent to resist the impulse to run away again. Knowledge of motivation enables greater success in direct treatment (Bandura, 1977), case management (Wiltse and Remy, 1982), and even community organizing and child advocacy (Weisner and Silver, 1981).

Child helpers with adequate knowledge of motivation shun the commonplace and egregrious notion that motivation is inside a child or caregiver. *Motivation* is a noun. This suggests that it is a "thing"—like a tooth—that a person has or is missing. Motivation is not a thing; it is an interaction between individuals and their environments. To carry the biological analogy forward, motivation is like muscle; it becomes larger or smaller as a result of activities that involve individuals and the press and pull of their worlds. Motivational deficits are not the fault of the caregiver or child. If a child is not striving for the goal that the child helper wants, then the child helper has failed to provide adequate social or material incentives or to address cognitive constraints on the child's or caregiver's appraisal of those incentives. Techniques for increasing motivation are discussed throughout this book.

The preconditions of troubled development and child helping are many. Changing the conditions at all levels of a child's ecology is not possible. Fortunately, such universal change is not essential to providing significant help. Changes at one level or in one part of a child's ecosystem may result in broad changes. Similarly, simultaneously mastering all child-helping competencies is not a necessary precursor of helping. A basic understanding of the principles of development and the contributors to maladjustment can be supplemented with knowledge of the development and course of the problems of children and their families that are particular to each setting. (Later chapters provide specific information about problems seen in many child-helping agencies.) In all cases, the child helper can call on his or her competencies, the competencies of the social ecology, and the competencies of children and their families to make small and durable changes that lead to new competencies and resources.

2

Assessing Children's Problems and Environments

The possibilities of helping begin with the first contact between the child helper and the troubled child's social ecology. The possibility of help may become help in reality as a result of many actions; or it may remain merely a possibility. The helper may conduct classic, face-to-face therapy with the child in a clinical milieu, may include a large part of the child's network, or may work with only the child and one caregiver. The child helper may work with people who previously knew nothing about the child—for example, a director of a distant special school—or who already knew too much about the child—as might the sibling of a mentally retarded child. This chapter will describe the beginning of the helping process. The model presented in this and the following chapters can be applied to a range of intervention strategies and a broad array of client problems.

The structure of helping is built around the tasks of helping. Actions within each of the components of the helping process are expressed through specific child-helper and client tasks. For a description of these components, I draw on Pincus and Minahan's (1973) systems approach; the task-centered approach described by Epstein (1980) and Reid (1981); Kanfer and Grimm's (1980) process model of therapy; and Stein's (1982) case-management perspective. These components are: (1) initial contact and decision making, (2) engagement and role orientation, (3) problem identification and ranking, (4) development of a service agreement, (5) problem analysis, (6) selection of an intervention, (7) development of a plan, (8) completion of the plan, (9) promotion of post-treatment success, (10) monitoring and evaluation of progress, and (11) termination and transfer. This chapter will address the first five elements—the basic components of assessment. The other elements focus primarily on intervention and will be discussed in Chapter Three. Before proceeding to discuss these components of helping, we will first consider the issue of relationship.

Relationship

Relationship is a summary label for many social and cognitive responses. The list of characteristics that may be key contributors to relationship is all but endless; humor, warmth, empathy, genuineness, nonjudgmental acceptance, concreteness, appropriate self-disclosure, attentiveness, and flexibility are but a small sample. Relationship and structure are partners. The essential role of relationship is motivation; the social rewards and punishments involved in relationship motivate adherence to the helping structure. Other sources treat the subject of relationship comprehensively (see, for example, Perlman, 1979) and describe the components of relationship-enhancing behavior (Egan, 1977; Gambrill, 1983), so this discussion will instead focus on identifying some misconceptions about relationship.

First, relationship is a result of, rather than a prerequisite to, work on clients' problems (Perlman, 1979). Clients do not come to the child helper for relationship; they come to alleviate problems (whether these be problems they see in themselves or those that others have labeled them as having). Few clients would complain if they were denied a relationship with a child helper. The relationship is for the child helper's use more than the client's. Clients do, of course, welcome relationship when it arises and reap benefits from relationship that may be separate from those specifically related to their problems. The vagaries of teaching, child care, parenting, and childhood are great, and all parties profit from the opportunity to turn to someone they find helpful and enjoyable. But helpfulness and enjoyableness are not interchangeable. Enjoyable exchanges have their place during most of the client's and child helper's work together and help motivate continued contact, but they are not the reason for relationship. Task accomplishment is the reason.

Second, the child helper should not endeavor to make his or her relationship with the client unique and special. The child-helping relationship should be genuine, positive, and appealing, but it should not compete with relationships between the client and members of his or her social ecology. The child helper should strive not to become the client's only confidant or a fantasy parent or spouse. Such transferences are not an inevitable part of the helping relationship and should be minimized. The socio-ecological perspective encourages inclusion of other models of competent performance and promotes attractive relationships in the family and community that endure long after the child helper has closed the case.

Third, although the child helper should certainly model an egalitarian and fair style of coping with people and situations, social reform is not the central goal of helping. The super-ordinate goal is to help families and their children manage adequately within their social ecologies. Only when clients' attitudes and actions (however acceptable or unacceptable) prevent self-protection or preempt the competent use of cognitive and social resources should they be a target of change. As Alexander and Parsons (1982) write, "if families terminate therapy because we blatantly ignored or even opposed their expectations, then we have failed no matter how noble our social ideals. In other words, we feel that our goals in family therapy should be kept separate from our ideals and goals as members of society" (p. 97). Child helpers can strive to maintain their own ways of relating in the treatment setting, but their commitment to their own cultural biases should yield when client welfare calls. As the child-helping relationship progresses, true colors may be more freely flown.

Fourth, nonjudgmental acceptance need not be a goal of child helping. Children and their families sometimes do terrible things to themselves and others. Child helpers must make difficult decisions about reporting their clients' physical or sexual abuse, substance abuse, neglect, delinquency, robbery, or burglary. Sometimes as difficult to label and confront are failures to complete agreed-on tasks, the use of threats in solving problems, and the invocation of cultural traditions and stereotypes to justify harmful acts. New relationships may not be able to withstand much confrontation, but the child-helping process often cannot succeed without it.

Fifth, the child helper need rarely fear that children or their families will develop such a dependence on them that they will cease to function on their own. Dependence involves the suspension of habitual patterns of coping while borrowing and testing new ways. This is the pathway to change. The client's dependence on the child helper is an acknowledgment that the child helper's ways are worth trying out. Learning new ways takes time and may require an intensive and extended period of consulation, problem solving, and general hand holding. Phillips and Wolpe (1981) reported a case of a severly ritualistic and phobic twelve-year-old who had been largely housebound for two and one-half years and who had an alcoholic father and an agoraphobic mother. Therapy required eighty-eight sessions over more than a year's time. At some point in this process every family member relied on the therapists for instruction, reassurance, and hope. Two years later the child was free of rituals and constraining fears; new skills learned during an extended dependence on child helpers led him to a heretofore unknown independence.

Initial Contact and Decision Making

Child helpers' expectations of clients and potential clients change over the course of helping. At the initial contact, the child helper's central task is to make decisions about the course of helping. The client's central task is to give and get information that will help him or her and the child helper decide on the best treatment. This decision must be based on answers to the fundamental helping questions: Are services needed at all? If so, what services does the client need? What role should the child helper play in delivering those services and who else should be involved? As these questions are answered, the expectations of clients and helpers change.

Are Services Needed?

Many children can benefit from services; fewer would not improve in time without services; a few may be harmed by services. Treatment should not begin until child helpers are reasonably assured that the problem will not worsen as a result. This seems an obvious point, but it is one that is routinely disregarded. The history of treating status offenders, for instance, is a striking example of providing services to young people who might have done better without them (Sarri, 1980). Many interventions are not based on solid evidence that the problem to be treated is stable or will have deleterious long-range effects if not treated (Edelbrock and Achenbach, 1980). It is not clear, for example, that early childhood fears and social isolation are stable and harmful problems. Some interventions, including treatments of children's alternative gender choices, obesity, and sexual activity between minors, may arise from the helper's personal preferences and so require scrutiny. Decisions about the need for services must call on the child helper's ethics as well as his or her knowledge of development.

What Services Are Needed?

Early contacts with clients often result from referrals. Referrers often lack a full understanding of other agencies' services and may base the referral on a limited or even incorrect understanding of the client's problems and of alternative services. Fewer misreferrals occur when child helpers fully communicate their understanding of their client's problems and why the client was referred to them. This shared perception of the referral helps delineate the cases in which the service that the child helper and his or her agency can offer is the most fitting source of help. With the inevitably fragmented continuum of services, child helpers in all agencies must recognize the broad possibilities of their agencies and overcome agency limitations and at the same time strive to organize and coordinate allied services.

Determining the match between clients and services calls for the best available understanding of case specifics and a few generic rules for evaluating services. Client problems limit the range of services that are potentially appropriate, although child helpers often err, first in thinking that family problems are mental health problems, and second in concluding that treatment should necessarily be sought from mental health services. A range of alternative services and resources may provide families with much of what they need. Regardless of the problem presented for therapy or the source of a referral, the following issues should be considered.

Available Models of Competent Performance

1. Culturally acceptable mentors and models
2. Cross-aged or more seasoned same-aged models
3. Models of skills needed in the next treatment setting or for independent functioning

Least-Restrictive Necessary Service

1. Child has opportunities for successful contact with other people and settings
2. Within-setting opportunities vary as child's self-management skills increase
3. Structure is sufficient to motivate learning and use of competencies

Assistance in Obtaining Material and Social Support

1. Contact with nonprofessional others is maximized
2. Material aid is provided as available and needed
3. Opportunities to maintain contact with families, peers, and communities of origin are maintained
4. Inter-generational ties are supported

Between-Setting Coordination

1. Consistent application of social and cognitive teaching and motivation systems
2. System of communication between treatment settings or individuals
3. Established aftercare follow-up program

Service Standards

1. Data-based approach to target problem(s)
2. Ethical practice
3. Outcome evaluation

Available Models of Competent Performance. Services must include models of the desired client performance. Simply uncovering concerns, discussing problems, and considering alternatives are often not enough. Instruction and example are in many cases irreplaceable. Agencies or individual clinicians can arrange access to other competent professionals. Fully or partially residential services offer less-skilled youth the chance to learn positive coping strategies from older residents or ex-residents (Wolins and Wozner, 1982). For children in settings (such as day treatment, full-week foster care, and special education classrooms) that are not intended as their final destination, the competencies should prepare them for their next settings (for example, special education classrooms, weekday foster care, or mainstream classrooms). This requires knowledge of the social ecologies in a child's future. As in the Re-ED model (Hobbs, 1982), child helpers should begin to develop plans for children's next settings from the very start of services and should deliver services with the guidance of those plans.

Least-Restrictive Necessary Service. The least-restrictive necessary service is the preferred service. This commonly accepted principle should not be used to support undersupervised placements or to argue for a closing of residential facilities. Undersupervised placements are unjustifiable in all cases, and residential facilities can be justified in many cases. Least-restrictive placements are those that provide the structure necessary for learning new competencies in a safe and reasonably secure setting. Research shows that placement of children in mainstream settings that provide insufficient structure may, though they promise the freedom to associate with competent peers, be unsuccessful and unhappy placements (Leinhardt and Pallay, 1982). Services with only the most necessary restrictions provide children and youth with the chance to learn to problem solve in a wide range of situations and to participate in social ecologies with opportunities for responsibility and reward (Madden and Slavin, 1983). Although unrestricted access to such situations does not ensure that effective problem solving will occur (this requires instruction), overly restrictive settings often ensure that such problem solving does not occur.

Assistance in Obtaining Material and Social Support. Services that do not provide clients with assistance in obtaining needed material and social support rarely merit referrals from child helpers. Treatments that focus solely on a child's or caregiver's inner experience and are not directly intended to enable greater access to or use of community resources are unlikely to lead to long-term change. Children discharged from residential care without improved linkages to social supports in the community quickly return to their pretreatment behavior patterns (Whittaker, 1983). Even though not all service providers can deliver material services, those who shun that role or do not provide clients with ample guidance in obtaining needed financial assistance provide incomplete services. Similarly, services that do not provide skills for increasing the yield from social-support networks are not fulfilling their helping potential.

Between-Setting Coordination. Commitment, personnel, and skill for between-setting service coordination are crucial to service delivery. For example, residential treatment staff should have the training and the time to meet with families, contact school teachers about attendance, meet with social service and mental health case managers, and identify after-school learning opportunities that will promote the attainment of the child's discharge plan. One group home that the author evaluated had a liaison specialist on staff. Demands on his time for supervision of the children in the house were so great, however, that he cut back his community-contact hours and limited his liaison role to the schools. He could not find time to work with the youths' families. Services that do not support their liaison positions are unlikely to serve children and their families well.

Service Standards. The standards of service providers are also critical to the choice of services. That ethical practice is of foremost importance is easy to concede; more difficult is determining which services are ethical. Providing "usual and customary" services, if these are shown to be ineffective or inferior to other services, can be viewed as unethical because this misleads clients into believing that they are being helped. Although no child helper can guarantee that his or her services will help, those services based on procedures supported by research and those that monitor client changes during treatment will most probably be helpful and most assuredly be ethical (given equivalent respect for other ethical standards).

What Role Should Child Helpers Assume?

Child helpers often decide to work as change agents directly with clients or as consultants or case coordinators—or some combination of these. This decision, like most others, emerges and changes over the course of the helping process. The helping role often depends upon agency dictates. Many agencies deal with the child and family in segmented, specialized fashion, so that the parents are seen by social workers, and the child meets with psychiatrists and psychologists for "psychotherapy" and with special educators for "academic therapy." In such agencies, the opportunities for role change are typically small, and the coordination of services is well defined. When interagency coordination is attempted, the opportunities for changes in roles are greater, and the choice of roles is more difficult. Convening an interagency staff meeting may be required to identify the roles of each agency and staff member (Kaersvang and Clark, 1982). Child helpers with uncertainty about the parts they play or who doubt that the client's interests are efficiently served should vigorously pursue clarification and change. This uncertainty may reflect an uncoordinated effort in need of redress.

Direct treatment, directly assuming responsibility for treatment, is a popular choice among child helpers. The treatment role is attractive and useful, and this book attempts to articulate its possibilities in the majority of its pages. Consultation and case coordination are also rewarding and useful roles. Other sources (for example, Bertsche and Horejsi, 1980; Curtis and Zins, 1981; Weil, Karls, and Associates, 1985) articulate the activities and responsibilities of these roles more fully than space in this book allows. Some discussion of the relationship among direct treatment, consultation, and case coordination is warranted nevertheless, for these roles converge in the practice of child helping.

Consultation in child helping dates back at least to the visiting teachers of the 1900s (Levine and Levine, 1970). Consultation continues to play a key role in child helping, although it often is subjugated to more glamorous direct treatment. Consultation involves informing, instructing, modeling, and assisting other child helpers or potential child helpers. Like direct treatment, consultation has too long relied on strategies designed to change the consultee's perceptions in the hope that these changes will translate into changes in the consultee's behavior and, finally, changes in the behavior of the child. The effectiveness of this "therapeutic consultation" strategy has not been confirmed by research (as discussed in Alpert, 1976). In response to these discouraging findings, more recent attempts have used techniques based on social learning theory and instructional models (for example, Bergan, Kratochwill, and Luton, 1980; Russell, 1978). These programs offer more optimism as to the effectiveness of consultation (Mayer, Butterworth, Nafpaktitis, and Sulzer-Azaroff, 1983).

Consultation should increase the resources of the target child's social ecology in a lasting way and, therefore, result in enduring improvement in the child's behavior. Further, by increasing the skills of child helpers or caregivers in the child's social ecology, consultation should increase the resources available to other at-risk children. Consultation with caregivers or, when possible, other child helpers with greater influence on the child should be the intervention of first choice. Consultation will be discussed in Chapter Four.

Case coordination, also known as *case management*, involves contact with children and other child helpers. Effective case coordination involves such tasks as assessing the client's eligibility for services and authorizing payment for services, assembling significant members of the child's social ecology and formulating goals and intervention plans, monitoring adherence to these plans, completing the paperwork needed to document adherence to the plans, helping the client and his or her caregivers complete the plans, providing support to the client in times of crisis or difficulty with other service providers, acting as liaison between the client and informal resources, and modifying service delivery systems as needed (Bertsche and Horejsi, 1980). Knowledge of case coordination also helps child helpers in direct-treatment roles. Because case coordinators often determine whether agencies receive referrals and reimbursements, child helpers must understand how to collaborate with case coordinators. Case coordination is discussed further in Chapter Four.

Engagement and Role Orientation

Beginning with the initial contact, child helpers shape clients' commitment to treatment and facilitation of social and cognitive change. During this time of problem definition and decision making, families are often embarrassed, hesitant, and cautious. The child helper's goal is to encourage all family members to commit themselves to the structure of treatment and its many demands for changes in beliefs and behaviors. How the child helper can help engage hesitant clients in useful roles is illustrated in the following exchange:

Child helper: Mrs. Montana and Jeanne, welcome. I'm pleased to see you. Mrs. Montana, when we talked by phone you described the difficulties that you and Jeanne have been having with her not going to school. Please tell me more about what you see as the problem.

Mrs. Montana: Well, there are a lot of problems between us. I'm not sure where to start or that we can really do anything. Maybe fighting is just part of living with teenagers. Or maybe Jeanne just has problems that can't be fixed.

Child helper: When you called before, you told me that, in your words, what is going on is just not right and that you wanted to change it. It sounds like you are now wondering whether you just have to live with these problems.

Mrs. Montana: You're right. I do want to try to make life at home better. I can always live with them if I have to, but I still hope these problems will end.

Jeanne: You talk about these problems, but you really mean me, don't you? Well, then, I should say that I think there's a problem—but not one that you can solve unless my mother learns to let me grow up and make my own decisions about what is best for me.

Child helper: You two clearly have something valuable to talk about—each of you seems to want to make the case that the other is mostly the cause of your problems. That's natural. I don't usually find that very helpful, however, sc I will try to distract you from debating who is at fault by getting you to talk about what you find to be a problem and what each of you can do differently about it. I won't expect you entirely to stop pointing out how you think the other person is responsible for the problem, however, as that is usually informative and can also tell me a lot about your role. I will expect, though, that you do more than just blame each other.

The child helper works to engender hopefulness in the client and the client's system. More specifically, after the initial interview or two, each participant should agree that the child helper "was as much on my side as anyone else's, saw how my life is made tougher by the family problems, helped me to begin sorting out the problems, left me thinking that the way I understood the problems might not be the only way to view them, and made me believe that the problems can be reduced" (Alexander and Parsons, 1982). These impressions usually should be fostered through an orderly interview. At this early point of treatment, the child helper should avoid situations where the families act "naturally." Family relationships and rules should be of interest to the child helper only because they may hinder the solution of the problem. Clients should not be allowed to digress ("You've been telling us many things that we can get back to—right now I would like to hear more from you, Mrs. Montana, about the difficulties this problem causes you"), interrupt each other ("Mrs. Montana, hold that one moment while Jeanne finishes"), or blame one another ("Hold on, Mrs. Montana! You may not be aware, but you are saying it's Jeanne's fault again. That's interesting, but you had been saying what you thought you contribute to this problem. That's very helpful, too. Please say more"). With warmth, good humor, and control, the child helper facilitates each client's entry into the structure of treatment. In short, the child helper must be directive to keep the meeting from becoming a forum for blaming or pessimism or being dominated by one person.

The initial contact is a time for symmetry. No matter who starts and what order families choose, everyone should get a chance to describe what aspects of the current situation are a problem for him or her, identify what he or she would like to be changed, and help to compile and order a list of problems. This is a time for minimal interpretation, confrontation, and self-disclosure and much simplifying and rephrasing of family concerns. This is also a time for attention to the strengths and potentials of the family and all of the relationships within it (Jacobson and Margolin, 1979; Patterson, 1982; Satir, 1967). The interviewer should not dredge for guilt, worries, anger, or frustration, but instead pull out positive feelings, initiative, and a sense of the possibility of change.

Determining the Child's Role. Helping a child find a valuable role in treatment is important. The child's contribution to treatment will improve with adequate role orientation. Whether the child is seen as part of a family in family treatment, as the focus of parent training, or as the client in child therapy, the child's role has certain characteristics. First, children should understand that the child helper is interested in their experiences and in any ways that family or school life could be better for them (DiGiuseppe, 1981). Children should then come to see that they and their families are going to learn new ways of interacting to make life in the family better for everyone. Like learning other new skills, this will take time and practice and will probably involve trying some things that at first are uncomfortable or difficult. Because children are rarely effusive or problem oriented at first, child helpers often have difficulty knowing whether they understand these points. This need not stall the helping effort. Children, like their parents, often respond more to expectations for role fulfillment than to statements of intentions. Child helpers can underscore their commitment to problem solving and learning and to incorporating children's perspectives at many points in the helping process. Kendall (1981) and others (for example, Barbrack and Maher, 1984) have shown that including children's perspectives and providing many opportunities for children to choose the problems to be discussed and the events, tasks, and rewards of treatment do improve outcomes.

The child helper should, if anything, err on the side of including children in treatment. Inclusion does not, however, mean that the child must be part of every transaction between the caregivers and the child helper. The child's inclusion underscores the importance of the child's ideas and efforts, but the child must also learn that parents have a unique role that includes privileged discussions. Certainly children who are very young or incapacitated will not be able to contribute significantly to discussions. Their presence in the discussion may still be useful to them and encourage their later participation in changes that the family agrees to make. Especially if parents have not previously been involved with special services, talking with parents before children participate in treatment sessions may help reassure them that the helping process is designed to increase their ability to give their child a bright future and not to undermine their parental position. (Implications for the use of family-therapy or parent-training approaches to treatment are further discussed in Chapter Four.) Several ways of including children in treatment and some reasons for choosing one way or another are listed in Table 2.

Cultural Concerns. Role orientation and engagement differ by culture. Whether a person is white, black, Latino, or Native American; male or female; literate or illiterate; or rural, suburban, or urban affects the expectations the person brings to treatment. Some people expect to "get it all out on the table," and

Table 2. Considerations in Deciding Who to Include in Treatment.

Format	Indicators
1. Child only	1. Child's caregiver has been or may be assaultive, is in a temporary role, or is not capable of treatment because of substance abuse or individual problems
2. Caregiver only in infrequent meetings	2. Caregiver is very busy or able to carry out limited behavior-change program without much help, or child's problem does not occur in setting supervised by caregiver
3. Caregiver only in frequent meetings	3. More complex and enduring child needs (e.g., developmental delays) of very young or incoherent child; the child is not residing with the caregivers, who must reorganize their life-styles to achieve child's return; caregivers are uncertain about their desire to change and be reunited with child
4. Caregiver only, then caregiver and child frequently, then less frequently	4. Younger child, limited intervention by caregiver
5. Caregiver at first and then caregiver and youth	5. Crisis intervention for adolescents; need to establish parental involvement or authority; many family crises
6. Caregiver and youth together at all times	6. Chronic family problems, adolescent who is hostile or suspicious or adolescent who is prepared to handle all family information
7. Caregiver and child or caregiver alone plus couple therapy	7. Caregivers disagree on or cannot consistently apply roles because of limited problem-solving skills

some expect only to provide simple responses to the child helper's questions. Some clients need to learn that the purpose of treatment is problem solving and task accomplishment and not catharsis or lament—welcome news to many families who prefer child helpers to teach skills and problem-solving techniques rather than to emphasize insight (Bernal, Klinnert, and Schultz, 1980). Minority clients may especially benefit from direct instruction or videotape models of key treatment components. This would encourage them to (1) not hide their problems, (2) say what they think about what is going on, even about their therapist, (3) tell their therapist if they plan to miss an appointment, (4) tell their therapist if they think treatment is taking too long, (5) talk about any problems they wish to—no problem is too small to talk about, and (6) try to talk about problems, even if this is embarrassing or difficult (Acosta, Evans, Yamamoto, and Wilcox, 1980).

Cultural perspectives on including significant others also vary. Native American families typically include extended kin and tribal members in their unstated definitions of family, whereas clients from English or Chinese background may define family membership more narrowly and resent sharing personal matters with their extended families or neighbors.

Information from many sources interacts with clients' cultural backgrounds to shape expectations. Movies and television, columnists, friends and acquaintances, and previous experiences influence clients' behaviors. The referring agent is a crucial source of information for parents and adolescents not living at home; for children, parents normally assume the not-so-easy task of explaining the purpose and process of treatment. The best and worst referrers have one thing in common: whatever they say will be reinterpreted by the client to yield a conclusion that does not perfectly match what they want. Time spent learning what clients believe about treatment goals, procedures, duration, costs, and outcomes will be well spent. The child helper need not ferret out clients' expectations regarding all of these matters but only inform them of what is correct and be aware of preconceptions that may interfere with clients' engagement in the change process. With example, selective encouragement, and respect for general classes of desired behaviors rather than demand for familiar client responses, child helpers can accommodate both the clients' expectations and the requirements of problem-specific, goal-oriented, task-centered practice. Some common pretreatment expectations and the expectations that the child helper should foster are listed in Table 3.

Table 3. Common Pretreatment Expectations of Parents and Children.

Pretreatment Expectations	Corrected Expectations
Treatment Goal	
Parents: To figure out why our child acts like he or she does.	*Parents:* To develop new family patterns that will be more successful.
Child: To be left alone and have problems go away.	*Child:* To develop new skills for handling problems.
Procedure	
Parents: To talk about our feelings and uncover the problems.	*Parents:* To improve our problem-solving skills and to plan for and implement new actions.
Child: To play with toys a lot and just act like myself.	*Child:* To try out new ways of handling situations that trouble me and my family.
Duration	
Parents: Until the child helper gets to the bottom of all the problems or until the mandated time is up.	*Parents:* Consider stopping after every month and any time that the child helper decides.
Child: Forever.	*Child:* If after a month you do not want to come, I will support your decision.
Costs	
Parents: Well, you know how much doctors cost.	*Parents:* According to our ability to pay.
Child: (None)	*Child:* (None)
Outcome	
Parents: Everything will be better afterward—or, these people cannot really help.	*Parents:* Hard work and persistence will yield some small but important changes.
Child: I will learn to follow rules and feel better about myself.	*Child:* I will learn to act more successfully and manage situations that do go wrong.

Problem Identification and Ranking

Paramount to determining service and treatment needs is identification of the presenting problem. The presenting problem is at times obvious and at times obscure. At this point in the treatment structure, the goal of the assessment is to ascertain what problems the client must address and what problems the client chooses to address (Epstein, 1980). *Mandated* problems are those identified by a social, educational, or legal institution as needing attention. If the mandated problem is not corrected, sanctions will be invoked. *Client-chosen* problems are problems related to the mandated problem. Tammy's mandated problem is her stealing. She will be suspended from school unless she shows that she will no longer steal class materials and peers' possessions. In her meeting with the child helper she says that everyone picks on her and makes up lies about her stealing. She agrees that she would like to be treated more positively by professionals and children. This is her client-chosen problem.

For children, most problems are mandated. Few children understand or agree with reasons for treatment. Although parents are more likely to seek changes in their children's behaviors, many parents at the same time resist changing their contribution to children's problems until mandated to do so. Juvenile justice and child welfare services (more than mental health or educational institutions) often mandate changes in family behaviors to facilitate such desired outcomes as unifying the family.

Child helpers must consider their ability to help clients alleviate mandated and, to a lesser extent, client-chosen problems and the ability of alternate services to orchestrate and deliver child-helping services. Clients are held accountable for their failure to achieve mandated change. Failures occur in all child-helping agencies, but they should not be the fault of poorly conceptualized or delivered helping efforts. Child helpers who are not able to deliver services to help clients with their mandated problems—to alleviate, for example, the unchecked bed-wetting of a child who is otherwise ready to move from institutional care to a group home—should seek assistance from other service providers. Many parents are naive about the need for help or shrewdly avoid professional services until professionals inform them that they have a problem by virtue of an administrative or legal mandate. By compelling behavior-change efforts, mandates can serve the client. For example, many child helpers have sought legal or administrative sanctions to motivate clients to attend and participate in behavior-change treatments.

Mandates and sanctions are not enough, however, to promote behavior change. Consider how often maltreating families confronted with the loss of their children still fail to provide the minimum sufficient standard of care (Borgman, 1981) and adolescents drop out of school rather than follow mandated guidelines (Children's Defense Fund, 1974).

Clients are often more motivated to solve client-chosen problems than mandated problems. Such problems are often of central significance to clients. A child with impulse-control problems may articulate this problem as "I wish everybody would stop worrying about me and treating me so mean." After some prompts to elicit more specific responses about what part of the child's daily life might improve, the child might describe the problem specifically as "I want to be in a new reading group and not to have to keep sitting on the bench at recess and lunch." Child helpers need not wring problem statements out of a child who does not quickly nominate a problem. Younger children often suspend disbelief and engage in activities whose rationale they do not understand. Relationship, encouragement, structure, and social reward for tackling tasks may prove sufficiently motivating. Undue emphasis on problems may make the child's experience unnecessarily stigmatizing.

Decisions also must be made about which problems to address and in what order to address them. Two or three problems are enough (Epstein, 1980). Choosing problems is far easier than sticking with those choices. The failure to choose a problem and commit one's efforts to addressing that problem is perhaps the most common and most harmful failure in child treatment. Abandoning treatment goals costs time, momentum, and confidence. Regular shifting of goals also provides clients with a poor model of problem solving. Shifts often are rationalized on the grounds of need for spontaneity, sensitivity to client-stated changes in needs, and relief from the frustration of solving agreed-upon tasks, but the gains are rarely as great as the costs.

Proper problem selection and ranking can often prevent switching problems later. Consider fourteen-year-old Jacky. He is a typical referral to a school district's interagency team. He is frequently truant, uses alcohol and drugs, gets into racial fights, threatens teachers and peers, and performs poorly academically. Each of these problems deserves prompt attention. In collaboration with Jacky, one mandated and one client-chosen problem—fighting and school performance, respectively—are chosen. Goals and objectives (activities directed at goal attainment) are chosen through discussion with Jacky. Jacky, as most children would, may temporarily fight less to avoid the threatened expulsion. With this problem apparently corrected, the child helper is tempted to take on a third problem: Jacky's distress because of his girlfriend's pregnancy. The child helper in this case resisted the temptation—instead referring Jacky to a Planned Parenthood counselor—and continued to work on objectives in support of the key problems' resolution. When Jacky's initial resolve to stop fighting wanes, he will have had a longer preparation period in which to learn to control his fighting.

Criteria for ranking problems, goals, and objectives are straightforward. Little empirical data now informs the problem-selection process, and until more investigations are concluded a child helper can justify many different approaches to problems so long as they make sense to the child helper, the client, and those responsible for the client. A few rules should be followed, though. Mandated problems are ranked highest along with matching client-chosen problems. Correcting easier client-chosen problems can give an early boost to commitment and so often should be tackled first. Problems that are closely connected to others' problems offer the promise of a large impact should they be ameliorated, but they may also be the most recalcitrant. Such problems include alcohol use, academic failure, and unstructured home life. Problems whose resolution will be supported by the social ecology also deserve priorty (Baer and Wolf, 1970).

Problem identification and ranking continue well past the initial meetings with clients. Clients will develop new problems and reveal longstanding problems at later times. New information does not necessitate changes in problem ranking. Learning that a mother drinks to excess may require a referral to an alcohol-treatment program but ought not change the goal of strengthening her caregiving skills. Child helpers should, on the whole, continue to work on old problems rather than shift to work on new ones.

Development of a Service Agreement

Goals, plans, and tasks stem from problems. *Problems* are what is wrong, and *goals* are the desired improvements. *Plans* are the general strategies for achieving goals that incorporate treatment. *Tasks* are actions by child helpers or clients that lead to the accomplishment of plans. Tasks are the substance of helping and include phone calls, homework, practice, keeping records of one's own performance, reading instructions, implementing new reward systems, and talking to significant others. Tasks need not be included in the initial service agreement but are agreed on and recorded in the course of helping.

For Jacky, the first problem was fighting, and its reduction was mandated. The goal was to help Jacky develop social and cognitive skills for not fighting. (*Not fighting* could be more positively labeled *cooperation* or *self-management*, but for children and youth, the simplest terms—even if they are negative—are often the best.)

Jacky agreed to attempt four tasks to meet this goal: (1) to meet with the counselor to practice handling racial comments, (2) to contact one friend outside of the fighting group, (3) to talk to his math teacher and pledge to attend class every day during the next week, and (4) to talk to his girlfriend about tutoring him in English. The counselor agreed to complete two tasks: (1) to meet with Jacky each week to assess his progress, help him improve his skills for keeping calm, and develop new tasks to help him reach his goal; and (2) to talk to the vice-principal of the school about Jacky's plan.

A written service agreement between Jacky and his school social worker Mr. How, is shown in Exhibit 1. Service agreements are not legal documents but are guides to action and statements of intention; they are not unalterable contracts. Service agreements that are highly specific may be too binding and cumbersome. A service agreement is minimally complete when it includes a problem, a goal, a plan, and some indication of the commitment of the people involved in pursuing the plan. Agreements can be tightened if the parties disagree on what they really mean.

Exhibit 1. Sample Service Agreement.

This agreement is between:

Client's name: Mr. Jacky Jaxxi   Child helper's name: Mr. Paul How

Problem 1: Jacky's fighting and his threatened expulsion for it.

  Goal 1: To reduce Jacky's fighting to one time in the next month and 0 times thereafter.

  Plan: (a) Increase involvement with nonfighting friends, (b) practice social skills for handling racial comments that upset Jacky, (c) practice cognitive skills for keeping calm, (d) find after-school job.

Problem 2: Jacky gets hassled by his teachers.

  Goal 2: Increase number of days Jacky attends class and is not hassled.

  Plan: (a) Set up conference with each teacher, (b) improve attendance and classroom behavior, (c) develop system for getting homework done, (d) get tutoring in one subject from girlfriend.

Schedule for meetings: Every Tuesday this month.
Schedule for agreement review: End of each month.
Target completion date: Three months.

We agree to meet to achieve our goals and to review this agreement on schedule.

Client's signature: _____   Date: _____

Child helper's signature: _____   Date: _____

An experimental investigation of the different effects of written and verbal service agreements in family therapy confirmed the importance of written agreements in helping clients maintain awareness of the goals of treatment, distinguish between goals they initially agreed to work on and other goals, and believe that treatment will primarily address those goals agreed upon (Klier, Fein, and Genero, 1984). Families with either written or verbal contracts were equally likely, however, to continue in treatment, to state that they had accomplished most of their treatment goals, and to maintain the improvement they had achieved after three months. (For additional discussion of purposes for, formats of, and issues in using contracts and service agreements, see, for example, Gambrill, 1983; Pincus and Minahan, 1973). In almost any format, and even with small and handicapped children, the message of service agreements seems to come through: that "we are committed to work together on a sound plan to make a limited number of changes that will help make your experience more positive."

Service agreements may, nonetheless, cause trouble. Forethought may help prevent this trouble and help child helpers recognize difficulties as they arise. The first parameter of service agreements that requires consideration is the *timing* of the agreement. Service agreements developed before a satisfactory relationship with the client is established and before an adequate assessment is completed may not reflect the optimum goals and the most feasible plans. A service agreement drawn up too late may allow the child helper and client to drift from problem to problem and may not communicate the seriousness of the working agreement and the responsibility of all parties for its implementation. Second is the issue of *reasonableness*. Agreements should not contain overwhelming and immobilizing expectations of client change. Including mandated and client-chosen problems ameliorates this concern somewhat, but child helpers must be sensitive to the pressure on a child to make an agreement and not use that pressure to demand too much. If too much is demanded, it is likely that too little will be accomplished. Last, goal and plan *specificity* must be considered. The correct level of specificity is difficult to estimate. When the client follows the service agreement, then specific goals and plans are helpful. When goals and plans change, however, then more specific goals and plans quickly become obsolete, whereas broader ones continue to be relevant. Periodically revising service agreements reduces the problems that arise when goals and plans are too loose or tight. Moving toward a more general agreement as progress is made is another strategy for helping clients assume self-management. Finally, goals and plans should encourage child helpers to emphasize successful efforts, even when they are not fulfilled. Otherwise, clients may appraise their efforts as unrewarded.

Problem Analysis

The success of the specific actions of the plan relies on an understanding of the cognitive and social conditions that maintain the problem. Whereas goals and plans require a general analysis of what contributes to problems—an analysis achieved as much by study and experience as by specific inquiry—objectives and tasks require an analysis of the changeable conditions that maintain the problem (Ferster, Culbertson, and Boren, 1975). In a problem analysis the child helper and client strive to go beyond their abstract knowledge of general influences on behavior (including those discussed in Chapter One) and identify the specific social and cognitive events that contribute to the current difficulty. The analysis attempts to answer the question "What motivates the client to act this way?" rather than "How is the client acting?" This analysis informs the child helper and client of the tasks that might help create conditions to motivate more competent performance.

Problem analysis includes consideration of social and cognitive competencies and incentives. The competencies needed for minimum success in problem reduction or resolution are identified and contrasted with the competencies of the child and other members of his or her social ecology. Analyzing the incentives for behaviors that promote the current problem entails reviewing family, school, and community norms, models, rewards, and punishments.

A complete problem analysis prior to intervention is, therefore, not usually possible. Client problems cannot be fully understood. The pursuit of a complete understanding prior to intervention often leads to unprofitable expenditures of client and child helper time and effort and to information that is not useful to task design. Although a thorough preliminary assessment increases the odds of a successful start, child helpers will learn about the contributors to a child's behavior as they try to change them. Assessment flourishes during intervention. Assessment and intervention begin together during initial contact while the child helper appraises and shapes the client's expectations, and they proceed side by side during the course of treatment. At the outset and throughout this process, child helpers should look for some of the contributors discussed on the following pages.

Expectations

As described in Chapter One, the child-helping process involves reducing the discrepancy between the expectations of the social ecology and the resources of the child and family. Cultural expectations influence the incentives for skillful performance by determining which competencies are rewarded or punished. Clients' appraisals of the expectations of significant others also contribute to the incentives for action. Thus, if Mrs. Montana assumes that Jeanne will not expect her to confront her for talking back and that she will become irate if a confrontation does occur, Mrs. Montana will have an incentive to more effectively assert herself. Thus, others' expectations become one's own expectations. Jeanne may come to think, "If my mother doesn't expect me to listen to her and do what she says, then I guess this behavior is not going to be rewarded for me." Rigid appraisals of expectations may make clients miss or misunderstand changes in their social ecology. Chances to gain rewards may be missed if expectations preempt effort. Assessment must, then, tap (1) the expectations in the client's culture, (2) the expectations of members of the client's immediate social network, (3) the client's understanding of others' expectations, and (4) the client's expectations for himself or herself and others.

Children and caregivers often have a neighborhood culture, a family culture, a school or work culture, and at least one culture from a community of interest. These cultures typically expect different actions and offer competing incentives for action. One may reward combativeness and another passivity. Each provides social rewards and privileges according to its own criteria for competent behavior. A thorough problem analysis will ascertain the most important influences on performance in each culture in which a behavior is targeted for change.

Information on incentives influencing the behavior of a single member of the child's ecology can be obtained directly from other significant members of that ecology. Assessment of caregivers' ideal standards and their minimum acceptable standards will help a child helper identify the range of the child's behaviors that may be rewarded or punished. The differences in expectations among different caregivers (for example, the expectations of caregivers within two-parent families, schools, and group homes) are often striking. Problem analysis can illuminate behaviors that are rewarded, ignored, or punished by each caregiver.

Clients' assessments of the expectations of significant others are also key to their reactions. As indicated in the discussion of motivation in Chapter One, clients act according to their anticipation of the likelihood that the givers of rewards and punishments will find their performances satisfactory, will offer desirable rewards, and will deliver those rewards when they have been earned. Clients' reactions may be detrimental when their expectations of significant others differ from the expectations those others themselves hold. This can cause clients to pass up easily obtainable successes—"I never knew that you wanted to talk to me more, Pops; you're always so busy"—or to ignore a true change in family rules and so suffer the consequences—"Yeah, I know you said that, but you always say that, and you never kept me in on the weekend before, so I headed out."

Clients' expectations regarding their own performances also influence their actions. Depressed children and caregivers may have unrealistically high standards for their own performances (Petti, 1983; Heiby, 1983). These standards may leave them unsatisfied with their own performances and with the performances of others. For example, depressed mothers may be more irritable with their children than nondepressed mothers (Patterson, 1982). Children who estimate that they have little hope of succeeding may refuse to go to school and may be more prone to eating disorders and suicide (Wells and Stuart, 1981). Caregivers who cannot meet their expectations for fulfilling certain caregiving roles—"I can never get him to listen"—may abandon those roles and deplete the resources available to their children and their fellow caregivers.

Opportunities to assess expectations may occur during individual and family or other group interviews and during observation of children and their caregivers in their homes or in the community. Homework assignments and checklists also offer assessment opportunities. Asking youth and caregivers to describe each other's behavior if it were the way they wanted it to be and, alternately, if it were just adequate can provide child helpers with information about desired and acceptable changes. Checklists like that shown in Exhibit 2 can identify the expectations of different caregivers and provide a clear indicator of differences. These differences cannot always be reduced, but highlighting them will improve a child's chances of meeting various people's expectations. When expectations are written, ignorance of them is inexcusable. Further, having caregivers articulate their expectations can help them notice when children fulfill these expectations.

Resources

The client's ability to meet the expectations of the social ecology and obtain the resources needed for success must also be assessed. Materials and services, interpersonal skills, general self-management skills, and task-completion skills all contribute to a client's success.

Materials, Information, and Services. Comprehensive assessment must include consideration of the services the child currently receives and the material goods the child needs for adequate performance in his or her social ecology. Careful assessment of classroom instruction, goal and progress records at a group

Exhibit 2. Sample Classroom Rules.

This form is to help clarify classroom expectations. There may also be specific rules for situations not listed (feel free to add these).

Out-of-Seat-Rules	*Permission Never Needed*	*Permission Always Needed*	*Other (Please Explain Below)*
1. Out of seat during work periods	_____	_____	_____
2. Out of seat after work is finished	_____	_____	_____
3. Out of seat to approach teacher	_____	_____	_____
4. Getting a drink or using bathroom	_____	_____	_____
5. Pencil sharpening	_____	_____	_____
Talking-in-Class Rules			
6. Talk to teacher during academic work periods	_____	_____	_____
7. Talk to peers during academic work periods	_____	_____	_____
8. Talk to peers after work is completed	_____	_____	_____
9. Hand raising to answer questions during class discussion	_____	_____	_____

Other (Specific rules of school or class that need clarification)

_____

_____

_____

_____

home, or interactions with day-care providers and other ecologies in which the child operates is critical to increasing the child's fit into his or her environment. The criteria previously described for choosing appropriate services can help the child helper assess current services.

Children also need adequate material support for performance. Consider, for example, the eager, bright, obese adolescent who began to miss school because she had only one outfit that fit her. Her social worker obtained an emergency grant to buy her another outfit and some cloth and taught her to sew new outfits. Or consider the seventeen-year-old girl who wished to learn job skills to gain employment to get herself and her young son off AFDC. Her dream was to be trained as a beautician. Inadequate material support prevented her from entering a beauty school. Finally, through the assistance of her foster mother, she obtained a tuition grant from the foster-child scholarship fund and purchased the mannequin and uniform required of entrants to the beauty school she wanted to attend.

Interpersonal Skills. Interpersonal skills are resources for obtaining the benefits of informal supports and more formal work and school experiences. Possession of the social competencies described in Chapter One enables children and their caregivers to obtain resources that are rightfully but not automatically theirs. Standardized role-play and self-report assessments of social skills are available to child helpers, but their results generally are not very consistent or accurate predictors of performance in natural settings (Edelson, Ordman, and Rose, 1982; Michelson, Foster, and Ritchey, 1981). Problem-specific rehearsals of the social situations that clients must manage are a preferable assessment strategy and, along with a post-rehearsal discussion, can help identify cognitive- and social-skill deficits that impair clients' abilities to obtain resources. Social skills are as important for caregivers as for children. For example, the mother of a twelve-year-old boy with school problems had great difficulty contacting school teachers or administrators to learn whether her son had accomplished such daily goals as attending class, not fighting on the playground, and staying in his seat for most of class. The child helper quickly addressed her difficulty in contacting the school by designing a school-home note system that allowed her to get a written report of her son's behavior each day. Without a more complete assessment and amelioration of her difficulties in making social contact with the school, however, the intervention was doomed to failure. Her son understood the significance of her social-skill deficits better than the child helper and, knowing that his mother would not call the school to check up or troubleshoot, began to manipulate the note system. Improvements in his mother's ability to contact and engage in problem solving with school personnel were necessary to a smooth communication system.

Self-Management. Standardized techniques for assessing self-management skills are being developed but are still unsophisticated (Karoly, 1981; Kendall, 1981). Most often, self-management skills can be inferred from watching clients' compliance with naturally occurring rules and incentive systems (Karoly, 1981). Further assessment of self-management deficits should follow observation of a child's response to a rich, tailored incentive system. Unless the child is unable to obtain a clearly attractive reward or is unable to define any rewards that are desirable, then deficits in performance may result from deficits in environmental incentives, not in the child. Assessment of self-management skills must also include assessment of the child's knowledge of the operating rules and reward systems. The assessment of self-management skills also assumes that the child possesses adequate performance skills. When a child has good performance skills but still displays inconsistent performances under low-stress external reward systems, self-management deficits may be indicated. In the event that a child expresses consternation about not performing more consistently, self-management deficits may be responsible (Karoly, 1981). Because better self-management skills will aid most children and caregivers, the institution of self-management training based on the erroneous conclusion of self-management deficits would not seem to have untoward side effects. Yet, because self-management training is complex, more direct and simple environmental changes are often more feasible for child helpers to institute.

Task-Completion Skills. Adequate resources, social skills, and self-control can provide opportunities for children and caregivers to accomplish tasks that advance their welfare. Success may still be blocked by gaps in task-accomplishment skills. Reading, making change from a dollar, filling out applications, record keeping, playing sports, and budgeting are but a tiny sample of the skills that children and caregivers may need to function successfully. This point may seem obvious, but it is often missed. The humiliation of language, math, or reading illiteracy is a strong incentive to develop refined strategies for hiding task-completion-skill deficits from peers and child helpers. Many situations can be mastered by caregivers or children lacking a full set of academic competencies; others, like reading about reward systems or budgeting for independent living, cannot satisfactorily be negotiated without the requisite skills. Child helpers often must overcome their own chagrin to assess performance by such acts as asking an adult to read out loud from the form that he or she has not been completing. Frustration for the client and the child helper will result from a failure to do so.

Conducting the Problem Analysis

Information about conditions comes primarily from interviews with clients and members of their social ecologies. Checklists (see, for example, Goyette, Conners, and Ulrich, 1978) can provide reliable information about children's behaviors. Such trace measures as attendance records, completed math quizzes, and disciplinary reports are rich sources of information about children (see, for instance, Webb and others, 1981). Observing clients in their natural environments to gain an independent assessment of their functioning is, in exceptional situations, also a useful adjunct to interviewing (Swan and MacDonald, 1978; Wade, Baker, and Hartmann, 1979). Standardized psychometric and achievement tests (such as Wide Range Achievement Test or California Test of Basic Skills) are valuable for estimating educational achievement and, to a lesser extent, educational ability and the discrepancy between achievement and ability.

Interviews. Interviews with caregivers, auxiliary child helpers, and children are the most flexible, convenient, and useful forms of assessment. Heavy reliance on interviews by members of all factions of the helping professions suggests their value

(Swan and MacDonald, 1978). Although additional assessment procedures can supplement interviews, intervention cannot succeed without the careful interviewing of members of the client's social ecology.

Interviews that include children and caregivers or auxiliary child helpers are usually the most efficient means of understanding the various perspectives people have on a problem. Some caregivers will want to meet with the child helper separately to candidly share their observations of a child. This is often useful and satisfactory at the outset, but later interviews usually should include the child. (Instances where interviewing all members of the social ecology together is not important are few; these are discussed further later.) Interviews are most useful for learning about the caregiver's appraisal of just what the problem is and what events or conditions contributed to the problem. Although many children, caregivers, and child helpers will argue that the problems are *in* the caregiver or *in* the child, the child helper can encourage discussion of interpersonal exchanges and external events associated with the problematic events.

In general, child helpers should adapt their interviewing styles to their clients, but problem-specific interview formats can provide a useful structure across different families (Mash and Terdal, 1981). For example, if a child has a seizure disorder, the child helper could use the Seizure Disorder Interview Schedule (Balaschak and Mostofsky, 1981) to guide the interview and guarantee that observable features of the seizure; possible precipitants of the seizure; relevant medical, surgical, and pharmaceutical histories; associated complaints; subjective impressions; and testing results are covered. Child helpers need not feel unpolished or awkward when referring to a standard interview protocol. These are aids, not crutches.

Interviewing the child alone may prove helpful, especially when caregivers are unavailable for meetings that fit the child helper's schedule; when a child is fearful of a caregiver and is unable to contribute information about family functioning in family interviews; and when the problems are very specific to a caregiver's behavior, and treatment focuses on the child's response (for example, when the caregiver is a substance abuser or is incapacitated by mental or physical illness). When meeting with a child alone, confidentiality may be an issue (although younger children may not understand the concept or worry about the implications). If confidentiality is a concern, then child helpers may want to tell children that they will not tell anything to the parents unless they have the children's permission. Nonetheless, and when relevant, children should be warned that any suspicion you have that they have been physically abused or sexually assaulted will require discussion with caregivers. Parents can usually accept this idea so long as the child helper supports the parents in front of the child at every opportunity and does not threaten their authority.

　　The goals of assessment interviews with children are to elicit the child's description of the specific characteristics of the problem and surrounding events, the child's appraisal of what contributes to the problem, and the child's sense of how his or her life could be better. Child helpers may begin the interview by stating the reason that they are meeting with the child—for example, "Your mother is very worried about the fighting between you and your father." Children and youth may be reluctant to discuss problems or to admit that the problem is theirs rather than the school's or their parent's or the law's. The child may appreciate knowing that the mission of meeting together is to better understand what is going on from the child's side so you can help child and family develop a way to handle the problem so that everyone will be happier. A clear statement of the expectation that the child or youth can be important in solving the family problem may be warmly received by the child. This approach emphasizes the shared responsibility for the problem and the need for mutual change. When necessary to gain the child's collaboration in the assessment interview, however, the problem can be restated as though it were caused by the authority—"So, the way that you see your problem is that your father doesn't treat you right and gets mad. Tell me what happens just before your father gets mad. Okay, your father gets mad when you hit your little brother. What happens just before that?"

　　Helping the child communicate freely may require other techniques. Reenacting situations may also be necessary for obtaining specific information from younger children. Dolls or drawings may help the child communicate. For older children, walking, driving, or eating seems to increase the fluidity of the interview without compromising the needed structure. Adams (1982) provides many practical suggestions for handling problems that arise when interviewing a child alone, including the child who will not budge from the car, the child who is afraid to separate from a caregiver, and the parent who wants to be included in the interview. Encouraging family interviews and taking an ecological perspective decrease the need for solutions to the latter two problems.

Whether interviewing caregiver or child or both, child helpers must continually remind themselves and their interviewees that their reports are their appraisals of the situation. Beginning paraphrases with such clauses as "So the way that you see this is . . ." and "Ah, so you figure that . . ." will underscore the message that each participant has a unique view. This is not to suggest that the child helper take these appraisals lightly. Researchers (such as Lobitz and Johnson, 1975) have found that parents' perceptions of their children are better predictors of parents' complaints about their children than are the children's objectively measured behaviors. Further, parents who fail to recognize objective improvement in their children's behaviors are likely to treat them as if they had not improved (see, for instance, Schnelle, 1974).

Checklists. One strategy for improving observation is to provide the observer with a checklist of behaviors to watch for and assess. Checklists that identify undesirable or desirable behaviors and require caregivers to mark whether those behaviors occurred during a recent time period may be especially helpful to child helpers. These checklists (also known as behavior-problem checklists because they typically focus on deficits rather than skills) are a popular assessment technique among clinical researchers. Ciminero and Drabman (1977) identify several advantages to checklists, including economy of cost, effort, and time; focus on the problems of interest; and ease of administration and scoring. Another advantage is that their purpose is obvious to teachers and parents and other checklist users; this may improve cooperation with the request to complete the checklist on a regular basis. This face validity often belies checklists' unknown test-retest and internal consistency reliabilities and modest correspondence with observed behavior (Eyberg and Johnson, 1974; Achenbach and Edelbrock, 1979).

Some checklists focus on specific problem behaviors like hyperactivity (see, for instance, Conners, 1970) whereas others are more global (see, for instance, Achenbach and Edelbrock, 1979; Quay and Peterson, 1979) and list a range of asocial or antisocial behaviors. One of the best standardized global checklists and the only children's checklist known to this author that includes positive as well as negative child behaviors is the Daily Child Behavior Checklist for two- to eight-year-olds (Furey and Forehand, 1983). Although a checklist for nearly every occasion has been developed—see McMahon and Forehand (1984) for descriptions of checklists—child helpers may find that constructing their own checklists is an attractive alternative to borrowing and retailoring a checklist that never quite fits the problem of interest. The disadvantage of creating a new and unstandardized checklist is its uncertain reliability and validity (although even when the construct validity and internal consistency of the checklist are in doubt, the child helper can use the individual items as cues for further inquiry during the assessment interview).

Scores from checklists can be used to estimate the difference between a child's behavior before and after treatment. Such estimates must be made cautiously, however, in view of the uncertainty of checklists' test-retest reliability and because caregivers may begin to observe *more* misbehavior as a result of learning such skills as how to define and track problem behaviors. In one case of the author's, a boy's father scored the child as nearly problem free early in treatment and as quite troubled at the midpoint in treatment, while the mother's scoring was the reverse. These results can be interpreted to indicate that the father became more involved in and aware of the boy's problems, and the boy's mother felt that the boy's behavior was improving. This information was useful to the author and the family and led to intensified efforts to reverse the father's appraisal by finding enjoyable activities for the boy and his father to do together and helping the father track some of his son's improvements.

Trace Measures. Child helpers often rely on extant records of a child's performance. This is sensible and requires little comment. One caveat is, however, in order. Trace measures like attendance records, grades on tests, and numbers of fines in a group home may be even less dependable than the measures previously discussed. Because multiple record keepers and changing standards make individual trace measures difficult to interpret, child helpers should understand the context in which the trace data was collected and, whenever possible, use several measures of the same target performance. This will lessen the chance of unjustifiable gloom or optimism about changes in performance that are more a function of measurement error than genuine improvement or deterioration.

Observation. Observation of clients in their social ecologies can contribute important information to assessment. Observation can provide information about base-rate performance, events occurring just before and after the problem behavior, patterns of behavior, and helpful and unhelpful caregiver responses to the child's misbehavior. Even though observation is time consuming and its results often imprecise—highly trained raters even have difficulty agreeing on what they see (Kent and Foster, 1977)—it has unique value as a source of hypotheses about contributors to problem behaviors. Because child helpers with well-developed social-ecological perspectives understand what they see differently than caregivers or other child helpers, observation may give child helpers ideas about problems that were not offered by others. Because few observers have the opportunity to watch clients at length in their own environments, and because children and their caregivers may act differently when observed (Hughes and Haynes, 1978; Johnson and Eyberg, 1975), the evidence from observation should be accepted tentatively and compared against verbal reports and other indicators (Wolf, 1978). Further discussions of the problems, advantages, and methods of observation are available elsewhere (see, for instance, Haynes, 1978; Kent and Foster, 1977).

Observation of specific skills during structured activities may have the best chance of providing information that can guide treatment. For example, watching for a family member's ability to define a problem, stay on task, and not interrupt during a structured assignment to choose and solve a family problem may inform the child helper of where retraining is most needed. Although such assessments cannot be expected to show how a family solves problems on its own, conclusions can be drawn as to how the family solves problems in structured problem-solving meetings. If increasing the occurence of problem solving and the skills necessary to it in these meetings is a goal of treatment, then this information will be helpful.

Standardized Tests. Standardized aptitude and achievement tests for children are much maligned and misunderstood. Although aptitude tests such as the WISC-R (Wechsler, 1974) may not accurately indicate a child's potential and are certainly culturally biased, they are useful predictors of children's school achievement (Kaufman, 1979) and indicators of children's relative academic strengths and weaknesses (Palmer, 1983). The cultural insensitivity of these instruments should not fool child helpers into minimizing their results (see, contrarily, Mercer, 1979). Minority students must perform at levels that are acceptable to teachers, employers, and friends from mixed cultures. Assessment of normative performances vis à vis their own culture is not enough. If youth are performing well below mainstream society's norm, they deserve special attention and help. Minority children should not, of course, be penalized for scoring lower on standardized exams by being placed in classes with fewer appropriate learning opportunities. Nor should they be penalized by placement in classes that are beyond their achievement level because estimates of their aptitudes were adjusted upward in allowance for their cultural disadvantages. Because the old saw about standardized assessment instruments is true—that is, that they are only as good as the assessors who interpret them— child helpers must learn to interpret them (see Green, 1982), to assess their meaning with cultural sensitivity (Clarizio, 1982), and to use them for prescriptive programming (Clarizio, 1979).

Achievement tests such as the Wide Range Achievement Test, or WRAT (Jastak and Wilkinson, 1984), are reliable, useful, and accepted indicators of a child's academic skills (more precisely, spelling, arithmetic, reading recognition, and reading pronunciation). Achievement tests are easy to administer and interpret and do not require the extensive training required for IQ tests. (Child helpers whose intervention leads to accelerated increases in the month or year of children's achievement levels will be appreciated by educators.) Discrepancies between scores on aptitude and achievement tests can indicate learning handicaps. Children with higher aptitude than performance scores may have visual-perceptual or perceptual handicaps or behavioral disorders that interfere with achievement.

In the assessment process, more is better: more indicators provided by more sources using more types of data collection yield more useful results (Barth and Sullivan, 1984). The exigencies of practice often thwart child helpers' efforts to interview or to observe as much as they would like to. Enlisting children and their families as data collectors is one strategy for learning more about situations. Child helpers can coach parents in skills for interviewing teachers about their expectations for their classes and the problems they see in their classes. Providing parents with some guidelines or a checklist can give structure to the interview and ensure that especially pertinent information is gathered. House parents, aunts and uncles, and older siblings can observe classrooms, meet with coaches, and contact preschool teachers. Many families are overextended and communicate infrequently with service providers. Troubled families especially may seek to minimize contact with services (Egeland, Briefenbacher, and Rosenberg, 1980; Wahler, 1980). Child helpers' efforts to include such clients in data-gathering meetings and interviews will allow them to better assist caregivers in the short term and will give caregivers skills to aid themselves and their families over time. Clients are the experts on their own ecologies. With consultation, training, and support they can become invaluable contributors to the assessment process.

Assessment should yield trace or numerical indicators of the client's current level of functioning and so provide the child helper and family members with a pretreatment baseline for comparison during later points in the treatment. Indicators of what clients and caregivers said, and clients' and caregivers' expectations about themselves and others, self-management skills, social integration, task-completion skills, and resources are critical to assessing change. Collecting assessment information in order to aid practice is not, however, problem free. The process of identifying key performance indicators and arriving at satisfactory measurement strategies should begin during the initial assessment. At that point, most child helpers will not arrive at highly reliable conclusions about the efficacy of various parts of their intervention but can estimate changes in problem behavior and a rough correspondence between those changes and child helper and client efforts.

In many settings, an assessment requires a diagnosis using the third edition of the American Psychiatric Association's *Diagnostic and Statistical Manual of Mental Disorders* (DSM-III) (American Psychiatric Association, 1980). Such diagnosis often occurs early in the assessment process and may contribute but a small amount to problem analysis and the planning of the intervention. Still, the third edition of this measure has far more to offer than its forerunners. Each diagnosis includes essential and associated characteristics of the problem and clarification of which factors rule out this diagnosis. While confirming or disconfirming these features, the assessor can also forward problem analysis. Additional assessment will certainly be needed, as the DSM-III assumes that children's problems reside within children alone rather than within children and their families and social ecologies. (Those who want to know more about the DSM-III classifications of infancy, childhood, and adolescence are referred to many fine resources, such as Rapoport and Ismond, 1984; Spitzer and Cantwell, 1980. Those interested in the relationship between the DSM-III and other assessment strategies should consult Kazdin, 1985.)

The goal of assessment is to make a decision about what to do. The outcome of assessment should include enough information to identify specific alterable personal and environmental contributors to problems. Assessment has no value if the information obtained does not facilitate the choice and application of an intervention strategy. The initial plan of action may be modified markedly by further assessment or gain new definition as more information is gathered. The assessment should provide information regarding the social and cognitive contributors to the problem as well as the resources that might facilitate the achievement of the problem-solving plan. Such information will improve the plan's chances of success. Still, few child-helping efforts are quick successes. More will be learned as plans break down, resources shift, and the client's and child helper's knowledge about each other and the social ecology mounts.

◊◊◊◊◊◊◊◊◊◊◊◊◊◊◊◊◊◊◊◊◊◊◊◊◊◊◊◊◊◊

3

Choosing
and Implementing
a Treatment Plan

No two child-helping interventions are alike. Even when treatments for such problems as bed-wetting, social aggression in young children, and school phobia are well detailed and documented (see, for example, Doleys, 1983; Kennedy, 1965; Ross, 1981), their implementation requires many decisions and assumes a unique form. Case-specific planning is essential to treatment success, even when research indicates that a specific intervention has an excellent chance of working. The most effective treatments for such problems that plague families and child helpers as running away, suicide, and truancy are less certain, and the context of the intervention is more unpredictable.

This chapter presents a framework for interventions to change the social and cognitive behaviors of children, youth, and caregivers, whether these interventions are largely predetermined and follow demonstrated protocols or the child helper must piece together bits of empirically supported interventions in response to a unique circumstance. Elements common to both situations will be considered. These elements are selection of an intervention, development of a plan, completion of the plan, promotion of post-treatment success, monitoring and evaluation of progress, and termination and transfer.

72

Selection of an Intervention

The choice of the intervention plan depends on the formation of a reasonable goal. The child helper's efforts would be simplified if the goal of treatment was to eliminate the problem. The accomplishment of this goal is what many caregivers expect from child helpers and what many child helpers expect of themselves. Most often, however, the child helper can offer hope for only partial resolution of problems and maintenance even of those gains only if clients and their families maintain their efforts. Problem amelioration is more often the outcome sought. The goal cannot always be determined at the outset of treatment, because the total problem most likely will not be revealed by the end of the assessment phase. Given the research indicating that most treatments last less than six sessions (reviewed in Wells, 1981), the importance of identifying a manageable goal is clear. As previously discussed, this goal should, as much as possible, be determined by the client.

Whether the intervention strategy should be determined by the child helper or the client is a more difficult question. Certainly the child helper must consult with the client concerning the acceptability of interventions. For example, despite proven efficacy, families are sometimes unwilling to implement a protocol for dry-bed training because it requires awakening every hour for a full night (Azrin, Thienos-Hontos, and Besalel-Azrin, 1979). Although this program may be the first choice of the practitioner, using a documented but potentially less effective approach like bell and pad training that the family prefers may be necessary. Involving clients in the choice of goals and the tasks chosen to meet these goals increases the likelihood that clients and caregivers will gain from treatment (Clark and Macrae, 1976).

Child helpers have responsibility for suggesting interventions that they believe to be effective. As others also point out (Fisch, Weakland, and Segal, 1982), caregivers typically attempt to solve their problems by doing more of whatever they have been doing (for example, yelling more often, grounding more, expressing more sympathy following school absences), and they thus become increasingly unable to resolve their problems. Child helpers can and should offer alternatives. Persuasive descriptions of the treatment of choice and accompanying rationale do not violate client self-determination as long as the client can veto the intervention. Clients often veto disliked interventions through inaction.

A client may choose a reasonable goal (for example, less fighting in the family), seek the child helper's suggestions about how to achieve the goal (for example, giving privileges according to the performance of behaviors that prevent fighting), and then determine that the intervention strategy is unacceptable. Caregivers' pretreatment strategies—that is, what they did that failed to solve their problems—may result from unfamiliarity with alternative intervention methods or from beliefs that prevent their use of more effective strategies. For example, many families have difficulty treating one child differently from another. This limits the use of special rewards for one child's performance. Other families do not believe that any child should be rewarded for showing appropriate behavior. Some do not believe that privileges should depend on performance, that medication should be used to control children's behavior, or that requiring crying children to stay in their own beds through the night is humane. These are reasonable beliefs that may prevent the use of effective treatments for social aggression, hyperactivity, and sleep problems, respectively (Barkley, 1981; Morris and Kratochwill, 1983; Patterson, 1982). The child helper cannot employ even the best interventions if the beliefs of caregivers or children prevent completion of the tasks required for implementation. Some clients respond to a request to suspend their disbelief and act "as if" the plan will work, while others accept only less effective treatments.

Development of a Plan

Intervention is as fluid as assessment. Assessment and intervention activities crisscross work with clients. Just as assessment of activities, such as monitoring how a caregiver responded to a child's threats, may lead to behavior change, so, too, the activities of intervention lead to better understanding of the causes of problem behavior. The plan may be based on the initial assessment but may later incorporate additional assessment. For instance, attempting to improve a child's reading skills informs the child helper about the availability of such necessary environmental conditions as a quiet place to read, reading materials, and when called for, eyeglasses; the child's interpersonal skills as reflected in asking for help with difficult work before frustration sets in; the child's self-management skills as reflected in the child's sitting still and reading; and if they exist, the child's visual-perceptual deficits.

A thorough problem analysis will help the child helper determine what interventions might be effective and develop an intervention plan. As discussed, the problem analysis should provide information about caregivers' and children's shortages of materials, information, and services; interpersonal skills; self-management skills; and task-completion skills. All of these contributors to children's and caregivers' problems will not be salient for all problems, with all families, or in all settings. Nor must all of these contributors necessarily be assessed or changed in pursuit of goals. As Wells (1981) points out, there is a certain monotony to client problems. Knowledge of research regarding contributors to client problems may serve as the major part of assessment and lead to speedy and accurate estimates of what intervention plan will help. Intervention plans in such cases focus on adapting the protocol to the unique characteristics of the child and caregiver in the social environment.

Once an intervention strategy is chosen, the child helper and client develop an implementation plan. This plan includes a review of the larger accomplishments that must precede goal attainment and the people who might facilitate or hinder those accomplishments and the likely settings of interactions with these people. The plan also includes alternatives in the event that the initial strategy fails and child helper, caregiver, or child must quickly implement an alternative or obtain additional consultation.

The plan later involves breaking the implementation strategy into actions, or *tasks*, that the child helper and client agree
to try to accomplish. Tasks are the building blocks of behavior
change (Reid and Epstein, 1972). (Tasks are also called *homework
assignments* by some authors; however, some youth and caregivers
have longstanding commitments to not doing "homework," so
this word should be used judiciously.) Task agreements may
involve identifying outcomes that the client or child helper will
achieve ("I will talk to your mother, Jacky") or performances
that the client or child helper will attempt to complete ("I will
try to call your probation officer tomorrow and Wednesday—I
hope I can reach him"). Each approach has disadvantages, with
the former more likely to be out of the task attempter's control
and therefore unattainable, and the latter encouraging pro forma
attempts.

Careful task selection facilitates task and goal accomplishment. Since clients only gradually grasp the rationale for task
selection, they are characteristically unable to at first identify
tasks that contribute to goal attainment. Still, they are experts
on the practicality, attractiveness, and likely outcome of tasks.
Task selection must also address the types and sources of tasks.

Types of Tasks. The type of task that child helpers, caregivers, and children agree on is bounded only by their collec-
tive creativity. Tasks may be personal or interpersonal (Reid,
1981). One example of a personal task is writing down the difficulties likely in implementing a plan and describing alternatives. Reading a self-instructional text on changing a child's
behavior (for example, Patterson, 1976b) is another type of personal task. Although behavior problems often involve problems
in personal interactions, child helpers can suggest tasks that
will help clients improve their personal contributions to interpersonal relationships.

Interpersonal tasks include one caregiver problem solving with another caregiver, a youth in emergency foster care
talking with one other youth one time each day, and a caregiver
rewarding a child every time he or she is quiet for ten minutes
between five and six o'clock. One kind of interpersonal task is
the joint task that is attempted with other members of the social

ecology (Reid, 1981). Conducting family problem-solving meetings is a common joint task in the latter stages of working with families in conflict (see Chapter Eleven). The task of explaining time out to a child and rehearsing its use with that child may be a joint task that follows the personal task of reading about time out and precedes the caregiver's interpersonal task of using time out to control the child's aggressive behavior. The child helper and child may also decide to attempt joint tasks. One such opportunity arose for the author as part of a self-control training program. The author and an adolescent agreed to audio-tape descriptions of five interpersonal events that made them angry and five interpersonal events that made them laugh during the week. This task was only partially accomplished by both parties, but it provided a boost to the relationship and some specific examples of how much anger or laughter depends on our own decisions.

Sources of Tasks. Much clinical lore and several studies show that tasks identified by the person who will have to implement them are most likely to be achieved (see, for example, Kanfer and Grimm, 1978; Kendall and Braswell, 1982). Clients, however, initially have difficulty thinking of tasks for themselves or others. The principles of self-change are easier to practice than to conceptualize, and the logical relationship among goals and tasks and personal skills may at first be obscure to clients. In the beginning, child helpers may identify and volunteer to complete tasks within their areas of expertise. Once the client has begun to understand the task orientation of the work and the distribution of tasks, child helpers may ask clients to identify tasks that they would like the child helper to do. (This request will not accomplish its purpose if it predates clients' understanding of the problem-solving process.) In time and with child helper assistance, clients will begin to develop personal tasks as needed.

The source of task assignments should be consonant with the overall goal of improving problem-solving performance in the social ecology. If a young child is unable to take directives from a caregiver appropriately, then the child helper may at first assign tasks to the child and then, once the child has developed a pattern of compliance, slowly transfer task assignments to the primary caregiver. Contrarily, if an older child deserves more recognition for his or her contributions to family problem solving, then the child helper may want to provide opportunities for that child to assign tasks to himself or herself and to recommend tasks for others. Most important is that everyone in the family or system agrees to do something about the family's problem (Thomlison, 1982).

Child helpers often assign tasks to improve caregivers' abilities to use assessment and behavior-change procedures. This is particularly true during assessment when child helpers guide the collection of information that may help to explain the contributors to problems and that will provide a basis for evaluation of the effectiveness of the intervention. The intervention protocols described in later chapters also require task assignment by the child helper.

Completion of the Plan

Task accomplishment is essential to helping children and youth. The reason for meetings of child helpers, caregivers, and children is to develop plans that are likely to lead to reduction of problems, to develop tasks that are likely to lead to accomplishment of those plans, and to develop strategies and incentives that are likely to lead to achieving those tasks. No aspect of child helping is more difficult and more deserving of concerted effort than encouraging clients to complete agreed-upon tasks. Without devotion to encouraging clients to practice cognitive and behavioral programs in the social ecology, skills will not be learned or maintained after the program ends (Wahler, 1980).

Many explanations for failure to achieve tasks have been proposed. The most common reason seems to be some variation of the idea that "the client must not want to change." Although this assumption cannot be proven or disproven, it lacks utility. Active resistance may, of course, occur when clients conclude that the changes are not in their best interests or that they will lose the freedom to choose for themselves if they agree to implement someone else's choices. These contributors to active resistance can be minimized by the conditions of mutual agreement to complete tasks (Goldfried and Robins, 1982; Reid and Epstein, 1972).

Alternate explanations for the failure to achieve tasks are provided by every clinician who uses a treatment that requires the client to complete between-session tasks. Common explanations include: (1) the social environment is perceived to provide insufficient rewards for task accomplishment, (2) the client believes that task-achievement will require more effort than task achievement is worth, (3) the client believes that he or she lacks or actually does lack the capacity or skills to achieve the tasks, (4) the client lacks the concrete resources needed to achieve the tasks, (5) the client is overburdened with other tasks (most of which the child helper did not help to formulate but that are no less important to the client). Recognition of these causes of failure to complete tasks can guide the child helper's efforts at facilitating task accomplishment.

Task Planning. Careful cognitive and behavioral rehearsal of task accomplishment has been shown to contribute to task completion (Reid, 1978; Shelton and Levy, 1981). The principle element in cognitive rehearsal is task planning. Task planning involves identifying what the client will do, when the client will do it, and what conditions the client predicts will precede and follow the task. A verbal plan serves as an implicit commitment to perform tasks. The specificity of the plan helps the child helper and caregiver or child begin the problem-solving process. Cognitive rehearsal of the task can go beyond specification of the task attempter's expectations and intentions. Planning should take into account what others might do that will threaten task achievement and anticipate what the task attempter can do in response. The plan also should not neglect to identify what the task attempter might do that will threaten task achievement and what can be done in response. This rehearsal might include a thorough review of the client's statements regarding what may block task achievement. Exhibit 3 illustrates a checklist of statements that clients may make during their efforts to accomplish tasks agreed upon with child helpers. When task attempters are frank, their self-review can neutralize beliefs that would otherwise prevent task accomplishment.

**Exhibit 3. Sample Checklist of Cognitive Contributors
to the Failure to Accomplish Tasks.**

The following is a list of reasons for not completing tasks. Because the speed of improvement depends primarily on the tasks that you are willing to do, it is of crucial importance to pinpoint any reasons that you may have for not doing this work. It is important to look for these reasons at the time that you feel a reluctance to do your task or a desire to put off doing it. Circle each statement that applies to you.

1. It seems that nothing can help me, so there is no point in trying.

2. I really can't see the point of what I'm supposed to do.

3. I think that I am a procrastinator and that I won't get around to the tasks.

4. I am willing to do some tasks if I remember to do them.

5. I think that I am too busy to do the tasks.

6. Doing something the child helper suggests is not as good as coming up with my own ideas.

7. I don't think that I can help myself, and I really don't believe that I can do anything that I choose to do.

8. I think that the child helper is trying to boss me around or control me.

9. I don't feel like cooperating with anybody.

10. I think that the child helper will disapprove or criticize my work. I believe that what I do just won't be good enough.

Source: Adapted from Beck, Rush, Shaw, and Emery, 1979.

One task-planning activity that clients may enjoy involves identifying the worst and best outcomes and the strategies clients will employ to cope with each result. Identifying worst outcomes is especially key when clients will be implementing tasks in cultures or settings unfamiliar to the child helper. The preparation that follows such rehearsal can reduce the risk that an untoward outcome will follow. This strategy may also increase the likelihood of task accomplishment by addressing clients' fears about attempting tasks. Visualizing exaggerated and dire consequences of failure to attempt tasks may also provide incentives for attempting tasks (see Chapter Five for discussion of cognitive rewards and punishments).

Rehearsing best outcomes may also motivate task attempts by boosting task attempters' expectations that they will obtain rewards. Such cognitive rehearsal should also include having clients visualize receiving rewards as a result of attempting or accomplishing tasks (see Chapter Five for discussion of covert reinforcement). Rewards must not be wholly dependent on task accomplishment, since this is often beyond the control of the task attempter. Rewards should also be visualized both for specific accomplishments and for trends in accomplishment (for example, "I'm sticking with my rules more than ever, and that's hard for me to do but good for my son"). Cognitive rehearsal should assume a *coping* rather than a *mastery* approach (see Meichenbaum, 1979). The coping approach demonstrates success at task accomplishment that follows an intermediate setback and shows how to cope with that failure in order to achieve the desired results.

Behavioral rehearsal is important when tasks involve interpersonal exchanges. Research frequently heralds the usefulness of practice for teaching new skills to child helpers, caregivers, and children (Blizinsky and Reid, 1980; Delamater, Conners, and Wells, 1984). Task attempters will improve their task-achievement skills through practice and should, again, have the chance to rehearse what they will say and do given the worst and best cases. (Role-play strategies are further discussed in Chapter Five.) Behavioral rehearsal of social interactions combined with cognitive rehearsal of what thoughts precede, accompany, and follow the social interaction may provide the most comprehensive rehearsal strategy. As Moon and Eisler (1983) show in their study of alternative cognitive and behavioral strategies for staying calm in anger-producing situations, cognitive- and social-skill strategies seem to accomplish this goal in different ways and, together, may provide the best outcomes. Behavioral rehearsal is not, however, a fail-safe strategy. Some caregivers and children dislike the demand to perform in front of the child helper or other members of their social ecology. For such people, this anxiety may discourage the continued use of services.

Task Sheets. ''The importance of the recording format as a means of training practitioners and of shaping practice can hardly be overestimated. The practitioner is not only reminded about the basic structural features of the model (target problem, contract, task formulation and review, and so on) but is required to practice within this framework in order to complete the guide in a reasonably correct and honest fashion'' (Reid, 1978, p. 284). Many systems for recording tasks have been developed. Behavioral contracts are a common format and some empirical data suggests that they do influence adherence to task agreements (Shelton and Levy, 1981). Task sheets and contracts have similar properties, as both ideally include space for identifying planned client and child helper activities and for signed commitments to the implementation of those plans. Task sheets do not, however, typically include any quid pro quo agreements or incentives for accomplishing tasks. Thus, task sheets may be used independently of contracts or may supplement contracts by identifying and encouraging the accomplishment of small activities that contribute to the completion of the overall contract. The task sheet that the author uses is called the Goal and Task (GAT) sheet and also includes room to identify the goal or rationale for the tasks (see Exhibit 4). Copies of task sheets should be left with clients to serve as cues to task accomplishment and as expressions of commitment to the shared goal of improving performance.

Task Review and Troubleshooting. The results of task attempts need review. As obvious as this seems, all but the most saintly child helper can recall failing to provide time for sufficient review of tasks. While time with clients is undoubtedly precious and should result in an action plan, planning and rehearsal should not keep the child helper from thorough review of all tasks planned during prior meetings. Task accomplishment should be warmly acknowledged. The character of this acknowledgment will vary according to client characteristics and the client's level of independent functioning. At the outset, the child helper may generously praise task-accomplishment efforts and approximations of task achievement. Later, inquiries about the client's level of satisfaction with task efforts or accomplishments may

Exhibit 4. Sample Goal and Task Worksheet.

Date _____

Goal I _____

Client's Last Tasks   *Client's New Tasks*

1. Achievement Rating[a]   _____   1.
2. Achievement Rating   _____   2.

Comments: _____
_____
_____

Child Helper's Last Tasks   *Child Helper's New Tasks*

1. Achievement Rating   _____   1.
2. Achievement Rating   _____   2.

Comments: _____
_____
_____

Goal II _____

Client's Last Tasks   *Client's New Tasks*

1. Achievement Rating   _____   1.
2. Achievement Rating   _____   2.

Comments: _____
_____
_____

Child Helper's Last Tasks   *Child Helper's New Tasks*

1. Achievement Rating   _____   1.
2. Achievement Rating   _____   2.

Comments: _____
_____
_____

_____   _____
Client   Child Helper

Date of Next Meeting _____. Location of Next Meeting _____.

[a]Achievement rating: (4) Completely, (3) Mostly, (2) Partly, (1) Minimally or not at all.

be more helpful than praise by the child helper, since much research underscores the importance of encouraging the client's appraisal of positive outcomes as a result of his or her own efforts (Brewin and Antaki, 1982).

Clients' or child helpers' failures to accomplish agreed-upon tasks also warrant full acknowledgment. Whatever the outcome, tasks should be reviewed without excessive disapproval or dismissal. Ideally, barriers to task accomplishment are evaluated during assessment and removed prior to task attempts. This is not, however, how intervention usually works. Each task assignment may involve client competencies or responses from the client's social ecology that cannot be predicted without impossibly time-consuming assessment. The troubleshooting of task failures often isolates one of several conditions.

Inadequate material resources—not having the requisite money, materials, transportation, or equipment—is the most obvious reason for task failure. Few child helpers would knowingly propose that clients attempt tasks without adequate resources. Still, this occurs. Clients are often woefully short of needed resources. Child helpers may assume—and clients may fail to correct them—that clients have cars, their own bathrooms, bus fare, telephones, books, televisions, radios, toys, a space of their own for relaxing, a bed for each child, money to purchase rewards, or paper and pencils. These assumptions always should be checked with clients. Such checking prevents mistakes like that of the author, who assumed that a family with difficulty getting their children to school on time possessed a clock.

Lack of child, caregiver, or child helper self-management is another cause of task failure. Without the ability to structure events and so increase potentially high-yield, long-term outcomes, children, caregivers, and child helpers are not likely to complete tasks. Self-management for completing tasks requires the arrangement of cues to prompt task efforts (for example, notes on or visualizations of target situations), retention of the plan, statements to oneself to encourage the achievement of the task while efforts are in process, and self- or externally administered rewards for task efforts or accomplishments. If self-management skills are not possessed prior to the assignment of tasks, they must first be developed, or they must be supplemented by high levels of external control. Child helpers who work with parents, for example, find that many parents are unable to use parenting skills until they develop adequate self-management skills (see, for example, Barth, Blythe, Schinke, and Schilling, 1983; Fleischman, Horne, and Arthur, 1983; Wolfe and others, 1982). (Self-management skills are further discussed in Chapter Five.)

Lack of interpersonal skills on the part of the child, caregiver, or child helper may also prevent goal attainment. For child helpers, interpersonal skills are necessary to be the client's advocate, to mediate between other child helpers, and to follow through with consequences despite strong opposition. Caregivers may need similar interpersonal skills, particularly as they assume the responsibilities of the child helper as they become more adept advocates, mediators, and facilitators of behavior change. Adolescents often need interpersonal skills to establish or reestablish positive contacts with peers and adults. Review and rehearsal of interpersonal strategies and skills are often key to helping adolescents achieve satisfactory outcomes with teachers whose classes they have shunned, peers in new programs that they enter, potential employers whom they meet, and probation officers whom they do not like. Children less commonly need strong interpersonal skills to achieve their tasks (which more often require self-control or technical skills); such skills are primarily important when children's treatment goals include improved interpersonal integration.

Lack of technical skills on the part of the child, caregiver, or child helper may hinder task accomplishment. Poor reading skills may make comprehending written instructions difficult; poor gross-motor abilities may prevent successful participation in recreational activities; the inability to make change for a dollar may hinder successful work experience; poor writing ability may make completing job applications difficult. Some poor technical skills may stem from physical handicaps; more often, they result from inexperience or lack of appropriate instruction.

Child helpers may conclude that building skills essential to accomplishing tasks is the best approach to remediating the problem situation. Alternately, child helpers may decide to work around skill deficits by teaching simple coping techniques and redesigning tasks so that the deficient technical skills no longer block task achievement. In the typically short-term treatments in which children and families participate, the latter strategy is most applicable. Referrals to obtain remediation of major problems, such as reading deficits, discovered during the pursuit of tasks should be made, but unless no alternative task-achievement strategies are available, this should not alter the child helper's efforts to see that designated tasks are achieved.

For example, consider the case of an assaultive Vietnamese refugee in group care who becomes particularly sullen and prone to assaultive outbursts at school or on his return home from school. This apparently is caused by his failure to comprehend much of what occurs in school. Helping this youth with his academic work should decrease his frustration and reduce his angry outbursts. He also has angry outbursts, however, when he is confronted about his schoolwork by female house staff and when he has been around other children or staff for a long time without any time alone. Rather than having him spend his one-hour-per-afternoon study period working on his reading, the child helper decides to focus on identifying the antecedents of his outbursts and looking for alternative cognitive and social strategies for diffusing these outbursts. Tutoring him in reading might also lead to a reduction in his angry and assaultive outbursts at school but may have less effect on outbursts in other settings. When he has completed the anger-control training program that the child helper designed, the child helper and he agree that more proficiency in academic skills will help him relax at school. He does not want to work with anyone else, however, and has only recently begun to admit that reading is difficult for him. The child helper decides that referral is not indicated at this point and decides, instead, to teach reading to the boy with just the help of materials provided by the school's special education resource specialist. When referral is not indicated, the child helper—whatever his or her professional training—must don a mortar board and teach children or caregivers skills as diverse as bus riding, writing down daily events, making change, using a telephone, and keeping an appointment book.

Task Revision. Task revision follows task review. When tasks have not been completed, they can be rescheduled for completion before the next meeting, modified, or eliminated. Old tasks may be discarded because the time for their accomplishment has passed and they have become moot, because the obstacles to task accomplishment are too great, or because the time and effort to complete them could be more usefully spent completing other tasks. Child helpers may find their clients stymied by task failure and may have to help them select new tasks, modify their approaches to old tasks, and reconfirm their commitment to task accomplishment. When the first tasks are not achieved—and some failure is inevitable in all cases—the child helper must grapple with several decisions.

First, the child helper must decide whether the client's motivation for task accomplishment has been diminished. This may be the case if the client is reluctant to meet, is hesitant about committing to a new task, or refuses the task-accomplishment strategies that the child helper tries to develop with the client. When this occurs, the child helper may wish to more actively structure the task-accomplishment experience for the client. Maintaining the client's engagement in treatment may become the foremost goal. If motivation does not seem markedly impaired, and the client seems interested in pursuing new tasks, then the child helper should consult with the client about the existing tasks rather than work with the client to develop a new task agreement. When clients seem to maintain or even increase their interest in task accomplishment despite previous task failures or obvious obstacles to task achievement, the task-centered approach is being used to best advantage. Cognitive and behavioral rehearsal of strategies for overcoming or circumventing obstacles to task accomplishment should follow task redefinition.

To facilitate task accomplishment, the child helper should consider the following strategies (adapted from Shelton and Levy, 1981):

1. Be sure that task definitions contain specific detail regarding just what should be done and when.
2. Anticipate the impediments to task accomplishment stem-

ming from service or material deficits and identify a plan to overcome or circumvent these deficits.

3. If necessary, demonstrate and rehearse the use of self-control, interpersonal, or technical skills.

4. Anticipate negative expectations of outcomes and have client cognitively rehearse positive outcomes and rewards for task accomplishment.

5. Attempt to strengthen the client's tendency to complete tasks by rewarding all efforts to complete tasks.

6. Keep task assignments simple at first and expect a small effort. Increase the complexity and amount of effort later, after the client has some success with task accomplishment.

7. Do not reward task failure or task achievement efforts that fail to match previous efforts.

8. Identify or arrange cues for the client to remind him or her to attempt the task (if needed, the child helper can provide the reminders).

9. Obtain a public commitment to complete the task by having the client state or sign an agreement that he or she will attempt to complete the task.

10. Anticipate and attempt to reduce influences in the social environment that will hinder efforts or accomplishment.

Motivation Maintenance. The arduous and painstaking adventure of changing one's own behavior and the behavior of significant others requires great motivation. Motivation levels need consistent monitoring. Client difficulties in maintaining motivation are likely when child helpers begin to think that they themselves are doing all the work, that they wish their client would not show up, or that nothing will get done between sessions. At these times, child helpers assess clients' satisfaction and the incentives and disincentives for completing treatment tasks. The check on satisfaction assesses the client's interest in the benefits of treatment as well as the client's appraisal of what is causing current treatment successes or failures. Clients shift their views about the causes of problems, the apportionment of responsibility for correcting problems, and the likelihood that treatment will be successful. However much a child helper encourages reasonable expectations and cautions against trying to make changes too quickly, caregivers and children want to get back to their old routines—minus their problems—without delay. Clients may achieve tasks and may be making lightning-fast progress by the child helper's standards but may be frustrated and may lose the motivation to continue making serious efforts to accomplish tasks.

A consumer satisfaction check may include a simple request for the client's appraisal of how things are going. For some clients, the child helper's perception that their motivation is waning may be useful—"You've missed two of the last four meetings and you haven't done any tasks for today. Are you wondering if what we are doing together will help?" Caregivers' satisfaction may be particularly low at the beginning of behavior-change efforts because of the strain caused by changing their own patterns of behavior and protest by children or youth about the changes. Child helpers should help caregivers anticipate this protest but not assume that this anticipation is sufficient. The amount, duration, and appearance of the protest may surprise the caregiver and may undermine the caregiver's commitment to change.

Efforts to maintain client motivation require the review of incentives for completing activities necessary to implement the treatment. Since long-term incentives are often less powerful than immediate benefits for families in distress, recognition of short-term incentives and disincentives is essential. The inconvenience of change is a common disincentive. Finding time and transportation to attend treatment sessions and complete tasks outside of treatment is an obvious—but underestimated—hindrance. Child helper flexibility about meeting in clients' homes helps lessen that hindrance. Another powerful incentive is the support of confidants and significant others for the efforts that change requires.

When support from confidants and significant others ebbs, caregiver skepticism may flow. At times these other persons should be incorporated into the treatment so that their concerns can be addressed. In one unsuccessful case in the author's experience, a child with infrequent but chillingly violent episodes was placed in group care by agreement of the youth's stepfather, county social services worker, and county mental health worker. The youth's birth mother acquiesced at first, but after some inattention on the part of the group-home staff and after the youth began to run away from the treatment home, she welcomed him and would not comply with her original contract to return him to group care. The stepfather finally yielded, and the child, still considered violent by the staff, went home. Staff failed to maintain incentives to encourage the mother's participation in treatment.

Evaluating Task and Goal Accomplishment. Task performance is the essence of competency building. Task accomplishment and goal accomplishment are not identical, however, and periodic checks of progress toward problem resolution may contribute to continued funding of the service; changes in responses to the client from the client's social ecology; and caregiver, child, and child helper morale.

Goal and task sheets provide useful and continuous indicators of the progress of treatment. Improvements in the rate of task achievement can show a caregiver's or child's growing competence and commitment. Recognizing the achievement of tasks that decrease the likelihood that a problem will occur is particularly vital when the problem rarely occurs but is catastrophic when it does. Setting a fire, running away, or hitting a child are examples. In one case in which a mother sometimes hit her daughter, arranging breathers (defined as moments *in* the house that are free from child-care responsibilities) and breaks (defined as moments *out* of the house that are free from child-care responsibilities) were agreed on as client tasks. The mother also noted her incidences of screaming at her daughter and crying and related these to her child helper every other week. Tasks to increase the use of breaks and breathers were inconsistently accomplished, but when they were, they were dramatically inversely related to screaming and crying. After a month, the child helper sketched a graph of this relationship on the back of a task sheet. The young mother and her mother—they had only six years of schooling in rural Mexico between them—understood the graph; they joked that "the picture says that if you don't get out of the house, you go crazy in the house." They became more consistent in arranging breathers and breaks.

Child helpers should obtain clients' evaluations of task accomplishment at every meeting. Task accomplishment will often be evident from the client's candid self-report or the events that follow. At other times, since children, youth, and caregivers may want to please child helpers with reports of success, more than client evaluations may be needed to ascertain task accomplishment. The incidence of erroneous reports may be reduced by the child helper's stressing that he or she wants to know "the good, the bad, and the ugly."

Sometimes more specific questioning and confrontation may be needed. Consider, for example, a child helper who attempts to encourage more positive interactions between a father and his son, Keith, who is home after a ride on a stolen motorcycle ended in the juvenile detention center. During the family meeting, father and son agree to go to a basketball game on Saturday. The child helper calls the following evening to find out how the outing went and talks first to the mother, who says that her husband is not home but that she thinks they had a good time at the soccer game; however, she was at her mother's on Saturday. The child helper then speaks with the youth, who says that the basketball game was "okay, but no big deal." This vagueness makes the child helper wonder, so, not wanting to put Keith on the spot, the child helper asks Keith to put his mother back on the phone. The child helper tells her, "I have the sense that Keith and his dad did not make it to the game." Her silence confirms the child helper's suspicion that this is the case. The child helper asks her if she is aware of any other activity they did instead for the same purpose of spending more positive time together. She says that they did work on Keith's bicycle some time on Sunday and that Keith was riding it Monday afternoon. The child helper tells her that that is good news and informs her that at the next family meeting they will discuss what obstacles get in the way of Keith and his father's spending time together and how they overcame these to work on the bicycle. During the next task review, the child helper discusses the value of faithful reporting on task accomplishment and how everyone learns from both successes and failures. Later, with more knowledge of the family, the child helper more directly discusses vagueness and discrepancy in reports of task accomplishment.

Repeated evaluation of goal accomplishment also is vital to the use of cognitive and social methods for helping children and youth. Without guidance from reasonable indicators of changes during treatment, the most sincere efforts of child helpers and clients may go astray. Child helpers most often evaulate progress in treatment by observing the perfomance of caregivers and children during treatment sessions. Less often do they confirm their deductions through reports from caregivers and children, still less commonly do they request confirmation of their impressions from other caregivers or treatment personnel, and perhaps least often of all do they attempt to observe clients' performances outside of the treatment setting.

Although child helpers may be keen observers, their judgments are a limited source of information. As stressed in the discussion on assessment, obtaining multiple indicators from multiple sources at multiple times provides the best chance of obtaining worthwhile information. Multiple measures may at times diverge, but this divergence may help highlight caregiver frustration despite observable improvement, unrealistically high expectations for change despite limited success, or differences in caregivers' perceptions that follow from their differing treatments of a child.

Promotion of Post-Treatment Success

Significantly changing the behavior of caregivers and children in any setting under any conditions is worthy of champagne. The best bottle should be saved, however, for celebrating changes that show in more than one setting, for several problem behaviors, and, particularly, for other siblings or classmates (for example, as demonstrated by Humphreys, Forehand, McMahon, and Roberts, 1978).

Increasing Generalization and Maintenance. Teaching caregivers and children to perform tasks under supervised conditions is necessary but not sufficient to helping. Advanced planning for application of new-found skills in different and future settings is essential if generalization and maintenance are to be fostered. Checklists outlining routine task-review procedures used by child helpers (such as the outline shown in Exhibit 5) will help clients

Exhibit 5. Sample Outline for Task-Review Interview.

Review of client's progress on tasks

Identification of indicators of task effort or accomplishment

- If task accomplishment:
  - Praise or elicitation of self-praise

- If limited or no task accomplishment:
  - Identification of reasons for limited task accomplishment
    - Material or service deficits
    - Self-control performance
    - Interpersonal performance
    - Technical performance
  - Development of plan for accomplishment of task during next task period *or* rationale for abandoning old task

Revision of old tasks or selection of new tasks

Development of new task plans

Cognitive and behavioral rehearsal for completion of revised or new tasks

- Commitment to new or revised tasks and plans

- Analysis of the plan in terms of:
  - Material or service needs and limits
  - Self-control strategies and skills
  - Interpersonal strategies and skills
  - Technical obstacles

- Information provision for the modification of material or service deficits
- Demonstration or rehearsal of self-control, technical, or interpersonal skills that will assist in modifying material or service deficits and ameliorate other task achievement obstacles

Summary and conclusion

- Finish and sign goal and task sheets

- Review accomplishments of meeting

- Review each person's agreement about future tasks

- Arrange next meeting times

Note: Discussion of the child helper's tasks may also follow this format but should not unduly interfere with the review of the client's tasks.

troubleshoot with minimum child helper guidance. Similar review sheets have been successfully used by Sanders (1982) to help families prepare for the exigencies of caring for difficult children during community outings. Clients should begin to use such checklists before the end of contact with child helpers and not after; as with other skills, preparing for the maintenance of treatment gains requires planning, rehearsal, repetition, and review.

Generalization of the treatment across settings to the community is promoted if the treatment occurs within the settings of greatest interest and among individuals who comprise the child's ongoing ecosystem. Lack of generalization across settings can be minimized by conducting most work in the desired setting, especially in the home or classroom (Haney and Jones, 1982; Lutzker, 1984). Sanders and Glynn (1981) had parents practice self-management skills in three out-of-home settings; these parents used better parenting behavior in all places. If treatment must be confined primarily to one setting, the degree of the improvement in that setting will predict improvement in other settings (Forehand, Breiner, McMahon, and Davies, 1981). Thus, child helpers who hope that a child's reduced noncompliance at home will be paralleled at school should encourage overlearning of competent responses at home. Some evidence also suggests that teaching the conceptual bases for performances increases the generalization (Bernstein, 1982). Others report the importance of teaching children to reward their own performances to help them generalize treatment effects (Prater, Wolter, and Clement, 1982). Above all, generalization training should not be a unique, additional part of helping appended during the last weeks. Preparation for generalization and maintenance should begin during the first moments of treatment and be encouraged at every opportunity thereafter.

Promoting Maintenance of Achievement. Maintaining the benefits of child helping is the optimal accomplishment; however, research on the longevity of treatment gains is not encouraging. Whittaker's (1983) review of the outcomes of residential treatment is only one of several reviews that suggest that the benefits of some treatments with some clients are only temporary (see, for example, Forehand and Atkeson, 1977). Whittaker concludes, " 'Success,' however defined, at the point of discharge or termination of services is not necessarily a good predictor of the child's ultimate adjustment to the community" (p.174). Yet, since short-term treatments are most commonly desired by caregivers, children, and funding sources, families commonly are left without skills for maintaining their treatment successes during independence (Whan, 1983).

"Practice makes permanent" is a recent twist on an old saw. Changing our own and our children's behaviors requires learning and applying many new behaviors and new ways of thinking. Child helpers can facilitate the learning of new skills with demonstration and repetition. The aforementioned formats for task review and task-accomplishment troubleshooting become second nature to child helpers and clients only after much repetition. As when one visits a friend for the first time, finding the way requires written clues, a few wrong turns, and repeated reference to the map. Over time, the number of wrong turns decreases, and the map becomes a comfort rather than a necessity. After a long lapse between visits or when distractions (such as talking to a friend or trying to quiet the wails of the infant in your car seat) draw one's attention, the habit will weaken and the map will again be necessary. Without further belaboring this analogy, learning is prompted by well-described, well-written, and well-rehearsed procedures that can be called on during times of stress, after disuse of the behavior, and when preliminary outcomes are not as one had hoped they would be.

Transferring the responsibility for problem solving and the future of family welfare begins with changes in the format of face-to-face or phone communications. The phrase "Let's start as usual by finding out how you did with the tasks from last time" is replaced with "Lead me through this meeting. I'll give you help with the agenda if you need it." "Okay, so that didn't seem to help; let's look at the surrounding events to see their effect on this" becomes "Okay, so what next?" These changes should be accompanied by encouraging the client to turn to other members of the family or social ecology at times of need rather than to the child helper. Allowing this mutual helping sometimes requires hard-to-maintain restraint on the child helper's part. Caregivers and children should also gradually move from daily monitoring of specific goals and tasks to weekly monitoring of general progress.

Child helpers must balance the sometimes competing demands of attracting clients to the change process and structuring the intervention so that it is successful and so that the methods of behavior change are repeated enough that clients learn how to apply them on their own. The tension between these two demands need not result in a tug of war. Excellent athletic coaches, trial lawyers, and child helpers combine personality and precision to achieve desired outcomes. Child helpers can find great rewards in demonstrating that there need be no dichotomy between a task orientation and spontaneity.

Relapse prevention techniques (Marlatt and Gordon, 1980) can help clients avoid returning to their old behaviors. Clients are asked to imagine the turning points in their treatments and to consider what they would do if each of their successes was undone. For example, in one case a parent after much effort was finally able to control his adolescent son's chronic wandering, running away, and stealing with the help of the child helper and a neighbor. While accomplishing this, he set and stuck by a strict curfew, lived through two brief episodes of his son's running away, and ignored his son's numerous threats. This parent was too exhausted and inexperienced to fully appreciate what the change process entailed and only felt lucky that the wandering and stealing had stopped. Reviewing these changes and the reasons for them and what he would do if the child again began to roam prepared the parent for the future.

The ecology-minded child helper may also be able to promote long-term benefits with attention to maintenance-enhancing strategies. Promoting maintenance also begins at the outset of child helping. Helping caregivers achieve the competencies necessary to helping the child maintain treatment benefits is the most obvious remedy for losing treatment efficacy with the withdrawal of the professional child helper. The convincingly demonstrated failure of individual child psychotherapy (Levitt, 1971; Barrett, Hampe, and Miller, 1978) contrasts sharply with the attractive, even though not unblemished, record of social and cognitive procedures (Horne and Van Dyke, 1983) and testifies to the value of changing the ecology as well as the child.

Services can also foster the client's ability to use naturally occurring resources and to create new resources. Wahler and Dumas (1984) report that mothers who learn to recognize the coercive behavior of children and of other inconsistent or ineffective adult caregivers may experience more durable increases in positive and effective parenting skills after treatment. Including friends in the treatment to provide a group sounding board may also help. School-age mothers, for example, have been trained in interpersonal skills to boost their abilities to resolve conflicts with members of their social-support networks (Barth, Schinke, and Maxwell, 1985). At the end of the group skills-training program, participants had only slightly higher levels of social support than at the start of the program, but at the four-month follow-up meeting, their levels were markedly higher, and participants reported regular use of conflict-resolution skills. These findings augur well for the lasting effects of the program.

Monitoring and Evaluating Progress

Although a child helper working in a community setting may have difficulty demonstrating unequivocably that his or her intervention was responsible for improvements in a child's behavior, this does not deprive the child helper of all opportunities to add to the research data of the field (Kazdin, 1981; Runyan, 1982). Although the implications of case studies have often been overestimated, single-case evaluation can help clarify the results and value of an intervention. Case studies are most informative and dependable when measures are believable and some basis for comparison exists.

The demands of data collection require scarce client resources and commitment and may tax the treatment relationship. Follow-up studies of social workers trained in graduate school to evaluate their practices show that only a small minority actually do so (Gingerich, 1984; Welch, 1983). Time demands and lack of agency support are certainly barriers to evaluation.

More optimistically, those practitioners who do evaluate their practices are often in child-helping agencies (Gingerich, 1984). Evaluation apparently is more feasible and rewarding with children. This suggests that evaluation is especially compatible with child helping. Perhaps this is because goals for children and caregivers involve situations that are observable and commonplace. Schools, juvenile detention centers, emergency shelter-care centers, group homes, and day- and residential-treatment programs routinely collect information on children's daily performance. Caregivers also may watch and count desirable and undesirable behaviors, a practice that may have salutary effects on treatment (Wahler and Dumas, 1984).

Collecting data for case evaluation may serve two purposes. This information may aid the child helper, caregiver, and child during the course of service. For example, weekly school reports of academic or behavioral performance may show progress that parents might otherwise not see. Demonstrations of improvement often are essential to maintaining the motivation of caregivers who have had many disappointments, and who see their children as incorrigible with little likelihood of change. For those who cease to implement behavior-change procedures after their initial efforts prove helpful, data showing decelerating performance illuminates the importance of resuming once-successful strategies.

Knowing case outcomes is also important to the child helper's practice. Although changes in the course of service for a single case may have little meaning, the aggregation of results for a specific type of case can be illuminating (Kazdin, 1982). Consider the child welfare worker who endeavors to increase parents' visiting of their children in foster care. Even though the child's return home often depends on their visiting, many parents do not visit regularly or on schedule. Children often suffer when their parent does not arrive as expected or arrives late and so must cut the visit short. Child welfare workers are often unsure about the effects of allowing visits that are not prearranged or that do not occur at the scheduled time. Disallowing unscheduled visits may encourage better visiting, or it may discourage all visiting; and allowing visits without condition may encourage even less frequent visits, or it may encourage more timely visits. Child welfare workers might collect data on case characteristics, parents' initial visiting patterns, parents' actions, and parents' subsequent behavior. Using data from many clients, many visits, and many years, each child welfare worker could build a personal data bank of outcomes divided according to the stringency or leniency of their approach to the supervision of visiting. Child welfare workers might, then, develop personal decision rules and influence agency policy to promote more appropriate approaches to visiting. Because other sources (for example, Barth, 1981; Kazdin, 1983b; Barlow, Hayes, and Nelson, 1984; Bloom and Fischer, 1982; Ollendick and Hersen, 1984) provide more complete discussions of research designs and data-collection strategies, this book will not go into detail. Only the most fundamental elements will be addressed: (1) the link between assessment and evaluation and (2) the logic of evaluation.

Even though this discussion of evaluation follows the discussion of treatment—as if evaluation is a last sacrament to be received after the client leaves the child helper alone—it should be recalled that evaluation was introduced in the assessment section of the previous chapter. Assessment is where monitoring and evaluation of progress begin. Monitoring progress can only occur if the child helper has identified the goal of treatment and the signs by which the client will know if he or she is moving toward the goal. In theory, monitoring progress is most effective if it is *continuous*; that is, if data is collected as frequently as is possible. Child helpers will more successfully collect data if caregivers agree that the data is important and if it can be easily obtained. Graphs of the frequency with which problem behaviors occur are good but are confusing to many caregivers. Diaries that fit into handbags or pockets for daily or weekly recording of events are more useful; the child helper can then transfer the information onto a graph if it seems that the graph will present a clearer and more motivating picture to clients.

Counts or estimates of amounts—of tasks accomplished, of Toughlove meetings attended by an isolated mother whose primary goal is to improve her child's adherence to family rules, of discussions between two caregivers about how they will respond to their child's aggression—can be used to keep track of intermediate treatment goals (Nelsen, 1984). Such indicators are particularly useful for clinicians who are attempting to see if some part of their intervention with caregivers—for example, role-play practice or giving clients maximum choice in decisions— is followed by changes in caregivers' performances. Changes in caregivers' performances can then be compared to changes in the child's overall behavior.

Evaluation is more than description. Evaluation requires comparison. Comparisons are most easily made between a child's behavior at the beginning and at the end of treatment. Comparisons with periods when other treatments (or no treatments) were in operation are also informative. Such was the basis for the conclusion of Koles and Jenson (1985) that their treatment of firesetting was effective. For one boy, the incidence of firesetting was reduced sharply following treatment, despite the boy's seven-year history of firesetting that started with his burning down his own home at age three. This design compared the boy's behavior during the three months preceding treatment (during which time he set twenty-four fires), the three months of treatment (during which time he set seven fires), and the year following treatment (during which time he set no fires).

The more comparisons that are made, the easier it is to tell whether the treatment reduced the problem behavior. The effectiveness of strategies for changing a single problem (such as a child's being out of his or her seat without permission) can be compared by alternating between two treatments that might work (for example, an incentive system operated by the child's teacher or a chance to have free time with an older peer). Comparisons can also be made across problem behaviors and across time by implementing one procedure to ameliorate one problem behavior (such as the child's being out of his or her seat without permission), and after a delay trying the same procedure on another behavior (such as the child's calling out without permission). If the behaviors change only when the procedures are operating, then a case can be made that the procedure works. Even in this relatively more sophisticated design, tenable explanation always exists that other factors besides treatment were responsible for the progress. Child helpers should not be daunted by this shadow of doubt. Few practitioners without significant research training and time can evaluate their practices with certainty. Yet by gathering information for progress monitoring and evaluation, most child helpers can improve their understanding of their practices and make better cases for continuing or changing treatment strategies.

Evaluations should include indicators of caregivers' and children's satisfaction with the child helper and treatment. Anecdotal evidence suggests that consumer satisfaction promotes the maintenance of treatment gains and that consumer satisfaction is important to evaluate, though this evidence has not been subjected to experimental test. Consumer satisfaction may increase the likelihood that clients will continue to employ successful change procedures, refer other families in need of services, and support the service if the retrenchment wolf comes knocking. Parents with positive relationships with child helpers and with the belief that the program they have completed is helpful may be more likely to seek aftercare programs that may be associated with long-term change. Satisfied parents also may become part of the service itself, as shown in Signell's (1972) description of a parents' group whose members so appreciated the assistance they received in adjusting to having their children enter kindergarten that they continued the group for new parents.

Although some popular programs are ineffective (reviewed in Witt and Elliott, 1985), this author suspects that treatment effectiveness is an important element of consumer satisfaction. Effectiveness is, of course, dependent upon the ability of the child helper to create initial expectations sufficient to gain caregivers' and children's cooperation with treatment procedures. Other contributors include the amount of time required to implement the treatment, treatment complexity, and attitudes about the treatment's acceptability. Child helpers should independently assess each of these.

Instruments for assessing consumer satisfaction with treatment are not well standardized or validated (McMahon and Forehand, 1983). By consensus, evaluation forms should be brief, clearly written, and private. Clients should be provided with a stamped, agency-addressed envelope so they can complete and return the consumer-satisfaction inventory on their own time. If they cannot read or write, they should be evaluated by phone or in-person interview by a member of the agency's staff other than the child helper they worked with.

Although evidence indicates that the benefits of the side effects of the social and cognitive approaches discussed here are greater than the costs, these data are normative; for each case, negative side effects may arise and must be monitored. For example, Balsam and Bondy (1983) identify one occasional side effect of reward programs, the "lawyer syndrome," in which children look for loopholes in agreements and then fulfill the literal but not the intended meaning. Forehand, Breiner, McMahon, and Davies (1981) found a corresponding increase in school misbehavior as home behavior improved for some children. Side effects within the social ecology may also result. For example, conflict between mother and grandmother about the risk of long-term harm from stimulant medications for hyperactivity is a side effect, even if the medication itself has positive results. Social criticism may arise from family members or extended kin when brief periods of social isolation are used rather than a smack on the head to interrupt a child's aggressive outbursts. Side effects should be addressed as the implementation proceeds. Because of the possibility of negative side effects, among other reasons, consumer-satisfaction queries should include the opportunity to mail an anonymous evaluation form to the child helper's agency, as well as discussions during and after the end of the treatment.

In keeping with a helping approach that values the client's agreement with and participation in the treatment, satisfaction ratings also should be obtained from children and youth. Bush and Gordon (1982) make a case for the value of children's evaluations of service delivery systems and find a discrepancy between what children and youth find acceptable and what service delivery systems offer. This discrepancy is difficult to interpret. The validity of children's assessments of the overall value of the services they receive seems questionable, given children's limited experience assessing alternative caregiving systems and the harm or good these systems do. Still, children should be encouraged to participate in decision making about their services in a way that is commensurate with their levels of competence (Gaylin and Macklin, 1982).

Ratings that reflect on the characteristics of the service are most useful. Since children are often involuntary clients, child helpers should endeavor to make their experiences in treatment as tolerable as possible. When evidence about the relative efficacy of treatment is unclear, then children's satisfaction with treatment is especially important. The reason for assessing children and youth is not just fairness. Kirigin, Braukman, Atwater, and Wolf (1982) reported that youths' evaluations of satisfaction with their programs were more strongly associated with the absence of criminal behavior after discharge than were evaluations by group-home parents, teachers, or birth parents.

Finally, the limits of consumer satisfaction must be recognized in view of human service organizations' sometimes passionate embrace of procedures without reliable data supporting their general effectiveness. Although "satisfaction with services is a relevant concern of the consumer, the society that must pay for it tends to place a somewhat higher priority on evidence that treatment enhances the patient's social effectiveness and thereby reduces the burden on society . . . " (Parloff, 1983, p. 246). Consumer-satisfaction data should supplement but not supplant other indicators of the worth of services.

Termination and Transfer

Treatment commonly ends because of such events as placement of children into other settings, relocation of families, the end of funding, or the conclusion of time-limited services. At other times, child helpers must decide if the benefits of continued regularly scheduled services outweigh the costs. Fleischman, Horne, and Arthur (1983) identified several indicators that the time has come to terminate treatment. These include consistent and coordinated implementation of new skills, changes in the behavior of siblings as well as of the referred child, the use of a cognitive and social perspective for problem solving, enjoyment during family interactions, and the appraisal that the family's major stresses are resolvable. Other indicators suggested by the author's experience include the caregiver's ability to distinguish and label successful and unsuccessful behavior, the creative use of primarily social rewards and penalties, and sufficient communication between joint caregivers.

For the majority of children who require continued services, termination of services may more accurately be described as *transfer*. Many children and youths transfer from programs with more restrictive to those with less restrictive settings—for example, from a special residential treatment program to a foster home. Special care should be taken to ensure continuity between the service settings for such young people. Research indicates that placement in a new setting causes great strain for families and youths; Cohen-Sandler, Berman, and King (1982) identify change of placement as a frequent antecedent to adolescent suicide, and Brennan (1980) notes its relationship to running away.

While the seriousness of these risks demands attention, a more common threat is that the loss of social supports will result in lost support for competent performance. Among the strategies that can help children and youths develop new social networks are buddy systems, orientation programs, and life books with mementos from previous settings (Fahlberg, 1979; Felner, Ginter, and Primavera, 1982; Jason and Bogat, 1983). Strategies that this author has found useful for promoting social integration include preplacement visits to the old program by staff from the new setting as well as visits to the new setting by the child, gradual—a few hours or days at a time—transition to the new program, sharing information with the new group about the child's interests to create positive expectations, offering the child some symbol (such as a tee-shirt) of membership in the new group, adding the child's name to the roster of youths who have been in the new program, and a structured opportunity for all participants to identify why they are in the new program and to state their goals. Finally, natural communities of identity arising from gender or cultural, religious, or ethnic backgrounds may provide support for the maintenance of treatment gains despite the stresses of new settings and services.

Many troubled families do not enter treatment with supportive social networks. These families are the most difficult to engage in treatment (Powell, 1984) and have the most difficulty maintaining their treatment gains (Wahler, 1980). Such clients—and they form a major part of the client population in many agencies—need assistance and support well after formal services end. Toward this end, services must from the outset attempt to involve clients' existing social networks and engage clients in new formal and informal service networks. For this reason, groups that stress sharing activities outside of the clinic are often preferred (see, for example, Barth, Blythe, Schinke, and Schilling, 1983). The helping literature's often excessive preoccupation with the traumas of termination from treatment fails to account for the many potential extratreatment resources available to clients. So long as child helpers are sure that a trampoline made of strong social fabric is available to their clients, they need not dread letting them somersault beyond treatment.

4

Working with Other Services and Helpers

The mission of the child helper is to promote the competent functioning of children and youth in minimally restrictive settings. At times this mission requires concerted and masterful training efforts to increase the cognitive and social skills of children, adolescents, and their caregivers. Skill training, however, is not usually the best opening move for the child helper to make. Efforts to change or enrich current services or environments often should precede skill training. Such efforts do not attempt to remediate personal deficits through retraining but, rather, endeavor to reshape the social ecology to provide needed support and resources for developing the capacity for positive change. Techniques for changing services and environment often are undervalued, unarticulated, and underresearched. Despite this neglect, skills in these techniques are valuable for helping. During these efforts, child helpers may collaborate with natural helpers within the client's own network, caregivers who can help the child to develop more competent behavior, family members, and other child helpers.

Social Networking

Most helping comes from informal networks of friends, family, clergy, and neighbors (Kamerman and Kahn, 1982).

Child helpers too often ignore these resources. The reasons for this reluctance to work with clients' social-support networks are unclear. Narrow conceptions of confidentiality that prevent discussion of children's problems with teachers, kin, peers, or friends may be partly responsible. The notion that the children child helpers assist are patients and their difficulties private is long-standing and widely recognized. Although physicians usually are bound by patient confidentiality, this is less true for other child helpers, since they treat unsuccessful social ecologies, not only patients (Speck and Attneave, 1973). As Moore-Kirkland and Irey (1981) discuss, confidentiality within a small social network is nearly impossible, as the problems and activities of clients are highly visible and public. Barriers between sources of information will likely impair a helping system's ability to find a consistent and effective approach to problem resolution and do not protect the client's best interest. Clients' rights to privacy warrant preservation, but so do their rights to effective treatment. Uncertainty about how to increase the strength of social networks may also dissuade the use of these networks. When the use of the social network is indicated and issues in assessing network membership, enhancing network support, and consulting network members are described in the following pages. Additional discussion can be found in Bertsche, Clark, and Iversen (1982); Collins and Pancoast (1976); Swenson (1981); and Whittaker, Garbarino, and Associates (1983).

Indications. Social networking is no cure-all. Networking is almost always an adjunct to other intervention plans. Evidence that negative community contacts diminish the durability of skills acquired in parent training (Wahler, 1980) suggests that the converse may also be true: positive community relationships may interact with services to support change and enhance competence. Community members can review and affirm the constructive changes arising from the crises of change. For example, Toughlove at its best offers parents of out-of-control children support for problem solving and implementing the solutions they choose in the face of threats, doubt, and fatigue. Social networking is particularly appropriate for situations in which parents support other parents' efforts to change. Even parents of very troubled children may have many competencies to share. Such parents may help other parents apply lessons that they do not always apply in their own parent-child relationships or which they learned late.

Mobilizing social-network support for families is perhaps most valuable when the families possess competent parenting skills but, because they are overwhelmed by other responsibilities, are not using those skills. Single, employed parents who are not in the home enough to provide developmental guidance or consistent disicipline may not need parenting-skills training but only the encouragement and opportunity to return to their effective parenting styles. Families with little income may exhaust themselves trying to stave off eviction or hunger and may find that the strain undermines their parenting. Stress from poverty and its accompanying disruptions is associated with poor parenting (Barth and Blythe, 1983). Although programs that provide economic sufficiency to all families are the most obvious solution, the provision of personal and social resources can shield families from stress. Families of disruptive and damaged children may be isolated (Kozloff, 1979; Schilling, Gilchrist, and Schinke, 1984). Services to these families will be incomplete unless they include a concerted effort to increase the families' social integration.

Social-network interventions can also serve children and adolescents. Most often this will involve a cross-age relationship, since older people are more likely to possess competencies and resources that can contribute to problem amelioration. (As will be described, peers may be of more service as mediators when their roles and responsibilities are clearly defined.) Child helpers typically need to be very active in arranging helping relationships within existing social networks. Such relationships require the acknowledgment of caregivers, and they require regular supervision. Cross-age helping relationships may involve interactions that leave child helpers uneasy; for instance, they may involve the use of guilt, sarcasm, or distraction from the "real" issues. Other more serious flaws may show over time—the helper may become unavailable or lose interest, strain may develop in the relationship, and client or helper may become frustrated. Such flaws must be watched for and counterbalanced against the oftentimes unique benefits of helping that occur within the social network. The case of Eric (described more fully in Barth, 1983) demonstrates the potential of helpers from the social network to provide models of competence and resources that professional child helpers cannot offer.

As consultant to a foster home, Mr. Fallon, a social worker, met a resident, Eric. This fifteen-year-old boy was bright, lonely, gregarious, and effeminate in manner; he frequented the nearby airport terminal looking for tricks, skipped school, and was prone to running away in stolen cars. The other foster children in his home disdained him because of his professed homosexuality and his incomprehensible interests. His foster parents were confused by his sexuality, enjoyed his wit and warmth, and lived in fear of a car theft and accident. The social worker concluded that Eric was often bored and unsupervised prior to his joy rides and airport rambles. After briefly chatting with Eric, his probation officer, and his foster parents, Mr. Fallon decided to help Eric make contact with a wider network. Mr. Fallon discussed his plan with Eric and then began to explore Eric's current and past support networks.

A social-network diagram helped Mr. Fallon locate Albert, a gay counselor whom Eric knew from a prior stay at a house for runaways. Eric indicated that he thought that Albert was a person who was easy to talk with about troubles and who might provide aid. Unlike other older contacts that Eric described to Mr. Fallon, Albert did not require personal compromises in return for aid. Eric and Albert, unfortunately, had lost track of each other; Eric thought that Albert had left his job at the house for runaways and was working for a furniture wholesaler. Mr. Fallon located Eric through the staff at the runaway shelter. He piqued Albert's memory and interest in Eric. Although wearied by the constant flow of runaways, Albert did enjoy helping— especially helping youths struggling with gay identification. With his foster parents' consent and after some rehearsal with Mr. Fallon, Eric contacted Albert, met with him once at the agency, and then began to spend Saturdays working at the showroom where Albert worked; Albert paid him with dinners and movies. Albert introduced Eric to his partner and shared with him a model of a loving, working, forward-looking, though unconventional, life. Albert at times provided special events for Eric following reports of school success but was reluctant to endanger the evolving relationship by delivering rewards or penalties based on Eric's performance. In this case, then, when resources and competencies lay outside the client's and child helper's singular possession but were available in the broader social ecology, the child helper brought these resources and the client together to help meet the client's needs.

Assessing Network Membership. Formal sociometric assessments of client networks are often unnecessary. Child helpers can learn about the networks of children, adolescents, and parents through careful listening and observation. In the course of investigating the client's problem and resources, child helpers will hear mention of friends, relatives, and neighbors with whom the client has positive contact. Child helpers can further determine network membership with such questions as ''Do your parents have any friends whom you also like?'' or ''Which of your neighbors do you like most?'' or ''What friends of yours can you most count on?'' or ''Is there anyone else you know who is in the same situation?'' Child helpers may know of other children, adolescents, or parents with mutual needs or available time and resources. Watching with whom children and adolescents spend time is also informative. The person who first reports that there is a problem in a family frequently is especially committed to the family's welfare (Bertsche, Clark, and Iversen, 1982) and so may be a source of support. Whether the family will be appreciative of or bitter toward this person must be ascertained before he or she is enlisted as a helper, but in any case the reporter of the problem often knows of other resources on which the family might draw.

Sometimes using specific network-identification techniques is advantageous. For people who cannot identify anyone within their social networks who might provide helping, the technique of the ''reconstructed week,'' in which the events and social contacts of the prior week are reviewed and discussed with others, may be useful (Pearson, 1981). Network diagrams, or ecomaps (Hartmann and Laird, 1983), may also help single parents, adolescents, and children to list the significant institutions and places in their ecosystem—schools, day-care centers, work, playgrounds, and clubs, for example—and then note the people connected with these settings who might be helpful. Visits to these settings may reveal additional information. Forms such as the Social Support Inventory shown in Figure 1 may prompt specification of what kinds of aid are available from network members. Discussion should, of course, determine personal costs to the family or child of requesting or receiving such aid, as some "gifts" come with strings—especially, the loss of autonomy—attached.

Helpers from clients' social networks may be most effective when they are identified and recruited by the clients themselves, often with the encouragement of the child helper. The child helper might suggest to a concerned mother that a neighbor might be willing to provide periodic after-school child care for her nine-year-old son in exchange for something (such as weekend child care) she can provide. The mother would then be helped to identify and recruit such a neighbor. Such collaborative recruitment of helpers within the client's social network usually follows the client's recognition of his or her problem, acceptance of the need for an intervention program, and development of a valued relationship with the child helper. These conditions help support clients when they discuss their experiences with friends, relatives, or neighbors and ask for their aid.

Enhancing Network Support. Child helpers may find outreach to network members enjoyable, profitable, and sometimes essential. In one celebrated case, networking efforts extended from Oakland to Mexico to identify the siblings of a child in need of an organ donor (Guendelman, 1981). A flight to Mexico to meet the child's birth family led to a joyful reunion and problem resolution. Young children in need of foster care have nominated day-care providers and schoolmates' families as people with whom they would like to stay. The child helper then visits the nominees to discuss their concerns and, if any of the nominees is willing and qualified, the child helper obtains a temporary license for the home so emergency foster care can be provided.

Figure 1. Sample Social Support Inventory.

On this form you will fill in the grid to indicate the kind of support you can expect from people you know. First, write people's names down the left-hand side. Then, put an X in the box across from each name and under each kind of support you could get. Then, *circle* each X that shows support you cannot get without doing something you really do not want to do.

People	Support	Share good times	Talk about troubles	Housing	Transportation	Money	New skills	Information
Friends								
1. _____	☐	☐	☐	☐	☐	☐	☐	
2. _____	☐	☐	☐	☐	☐	☐	☐	
3. _____	☐	☐	☐	☐	☐	☐	☐	
Family								
1. _____	☐	☐	☐	☐	☐	☐	☐	
2. _____	☐	☐	☐	☐	☐	☐	☐	
3. _____	☐	☐	☐	☐	☐	☐	☐	
Work or school contacts								
1. _____	☐	☐	☐	☐	☐	☐	☐	
2. _____	☐	☐	☐	☐	☐	☐	☐	
Relatives								
1. _____	☐	☐	☐	☐	☐	☐	☐	
2. _____	☐	☐	☐	☐	☐	☐	☐	
Other								
1. _____	☐	☐	☐	☐	☐	☐	☐	
2. _____	☐	☐	☐	☐	☐	☐	☐	

Source: Adapted from Barth, 1983, p. 329.

With sufficient rehearsal, clients can often contact network members themselves. Teenagers involved in Ala-teen, a self-help group for the children of Alcoholics Anonymous or Al-anon members, often arrange to stay at other members' homes during crises. Younger children often fail to recognize the resources embodied in their older siblings and miss opportunities to problem solve, have fun, and learn coping strategies. Parents also may overlook the benefits of contact with others who have learned from similar experiences, however successfully or unsuccessfully they first handled them. As with other encouragement child helpers give to children or parents, the suggestion to contact network members should be carefully discussed, contact strategies should be rehearsed, drawbacks should be noted, likely responses should be anticipated, and progress should be followed with interest.

Child helpers may also need to make contacts to strengthen the network themselves. In a school setting, this may involve arranging for a child who attends school regularly and who lives near a child with low school attendance to stop by each morning and provide a model and support for regular attendance. Such arrangements should be made only after discussion with the child who is to be helped and assessment of other possible barriers to or discouragers of attendance. Support for continued social contact can include attention for helping, recognition of the helper as well as the child being helped for changes in attendance, notification of parents and teachers that improved attendance is part of a team effort, and treats like soft drinks or comic books. Enlisting adult members of the network should also follow from assessments of the problem and the ecology. Single parents of troubled children often lament the unavailability of someone to give them a breather and to talk with about parenting decisions (Brown and Harris, 1978). Such resources may be available among self-help groups (Toughlove or Parents Anonymous, for example), other single parents identified by the child helper, or helpers within the community with whom the child helper maintains collaborative contact. Single teenage mothers from minority groups, whose children often have more than their share of difficulties (Kellam, Ensminger, and Turner, 1977), more effectively fulfill their parenting roles when they are paired with older single mothers (Blum, 1984; McHenry, 1980). Child helpers can locate potential helpers in communities of interest, within neighborhoods, or among people whose age, sexual orientation, religious affiliation, gender, ethnicity, or occupation is similar to the client's.

Consulting Network Members. Network members who seek to help a troubled child or family may sometimes find this work rewarding, and sometimes find it slow, confusing, and even disillusioning. Professional child helpers can help nonprofessional adult and adolescent helpers relinquish the myth that cure is the goal of helping and provide instruction in noticing and praising any gains in the client's behavior or in the competencies of the target social ecology. Supporting their judgment, resisting the temptation to oversupervise them, being easily accessible to them by phone, and organizing groups of helpers to provide the opportunity for all to share experiences can help maintain interest and optimism. The distribution of these services, however, should follow careful assessment of the incentives for helping. The majority of adolescent helpers known to this author prefer anonymity (in part to avoid the stigma of being called a "do-gooder"). More generally, altruists often lose motivation when externally monitored or rewarded (Wispe, 1978). The most subtle incentives may be the most effective.

Caregivers as Child Helpers

Closely related to social networking is engaging caregivers in child-helping roles. Caregivers who serve as child helpers are sometimes called *mediators* because they operate between the consulting professional and the child (Tharp and Wetzel, 1969). In this role, caregivers may teach the client new skills and provide incentives for their use, monitor their occurrence, and evaluate the client's progress in using them. Although caregivers may be nonprofessionals such as parents, siblings, friends, and coaches, they are equally often professionals, including teachers, nurses, group-home operators, foster parents, and juvenile hall staff. In the child-helping role, caregivers, in contrast to helpers from the social-support system, engage in concerted change efforts under the supervision of a professional child helper rather than in the unsupervised provision of supportive aid. These forms of helping, although conceptually different, are neither distinct nor incompatible.

Indications for Enlisting Caregivers as Child Helpers. Caregivers serving as child helpers can contribute to the majority of change efforts directed toward children, and to a lesser extent, those directed toward adolescents and adults. A few specific attributes of caregivers contribute to their success in a child-helping role. Some of the critical attributes of successful child helpers have been articulated by Tharp and Wetzel (1969). Practice suggests others and identifies client characteristics that might influence decisions about using a mediation approach.

A good relationship with the client is one characteristic of the caregiver who is also a successful child helper. To fulfill their roles, child helpers must be able to build new skills or motivate children to use old skills. A good relationship between the caregiver and child contributes to both motivation and learning. The child and caregiver will most likely know that each one is able to punish the other, but they should not have reached the point where positive exchanges are impossible. Caregivers must be willing to risk at least temporarily upsetting the relationship in order to deliver suitable rewards and penalties. A caregiver whose distaste for a child overwhelms his or her ability to recognize when the child has done well or to deliver rewards when they are deserved will have difficulty fulfilling the child-helping role. Child helpers who do not communicate well with a child's parents will also not help the cause. For instance, the father of a young stealer in a group home consistently failed to perform his weekend tasks because he did not take the group-home parents seriously. Without ever saying so, he thought that they should be as rough on the child as was the staff when he himself was in residential care during his adolescence. Taking away privileges did not seem like sufficient punishment for his son. Only after the child's mother began to successfully implement the program did the father begin to support her efforts to control privileges and provide rewards. The house parents did not know about the father's own experience in residential care until much later.

Naturally, the caregiver who is a successful child helper must have control over incentives that will motivate the child. For younger children, time to spend with the child often is a more valued incentive than money or goods. Alternately, for older children, child helpers need control over such privileges and material benefits as evenings out, television watching, bicycle riding, home video equipment, movie money, having friends over, and tickets to concerts. If a person with a good relationship with an older child—perhaps a basketball coach or an older cousin—lacks natural control over privileges or material benefits, child helpers can help this person obtain more control by working with other figures in the child's social ecology who control more incentives. For example, parents could provide an older cousin with money to buy a Friday-night dinner for two at a favorite fast-food restaurant if their adolescent child is home for dinner the first four nights of the week.

Caregivers who become child helpers must have the capacity to take on and complete the tasks of fostering children's behavior change. Most adults and some adolescents have this capacity. The notable exceptions are people who are unable to follow instructions, restrain impulsive actions, or distinguish differences in children's performances. People who are psychotically depressed, schizophrenic, alcoholic, rarely available for consultation, or hostile to the goals or methods of mediation also are among the modest-sized group of people who should not be enlisted to help. People who are only mildly depressed, disoriented, ineffectual, or unassertive may make good mediators, however, and the mediating process may, in fact, help them organize their actions and improve their morale (see, for example, McLean, 1976; Harris and Ferrari, 1983). Teaching potential child helpers self-control skills—with many preparatory simulations—before asking them to calmly provide rewards or penalties to children is one way to test their abilities to discontinue habitual and unhelpful responses to children's behavior (Fleischman, Horne, and Arthur, 1983; Wolfe, Kaufman, Aragona, and Sandler, 1981).

Few caregivers come to the child-helping role with mastery of all of the skills needed to teach new competencies to clients. Exceptions may be teachers, group-home staff members, or others with experience in instruction. For that reason, expectations for caregivers' instructional abilities should be limited. Without a major time commitment by professionals, caregivers who serve as child helpers are not likely to become competent at, for example, teaching self-instruction techniques, using fear-desensitization techniques, or discussing and rehearsing ways to protect against unwanted pregnancy (see Gilchrist and Schinke, 1983, for a discussion of parents' difficulties in counseling their children about sexuality). When a homemaker-services employee or Head Start aide, for example, has responsibility for more than a few clients, then coaching in skills for using complex behavior-change techniques may be worthwhile.

Nearly every caregiver who serves as a child helper will require training in discriminating between desired and undesired performances, and this is often the focus of consultation. With training, most will learn to label noncompliance, stealing, and wandering. Given these minimum qualifications, most mediators can help increase children's prosocial skills. Professional consultants whose expectations for changes in the caregiver's own behavior are modest will likely be rewarded with a caregiver who better executes the role of child helper. Through examples, encouragement, handouts, and feedback, caregivers can learn to teach children to operate token economies, relax tight muscle groups, sit during time out, and remember basic arithmetic. Over time, through repetition and example, some caregivers learn the principles basic to all skill building: rationale provision, demonstration, practice, and feedback.

To be effective as child helpers, caregivers must not only have access to rewards; they must deliver them in a timely, consistent, and discriminating fashion. This not only requires that the relationship incorporate limits and rewards but also that the caregiver be close enough to the child to observe and judge the child's performance (for minute-to-minute or hour-to-hour assessment) and to monitor and draw conclusions from the reports of other observers (for day-to-day assessment). The behavior of younger and less-sophisticated children is governed by more immediate consequences and, therefore, calls for more immediate responses. With older children, a correlation-based law of effect (Baum, 1973), in which delays between actions and consequences are bridged cognitively and rewards can be given effectively with less promptness, is in operation. Still, experience suggests that few youths can maintain a high level of improved performance without at least weekly review, acknowledgment, and reward. Less frequent contact is likely to hinder success.

Engaging Caregivers to Serve as Child Helpers. Effective mediators are not easy to find, recruit, keep, and supervise. The social
and educational backgrounds of mediators often differ from those
of professionally trained child helpers. By the time a child helper
makes contact with possible mediators, these mediators may be
frustrated with the child, have tried everything they know, have
decided that there is nothing anyone can do for the child, and
may hope that their interventions will lead to the child's removal
from their care through transfer to another school, another class,
another group home, or another family. Caregivers may not be
thrilled to be asked to learn new skills and to make new attempts
to correct old problems but may agree to do so because they
have the greatest stake in helping to improve a child's behavior.

Locating potentially effective child helpers among caregivers is difficult. Professionals must creatively scan the social
ecology for people with the qualities indicated earlier that contribute to success: a sound relationship with parent and child,
access to rewards, ability to discriminate among behaviors, consistency, and proximity. Beyond any rewards provided by the
professional child helper, the caregiver's world should improve
as the child's performance does. Caregivers should ultimately
be snared by the "behavior trap"; that is, improved circumstances that reward and sustain their helping efforts (Baer and
Wolf, 1970). While the professional must help sustain the caregiver's child-helping efforts during the tumultuous beginnings
of change, the changes in the social ecology (in this case, in the
caregiver's behavior) must persist beyond the period of consultation. Ironically, caregivers' indications of frustration and rejection (but not apathy or defeat) may signal their potential as
child helpers. Individuals who are upset are motivated to seek
change. The professional's role is to redirect and inform that
pilgrimage.

Caregivers who have themselves initiated requests for help
may have enthusiasm and confidence and be eager to undertake
a modified approach to helping. Others may be receptive to assuming a child-helping role because this is their designated responsibility, or they have learned to operate in this role. They
will be comfortable working with consultants and will be at least

half pleased when they see that the professional child helper's brand of consultation differs from the too-common therapeutic strategy of "discuss, dissect, and disappear." While an approach that offers more guidance and responsibility may seem more appealing, the increased expectations for performance and the greater accountability for implementing plans may initially awe or worry potential child helpers.

Cognitive and social barriers to engaging caregivers as child helpers can be anticipated. Caretakers other than parents (for example, day-care providers, neighbors, or relatives) may be reluctant to act toward the troubled child in a way that they do not act toward their own child or in a way that the parent does not act. Nonparental figures who assume a child-helping role may fear others' judgments or accusations of favoritism. Such potential mediators will likely benefit from a meeting in which the responsibilities of all members of the social ecology are detailed. To maximize commitment, the child helper should communicate the message that *everyone* in the social ecology is losing from the way the system currently works (Fleischman, Horne, and Arthur, 1983) and that *everyone*, therefore, is expected to change their behaviors and act "unnaturally." This message may relieve individuals' fears that they are the only members of the child's ecology expected to change. Acknowledging that members of the community at large may not understand that behavior problems are centered in the relationships between people rather than in individuals may give meeting participants a sense of membership in an exclusive and informed club. This may shield their decision to help from the pressures of their own social ecologies (Janis, 1983).

Time-limited agreements may also reduce fears that the enterprise will be too demanding. A two-week agreement is usually a good starting place for mediators from outside of the family (family members should be motivated to make longer commitments). Starting with a consensus that a problem exists; a rationale for the consistent provision of incentives (it may be wisest to phase in incentives without phasing out disincentives); permission from as many members of the social ecology as possible; and a plan for small, well-defined, short-term changes in behavior will encourage potential mediators to begin the process. Professionals should strive to boost caregivers' commitments to perform on behalf of themselves and the child of interest rather than for the benefit of the child helper. With much support and sufficient but not overbearing social reinforcement, the caregiver can overcome restraints, enter into the child-helping role, and start down the trail to the behavior trap.

Guiding Caregivers as Child Helpers. Child helpers will certainly confront difficulties in implementing their roles but will too rarely acknowledge them or request assistance in problem solving. Professionals will be unable to provide guidance unless they take time to observe or to ask pointed questions about the mediator's difficulties and successes. As for other behavior-change activities, the supervising professional must track the behavior, provide ample suggestions for improvement and reward, and help to predict and plan for events that might undermine success. Review of cognitive contributors to success can also help guard against caregivers' giving up their roles due to inaccurate expectations about the speed of behavior change or insufficient self-management skills that make using a strategy with short-term difficulties and long-term gains difficult.

Children may be the most significant influence on caregivers' successes as child helpers. Children who engage in low-frequency, hard-to-ascertain behaviors such as stealing will tax caregivers' abilities as child helpers. Unappealing children who soil, scream, spit, or use abusive language can make child helping an ungratifying job. For some children, creating frustrating experiences for the child helper is more rewarding than the privileges or rewards that the child helper offers. Such children seem to reject all efforts to add positive consequences to their typically negative world. The especially infuriating child who destroys a child helper's property may elicit a response from the child helper similar to that of abusing families: attack, counterattack, apology, remorse, appreciation, affection, still fiercer attack, and so on. During these episodes, professionals must reemphasize the importance of using self-control to minimize counterattacks, of consistently punishing the child's negative behavior regardless of remorse or forgiveness, and of maintaining a reasonable level of appreciation. When professionals enlist child helpers to work with unappealing, hard-to-reward, agressive children, they must provide careful guidelines and structured and frequent supervision to help them cope with these adversities.

Family Treatment

The family is usually the foremost social-support network and the fundamental provider of sanctions and rewards. Loosely applied, the term *family* can include group-home peers and parents, a single nonrelated adult who is responsible for a soon-to-be-emancipated youth's care, a great-grandmother and her teenage granddaughter and child, and a twice-married couple with custody of two children with no blood relationship to either of them. Propinquity provides families with unparalleled opportunities to shape each other's behavior and to disrupt healthful and unhealthful patterns of personal development. Because of families' unique contribution to the social and cognitive development of children, assisting families entails using the procedures described thus far as well as additional treatment strategies.

Indications for Family Therapy and Parent Training. Much was written about indications for family treatment in the heyday of individual therapy and when seeing families together was an exceptional practice. Now almost all client problems are deemed amenable to interventions that involve the family. The reemergence of fathers as important socializing figures (Lamb, 1976) and recent studies identifying the important contribution that father involvement makes to treatment outcome (Stanton and Todd, 1981; LaBarbera and Lewis, 1980) support the idea that full family involvement is critical. Even when the child has less of a problem at home than at school, child helpers can benefit from enlisting parents as coadvocates for corrective adjustments to the school environment (Barth, 1983; Pennekamp and Sarvis, 1974). In short, reasons for involving most family members in treatment are bountiful. The rare exceptions usually involve families whose members have been abusive to each other. If the father has sexually abused his child, total family treatment may have to await evidence that the child has adequate protection and that the offender is undergoing separate rehabilitation. Physically assaultive adults or adolescents may also undermine the ability of family members to engage in problem solving or nonviolent discipline. Self-control training for the violent family member may be a necessary precursor to family treatment.

A more common reason than violence for not working with families is the inaccessibility of family members to child helpers because of their schedules or jobs. Despite flexible hours and conscientious efforts to visit homes, child helpers cannot always meet with all family members. Whenever they can, however, they will benefit from incorporating members of the child's family or social ecology into treatment.

Thus, the question currently perplexing child helpers is not whether to include families but what kinds of family and child helper involvement are indicated. The two major forms of family treatment are family therapy and behavioral parent training. Recent interest in a synthesis of these approaches has produced structured family therapy (Alexander and Parsons, 1982), behavioral family therapy (Griest and Wells, 1983), and family training (Dangel and Polster, 1984). This amalgamation is laudable as the intent of most traditional family therapies, with the exception of strategic therapy, is to improve communication patterns, clarify family rules, and trigger changes in interaction among all parts of the family system. Restating these goals in language and procedures that emphasize instruction should increase the likelihood that they will be reached. Behavioral parent training has focused on teaching procedures for correcting children's aggressive and noncompliant behavior. Parent trainers have only recently begun to redress their earlier inattention to social-ecological and marital contributors to problems (Lutzker, McGimsey, McRae, and Campbell, 1983; Wahler and Fox, 1981). This trend suggests that parent training will increasingly incorporate marital and social-ecological factors and that family therapy may better articulate the family competencies it seeks to strengthen.

Child helpers must decide whether to work with both parents and children or only with parents. Parent Effectiveness Training (PET) and parent consultation models teach parents in the absence of their children, whereas parent-adolescent communication training, traditional family therapy approaches, and behavioral parent training work with parents and children together. Child helpers must also decide whether to teach families communication and problem-solving skills or behavior-management techniques. Consultation and individual parent training models are designed primarily to teach parents to control the behaviors of their children, whereas the other models aim to help parents and children arrive at mutually agreeable solutions to family problems. As shown in Table 4, these dimensions present four possibilities for intervention (compounded by the option of conducting each kind of intervention in a group).

Table 4. Types of Family Treatment.

	Behavior Management	Communication and Problem Solving
Work only with the Parent(s)	• Parenting Consultation • Teaching "Time Out" • Tracking and Rewarding	• Parent Effectiveness Training • Couples Therapy
Work with Parent(s) and Child	• Behavioral Parenting Training	• Parent-Adolescent Communication Training • Family Therapy

Available evidence suggests that each of the forms of intervention offers benefit to some clients, with the data on PET least persuasive (Berkowitz and Graziano, 1972; Cobb and Medway, 1978; Rinn and Markle, 1977). The single study that compares the consultation and individual parent-training approaches (Christensen, Johnson, Phillips, and Glasgow, 1980) suggests that these are equally effective in improving children's behavior and that the consultative arrangement is less preferred by parents but less costly to service providers. (Yates, 1982, reported that the consultative model was less costly than traditional clinic or group therapy.) Although definitive data is lacking, indications for each type of treatment can be briefly discussed. Decisions about the most appropriate treatment might consider the parents' current parenting skills, the child's age, the parents' relationship, the family's learning level, and the family's social integration.

Parents whose current parenting skills are poor may benefit most from the consultative and individual parent-training models, which are intended to instruct parents in the microskills of parenting, including self-control, labeling and tracking, delivering consequences, and issuing effective commands. These skills are also considered important in the alternative family-treatment models, but the concern of those models is more specifically focused on enhancing reciprocal communication to improve understanding between parent and child. The assumption of the communication and problem-solving models is that parents are providing the basic structure and relationship needed to promote healthy development but that inevitable conflicts of interest between parent and child must still be negotiated.

The child's age is an important factor in the choice of model. Families with older children find the least success with consultation and individual parent-training approaches (Horne and Patterson, 1979; Sadler, Seyden, Howe, and Kaminsky, 1976). One possible reason for this is that these approaches rely on parental control over family decisions and privileges, and the older child can figure out how to circumvent this control and obtain rewards elsewhere. Alternately, the communication models depend on the child's ability to problem solve with the family and to engage in the communication process. The treatment goal is to boost the family's ability to restructure communication and resource allocation to reduce the family's conflict. Since each family member is expected to have a say in this process, the ability to communicate is paramount. Even though communication can take different forms for children of different ages, these treatments seem most applicable to families with preadolescents and adolescents.

Congruence between parents is not assumed by any approach, but the communication and problem-solving approaches have more established procedures for incorporating the divergent perspectives of all family members. Classic family therapy has much affinity to marital therapy and offers considerable flexibility. Recognizing the limits of individual parent-training strategies, clinicians are simultaneously employing individualized or consultative parent training and consultation regarding couple conflicts; this is well received by parents (Griest and others, 1982; Schreibman, 1983).

The family's learning level is also a possible indicator of treatment type. Families with little experience using handouts or workbooks or keeping records are likely to need much individual attention. This does not mean that they cannot benefit from a didactic approach. Many nonreaders, for example, can sight-read words that are made familiar through frequent use or repetition. Using this approach, handouts and homework assignments have been successfully used in work with teenage mothers with low educational skills and with adult child abusers with learning handicaps (Barth, Blythe, Schinke, and Schilling, 1983; Barth, Schinke, and Maxwell, 1983). The goals of the program may have to be lowered, and modeling and practice may have to be repeated, but change is possible. Of course, limited learning levels make programmed texts or programs that require further reading by family members inappropriate.

Finally, families with limited social integration—perhaps by reason of language barriers, inadequate transportation, poverty, or disabilities—may not be comfortable in groups of any kind. These families are likely to drop out of treatment or to have difficulty adhering to any program (Griest, Forehand, and Wells, 1981; Wahler, 1980).

So far absent from these criteria is the type of problem the child has. This often is the first consideration in selecting a treatment. Indications for various problem-specific treatment approaches will be discussed in the latter chapters of this book, but some generalizations at this point may be useful. First, clinicians seem to overestimate communication patterns and personal reactions (such as unexpressed anger) as contributors to family problems. Early, methodologically unsophisticated research (for example, Bateson, Jackson, Haley, and Weakland, 1956; Bettleheim, 1967) is partially responsible for the continued fascination with the role of communication patterns in such conditions as autism and schizophrenia (see, contrarily, Torrey, 1983; Whittaker, 1976). Reliance on this research encourages the use of communication training for all family problems. We now know that children can operate very well under seemingly impossible circumstances and in the face of myriad communication styles (Garmezy, 1974; Robinson and Fields, 1983). The challenge of child helping is to change only those conditions that prevent children from adapting to their families or communities.

Unstructured approaches to family treatment may cast their nets so loosely and widely to capture flaws in family or marital communication that cognitive and behavioral contibutors to unsuccessful behavior patterns are missed. Narrowly focused parent training may suffer from the opposite problem, however, in not recognizing that key behaviors are often supported by parental disagreement, a parent's ambivalence about remaining in the family, the possibility of out-of-home care for the child, and social isolation. These conditions also require attention.

Finally, although differential assessment is often limited by the unavailability of service or treatment options, assessing the appropriateness of alternative family-treatment models is worthwhile. A single child helper can feasibly learn to deliver each form of treatment or combination of treatments according to family needs. For example, consider a family with an adolescent who ignores curfew, shoplifts, and has twice run away, and whose brother is developmentally delayed, destructive, and enuretic. In addition to investigating related services, the child helper might employ several family-treatment strategies. The child helper might use a communications and problem-solving approach to attempt to resolve the parent-adolescent conflict. At the same time the child helper might provide consultative parent training for the younger sibling (perhaps using the adolescent as mediator) and meet privately with the parents to discuss the strain on their relationship resulting from the family turmoil and help them develop compatible problem-solving styles. The near future will, it is to be hoped, bring additional research and case reports describing and testing integrative family-treatment strategies.

Recruitment and Relationship. The origins of children's problems are often the origins of the difficulties child helpers have recruiting families for treatment. Social isolation, single parenthood, full-time employment, children's mobility, and inadequate services keep families from functioning competently and from engaging in needed change programs. Successful recruitment, then, is itself the beginning of intervention. Relationship begins during recruitment and develops throughout treatment. Relationship provides the initial incentive for tolerating the difficulties and frustrations of learning new approaches to living in a family.

Recruitment may require considerable effort, but usually it is worth it. In families with younger children, the greatest recruitment challenge is bringing in fathers. LaBarbera and Lewis (1980) found a strong positive relationship between fathers' participation in child-helping interventions and their outcomes. Others have noted that fathers often abdicate responsibility for their children (see, for example, Kozloff, 1979). Fathers often have little involvement with child rearing and are especially unlikely to see family management as part of their role (Patterson, 1980). Yet their role is important enough to suggest that recruiting them for treatment—in order to recruit them to play a more responsible and complete parental role—may make a marked difference in treatment outcomes. Fathers, like other on-the-scene caretakers, potentially can contribute general support to mothers in their efforts to cope with parenting (Baumrind, 1979; Brown and Harris, 1978), play with children more than mothers do (Lamb, 1976), and provide an alternative perspective on child management (Patterson, 1982). Although less studied, other adult female caretakers, such as grandmothers, sisters, or lovers, in the same residence with the mother may have similar salutary effects on parenting and should also be included in family treatment.

The effort to recruit fathers and significant others requires child helpers to employ well-developed self-control skills. Time conflicts ("You have got to understand, he works two jobs"), hostility ("If you would leave the kid alone he would be all right"), and lack of interest ("I'm sure you can take care of it") are but a few of the problems child helpers encounter. Stanton and Todd (1981) made up to sixty attempts to recruit the families of young heroin addicts. Their efforts were repaid in dramatically better outcomes for addicts whose families finally did respond to recruitment. Some child helpers will have to contend with the disdain of supervisors or peers who believe that zealous recruitment is countertherapeutic and indicates that the families are not motivated and so treatment will not succeed. Several studies in which family members were paid for attendance and homework completion (Eyberg and Johnson, 1974; Fleischman, 1979) demonstrate the opposite; the children of parents on salaries improved more than other children. Child helpers might best begin the recruitment process with a firm commitment to enlisting family members and an awareness that this commitment will be severely tested by family members and colleagues.

Recruitment involves outreach, inducement, and coercion. Outreach to clients might include some of the strategies associated with job finding. Phone calls, letters, and finally just showing up will begin to express the sincerity of the child helper's interest in working with a person. Calls from other people who have received similar services can augment the child helper's efforts. In this way, the Whites, a Native American foster family struggling to maintain control over their children and to keep their license, were recruited to a foster-family problem-solving group. After no success in engaging the foster parents, two Indian foster parents who had been involved in the group made, at the behest of the social worker, independent visits to the troubled foster family. The group meeting was held at the Native American center, while one of the Native American foster fathers involved in the recruitment effort supervised the Whites' foster children. The first meeting resulted in many offers of aid and information and led to consistent attendance at group meetings by the Whites. As this case shows, program "graduates" are an excellent pool of credible recruiters.

The positive incentives for participation seem plain enough for family members to see, and it is aggravating to child helpers that the improved behavior of the child and a better future for all family members are not adequate incentives. Recruitment must overcome such disincentives as fear of being misunderstood, renegotiation of decisions that have already been made, and fear of being assessed as inadequate. Thus, additional incentives must line the way. Lee (1979) offered lottery tickets, certificates of participation, or cash to enlist the participation of parents and delinquent youths in a program. The enthusiasm of participants for the lottery tickets and certificates, as demontrated by their regular participation and stated preference, led to the end of the cash incentive program. Fleischman, Horne, and Arthur (1983) report a social-learning program for groups of low-income parents that replaced parenting salaries with raffle tickets earned for performance of assignments. Prizes included movie tickets, vouchers for fast-food meals, and money for baby-sitters. Even these prizes were phased out after three weeks as parents apparently found the socializing and opportunity to learn new skills incentive enough for attendance. Food is another appealing and nearly universal incentive. Child helpers may be surprised at the participation of clients when food is provided.

Coercion is perhaps the most powerful and common contributor to program participation. Coercion usually involves legal action, often stemming from charges of juvenile delinquency or child maltreatment. These charges and their consequences of lost rights are frequently not in and of themselves sufficient incentive for full program participation. Stanton and Todd (1981) tell reluctant participants that therapy meetings will involve making decisions about new ways for the family to function and about the reallocation of power. Such thinly veiled threats apparently coerced several hard-to-reach fathers into joining the treatment program to save their power. Coerced treatment was once anathema to human-service workers, who argued that their clients were victims and often sided with them against the law. This has changed for the better, inasmuch as fewer clients are now punished by law because of their morality, cultural background, or status. For those who are still mandated to obtain services, the power of the state may increase their likelihood of using these services (Sgroi, 1982; Ten Broeck and Barth, in press).

The pluralistic nature of families in conflict causes difficulties for child helpers endeavoring to establish relationships with everyone. This may explain some clinicians' reluctance to meet with the full family unit. Alexander and Parsons (1982) provide guidelines for developing relationships with all family members. At minimum, the early sessions should communicate the following message to family members: "First, the child helper sided with me as much as with the others. The child helper also led me to see how my behavior is related to everyone else's behavior. To do that, the child helper made it clear that I alone am not to blame, that everyone in the family contributes to the problem and is a victim of it, and that our problem does not result from different and contradictory goals but instead from not knowing how to resolve those differences. Finally, if I continue working with the child helper, I will be safer and better able to get what I want." The intent is to encourage attendance, an openness to new conceptions of the family, and a willingness to engage in the work of reeducating the family in more successful strategies.

Family members do not, of course, instantaneously substitute child-helper-supplied explanations of their family problems for their own longstanding views. Fisch, Weakland, and Segal (1982) argue that members of families in conflict may never give up their beliefs and encourage individual meetings with parents or adolescents to sympathize with their private versions of the family problem and develop an alliance with them and thereby gain their cooperation in implementing corrective action. In joint sessions, they concur with Alexander and Parsons (1982), the child helper must not take sides. Minuchin and Fischman (1981) describe techniques for joining with individuals during meetings with the full family. These include making inquiries and statements about the roles in the family and community that are not directly related to the presenting problem. In this way, relationships with individual family members are developed but not at the expense of relationships with other family members. Above all, the child helper must make all family members consider the promise of treatment to be greater than the risk, stigma, inconvenience, and tension involved. With authoritarian parents, this may require agreeing that the work ethic does not seem to mean much to children anymore. It may also mean avoiding the temptation to reinterpret anger or criticism as affection. With adolescents, simple confirmations of their positive efforts and qualities—"There's a lot of disagreement in this family, but you hang in there and keep looking for changes," for example—may begin to strengthen the commitment to treatment. With all family members, relationship building requires understanding and using their language and metaphors. With adolescents, understatement typically is the most effective means of communication; messages delivered in other ways may go unheard. With parents, the child helper often must speak the language of anguish, despair, confusion, anger, and outrage.

Child helpers express their recognition of the importance of the social and cultural context of practice through their involvement of natural helpers, mediators, and family members. This chapter only hints at the complexity created when the child helper begins to consider all the possibilities for including members of the child's or family's social ecology. Unfortunately, the questions that are raised by working with significant others do not each have a single correct answer. Involving other people to help the child does not ensure that the helping effort will be effectual and long-lived. But as long as the involvement of others does not harm the child, child helpers should pursue the collaboration of others because this will enable them to implement change strategies that will endure after they withdraw from the case. The failure to involve others all but dooms the helping effort to be ineffectual and short-lived.

Service Coordination

Child helping requires humility and the recognition that using additional resources may benefit the client. Sometimes, particularly when families are involved with child protection or mental retardation services, the responsibility for case coordination is clear, and the child helper knows that another case manager is helping the client obtain needed services. When a team approach to treatment is used, the responsibility for service coordination is more diffuse; at any given point in the process of service delivery, a child helper may undertake the case-management role. Many times, children and youth are not part of any identified network of services but come first to the attention of the child helper. Techniques for case coordination thus are necessary.

Planning. A thorough assessment, following the guidelines discussed in Chapter Two, will identify client assets and needs and suggest case goals and an intervention plan. This plan may draw on resources provided directly by the child helper and resources from other community members and agencies. Whatever the composition of the plan, it will be most effective if it is put in writing. Planning must involve both the child helper and additional child-serving agents. Monitoring the plan and whether or not it is completed are crucial to making changes in the child's social ecology.

Service coordination agreements fulfill the same purpose for interservice collaboration between child helpers that service agreements (discussed in Chapter Two) fulfill for collaboration between child helpers and clients. The objective is to clarify the role of each child helper and agency in delivering services for the client. Such agreements provide a framework for service delivery and pledge each party involved to (1) give priority to fulfilling those agreed-upon objectives for which they have the resources, (2) avoid working on objectives that belong to another party, and (3) not change or add new objectives without agreement by the service coordinator. The service coordinator may assume responsibility for specific service objectives and must assume responsibility for addressing service gaps, convening and calling meetings, and disseminating new case-related information. Exhibit 6 shows a service coordination agreement for Jacky Jaxxi (this case was first described in Chapter Two). In this case, the contract was drawn up after the service agreement with Jacky was developed. At the child helper's request, a Planned Parenthood counselor, Jacky's math teacher, and the vice-principal of Jacky's school attended a meeting to agree on the responsibilities each would have and the resources each would provide. Jacky and his girlfriend Jeannette joined the meeting during its last fifteen minutes. The contribution pledged by each meeting participant was recorded, and all participants were duly encouraged and thanked. The responsibilities agreed on verbally were written down, and a list of these responsibilities was sent to key participants.

Exhibit 6. Sample Service Coordination Contract.

This agreement is between Mr. Paul How, school social worker, Ms. M. Kim White, counselor at Planned Parenthood, Mr. John Copez, math teacher, Dr. Sandra Warren, vice-principal, and Ms. Jeannette Cartier, student, who will assist Mr. Jacky Jaxxi's achievement of the goals of his service agreement.

Mr. How agrees to meet regularly with Mr. Jaxxi, to contact each of the parties to this agreement monthly to collect and share pertinent information, and to address any new areas that may arise. Ms. White agrees to meet weekly or as often as agreed on with Mr. Jaxxi and Ms. Cartier to discuss pregnancy and contraceptive options. She will make one follow-up phone call if appointments are not made.

Mr. Copez agrees to first meet with Mr. Jaxxi and Ms. Cartier to provide a summary of past assignments and then meet once a week for one-half hour with Mr. Jaxxi and Ms. Cartier to help with their tutorial.

Dr. Warren agrees to meet with Mr. Jaxxi, Mr. How, and other interested parties to discuss actions to be taken if Mr. Jaxxi is caught fighting this month. In future months, Dr. Warren may call such a meeting or may suspend Mr. Jaxxi for fighting without delay because of the danger of harm to Mr. Jaxxi and others. Mr. Jaxxi may, of course, then request a hearing.

Ms. Cartier agrees to meet with Mr. How and Mr. Jaxxi to arrange the best procedure for helping Mr. Jaxxi with his math. She also agrees to accompany Mr. Jaxxi to Planned Parenthood counseling for an initial visit.

All parties further agree to report difficulties in implementing their roles to Mr. How, to attend future meetings as needed, to give priority to the objectives they are pursuing, and to avoid adding or changing objectives without discussing this with Mr. How.

Mr. How   Dr. Warren

Ms. White   Ms. Cartier

Mr. Copez

Making Connections. A child helper can rarely meet all of the service needs of a child, youth, or parent without drawing on the resources of others. Linking clients to resources is a central, though at times frustrating, task. Frustration may arise from difficulty arriving at a consensus as to the goals of treatment. This consensus must precede contact between the client and the agency or resource. If a child helper believes that a mother should get consultation in managing the behavior of her

six-year-old child, but the agency that the child helper wants
to refer her to wants to give her marital counseling and place
her child in play therapy, this should be discussed before the
client is referred. The client should only have to negotiate the
route to the next service, not broad treatment strategies. At least
an implicit service agreement must be reached between the child
helper and the agency receiving the referral before the client
participates in the linking process.

Once a service agreement is established, clients should
be encouraged to complete as much of the link on their own
as they can. Clients involved in the linking process are most
likely to follow through with the referral. Hopefully, they will
have a positive exchange with the staff member they contact.
The child helper should not, however, overestimate clients' interest in or ability to make connections themselves. Whatever
the benefits, receiving services is time consuming and usually
is accompanied by ambivalence. Many clients welcome the opportunity to reconsider their engagement in child-helping systems and use the referral point to drop out of services. Vague
indications by clients that they will make the call "later" should
cue the child helper that a skill or motivation deficit is likely
to disrupt the connection if it is not redressed. A range of connecting strategies, from those requiring the least practitioner
assistance to those requiring the most, are illustrated here.

- Give vague verbal instruction: "You might call the school
  counselor and talk to her about getting Josie tested."
- Give specific verbal instruction: "You might call Dr. Sandi
  Chavez in the counseling office, 123-4567, and set up a meeting time to discuss testing for Josie."
- Provide written instruction: "Let me write down the name
  and number of the psychologist at Martin Luther King
  School so you can call her and set up a time to talk."
- Write letter to contact: "I know Dr. Chavez. I will write her a
  letter describing your situation and telling her that you will
  call. I will send you a copy. When you get your copy you will
  know that she's gotten one too. Call her then, at this number."
- Rehearse call with client and have client call the contact while

child helper is present: "Perhaps you could call Dr. Chavez right now."

- Make call for client and rehearse behavior during visit: "Let me call Dr. Chavez while you are here so we can arrange a time."
- Make call for client and inform client of visit time: "I will call Dr. Chavez and then call you, certainly by the weekend, about the meeting time."
- Make call for client and arrange for helper from the child's social network to take client, or child helper goes with client: "Now that we have a meeting time, let's go together. Is that okay with you?"
- Make call for client and arrange for contact person to meet at a setting familiar to the client: "Dr. Chavez will join us here at the usual time."

Following Through. Making sure that the connection to the new resource is securely made, troubleshooting any problems that arise, and helping clients take full advantage of their new services are part of effective service coordination (Bertsche and Horejsi, 1980). Cementing the connection is especially critical with adolescents, who often "lose their way" to new classes, employment-training programs, mental health centers, and sports programs. The probability of a successful connection can be boosted by applying one or more of the following strategies (Weissman, 1976). In a *check back*, the client calls the child helper after contacting the resource to summarize what has happened so far. The child helper who, with the client's knowledge and approval, employs *haunting* contacts the client by telephone after the initial contact with the new resource has been made and after several subsequent contacts have been made. *Sandwiching* involves meeting with the client immediately before the connection and soon after to be sure that all is going according to plan. *Alternating* involves a series of interviews during the period of contact with other resources. Clients exposed to these techniques may feel hounded or supported. With many clients, it is hard to predict which response will be forthcoming, although the child helper's interest and time are often appreciated.

5

Using Basic Social and Cognitive Principles and Techniques

Enhancing the competencies of children, youth, and parents requires much knowledge and skill. Fortunately, new intervention techniques are being developed and gaining empirical and experimental confirmation. This chapter will familiarize readers with the underlying logic and purposes of core social and cognitive techniques for helping children and youth. Paralleling the order of most helping efforts, the chapter will first introduce less-structured intervention techniques such as giving information, demonstrating new competencies, and promoting practice. The latter part of the chapter will describe structured techniques for increasing desired behavior, reducing undesired behavior, and teaching self-management skills.

Indirect methods for helping (discussed in Chapter Four) may precede, follow, or coexist with direct methods. Certainly, child helpers have many occasions for encouraging changes in the performance of child and adolescent clients and for referring professionals, mediators, and family members. Understanding and, often, changing the cognitive and social forces governing the actions of members of the social ecology are central to effective work with children and youth. Because of this, these techniques should not be limited to application in face-to-face or one-to-one interviews with children and youth. With careful instruction and continued consultation, the social and cognitive methods described in this chapter can be learned and enlisted by caregivers, who then become child helpers.

Teaching New Competencies

Whether they are paraprofessionals, psychiatrists, psychologists, teachers, nurses, social workers, or parents, all child helpers also must be educators. They must become familiar with the core skills for building clients' abilities and methods for facilitating clients' expression of new, as well as existing but unused, competencies. Further, child helpers will profit from abandoning dated and absolute strictures against giving timely instruction, advice, guidance, and homework. As Adams (1982), a psychiatrist, relates: "One small token of our esteem for parents is demonstrated by our answering some of their questions. As we come to know them we try to be of service. Many young therapists, already cagey about parental wickedness, 'give the business' to parents who ask for some advice. The parent poses a question and the young therapist becomes devoutly 'Rogersian' in his refusal to cooperate—I tend to give sensible (I hope) advice to parents when they ask me about their child's sexuality, bedwetting, school phobia, custody changes, learning problems, physical and neurological problems, cruelty to sibs, and trouble with the law. I do not know of any area of practical childrearing that is sacred and can never be commented on during a contact with parents" (pp. 102–103). Instructing clients in new competencies and encouraging them to use behaviors that worked for them in the past often promote rather than usurp client judgment and competence.

Before child helpers give advice, they must determine that a person actually is a client. Then child helpers must (1) believe in the content of the advice and instruction they provide, (2) understand the process of instruction, (3) monitor and refute their own overstated and unhelpful admonitions about the dangers of instruction, (4) recognize opportunities for correcting helper-suggested actions that initially go astray, and (5) practice giving instruction. Confidence in the content of instruction comes with experience in applying the techniques and with careful review of the experimental evidence documenting their efficacy. Case examples in future chapters will provide vicarious experience in applying these methods. Additional hands-on experience will provide opportunities for child helpers to build additional competence in the educational skills of child helping. Concern about clients' misusing a technique that the child helper taught them (as in the recent case of an overweight mother who suffocated her son by sitting on him after being instructed to use her size in controlling his tantrums) will abate after parents' generally reasonable efforts to apply techniques have been observed. Careful demonstration and review of what the client is going to do and say in the situation calling for the newly learned skill will provide additional assurance. Ample use of role play also should give child helpers a good indication of a client's readiness to apply skills.

Last, as research thoroughly demonstrates (Bandura, 1977), nothing changes thoughts as well as changing behavior. New instructional techniques usually meet with some success rather than acute failure. As child helpers gain experience in giving instruction, they are likely to think, "I do not promote my clients' autonomy by expecting them to invent their own change techniques—I only frustrate them"; "If I give instruction and practice in using data-based techniques and these don't at first work, my client and I can recover—nothing ventured and nothing gained"; and "I wish someone had taught me about this method when I was going through it with my child." Further, clients themselves often express satisfaction with helpers' active instruction (Mayer and Timms, 1970; Sloane and others, 1975). This should not be mistrusted as a sign of overdependence. Clients familiar with instructional approaches know when they have worked hard, tried and mastered new competencies, and learned to independently manage environmental demands that previously managed them (Barth, 1983; Barth, Blythe, Schinke, and Schilling, 1983). Children, youth, and their families are busy with the hectic business of growth and deserve helping that is as brief, unobtrusive, and pointed as possible.

Giving Information. Reflecting back on the last time one gave a lost pedestrian directions to a familiar landmark can underscore the difficulty of providing information. This incident may have stirred such thoughts as ''Did she really follow all those instructions? I'm afraid I went too fast. I should have written them down. I wish my thinking was more organized. Oh! I forgot to mention that bend in the road; it's crucial.'' The road to giving useable information is paved with regret. Several principles may assist child helpers in giving information to parents, mediators, adolescents, and children.

First, be *orderly* and *clear*. Some of the best guidelines for communicating clearly come from principles of writing. Speaking in paragraphs is a useful starting point. This includes introducing what you will say, stating your point and providing an example, and finally, restating your major point and summarizing its significance. For example, note the paragraph structure of the child helper's response in this phone exchange (in contrast with the parent's less ordered comments):

Parent: Well, what do I have to do to get Lee back in school? I'm ready to scream. He's home, and I'm home watching him and missing work—this isn't right at all. I don't know what's wrong with that kid.

Child helper: According to the school's rules, two things are needed before Lee can get back in school. First, you and Lee need to come down and talk to me and develop a plan to help improve Lee's attendance. We should do that right away. Second, Lee will have to agree to the plan and take it to the vice-principal for his approval. So these two things, our meeting and Lee's meeting with the vice-principal, will get Lee back in school where he should be and let you get to work where you'd rather be.

An additional aid to effective information giving is the *linking sentence*. Linking sentences help the listener understand the logic of a series of questions or instructions. By revealing this logic, linking sentences model the problem-solving process for clients. Note, for instance, the difference between the following two versions of an exchange between a child helper and a parent. Linking sentences are italicized.

Version 1

Child helper: What happened before he started the seizure?
Parent: I told him he couldn't go out.
Child helper: Did the day have any unusual stresses?
Parent: Well, he didn't sleep well last night and was grouchy this morning.
Child helper: Had he eaten?
Parent: I'm not sure.
Child helper: What did you do right after the seizure?
Parent: I didn't do anything. I was too shocked.
Child helper: What did anyone else do?
Parent: His brother yelled at him and then took him to his room.

Version 2

Child helper: *To understand what contributed to his seizure, it will help to know what happened just before and after the seizure and if Jack was under any physical stress.* What happened just before?
Parent: I told him he couldn't go out.
Child helper: *I'm also wondering about other events that might set the stage for a seizure.* Did the day have any unusual stresses?
Parent: Well, he didn't sleep well last night and was grouchy this morning.
Child helper: *Being tired or hungry can also contribute to seizures.* Had he eaten?
Parent: I'm not sure.
Child helper: *Hmm! We should check with him on that, perhaps during our family meeting. Since some seizures may be accidentally encouraged by events that follow them, I'm interested in what happened after the seizure.* What did you do right after the seizure?

Parent:	I didn't do anything. I was too shocked.
Child helper:	What did anyone else do?
Parent:	His brother yelled at him and then took him to his room.
Child helper:	*That's a good start on figuring out what events might set up or support Jack's seizures.*

Although lengthening the amount of time child helpers talk, these instructional linkages provide coherence to the interview. Studies of client satisfaction suggest that clients respond positively to longer comments by therapists (see, for example, Sloane and others, 1975).

Although often vilified as impolite or condescending, *repitition* is key to providing information. Children and adolescents are especially tolerant of repetition, as shown by the frequency with which they enjoyably play the same games. Because clients are often preoccupied with their problems or concerned about the way that professionals will judge them, they often misinterpret euphemistic or cryptic comments. Like the earnest listener to a disc jockey's announcement of the number to call to win free tickets, the client will welcome repetition. The first pronouncement is often the attention getter, and subsequent repetitions allow the client to consider inconsistencies and ask for clarification. One technique deserving wider use is taping key meetings—especially conferences where diagnoses are presented, meetings where individual education plans are developed, or official proceedings—for clients to listen to when they get home (tape players are now found in most homes).

To adequately convey information, the child helper also must be sensitive to the *audience.* Communicating information to families asks much of child helpers. Developmental differences in family members require tailoring information for each person. In family meetings, parents or older children may be able to communicate more effectively with younger children. Most often, however, adult talk, so long as it is clear and orderly, will communicate as well as possible to children. Young children often do not understand, in the way adults do, life concepts—adoption, death, or abuse, for example—no matter how simplified their presentation (Furth, 1980; Harris and Ferrari, 1983). The author does not, therefore, advocate "kiddie talk" or using fantasies or allegories to present information. Crisp descriptions and occasional reviews seem most effective with children.

Child helpers must ensure that information is understood. Unfortunately, the families needing the most help often are the most reluctant to ask questions. Simply asking whether there are any questions is rarely sufficient. One technique for checking information reception is the *empathy probe*—saying to oneself, "If I were listening to this I might wonder, what should I do if . . . " or "If I were listening to this I might worry that I missed something. Is there a part of what I said that is unclear or wouldn't seem likely to help?" After a relationship is well established, the child helper can ask clients to repeat what they have heard. Asking clients to repeat too early in the working relationship may, however, be interpreted as patronizing. Thus, at first child helpers may want to summarize the information they have presented to clarify it for the client.

Clients' experiences with previous helpers can also influence their comprehension of new information. An adolescent girl who has endured years of court rulings and external control may not readily understand that she now has an opportunity to choose some of her own goals. Parents who were instructed by other professionals to "get in touch with their feelings" before deciding on a response to their child's behavior may not readily comprehend a system based on what their child does rather than how the parents feel about it. Adolescent clients with information on birth control obtained from peers, the popular media, or siblings may be slow to accept the information that foam alone is not adequate protection against pregnancy or that the pill does not cause breast cancer. Child helpers should probe further if they suspect that clients may have inaccurate information regarding the side effects or risks of carrying out prescribed actions. Many clients learn from popular writings and the media that problems start inside the person and must be solved individually. Few "Dear Dr. Helper" columns educate clients about the ecological perspective or accurately portray the complex interplay of thoughts, behaviors, and feelings that shape lives.

Demonstrating New Competencies. "So, show me what you mean—go ahead, you do it first." Unfortunately, these words are too rarely spoken. Few clients demand professionals to demonstrate what they are talking about. Equally lamentable, child helpers often miss opportunities to demonstrate desired skills. Demonstrating can help clients see what they are expected to do, how to do it, and the results of doing it.

Demonstrating competencies need not be show stopping; practitioners can slip a demonstration into an interview. For example, in helping a frightened child manage better in the dark (Kanfer, Karoly, and Newman, 1975) the child helper can say, "So, if I was starting to feel small and scared I might say to myself, 'even though I'm in the dark, I know just where everything is and can turn on the light if I really need it. I know that I'm in charge of my room even in the dark.' By saying that, I'd feel more calm" (p. 255). More dramatically, and at the risk of some nervous laughter, the child helper can turn off the overhead light, lie down on the floor, and repeat the modeling of fear-mitigating talk.

More structured demonstrations may rely on audio- or videotapes, puppets, fiction, or, in groups, peer models. Most important, the client should be prepared to understand the significance of the demonstration through descriptions of what the specific skills are, and when and where the demonstrated skills might be used. Exposure alone does not ensure that the skills will be noticed (Bandura, 1977). Thus, before reading a story to a child about a lion cub's new-found mastery of its fears about the dark, the child helper should tell the young client to listen for changes in the thoughts and actions of the cub that make it less afraid. The discussion that follows should emphasize the cub's shift to mastery and make obvious the comparison to the child's life.

Modeling should demonstrate not only the competency but also the consequences of using the competency. Thus, covert modeling (Cautela, 1979) that asks parents, children, and adolescents to visualize a similar person's exemplary action under difficult conditions should end with a vivid description of the positive physical, cognitive, and social consequences of the action for the model; for example, "After that he felt full of energy and warm inside, proud of his new way of thinking about the situation, and aware that others admired his easy way of handling the problem."

Promoting Practice. Practice has no substitute as a learning aid. Clients who first rehearse new competencies are more likely to believe in their ability to use them in the community and to actually do so (Bandura, 1977). Child helpers can provide practice opportunities for clients via role playing and homework. Practice should be graduated and should enhance generalization.

Role playing can be used for assessment, modeling (as earlier described), and practice and feedback. Clients' hesitancy to role play new skills usually lessens after they watch the child helper model the role play. Child helpers also can gently engage clients in role playing by asking, "So, what would you say to me if I said . . ." Although role playing is used most often by the child helper with a single client, parents and their offspring can also rehearse ways of handling difficult situations, and peers in groups can practice resolving conflict. Role playing can follow various sequences. One is shown here.

1. *The setting and the scene.* Ask the client to identify what typically happens just before the interaction to be role played occurs. Obtain a description of the client's thoughts that precede the scene. Have the client describe other surrounding events.

2. *Outcome goals.* Ask the client what he or she wants to accomplish the next time the interaction occurs. Agree on a reasonable goal.

3. *Performance goals and components.* Determine what the client wants to say and do to achieve those goals. If the client is unsure, then offer suggestions.

4. *Demonstration or client practice.* Go through the role play. Ask the client if he or she first wants to be shown how the child helper might handle the client's role or to practice his or her own role. If the first approach is used, then the discussion after the role play focuses on what the child helper said that the client can use in subsequent role plays, or in the real

situation. If the latter approach is used, then the child helper should forewarn the client that he or she will stop the role play to comment on what looks and sounds good, will suggest improvements, and will remind the client to use particular skills that were previously agreed on.

5. *Client and child helper feedback.* Ask the client, "What did you like about your performance? What could have been better?" Then praise a specific client behavior, suggest an improvement in another behavior, and again praise an aspect of the client's performance. Be specific. Say "I think you would sound more convincing if you made more eye contact and used shorter sentences without apologies" rather than "You seemed sort of passive and unconvincing." Give feedback as opinions or suggestions, not as facts: "If I were in that situation, I'd do it like this" rather than "You should" or "You didn't." Be positive but not overly protective; suggestions for change are important.

6. *Repetition.* Repeat the role play to ensure that the client really has command of the skills.

7. *Discussion.* Review what has been learned in the role play and any concerns, especially concerns about timing, what to do if the other person responds very differently than expected, and how a different setting or time might alter responses. Also check to see if the client believes that he or she can use the skills in the real setting and that the skills will be useful.

     Role playing can also provide opportunities for practicing the cognitive processes necessary for effective verbal responses. A role play between a man and a child helper playing the man's son Dale illustrates this technique (Barth, Blythe, Schinke, and Schilling, 1983). The lines in brackets are "self-talk," thoughts said aloud while facing away from the other person. (This role play excerpt corresponds to items 4 and 5 in the previous list.)

Child helper:	Okay, now, I'll be Dale.
Child helper as Dale:	Can I get a candy bar? Or cookies?
Parent:	[Oh no! Whenever this happens, it turns

into a battle! I've got to try something different this time.] No, Dale, we're going to eat soon.

Child helper as Dale: (Whining.) I'm hungry. I can't wait for dinner. Get me some cookies.

Parent: [I'm really tired. I'll have to watch it! I'd better get myself together.] I know you're hungry, Dale. I am too. It won't be long until we're home and can eat dinner.

Child helper as Dale: Can't I get something to eat? Just because you're fat, why do I have to starve?

Parent: [I'm not going to let him get to me. Oh, damn. The other shoppers are listening. It's time to take a deep breath.] Dale, I won't buy candy before dinner. [Good, you didn't yell—that only makes you and Dale more upset.]

Child helper as Dale: (Angrily and loudly.) You never let me buy anything. You're rotten. I hate you.

Parent: [Calm down. I don't have to get angry just because Dale did.] It's okay, Dale. We'll finish shopping and have dinner soon. That will really feel good. [I'm glad Dale and I didn't blow up at each other. All right, I sure handled that better than last time. I'll call and tell Gloria about it when I get home.]

Child helper: I made it tough on you, didn't I?

Parent: Yeah, sort of.

Child helper: What did you like best about what you did?

Parent: I didn't try to think up anything fancy to say.

Child helper: Anything else?

Parent: That's about it.

Child helper: I also liked the way you praised yourself right in the midst of all that for keeping calm. You might try getting down to Dale's eye level, getting up close, touching his shoulder, and then saying, "No." One other strength was the way you didn't bargain about the candy. That was not the place to cut deals, and you knew it. Such a role play could be reenacted with the real Dale. At home, under good conditions, he might first be prompted to complain a lot and to receive no redress and then be more compliant and receive praise and a favorite privilege: "Dale, you really listened and didn't back talk. How would you like to play cards with me after dinner?"

With children who are reluctant talkers, role playing may involve drawing figures, dolls, or toys and include commentary by the child or child helper or both. Encouraging the child to speak for the dolls is key and will permit direct dialogue after the use of the dolls is phased out. The child helper may use the figures to model prosocial responses. As in the sequence presented earlier, either the child or the child helper may show how he or she would like the interaction to go. Feedback and coaching can be directed to the figures or to the child.

In all role playing, efforts should involve graduated practice toward the final goal and promote generalization of performance to other settings and times. Clients and child helpers are often in a rush to change the conditions that are the cause of their collaboration. This rush may work against a gradual and thorough building of cognitive and social skills and lead to an unsuccessful and discouraging first attempt at using new skills in the natural setting. Assessing clients' current levels of skills and building from there will give clients the chance to test their use of new skills, personalize those skills, and anticipate a range of future challenges. Thus, an adolescent girl learning to control her anger when other residents of juvenile hall "call her out" might first practice an assertive response to very mild criticism, and build up to an effective response to more personal derision. Although clients should learn to handle increasingly complex and challenging situations, increasingly complex responses are not needed; simple ones may continue to succeed.

To help clients succeed in other settings and at other times, practice should take place under conditions similar to those in the client's own ecology. Delivering treatment in the target setting—parent training done in homes or self-control training done at juvenile hall, for example—facilitates the use of skills in situations when the child helper is not present. Still, parents will need to use parenting skills in supermarkets, and adolescents will need self-control during weekend visits home. Thus, practice should, as much as possible, prepare clients to use skills in various places and at various times.

Helping clients to identify or arrange circumstances common to the practice and performance settings strengthens generalization. After mastering a skill in the practice condition but prior to trying it in the target setting, clients can attempt to use the skill in other places. A school-phobic adolescent boy might first rehearse cognitive strategies for coping with a return to school at a family service agency and then practice the same exercises on the school grounds after school is out. Finally, he might employ his new but well-practiced abilities in class. Clients can select cues to trigger effective performance in new settings. Parents can use a radio station's half-hourly news program at home, in the car, or at grandfather's as a signal to look for and praise their child's positive behavior. Children can use the signal of a change in activities to take a deep breath, evaluate how they are doing, and if merited, use self-praise. Well-rehearsed cognitive strategies seem to best prepare clients to abstract needed cues and rewards for skill use from different locales and under different circumstances.

Helping Clients Regulate Performance

Knowing what competencies are and knowing how to use them do not ensure their performance, nor does such knowledge or ability ensure timely or appropriate skill use. Further, knowing what not to do does not ensure cessation of inappropriate behavior. Every child helper, parent, and child recognizes these performance gaps in their own and others' behavior. This section will review several techniques for increasing the likelihood that clients will perform as desired. Note that increases in positive behavior generally are accompanied by decreases in negative behavior and conversely. As will be shown in later chapters, these techniques are often used in combination with self-management skills. Techniques for promoting positive behavior are described before those for reducing negative behavior, since the ethical child helper uses competency-building techniques first.

Increasing Desirable Behavior

Competency building is often a slow and humbling experience. Recognizing the difficulties of changing one's own behavior helps the child helper understand the need to begin with small changes and gradually shape social or cognitive skills toward the desired end. This *shaping* process begins with a thorough understanding of the client's current level of performance and endeavors to build the briefest flash of successful performance into a better and more constant performance. This is done by rewarding each slight improvement over previous levels of performance. Child helpers must endeavor to recognize and be satisfied with small changes if they are to effectively apply the methods described here.

Positive Reinforcement. When a child helper gives a response to a client that increases the chance that the client will make a response, this process is called *positive reinforcement.* The response given by the child helper is called a *reinforcer* or, more appropriate for clinical use, a *positive consequence* or *reward.* Rewards can be given deliberately or by accident. Either way, rewards can strengthen both desired and undesired performances. Delivering positive consequences is not the sole prerogative of the child helper. Children also reward us with their touches, smiles, gifts, and words, and parents reward us and their children with their greetings, attention, praise, laughter, agreement, and attempts to change. This book presents many concepts and techniques, but no principle serves so many purposes with such flexibility and success as the principle that behavior followed by positive consequences is likely to recur with greater frequency.

Social consequences are perhaps the most ubiquitous shapers of positive behavior. Praise is a common social reward and, like other rewards, usually provides information about the adequacy of the performance as well as an incentive for continued performance of the behavior (Bandura, 1977). The value of praise as a reward is increased when it is linked to more tangible privileges and pleasures. Praise may be judged as insincere if it is not connected to other benefits, and in such cases, praise may not be reinforcing. In many families, especially those with agressive and disruptive children and those with parents who neglect or abuse their children, praise is seldom offered (Conger, 1981). In some of these families, a link between praise and privileges or pleasures has never been established. The relationship between praise and benefits should be close and specific at first—"You did such a good job by helping and not hitting your baby brother this last half hour that you get a kiss and you get to choose a dessert tonight." When the relationship is well established, timing and specificity become less crucial (Baum, 1973), so long as the general relationship between rewards and good performance is understood by both the performer and the rewarder, as evidenced in such statements as "The last half hour was so peaceful, William. We'll do something special later." After some time, the child understands that the tangible reward will eventually be forthcoming, and the praise alone serves as the incentive. This association is often learned early in life, but it requires relearning or strengthening in many troubled families and relationships. Praise and such other social rewards as smiles, embraces, nicknames, and keeping company are more versatile, transportable, and inexpensive than such tangible rewards as food. Nevertheless, social rewards can, like tangible rewards, lose meaning from overuse.

The opportunity to obtain *privileges* can also increase desired behavior. There are at least three kinds of privileges: (1) *access* (to television, tumbling mats, tape player, snacks, art supplies, bicycle, telephone, park, magazines, sports equipment),

(2) *choice* (of radio or television station, dinner, movie, story, dinner time, seating arrangements, roommate, rewards), and (3) *responsibility* (for collecting attendance slips, saying grace, calling siblings to dinner, camping cooking, using electric tools).

The reward value of privileges differs across individuals, across time for the same individual, and across age groups. In the author's special education classroom, washing the chalkboard was a privilege, whereas in the adjacent classroom it was a punishment. Later bedtimes, responsibility for room cleanup, opportunities to choose games, and opportunities to bring friends on outings may be reinforcers of children's behavior; weekend release, opportunities to choose radio and television stations and make phone calls, flexible schedules, and opportunities to exercise authority may serve for adolescents. Helpers from clients' social networks may be rewarded by opportunities to go to agency staff meetings, call in when they have difficulties or just want to talk, attend agency inservice training meetings, and borrow reading materials.

Using privileges as rewards assumes the existence of performance standards and, more fundamentally, the operation of rules that ordinarily restrict some benefits. Many families operate without explicit family rules and have difficulty granting privileges because children assume an entitlement to every pleasure they can obtain (Patterson, 1982). Small children may particularly expect that every freedom is theirs. Adults may feel unentitled or unable to confront this assumption. In such situations caregivers must first define and repossess privileges before using them as consequences.

Physical symbols, or *tokens*, can stand for parts of privileges or tangible pleasures and, when a sufficient and predetermined number are obtained, can be exchanged for the real thing. A token is a sign or symbol (Morris, 1969)—anything including a poker chip, paper slip, gummed star, checkmark on the chalkboard, dinosaur stamp, or mental note. Some child helpers find that the token acquires such reinforcing value that no other privilege or pleasure is needed—"No, I don't want any other prizes, I just want to finish my Little Orphan Annie star card and put it in my room." Child helpers and their child clients should, nonetheless, agree on a range of *back-up reinforcers*—that is, the privileges and pleasures that the token symbolizes—to be delivered when a specified number of tokens are saved. At first, few tokens should be required, and back-up reinforcers should be minor, easily available rewards—access to felt-tip pens, head rubs, pennies, new pencils, or food, for example. Tokens can then be cashed in frequently. Over time, children may learn to tolerate a delay between earning tokens and cashing them in and may go as long as a day or a week before collecting their booty. Intermediate symbols can also be used; for example, tokens can be cashed in daily for recording on a grid or in a bank book until significant savings acrue. High interest rates (for example, 50 percent) can help spur savings. Carpenter and Casto (1982) recommend the use of gift certificates and vouchers to be used in community stores and restaurants since retail stores typically have more appealing merchandise than token stores.

The drawbacks of token systems require anticipation. For active or distractible children, chips in cups may quickly become chips in mouths or chips all over. Star charts are better, but even then parents and teachers may run out of stars. Charts covered with clear contact paper can be colored and then erased when tokens are cashed in. If tokens are used for some but not all children in a family or class, other children may request the opportunity to earn tokens as well or may misbehave to earn the right to gain tokens. These effects usually are minimal and short-lived so long as high levels of attention and social rewards are provided to other children (Christy, 1975; Drabman and Lahey, 1974). The *positive* effects of the token economy on the target child may prove contagious to other children (Drabman and Lahey, 1974).

Self-rewards, rewards that are self-delivered, are convenient and can contribute to important increases in desired behavior (Robertson, Simon, Pachman, and Drabman, 1979; Shapiro, McGonigle, and Ollendick, 1980). Parents and mediators will usually learn the basic idea of self-reward quickly. They may restrain their use of self-rewards, however, until child helpers give them permission and encouragement to be self-congratulatory. Modeling self-rewards during naturally occurring events is also useful: "Sorry for the interruption—that was a phone call that I had been waiting for and, I'm pleased to say, I handled quite well." Adults also seem to appreciate the reasoning that no one rewards parents enough for their behavior, so if they want full credit they had best provide it themselves.

Children may have more difficulty learning to self-reward. The following well-tested procedure (see, for example, Robertson, Simon, Pachman, and Drabman, 1979; Shapiro, McGonigle, and Ollendick, 1980) should help them learn. The reason for teaching self-reward to children is to help them perform and recognize reward-worthy performances and self-administer rewards following such performances. Thus, procedures must provide a child with skills for (1) performing the behavior, (2) judging whether the behavior deserves rewarding, and (3) rewarding oneself. Following is a procedure for teaching children to reward themselves.

1. Child helper and child rehearse competent performance and agree on criteria for reward (for example, completing chores and homework and playing or watching television calmly until bedtime).
2. Child helper provides ratings for child's performance (for example, 1 is bad, 5 is okay, 10 is great) and verbally rewards child for competent performance ("You did quite well tonight. I rate your behavior as a 6"). Child rephrases child helper's comment into a self-reward for competent performance ("I did fine, I earned six points").
3. Child helper first writes down a rating of child's behavior. Child helper then prompts child to rate his or her own performance ("How did you think you did?"). Child helper and child compare ratings, and child receives a reward if the child's and child helper's ratings *match* within a broad range. Child adds cognitive self-reward for matching.
4. Child helper provides rewards only if child's performance meets criterion (for example, 7 on a scale of 10) and the match is within a narrow range (for example, child's rating is within one point of child helper's rating).
5. After child learns to consistently match child helper's rat-

ings, rewards are gradually given for child's performance alone rather than for matching (a bonus for matching exactly can be maintained).

6. Child helper reduces rewards for performance and for matching as child's positive behavior is maintained. Child continues to use cognitive self-rewards for accurately judging performance and for competent performance.

The complexity of the procedure can be adjusted. The procedure just outlined is one that the author has used with children in their preteens and early teens. Such youth may be able to aim for and then rate the attainment of several goals. They can also use a more sensitive, longer scale. A simpler system will help younger or less cognitively sophisticated children. *Yes* and *no* or numbers 1, 2, and 3 may be used as the rating system for a single behavior. Also, the time that elapses between the behavior and the rating should be short.

Less systematic procedures may be effective for some children. Queries such as "How did you do, Jacky?" and "Have you told yourself how proud you are of your work? I think you should give yourself a big round of applause" may prompt self-reward. Since results have an imperfect correspondence with effort, children should also learn to recognize and reward meritorious attempts—"Fran, I saw how long you ignored Roger's teasing. Even though you finally got mad, I hope you will reward yourself for such good ignoring. What nice words can you say to yourself about that?"

Negative Reinforcement. Ending negative experiences can also increase desired performance. Negative reinforcement involves strengthening the likelihood of a performance by ending a negative event just following the desired performance. Negative reinforcement, like positive reinforcement, strengthens the behavior that occurs just prior to the reinforcement. The behavior that is strengthened is that which ends the negative situation. Returning to Dale and his father at the market, if Dale's whining (a behavior that his father experiences as negative) stopped after his father provided him with a candy bar, the likelihood of his father's giving him another candy bar under similar circumstances would increase. The end of the whining would negatively reinforce the giving of the candy bar. As it turned out, since Dale's whining decreased after his father stayed calm and firm, the father's self-control was negatively reinforced and strengthened. An end to parental nagging is another negative reinforcer that often increases children's escape behavior. Unfortunately, as with much negative reinforcement, the escape behavior can be either positive (completing homework or chores, for example) or negative (for instance, lying about homework or running away).

The return of lost privileges also strengthens preceding performances. Thus, the calm deportment of a previously disruptive boy consigned to brief social isolation will be strengthened if the child is allowed to rejoin the group when he is sitting quietly (Hobbs, Forehand, and Murray, 1978). Contrarily, the undesirable deportment of the still-noisy child asked to rejoin the group after a similar social-isolation period is more likely to be strengthened by the ending of the negative condition. Many fears are strengthened by negative reinforcement. For example, the tendency to shun social situations will increase for a youth who avoids all private social moments because he fears that he will not know what to do or say. When he avoids a social encounter, he also, unfortunately, "escapes" from the opportunity for a profitable encounter.

Positive Practice. Little-used skills can be strengthened through positive practice. Routines for positive practice involve three steps. Consider the use of positive practice with a father having difficulty completing the task of supervising his children during meal preparation. The first step is identifying the correct procedure. The father is asked to describe the correct procedure and its rationale. "After I get out of my work clothes, instead of watching the news, I should spend time with the kids to keep them out of my wife's way and help them learn to play quietly and without fighting." Second, since describing what he intends to do next time is often not enough, the father is asked to repeat the *physical* movements of the desired practice. In this case the father would engage in changing clothes (that is, the last appropriate behavior prior to the error) and then walk into the kitchen to find the children rather than stay in the bedroom and watch television.

Using positive practice, on five occasions per night the father might sit on the bed, take off and put on his leisure shoes while reciting phrases to enhance task accomplishment ("Okay, I'll watch the TV news later—right now I'm going to do some fathering"), and then walk into the kitchen and check to see if his children are around. Finally, self-praise, the appreciation of significant others, and the approval of the child helper should follow positive practice. Repeated positive practice often helps break tenacious bad habits.

Positive practice with children may be useful in overcoming aggressive or impulsive behavior, toileting problems, and tics. Children unwilling or unable to perform positive behaviors alone can be firmly guided through the practice. For instance, a boy who straightens his hair, twirls it, and then pulls it out in hunks can be shown the appropriate behavior of straightening his hair and then taking his hands away, saying "hands down," and placing his hands flat on his desk. This can be repeated for five minutes (about fifty repetitions) each time he pulls his hair. A girl who frequently jumps up from her seat can be asked to practice starting to stand up, catching herself by saying "sit down," and then quickly sitting down. Such practice might occur for ten minutes several times a day until a change in her classroom behavior occurs. Severely disabled children may initially require physical guidance to prompt voluntary action (Foxx and Azrin, 1972). Although children are likely to experience guided positive practice as somewhat noxious, this feeling can be lessened by using the minimum force necessary.

Decreasing Undesirable Behavior

Child helpers would enjoy their work more if all problems could be solved with only positive means. Unfortunately, many problems of children and youth require efforts to decrease ineffective behavior. This is less pleasant but central to reducing the cognitive and behavioral barriers to establishing positive skills. The following techniques, presented roughly in order of their punitiveness, will provide child helpers with methods to complement positive, skill-building procedures. The latter techniques should be used only after positive consequences are in operation and, as discussed in Chapter Thirteen, with appropriate supervision and consent.

Reinforcing the Alternative Response. At times, negative behaviors yield to the increased strength of positive behaviors. Reinforcing a positive behavior incompatible with the negative behavior should always be the first intervention attempted. Alternative responses can be identified by such queries as "What do you hope that he will do?" and "How would I know she is doing what you expect?" Rewarding a boy for attending all of his classes, if effective, will preempt any need to penalize nonattendance because he cannot both attend and not attend. Rewarding cooperative play often reduces fighting.

Reinforcing the alternative response is, however, often a slow way to reduce aggression and self-stimulating behaviors that provide their own competing reinforcements. When a negative behavior represents a danger or a barrier to learning badly needed adaptive responses, quicker and more expedient methods are desirable and ethical.

Ignoring. Although a mild and nonpunitive means of reducing undesirable performance, ignoring may elicit strong reactions. Children may react to ignoring as they do to other changes in reinforcement: with upset. Thus, a boy expecting a teacher to offer comfort and reassuring words when he presents his hackneyed complaint about being pushed down by another child will likely complain exceptionally hard if the teacher suddenly seems uninterested in this behavior. Child helpers' cognitive preparation for ignoring requires understanding that newly ignored behavior often gets worse before it gets better.

There are two kinds of ignoring: total ignoring and selective ignoring. *Total ignoring* is used to reduce bothersome but not dangerous behavior (for example, whining, silly faces, begging for a change of rules), and *selective ignoring* is used to reduce behavior that is of secondary importance (for example, verbal noncompliance accompanied by behavioral compliance). Total ignoring and selective ignoring are compared in Table 5.

Table 5. Comparison of Total and Selective Ignoring.

Total Ignoring	*Selective Ignoring*
• Child helper informs child that he or she will be ignored as long as the negative behavior continues ("I will check on your readiness for recess when you are quiet. Until then I will ignore you").	• Child helper decides on the criterion behavior to reward and prepares to ignore extraneous behavior.
• Child helper turns away from child and makes no eye contact.	• Child helper turns toward child and makes eye contact or looks at the part of child that is behaving well (for example, the hands if the child is working).
• Child helper does not talk to child.	• Child helper verbally rewards competent performance ("Good! You're finishing your work and getting ready for recess").
• Child helper reinforces child's first prosocial response ("Let's see, Hua, you are quiet and have your work finished—RECESS!").	• Child helper rewards additional appropriate behaviors as they appear ("You are working hard and are quiet. Lovely! That will help you earn recess").

Both versions of ignoring require cognitive preparation and on-the-scene concentration. Ignoring has little of the immediate satisfaction of an active approach like positive reinforcement, nor does ignoring have the speedy results of punishment. The technique is considerably less punitive, however, and in combination with positive rewards is often an effective tool. The ignorer will be most successful if he or she is convinced of the value of the method and steeled by a well-rehearsed set of self-control statements ("I'm not going to let this get to me; I'll think about the positive; nice work, you're doing fine and staying sublime").

Following is an example of selective ignoring by a psychologist in an adolescent day-treatment center.

Child helper: So, as I said, it's time to return to class. (Stands up.)

Youth: I'm not finished talking. You never give me no time. I'm not going back yet. Besides, those other kids are crazy. (Stands up.)

Child helper: What's next on your group's schedule? (Opens door of office and motions youth through with eyes and head.)

Youth: Look! I'm telling you that I'm not through talking to you. How 'bout if we eat lunch together? (Walks out door.) Don't just ignore me, I'm talking to you.

Child helper: I'm ignoring your efforts to stay out of class. I like your idea of lunch, though; we can arrange it next time if you remember to tell me when it is time for you to return to class. (Continues to walk down hall.) You worked hard on your drinking-control plan today. I look forward to doing more on that next week.

Youth: Yeah. (Walks along behind.) Right. See you later. (Heads toward class.)

In this dialogue the child helper attends to the youth's positive nonverbal and verbal cues (that is, moving toward the classroom and an appropriate request to have lunch) and his recent cooperation. The child helper ignores the complaint about the short time, the comments about the other youths in the program, and the attempt to end the ignoring. As the youth's skills increase and the treatment relationship develops, the child helper could, if time permitted, extend confrontation and consequences to these latter issues.

Response Cost. Response cost involves the measured taking away of a pleasure or privilege following an undesirable response (Kazdin, 1972). Response cost is often used in token economy systems with aggressive and impulsive children and following low-frequency but highly disruptive or dangerous behavior. Costs of inappropriate behavior are predetermined and may include loss of points or tokens, opportunities for bonuses, and privileges. Some nonexclusive response costs for the home, classroom, and clinic are listed here.

- *Home:* Bedtime snack; use of bicycle; outside time after school or dinner; allowance; phone privileges; weekend nights out; having friends over; using television, radio, or records; points toward prizes
- *Classroom or school:* Tokens, story or joke time, break time, background music, points toward field trip, time at recess
- *Clinic:* Choosing order of activities, points toward inviting a friend to a session, points toward fast food, total time together in sessions

Many more response costs can be generated or found in the Children's Reinforcement Survey Schedule (Cautela, 1977).

Most response-cost systems involve the loss of points previously gathered as reinforcers. This is an ideal approach but requires that rewards and a point system already be in place. In this arrangement, privileges and pleasures are lost or gained gradually as a result of the aggregate success of the child's behavior. This compares favorably to response-cost systems that use an informal quid pro quo arrangement: ''Hal, you're swearing. What is the cost of that? Hmm. I think you should lose your snack tonight.'' The latter has several disadvantages: (1) fairly matching the cost to the behavior is difficult, (2) the corresponding rewards for *not* engaging in the behavior may get neglected, (3) once the reinforcer is lost, the performance incentive is also lost (the child can only lose tonight's snack once) and, following upon disadvantage number three, (4) marginally inappropriate behavior often elicits a threat rather than the full response cost because once the response cost is invoked, control is lost. This may increase caregivers' use of threats but may not decrease children's negative performance.

Several guidelines can benefit users of response-cost systems. First, children and youth should have the opportunity to discuss and rehearse successful and unsuccessful ways of coping with response costs. Economically deprived children may have much difficulty giving up reinforcers, for example, and should have a chance to prepare themselves for this (Kendall and Braswell, 1982). Second, the time between the behavior and the cost should be short (youth can often tolerate *slightly* longer delays than children). Third, children and youth should have the opportunity to earn back costs with especially competent behavior (including accepting the penalty with equanimity). Fourth, the association between the response and the cost should be highlighted ("Now that I've explained what I saw you do and what the penalty is, can you explain it to me in your own words and tell me what you have to do to earn your privileges for tomorrow?"). Finally, the response cost alone should be sufficient to influence behavior and should not be exaggerated with personal attacks or disparagement. After all, the intent of reward and cost systems is to provide child helpers with instruments of behavior change other than sarcasm, force, and overdeveloped vocal cords. Overreliance on any of these instruments signals a breakdown in current reward and response-cost systems.

Time Out. A variant of response cost, time out temporarily removes the child from opportunities for reward. This can be accomplished by removing the child from the reinforcing environment or by removing reinforcers from the child (Ollendick and Cerny, 1981). Time out is a frequently employed method with thoroughly documented effectiveness for reducing aggression and many other inappropriate behaviors in homes, classrooms, and even shopping centers (Wilson and Lyman, 1982). Because time out involves time away from rewards, the procedure, like other procedures whose goal is reducing inappropriate behaviors, should not be used without a coincidental reward system. Indeed, time *out* is not likely to motivate improved behavior if time *in* is not rewarding. The basic steps for setting up and implementing time out are as follows:

1. Explain the rationale for using time out (T.O.).
   a. T.O. helps decrease unwanted behavior.

    b.   T.O. keeps a child briefly away from situations that reward the child for poor behavior.

    c.   T.O. can be used often to keep a situation from blowing up and to avoid hitting and scolding.

    d.   T.O. should only be used if a reward program is also in use.

2.   Select a behavior to decrease and count it.

    a.   Define the behavior clearly.

    b.   Determine that the opposite behavior is regularly being rewarded.

    c.   Inform caregivers that they should not quibble with the child about the definition of the behavior; the adults' words should be fair but final.

    d.   Count the behavior (if this was not done when the positive program was begun). If the behavior occurs very frequently, such as interrupting or yelling, it can be counted during a meeting with the family. If the behavior occurs infrequently, delay the commencement of the T.O. program until the family can confidently estimate the current rate.

3.   Pick a T.O. location.

    a.   Determine that it is free of distractions.

    b.   Determine that it is free of danger.

    c.   If a "quiet chair" is being used, inform the other children that they are not to talk with anyone in T.O.

    d.   Explain that it may be tempting to mess up the T.O. area but that it will require cleaning up afterward.

4.   Consider the timing of T.O.

    a.   Determine that there is a suitable timing device available (such as an oven timer, a portable kitchen timer, or an egg timer).

    b.   Remember that the standard length of time for T.O. is five minutes, or one minute for each year of a child's age.

    c.   Remind the child that the time spent in time out will start over again from the point of any disruption.

    d.   Determine the absolute time limit and backup costs

in privileges if the child goes over the time limit because of consistent disruption (fifteen to thirty minutes are reasonable time limits, depending on the child's age, the parent's tolerance, and the history of the parent-child relationship).

5. Treat troubled and untroubled T.O.'s differently.
    a. Praise the child after a good T.O.
    b. Remember that T.O.'s should be used consistently and that they are portable to other places (such as the market); a park bench can serve as a "quiet chair."
    c. Rehearse what to do if the child refuses to go into T.O.: repeat the command one time, assist the child to T.O., repeat the consequences of refusal *and* of compliance, and use a backup response cost.
    d. Provide a cue for avoiding T.O., such as "Jimmy, that's yelling—next time will mean T.O." Never use the cue more than once per incident; the very next occurrence earns time out: "Jimmy, that's yelling—go to time out." It is best not to encourage caregivers who often make unenforceable or idle threats to use warnings.
    e. Debrief the child after the time out: "Your time out for yelling is over. Talking and not yelling will keep you out of time out." Praise the positive completion of time out: "Jimmy, you handled that time out very well."

6. Keep T.O. going.
    a. Determine that other significant people have been informed that the T.O. procedure will be used.
    b. Post T.O. rules and reminders.
    c. Demonstrate (model) the use of T.O.
    d. Have parents/teachers rehearse the use of T.O.
    e. Provide the parents/teachers with an emergency number or strategy to use in case any problems or questions arise.

Child helpers may grapple with several questions while teaching caregivers to use time out. Fortunately, much evidence now provides answers to these questions (Wilson and Lyman, 1982).

How much needs to be said about the time out? Consistent with a cognitive perspective, telling children the reason for time out and warning them about behavior that will warrant time out seem to foster improved performance. The efficacy of discussing the reasons for time out and the desired behavior that follows it is not proven, but this also seems like sound practice.

How long should time out last? Shorter durations seem suitable for younger children and children with shorter attention spans. One minute for every year of the child's age (beginning with age three) is an often-cited rule of thumb. Longer time-out periods may suppress behavior somewhat better, but they also remove the child from learning opportunities and may increase the child's frustration and hostility. For older children, longer time-out periods may be needed. To markedly reduce the antisocial behavior of detained juvenile offenders required time outs between fifty and eighty minutes in length according to a carefully executed study by Carbone (1983). Somewhat longer time-out periods for especially bad behavior may effectively communicate the unacceptability of the behavior.

When should time out take place? Time-out rooms usually are not necessary except for children who cannot control themselves in a shared space. A "quiet chair" in the kitchen or in an uninteresting but observable and uncluttered part of the house is often suitable. The bathroom is useful for very combative children, but it must first be child proofed. Some of the inconvenience of this can be reduced by having family members put their important items in bags that they can take out of the bathroom with them. Time out can also be implemented in homes, classrooms, supermarkets, or parks by having the child sit out of the way or by marking hands or cards to indicate the need for transfer to time out upon return to the standard time-out area (Drabman and Creedon, 1979). Other peer and adult members of the child's immediate social group should also be told that the child is in time out and that social or token benefits are momentarily suspended. (Time out is considered further in Chapter Six.)

Restitution and Overcorrection. Restitution is kindred to positive practice. Both require repeated efforts to counteract the otherwise positive short-term consequences of inappropriate behavior for the child. Overcorrection requires that the child restore the environment to an improved state. Thus, a girl who threatens another girl with a brick to get her cookies may be required by a teacher employing restitution to apologize to the girl and push her on the swing for half an hour. An overcorrection procedure might include requiring the misbehaving girl to share her dessert for the rest of the week and to pile up all of the stray bricks in the park. A boy who wets his bed may be required to change his clothes, wash his clothes and sheets by hand, and put clean linen on his bed. Restitution and overcorrection, like many social-learning practices, are straightforward: when children act badly, they must do extra good deeds as special reminders and to mend bad feelings. The systematic use of restitution and correction deserves more attention than it now receives from child helpers.

Several procedures for using restitution merit use (Ollendick and Matson, 1978). First, restitution should have a direct relationship to the undesired behavior. This relationship should highlight the appropriate or desired action and serve an educational purpose. In the examples just cited, cooperation and responsibility for personal cleanliness are stressed. Requiring an hour of math homework or window washing might also reduce the undesired behavior through their punishing effects, but these do not possess relevant educational value. Second, restitution should closely follow the inappropriate behavior. This is a sound principle of learning and minimizes the reinforcement of the improper behavior that might otherwise result (Foxx and Azrin, 1972). Thus, immediately having to do cleaning chores after bed-wetting makes the pleasure of emptying a full and uncomfortable bladder short-lived. Next, restitution should span a long enough time to remove the child from the reinforcing situation and to ensure that the child has the opportunity to learn the appropriate behavior.

Punishment. Punishment involves the application of an aversive experience toward reducing undesired thoughts or actions.

Although once thought to be less powerful and less enduring than reinforcement and generally expendable if alternative positive behaviors were reinforced (Skinner, 1971), punishment has an important place in the array of techniques appropriate for the child helper. Especially when used to change self-destructive behavior, punishment may have positive effects (Harris and Erner-Hershfield, 1978). Child helpers should not fail to use punishment when it might eliminate behaviors that would otherwise keep a client in an excessively restrictive environment (Repp and Deitz, 1978).

Professional child helpers may have difficulty using punishment at all, and caregivers often use it improperly and too much. Central to using punishment properly is careful attention to ethical judgment and procedural guidelines (Repp and Dietz, 1978). Foremost among the ethical questions that require resolution prior to using (or encouraging the use of) physical punishment are: Have nonpunishing methods been competently and thoroughly tried? Is the client's current behavior injurious to the client or others, or is it merely annoying or unattractive? Does available research indicate that punishment will result in significant and lasting reduction in the target behavior? As with medical procedures like surgery, the balance between client welfare and discomfort or risk must be carefully considered (Harris and Erner-Hershfield, 1978; Moffitt, 1983). The more punishing the procedure, the more evidence is needed of the risk to the client's welfare of continuing the current behavior.

Caregivers and youth can learn to reduce unwanted behavior through *cognitive self-punishment*, or by punishing it themselves. Cognitive self-punishment involves presenting oneself with a negative experience after engaging in the undesired behavior. Salend and Allen (1985), among others, have shown that young learning disabled children can manage their own behavior by taking away their own rewards after undesirable performances. Similarly, children and caregivers can reduce unwanted behavior through punishing self-talk after they engage in inappropriate thoughts or behaviors (Cautela, 1979). Cognitive self-punishment involves clients in a variant of the following procedure, which is initially guided by the child helper. Clients are asked to:

1. Imagine themselves in a situation that is associated with a desirable but inappropriate activity (for example, stealing a bicycle).
2. Begin a typical approach to the activity (for example, walk toward the bicycle while looking to see if anyone is watching).
3. Begin to experience an immobilizing discomfort (for example, feeling very hot and sick to the stomach).
4. Stop to further experience this discomfort (for example, a deepening sense that they will pass out or vomit or both).
5. Escape from the situation to another appropriate situation (for example, start to walk toward school).
6. Experience the satisfaction of new comfort (for example, a cool breeze and a clear head) and of avoiding the temptation.

After obtaining some details about the typical high-risk situation, the child helper talks the child through the visualization of the experience. A prearranged signal such as a head nod allows the child helper to see whether the child is experiencing each part of the story before the child helper continues. A sample script is provided in Chapter Nine.

Such procedures have typically been used to help children and adults avoid such pernicious behaviors as stealing, setting fires, or hurting oneself. As with other forms of punishment, cognitive procedures should not be overused. These procedures are difficult to abuse, however, because they can only be used with the client's full participation. Also, because human-service professionals often learn early in their training to help people avoid saying unkind things to themselves, this procedure is probably rarely considered for use. Cognitive self-punishment should probably not be used when a tangible event could be witnessed instead. For example, Koles and Jenson (1985) took a chronic firesetter to meet a badly burned young firesetter at a burn unit instead of using a cognitive self-punishment procedure developed by McGrath, Marshall, and Prior (1979); Koles and Jensen argue that their procedure may have been more powerful and taken less time than repeatedly asking the child to visualize a murderous fire.

Although cognitive self-punishment has been a part of several successful treatment programs, the efficacy and risks of cognitive self-punishment are largely undocumented. Possible threats to the success of cognitive self-punishment are: (1) clients may not be able to visualize a punishing scene or experience, (2) consistency and regularity of the program may be difficult to monitor and maintain, (3) the use of the strategy may be short-lived because people are fundamentally unlikely to want to punish themselves, and (4) the undesired behavior may continue; the client will simply be more troubled by it. Because of these possible problems, cognitive self-punishment should be used only in conjunction with positive strategies, only when a dramatic reduction in the undesirable behavior is needed (as is the case, for instance, with firesetting or stealing), and only with people who are not likely to be seriously troubled by excessive self-disparagement.

Reprimands are a relatively mild form of punishment. Firm, face-to-face, behaviorally specific reprimands have the most likelihood of suppressing noxious behavior (Van Houten and others, 1982). Reprimands may have a spillover effect and also reduce the disruptive behavior of nearby vicarious learners. Reprimands may be strengthened by holding—but not pinching—a child's upper arms. They are less successful when issued from a distance. Voice volume seems unrelated to success. Effective reprimands should also include eye contact, a description of what the child did incorrectly, a brief statement of what the child should do instead, and approval of good behavior that follows the reprimand. This technique loses its impact and requires greater intensity if it is overused. Like other punishments, reprimands will increase the likelihood of a child's wanting to escape from or avoid the situation and the people associated with it and so should be coupled with rewards.

Satiation and Negative Practice. Some troublesome behaviors diminish with continued and exaggerated use. *Satiation* attempts to remove the reinforcing value of a stimulus through repetition. This method seems preferable to child helpers who are uncomfortable with punishment or limit setting. Thus, a girl who jumps up from her work to the window and yells "fire" every time a siren is heard might be satiated by taping a siren and allowing her to replay it during recess and lunch and after school. In this way, a child may become bored with the activity and, because the activity is now permitted, lose the incentive of upsetting or surprising classmates and teacher.

Negative practice is a form of satiation that involves an additional step: the child is *required* to repeat the undesirable behavior (for example, to listen repeatedly to the tape and jump up to the window to yell fire during recess, after eating lunch, and after school). Thus, satiation involves the *voluntary* repetition of a behavior until the behavior loses its reinforcing behavior, and negative practice involves the *required* repetition of the behavior. The latter is more aversive.

The effects of both methods should be carefully monitored because some tics, swearing, fire play, and screaming behavior may increase with practice. The vital importance of carefully administering satiation and negative practice is shown in three treatments of firesetting (these are more fully discussed in Chapter Ten). In a study reported by Carstens (1982), a mother attempted to satiate her son's interest in fire play by having him throw matches into a puddle under her supervision. His fire play was unabated, and he later set fire to the house. Welsh (1971) and Wolff (1984) had greater success using negative practice that required children to continue to light matches even when they wanted to quit. Yet Wolff's case required ten times as many sessions as Welsh's before satiation was fully achieved; only by persisting with negative practice for one hundred sessions did Wolff obtain the desired result. Collecting baseline data and recording occurrences of the behavior during intervention (see Bloom and Fischer, 1982; Jayaratne and Levy, 1979) are essential to monitoring the possibly untoward outcomes of these techniques.

Physical Punishment. Noise, unpleasant tastes, hand slaps, spankings, and shock are the most common physical punishments described in the professional literature, although even these are rarely used and are always a treatment of last resort. Shock is used primarily with the most disturbed, isolated, and self-destructive children (autistic and severely mentally retarded children, for instance). Less painful physical punishments serve similar purposes for other severely disturbed children. Loud handclaps and buzzers may gain a child's attention, signal a reprimand, and reduce loud or self-stimulatory noise. Mouthwash, lemon juice, and shaving cream have been sprayed in children's mouths to disrupt temper tantrums (Conway and Bucher, 1974), life-threatening self-induced vomiting (Sajwaj, Libet, and Agras, 1974), and biting (Matson and Ollendick, 1976). Hand slaps and spankings may discourage self-injurious behavior, but they have little efficacy in teaching other, appropriate behaviors.

It is important to note and to inform parents who rely on physical punishment to control mild problems that punishment has an information function. The punisher informs the punished child that the criterion behavior was not met. Other signals of disapproval and related consequences, such as time out and response cost, may make this point equally well. Even so, caregivers often attempt to justify their use of punishment and continue to use it despite child helpers' efforts to provide alternatives. Although some intensive efforts to teach alternative parenting behaviors to parents who use physical punishment have been successful (see, for example, Barth, Blythe, Schinke, and Schilling, 1983; Reid, 1985), these demonstration efforts are often more than most clinicians have the time or skill to manage. Ironically, then, teaching caregivers alternatives to out-of-control and ineffective punishment can spare children from harm and reduce caregivers' risk of becoming child abusers. Effective reprimands (see Van Houton, 1980, for a useful workbook) paired with time out can reduce yelling and hitting. Professionals should inform parents that spanking is ineffective and unfair and that they must by law report any suspicion of physical abuse—that is, any punishment that bruises or endangers a child. Indicating that hitting a child with an object or a closed hand is grounds for a report should further clarify the difference between punishment and abuse and emphasize the expectation that parents not hurt their children.

Before using punishment, the child helper interested in curtailing serious self-injurious behavior should consult other resources (for example, Lovaas, Young, and Newsom, 1978; Romanczyk and Goren, 1975), because the brief discussion provided in these paragraphs is insufficient to guide the use of punishment. Punishment should be used only after much study, under skilled supervision, with parental consent, and following documented attempts at change using positive techniques.

Contracts

Most helping efforts combine several of the previously described techniques and endeavor to reduce ineffective performance while building new skills or increasing the use of old ones. Contracts provide structure for the specification of problems; for the delivery of positive reinforcement, response cost, and negative reinforcement; and for performance feedback and discussion. Perhaps most important, contract development offers a structure for mutual problem solving, cooperation, and reciprocity in relationships with shortages of those characteristics.

The following guidelines can be used to help a child helper and child develop a contract (adapted from DeRisi and Butz, 1975).

1. Select one behavior for the child to work on first (start modestly).
2. Describe the behavior so that it can be observed and counted.
3. Be sure that the child has the skills to perform the behavior.
4. Consider what difficulties the child will have performing the behavior.
5. Identify rewards and penalties that will help provide motivation to do well.
6. Identify someone who will help keep track of the behaviors and give rewards or penalties.
7. Write the contract so that everyone can understand it.
8. Try out the contract.
9. Troubleshoot the system if the desired behavior does not increase.
10. Continue to monitor, troubleshoot, and revise until there is improvement in the behaviors that were troublesome.

Whether the contract is written or verbal, it should include:

1. Date agreement begins, ends, or is renegotiated.
2. Behaviors targeted for change.
3. Amount and kinds of rewards and penalties to be used.
4. Schedule of reward delivery or beginning and end of penalty.
5. Agreement of all involved.
6. Schedule for review of progress.
7. Bonus clause for sustained or exceptional performance.

Contracting with older children and adolescents is similar but often requires considerable negotiation; behaviors of caregivers as well as of children are selected for change. Developing contracts between caregivers and adolescents is discussed further in Chapter Eleven.

   With younger children, contracts that involve only one behavior and one type of reward and penalty as consequences may have greatest success: "If you do your homework between now and dinner, we'll have ice cream for dessert." Points add flexibility and more closely mimic the characteristics of human relationships—that is, good deeds are not always rewarded right away. For example, a six-year-old child who is expected not to fight with a younger sister after dinner can earn five points for not fighting at all and have time out for fighting. He might earn his reward—perhaps a special half-hour of time with his parent—when he reaches ten points. Initially, only a very short time should be allowed to elapse between the earning of points and the reward that a child earns. Following a few successes, he might have the chance to earn a different reward or privilege but be told that he has to earn twenty points. Points and penalties can also be given depending on the quality of performance—five points for getting home right at 3:30, two points for getting home by 4:30, and one point for getting home by 5:00, for instance; if the child arrives home after 5:00, chores can be assigned.

   Because of their flexibility, point systems are especially useful with children about eight years of age or older, who may simultaneously work on several behaviors—for example, not back talking, doing chores without reminding, going to school, bringing home homework, and not swearing. If each of these items is scored on a *yes = 1, no = 0* scale, then the calculation of points (in this case, 0 to 5) is straightforward (the more important items can be assigned extra points). Obtaining the maximum number of points (that is, five) would earn a special privilege (such as an extra weeknight phone call), a specified low number of points (for example, two) would result in no privileges (for example, no television, snacks, or phone calls) but no penalties, and one or no points would result in no privileges and two hours of chores. Contracts should be reviewed regularly by child helpers and families together, and then, under the child helper's watchful eye, families should learn to adjust and renew contracts on their own.

If caregivers or children balk at participating in contracts, the ideas that undergird participation should, if necessary, be promoted through example and exhortation. These ideas include the following: (1) the receipt of positive experiences in interpersonal exchanges is a privilege, (2) good relationships include a fair and reciprocal exchange of positive experiences, (3) the value of a relationship increases when the frequency of the exchange of reinforcers increases, and (4) rules create freedom (Stuart, 1971). Although child helpers and children may engage in contracts without full adherence to these beliefs, the vehement rejection of any belief will undermine contract development. For instance, the father committed to the belief that his daughter owes him unconditional respect (in violation of the first assumption) will be difficult to engage in contracting. Similarly, an adolescent convinced that "my parents don't trust me and never will" (in violation of the third assumption) may only reluctantly enter into a contract.

Careful monitoring of contract development and implementation is also necessary. A contracting game (see, for example, Blechman, Olson, and Hellman, 1976) can help teach the family to develop workable contracts. Still, initial goals may be too high, or the time between performance and consequence too long. Disputes about whether or not the performance met the criterion (and whether or not the reward was as promised) may aggravate mistrust. Contracts that lead to expensive rewards may inspire bitterness from mediators required to provide those rewards and lessening of internal attributions for competent performance. Contracts in which penalties are more common than rewards may promote escape rather than effort. To provide clients with the full benefit of contracting, closely spaced contracting sessions, careful monitoring of any concerns via between-session phone calls, and other safeguards should accompany contracting efforts.

Self-Management Training

Children and adolescents are often prepared to build new competencies and willing to labor at them. With the aid of an instructive and reinforcing milieu, young people can use self-management techniques to augment the lessons of the social environment. Self-management training can occur in individual sessions (Kendall and Zupan, 1981), small groups (Camp and Bash, 1981), and classrooms (Kneedler and Hallahan, 1981); with children of elementary school age (Camp and Bash, 1981) and adolescents (Snyder and White, 1979); with hyperactive children (Cameron and Robinson, 1980; Meichenbaum and Goodman, 1971), children with learning handicaps (Mickler, 1984), angry children and youth (Kennedy, 1982; Saylor, Benson, and Einhaus, 1985), and children with other clinical problems (see, for example, Bernard, Kratochwill, and Keefauver, 1983).

Self-management programs vary depending on what child helpers are attempting to teach children. Chapter One described the common components of self-management programs: (1) enhancing commitment, (2) identifying and managing arousal, (3) assisting with goal setting, (4) developing plans, (5) self-monitoring, (6) self-evaluating, and (7) self-praising or coping. Some have a more interpersonal approach and teach children to solve problems in social situations—Camp and Bash's (1981) Think Aloud program is a fine and well-evaluated example. Self-instruction training (SIT), a form of self-management training, is typically used for teaching academic skills. Self-management training also encompasses anger control and other personal and interpersonal behavior. The best descriptions of the elements of the SIT procedure as applied to academic work are available in Meichenbaum (1977) and Kendall and Braswell (1985). Table 6 shows the relationship between self-management and self-instruction training. Procedures for building young people's self-management competencies are briefly considered in the remainder of this chapter; the remaining chapters of this book describe additional applications of self-management training.

Table 6. Self-Instruction Training as a Type of Self-Management Training.

Self-Management Training	Self-Instruction Training
Enhancing commitment	1. Involve the child in decisions about the training 2. Establish incentives
Managing arousal	1. Relaxation training or physical warm-up
Assisting with goal setting	1. "What am I supposed to do?"
Developing plans	1. "How can I do it?" or "What is my plan?" 2. Go slow and step by step
Self-Monitoring	1. "Am I using my plan?" "Am I focusing in?"
Self-Evaluating	1. "How did I do? Did I: Go slow? Step-by-step? Get the answer right?"
Self-Praising or coping	1. "I'm proud." 2. "I goofed! I can do better if I go slower."

Common to most procedures for teaching self-management is the approach of "talking through" and demonstrating the procedure while the child observes. This "talking through" differs from explaining in that it shows the self-talk ("Okay, first I ask myself 'What am I supposed to do?'") and activities involved in implementing the procedure. Next, the child performs the task instructing him- or herself out loud (this is facilitated by a chart or deck of cards with the steps written on them).

The adult model again demonstrates the performance while softly saying the self-instructions and acting out the role. The child then completes the task while whispering self-instructions. The child helper next performs the task with pauses and nonverbal signals that suggest thinking and whispers or writes down the needed self-instructions. Finally, the child performs the task using self-talk.

Although self-management training can be presented as a standard package, it is most useful when tailored to the readiness, interests, and problems of the particular child; presented in small rather than large groups; and applied by the child helper to illustrative practical problems in the child's and child helper's activities (for example, getting to sessions on time, remembering materials or homework, handling interruptions, and coping with hunger and tiredness). Readiness will partly determine whether a child can learn the self-management procedure. Camp and Bash (1981) assessed and built the readiness of six-year-old children to learn from teacher demonstrations of cognitive and social skills with games of copycat that require the child to say and do what the program leader does. Several investigators (for example, Kendall and Wilcox, 1980) have found that younger children benefit more from concrete and specific self-instruction (for example, "I'm supposed to look at the numbers") rather than more conceptual self-instruction (such as, "I should think about what I'm doing right now"). Flexibility should be used in implementing the procedure.

Enhancing Commitment. Learning self-management requires an initial commitment of effort. This commitment can be motivated by external incentives ("If you use these self-management methods you will earn this privilege . . . "), or by personal incentives to perform better, save money, or defeat self-destructive health habits or immobilizing fears. With younger children commitment often arises from a willingness to please adults and requires no significant reflection. Braswell and colleagues (in press) found that statements of encouragement (for example, "keep up the good work") were more motivating than simple acknowledgments of correct answers. With older youth, pleasing others may provide less incentive, and other motivational aids must be brought to bear. Positive models (such as actors or athletes), graphic depictions of negative outcomes (for example, the display of tar-filled lungs), and bonuses (such as additional privileges after a self-managed delay) may provide incentives. Methods for building and sustaining sufficient motivation are less well studied or circumscribed. Once a commitment is made, several methods can be used to help sustain it. Helping children to imagine successful performance, future rewards, or an end to current deprivations may all provide motivation (Upper and Cautela, 1979).

For many young people, external rewards may initially and periodically be necessary to support efforts made to develop self-management skills. Kendall and Braswell (1985) recommend the use of a reward menu and a response-cost system (using chips) during SIT. Such systems have the advantage of requiring few interruptions (assuming that the child follows the procedure more than half the time). They should be balanced with periodic encouragement for correctly following the procedure and ample prompts for the child to use self-praise.

Expectations of success may also be increased with exposure to models of similar and successful youth. Child helpers may help youth increase motivation by decreasing their adherence to self-limiting beliefs, such as "what difference does it make?" and "I can (not) do it even if I don't (do) try." McMullin and Casey (1975) have described others, and their alternatives, in a booklet for children. Although such self-limiting statements are hard to budge except through the child's becoming more successful, seeds of change can be planted by identifying such beliefs and asking children and youth if they can think of alternatives. Typically, children will struggle with this request and then start to state beliefs that are totally contrary. Encouraging more realistic beliefs takes time.

It is especially important to involve the child as much as feasible in every decision and activity about the structure and process of the training. Braswell and colleagues (in press) have demonstrated that the amount of the child's involvement in the delivering of the intervention is strongly associated with the intervention's effectiveness. To provide youths with some feeling of control and an enhanced sense of the possible, child helpers can help them solve problems of their own choosing. Rehearsal of personalized statements—"If I go slow and learn to add, I will be able to make change at the store," rather than "Going slow helps you get the right answers"—may also help provide extra motivation (Gilchrist, Schinke, and Blythe, 1979).

Managing Arousal. Upset, hyperactive, tense, and angry children often face too many difficulties to use self-management. Self-relaxation is another means of managing overarousal and has been used effectively as part of self-management training and in the treatment of children's and youth's anxiety, insomnia, and headaches (see the review by Richter, 1984). After learning deep muscle relaxation that involves tensing and relaxing key muscle groups (see Koeppen, 1974; Ollendick and Cerny, 1981), children and caregivers learn to achieve a relaxed state with a cue word such as *relax*. Supplemental procedures include the use of deep-breathing exercises and soothing mental imagery (Stroebel, Stroebel, and Holland, 1980, have published a relaxation program endorsed by the National Education Association for use in classrooms). Kendall and Braswell (1985) suggest simple games such as rag doll and contracting and releasing all muscle groups at once when a child seems tense before sessions; if the child's tension is chronic, time may need to be devoted during each session to more thorough relaxation training. With children who are more aggressive or prone to destructive acts when under stress, relaxation training may require particular attention (Koles and Jenson, 1985).

Graduated practice should be used by the child helper to keep the youthful self-manager from overstimulation. Arousal is less likely to become incapacitating if exposure to tasks is provided in a step-by-step manner. Calming self-statements can also keep arousal manageable. Cognitive strategies can help increase tolerance of delayed gratification (Mischel, 1983); forgoing lesser, short-term rewards and instead waiting for better, long-term outcomes is facilitated by encouraging the child to think about "fun" distractions rather than the long-term reward, or about the less salient features of the reward rather than about its most appealing characteristics. Fear of the dark, on the other hand, seems more manageable when children learn to think about mastery of the dark and not to think of distractions (Kanfer, Karoly, and Newman, 1975).

Assisting with Goal Setting. Goals help guide children's performance by helping them to know what is expected and serving as a basis for later evaluation and reward. *Correspondence training,* a little studied but sensible and promising procedure by which children learn to identify what they will do and then report on whether they accomplish it, can help build goal-setting skills. Rewards initially are given for the correspondence between setting and accomplishing the goal and later are given for making goal statements alone. In this manner, goal setting is encouraged by requiring it at the end of every day or class or treatment session. Before bedtime, children in group care, for example, can be asked to review their day's successes against the goals set the night before and then asked to set goals for the following day. The repetition of this process sharpens their goal-setting abilities. Disabled children may need considerable rehearsal at first but can learn to independently articulate goals (Whitman and others, 1982).

In SIT, the goals are given to children—that is, to follow the procedure, to go slowly, and to answer the problem correctly. The procedure also asks the child to restate the goal of the specific task (for example, completing a maze or math problem) in his or her own words by posing and answering the question, "What am I supposed to do?" Then the child answers the question, "What is my plan?" The answers to the latter— previously modeled by the child helper—are likely to include "to go slowly" as well as the specifics of the problem to be solved ("I'll start on the right side and go across to the left," or "I'll say each sound out loud before I try to put the sounds together into a word").

Developing Plans. Just as plans are essential to child helpers using the task-centered treatment approach, plans are essential to children's success as well. In the problem-solving paradigm, a plan comes from generating as many feasible options as possible. Children or youth are taught a model like SODAS (Barth and Maxwell, 1985), which involves Starting the problem-solving process at the first sign of difficulty, generating *O*ptions, *D*eciding on the best option, *A*cting out the plan, and *S*elf-rewarding successful execution of the plan. For younger children, the idea of trying to come up with different ideas rather than to agree with the first or dominant idea may come slowly. To teach the skill of generating alternatives, Camp and Bash (1981) model the use of a plan by Ralph the Bear to build a birdhouse, go on to get students to develop a plan for completing a puzzle, and finally, tackle the problem of a girl who wants scissors that a boy is using. In SIT, the plan for tackling an academic problem is usually less dependent on generating a large number of alternatives needed to solve social problems, but it does seem to succeed better if children restate the procedure they will use in their own words. The key question regarding developing a plan in SIT is "What is my plan?" or "How can I do it?"

Self-Monitoring. Self-management strategies for children and youth provide guidance as well as incentives for task accomplishment. Self-instructions about implementing the plan include statements that answer these questions: "Am I focusing on the problem?" "Am I going slowly?" "Am I ignoring distractions?" Once a plan has been embraced and performance is under way, children and youth can profitably focus on whether or not they are implementing their plans. Depending on the nature of the performance-monitoring task, self-comments might include: "I'm staying calm and not getting mad," "I'm watching what I'm doing," "That's two classes I went to—only three to go," and "I'd better check on what I'm supposed to do again." Self-monitoring is the inner ear of performance, guiding the child down the winding and uneven path to goal attainment. As will be described in Chapter Seven, child helpers can promote the development of self-monitoring skills by periodically cueing (with a question or a tape-recorded sound) children to observe their own performances.

Self-Evaluating. Judging the success of personal effort involves comparing the actual performance and outcome with the initial performance and outcome goals. Self-monitoring plus evaluation have been proven to increase appropriate behavior (see, for example, Sagotsky, Patterson, and Lepper, 1978;

Ollendick, 1981). When accurate self-assessments are initially rewarded by child helpers, they may help prolong competent behavior even after rewards are discontinued (Wood and Flynn, 1978). Evaluating performance is closely linked to self-monitoring and addresses the questions "Did I do what I planned?" and "Did I achieve what I wanted?" The distinction is not difficult for child helpers to see, although children and youth may have less acuity. Child helpers can model this difference by recognizing children when they have completed the tasks of self-management (for example, going slowly), even if the outcome is not correct. After children begin to understand the procedures, child helpers must carefully listen to and change their inner and outer speech to avoid evaluating children's achievements ("All right! You went slowly!") and to instead give children opportunities to evaluate themselves ("How did you do?").

When achievement does not match effort, children should be encouraged to evaluate their use of self-management skills ("I got the problem wrong. At least I did the first three steps before I guessed. That's better. I'll try extra hard not to panic next time. I'll stay calm"). Evaluation of outcome is straightforward if goals have been carefully defined. Self-evaluation skills are learned by matching evaluations with the standard setter. A simple five-point scale for evaluating one's own performance, where 1 = not so good and 5 = super, may help youth judge complex problem-solving or interpersonal performances (Urbain and Kendall, 1980). As previously discussed, youths may improve their ability to accurately evaluate their performance if they are rewarded for doing so. In this way, children who consistently underrate or overrate themselves earn more points as they improve the match between their assessment and that of others. This may be as important to helping overly critical or depressed children as it is children with low standards for themselves.

Self-Praising or Coping. Children can learn to administer points and positive self-talk that corresponds to their achievements. Phillips (1984) reported on the effects of teachers' praise following legitimate positive comments by elementary school students about themselves (for example, "I am happy about this," and "I am proud of myself"). Teachers responded to some of their students with such comments as "I would be happy also if I were you," and "You are right to be proud of yourself." Students who were praised nearly tripled their use of self-praise and significantly raised their scores on a measure of self-esteem. (Students who were not praised but who listened to other children being praised also increased their positive self-talk but not their self-esteem.) Demonstration of self-praise by teachers in incidental or planned circumstances should further boost students' skills in its use.

Youths who have difficulty developing a repertoire of self-congratulatory statements can begin by writing down things they might say to someone they admire and then converting these to the first person and using them on themselves. Youths who are still reluctant to give accolades to themselves can be asked how they would change these statements to fit themselves. (The relative generosity of self-praise is probably less important than the difference between new and past levels of self-acknowledgment.)

Coping statements are critical to impulsive and aggressive children who take failure very hard and whose reaction disrupts opportunities for learning. Such children, like John described in Chapter Eight, can benefit from thorough rehearsal of responses that redirect their efforts back to solving the problem. Such responses include: "I got it wrong. I guess I didn't follow my plan. I'll start again and go slowly and take each step one at a time." Young people may enjoy more global coping responses like: "I got it wrong. Well, that's too bad, but at least there is still pizza and punk" (or baseball or whatever a youth likes). "I guess I can go on living and start again and go more slowly this time."

Child helpers trying to get their own ego strengths to rub off on their young clients and parents struggling to show what it means to "grow up" are, in their own ways, teaching self-management. Fortunately, related research is increasing and helping to guide more systematic and successful self-management instruction (Copeland and Hammel, 1981; Kendall, 1977; Kendall and Braswell, 1982; Kendall and Wilcox, 1980; Kendall and Zupan, 1981). The basic instructional strategy involves graduation (1) from easier and shorter to more difficult and longer tasks, (2) from the child helper's modeling and the child's practicing task-management statements out loud to the child's practicing self-management statements silently, and (3) from the child helper's cues and rewards to the child's self-administered cues and rewards. Self-management also helps parents to use more effective parenting skills in several settings (Barth, Blythe, Schinke, and Schilling, 1983; Sanders, 1982). As with other techniques described here, child helpers may also use self-management methods to improve their own professional and personal performance.

Treating Behavior Problems: Specific Strategies and Illustrative Case Histories

The chapters in Part Two address problems that are rarely written about but often confronted by practitioners. These problem-focused chapters have parallel formats. To clarify treatment rationales, each chapter provides information about associated child and family characteristics. Issues in assessment are then described, as is the assessment of each case. Social and cognitive treatment methods are then reviewed. A continuing discussion of the case throughout the chapter illustrates the application of these methods. The concluding chapter in Part Two discusses strategies for applying these innovative techniques despite the shortage of supervisors and peers who are skilled in their use. It also provides guidelines for using these techniques while protecting client rights.

6

Aggressive Behavior

Of all children, aggressive children are at the greatest risk of growing up to be incarcerated or hospitalized for mental illness (Robins, 1981). Child-care facilities increasingly serve aggressive children and youth; 44 percent of all group-care facilities reported increases in physical and verbal abuse by their residents in the last five years (Russo and Shyne, 1980). The latest edition of the *Diagnostic and Statistical Manual* (DSM III) includes aggressive children under the larger category of conduct disorder (American Psychiatric Association, 1980). The aggressive subtype includes children who are violent toward people or property or who are firesetters (firesetting will be discussed in Chapter Ten). Aggression results in personal injury, psychological degradation, or the destruction of property (Bandura, 1976). Aggression, as discussed in this chapter, does not occur in self-defense or in extravigorous use of socially acceptable strategies for pursuing acceptable goals.

Aggressive behavior is learned early and well. Reviewing sixteen studies of the stability of aggression in males, Olweus (1979) reports that patterns of aggressive behavior are well established by age three. Lambert's (1982) findings, alternately, suggest that fighting and quarreling among first graders does not predict conduct disorders, but fighting among fifth graders does. Farrington (1978) found that half the children between the ages of eight and ten rated as aggressive by teachers committed violent delinquent acts by age eighteen. Eron (1980) found that third graders rated by their peers as aggressive were remarkably likely to be perceived as aggressive twenty-two years later. Children rated as aggressive at age eight were three times

187

more likely to have police records ten years later. The consistency was less for females than for males but was, overall, "comparable to the predictability of intelligence test scores over a similar period" (p. 246).

Family and Child Background

Families with aggressive children often have weak and punitive family-management skills and limited problem-solving and communication skills. Child and caregiver conditions associated with aggression in boys include the mother's negativism, the mother's permissiveness regarding aggression, the mother's and father's uses of power, and the boy's temperament (Olweus, 1980). Similarly, McCord, McCord, and Howard (1961) noted erratic discipline, minimal supervision, punitive parents, and parental conflict in the families of the most aggressive of their sample of nondelinquent boys. Eron (1980) identified the antecedents of aggression as punishment for aggression at home and at school, and little identification of the child with either parent (which reduces the effectiveness of parents' ability to influence aggression). Huesmann and Eron (1984) found parental disparagement and the public shaming and punishment of children related to children's aggressiveness twenty-two years later. Pfeffer, Plutchik, and Mizruchi (1983) found that parents' assaultive behavior was a strong predictor of assaultive behavior in latency-age children. Harbin and Madden (1983) found that the decision-making styles of families with a violent adolescent consigned to an inpatient unit differed from those of families with nonviolent adolescents. Families with violent adolescents had less agreement when making choices as a group, sons who had less influence in the families' choice of activities, and mothers who dictated family decisions.

The socially aggressive child is not consistently punished for aggression. Patterson's (1982) painstaking research shows that families of aggressive children reward their children's aggressive behavior more than half the time by such means as the families' dropping their requests or giving the children what they demand. According to Patterson and others (for example,

Berkowitz, 1973), punishment, although not the inconsistent or violent version that is too often used, is needed to control children's aggression. Families that "natter," that threaten punishment for aggressive behavior but in fact provide no negative consequences, are more likely to have aggressive children.

The Development of Aggression

A child's aggressive behavior originates as an effort to attract attention and to prompt caregivers to reduce the distress created by a child's bodily needs. Noxious or aggressive behavior occurs most frequently in the early years; on the whole, three-year-olds exhibit more noxious behavior than do members of any other age group (Patterson, 1980). Preschool children are more aggressive than elementary school children (Hartup, 1974), and junior high school youth are more violent than elementary or high school youth (Duke, 1976). The development away from aggressive behavior probably reflects an increased understanding of the costs of aggressive behavior as well as greater ability to delay action until alternative, nonagressive solutions are identified. *Control* theory (Hirschi, 1969)—which posits that individuals restrain from aggressive acts in direct relationship to the cost of being apprehended for those acts to their personal investments in family, career, friendships, and education—is consistent with the idea that children become less aggressive over time.

Like other behaviors, aggressive behavior is learned largely by observation. Instinctual aggressive actions may also contribute to early childhood agression, as even primates have temper tantrums (Hamburg and VanLawick-Goodall, 1974). Males are certainly more aggressive than females in Western cultures and, with few exceptions, in all other cultures. Primarily, though, aggression is learned through watching and is strengthened or weakened by its success or failure in reducing the discomfort that comes with deprivation and by its effectiveness in maintaining the pleasures of the status quo.

Parents and children often teach each other to be aggressive by accident. Children teach parents who never dreamed of being aggressive toward their children to be just that (Patterson,

1975). One common sequence of events showing the development of increasingly powerful attacks of family members on each other is described in Table 7. Vignette 1 is a common exchange between a caregiver and child. Exchanges result in two common outcomes for both caregivers and children. First, the child or caregiver who persists and achieves his or her goal in the exchange will be more likely to persist again. Second, the loser will learn either to yield more readily in future exchanges or to persist at a level that surpasses previous effort. Varied selection of these two options in part explains the uneven course followed by caregivers and children while they train each other. The three vignettes that follow show variations of this course. In Vignette 2, after the child yields to the caregiver's command, the caregiver is more likely to give loud and threatening commands, and the child is more likely to comply; the child who does not comply, however, learns to fight harder. Because children and caregivers learn on several dimensions, they learn unevenly; thus, child helpers must recognize that much repetition is needed before more prosocial responses are firmly shaped. In Vignette 3, the child refuses to comply with the command, and the caregiver rewards this noncompliance by withdrawing the request. The child learns that the caregiver's command may only be nattering, and the caregiver learns that another command must be used or commands must be backed up by consequences. In the final vignette, the caregiver follows through with consequences, and the child complies; the child is thereafter more likely to comply earlier to avoid consequences or to fight harder to override consequences (if the consequences are given consistently, the child will soon despair of overriding consequences).

These vignettes show the *escalation* of aggression so elegantly articulated by Patterson and his colleagues (Patterson, 1982; Patterson, Reid, Jones, and Conger, 1975). The caregiver and child begin with low-intensity commands and refusals and, in each vignette, increase the intensity and aggressiveness of the responses. The culmination of these escalating exchanges may be child battering or, in adolescent-parent dyads, parent battering (Harbin and Madden, 1983). In this common and frightening game, each player believes that he or she must not

Table 7. How a Caregiver and Child Teach Each Other to Be More Aggressive.

Vignette	Events	Result
Vignette 1	1A Caregiver commands child to stop a rewarding activity.	1C Caregiver is distracted from or withdraws the command (i.e., caregiver rewards child's noncompliance).	1D Child is more likely to ignore, whine, or complain.
	1B Child ignores, whines, or complains (i.e., child punishes caregiver).		1E Caregiver is less likely to use only that command or, if he or she does, to persist.
Vignette 2 1A + 1B	2C Caregiver persists by making the command louder and adding a threat to punish the child if child does not comply.	2D Child complains but fulfills the command (i.e., child rewards the caregiver but attempts to punish command giving).	2E Child is more likely to comply the first time or to persist in efforts to defeat the command.
			2F Caregiver is more likely to persist in giving commands and to threaten.
Vignette 3 1A + 1B + 2C	3D Child complains, threatens or dares caregiver, and does not fulfill command (i.e., child punishes the caregiver for the command).	3E Caregiver is distracted from or withdraws the command (i.e., caregiver negatively reinforces the child's noncompliance).	3F Child is more likely to ignore, whine, complain, and threaten.
			3G Caregiver is less likely to use only that command or, if he or she does, to persist with threat.
Vignette 4 1A + 1B + 2C + 3D	4E Caregiver begins to institute punishment or does institute punishment (i.e., hitting or yelling).	4F Child complies.	4G Child is more likely to comply the first time or to persist in efforts to defeat the command.
			4H Caregiver is more likely to persist in giving commands, threatening, and using punishment.

give in because yielding may result in losing liberties or rights that can never be reclaimed. This belief is partly correct, as each completed exchange moves the power slightly toward one party or the other. Caregivers or children may then believe that more aversive responses are necessary to reestablish the previous equilibrium of power. Children and caregivers commonly emit their strongest protest behaviors—known as *extinction bursts*—just prior to yielding their power. If the burst succeeds in diverting the foreseen loss of rewards, the likelihood of future and more intense bursts is increased. If the burst is not followed by success, then future bursts are less likely and, if they do occur, will be less intense. The shift in control between caregiver and child may be very slow and beset with difficulties, or it may occur quite suddenly if the child or caregiver generalizes the exchange to all future exchanges.

Fred Fitt: Background of a Case Study

Fred's mother was murdered on the street, and he never again heard from his father. Fred, age fourteen, has lived in a group home with his twin sister, Annette, in the nine months since he became parentless. Fred reports that he enjoys the life of the group home and finds more to do there than he did living downtown. Fred is withdrawn according to his group-home parents, the Sharps, who attribute this to the loss of his parents. Fred's aggressive outbursts include destruction of property and fighting with other youths in the group home and, to a greater extent, at school. Fred has been suspended from school for fighting three times in the last seven months and is one suspension short of expulsion. At school, the fighting occurs after such provocations as comments about Fred's mother, race, living in a group home, and speech problem. Fred has few successes at school, although he has become friends with two other black youth.

At the group home Fred primarily fights over his possessions or privileges. If another youth does not make his target weekly school attendance and costs the entire group their Friday

night movie, Fred becomes enraged and assaultive; if not supervised, he will attack the youth. Fred is also fiercely defensive of his
belongings and will attack anyone who he suspects has taken anything from him, whether it is a few splashes of cologne, clothes,
or a pen. Most troubling to the Sharps, Fred's destructiveness
follows the loss of privileges. Fred typically leaves the scene of the
confrontation with the group-home parent and hurls, kicks, or
punches something on the way to his room or in his room.

 Mrs. Sharp spoke to the consultant from the social services agency about three of Fred's problems: (1) his fighting
at school, (2) his destructiveness upon receiving response costs,
and (3) his possessiveness about personal items that leads to
fighting in the group home. The Sharps wished to keep Fred
in the home and did not want to separate him from his sister
(his sister had made an excellent adjustment to the home and
school) but could not tolerate his destructiveness in the home
and were concerned about having Fred at home in the daytime
should he be suspended from the continuation school.

Assessment

 A functional analysis of aggression must thoroughly consider the setting and antecedents of aggressive behavior as well
as the consequences. Although much experimental evidence and
clinical lore show that consequences of actions determine future
actions (as previously shown in Table 7), more recent evidence
shows that specific events can be powerful triggers of aggression. Patterson's (1982) research shows that roughly one-third
of coercive child behaviors are *counterattacks*, or reactions to in-
trusions by others. Much aggressive behavior of children may
have the primary purpose of stopping the aversive behavior of
caregivers or siblings. Caregivers' and siblings' behaviors have
their own antecedents, including (1) a child who is difficult to
care for; (2) other household members who are coercive toward
the caregiver; and (3) unpleasant community contact with individuals, agencies, or institutions that pressure the caregiver
to change (Wahler and Dumas, 1984).

Family Management. Child helpers must understand a family's rules and their enforcement. Asking all family members about their rules and which ones are obeyed often leads to surprising candor and information. The assessment should focus early on aggressive behaviors that occur in and around the caregivers, since these will be easiest for caregivers to monitor. Verbal and nonverbal threatening behavior should be included in the definition of aggression. Some caregivers may at first be hesitant to identify behaviors that they view as threatening to them because they may see this as an aide to older youths who will then know better how to intimidate them. Hesitancy can be overcome and the full range of aggressive behaviors identified. After all, in many major crimes (including extortion and robbery), the weapon is nothing more than a verbal threat. Once the aggressive behavior of greatest import is defined (it may be unwise to tackle all aggressive behaviors at once), an estimate of its frequency of occurrence should be made. Aggressive behavior should be labeled as such, regardless of its intent. Caregivers and children must concentrate on acts and outcomes, not intent; an act that produces harm is aggressive.

The youth's view will facilitate assessment. If the child helper fears that the caregiver is also assaultive, then the child should be interviewed alone (in the extreme case that parental disciplining is abusive, then a report must be filed with the social services department as well). A youth's-eye view of the precipitants of aggression at home will contribute to the assessment of the phenomenon of attack-counterattack. Caregiver commands can also be observed during less structured times before or after consultation sessions—especially if sessions are conducted in the home or school—and in simulated situations that require a caregiver to gain the attention and compliance of the aggressive child.

Some caregivers describe responses to aggressive behavior that sound reasonable and effective (for example, "I make him leave the TV room when he fights with his brother"). If the child is very aggressive, it is almost safe to assume—but further inquiry will ascertain—that the consequence is used irregularly. If it is and if the caregivers have the time and ability, the caregivers can note the thoughts or activities that keep them from using the consequence regularly (for instance, "I'm never sure who is to blame," or "There's no place else to go except the kitchen, and I'm there and he'll drive me crazy"). The cognitive barriers to family management deserve assessment and may be influenced by offering alternative self-talk.

Because the quality of caregiver commands partly predicts the aggressiveness of the child's response, assessment of antecedents should include these commands. Forehand and McMahon (1981) have distinguished between doable and undoable commands (which they call alpha and beta). Doable commands are those rules, suggestions, and statements that are appropriate and that can be complied with. Undoable commands cannot be complied with because they are so vague that compliance with them cannot be ascertained (for example, "Be good"), interrupted by other commands or talking before enough time (at least five seconds) has elapsed to do them, or carried out by the caregiver before the child can begin to accomplish them. Undoable commands are more likely to be followed by noncompliant behavior and escalation of aggression (Williams and Forehand, 1984).

Assessment Instruments. The goal of assessment is to identify the current level of aggressive behavior and the behaviors that maintain aggression. Checklists are well suited to determining the rate of occurrence of aggressive behaviors, and interviews and observation reveal more about the events surrounding the aggressive behavior. The Walker Problem Behavior Identification Checklist (Walker, 1976) has been widely used with families. It includes a subscale with indicators of the child's "acting out" behaviors, each of which may be given a rating of up to five points. This allows caregivers to rate their agreement with statements about the child (such as "has temper tantrums"). The Child Behavior Checklist (Achenbach and Edelbrock, 1979) asks caregivers to identify which aggressive behaviors occurred during the last six months (there is a separate form for teachers). This checklist is the only one that has the advantage of norms for boys and girls and for children from ages two to three, four to six, and six to twelve. Such instruments are useful for identifying long-term changes across a range of behaviors.

Problem-specific checklists that describe only the problems on which the caregiver and child are working (such as "responds to first request to come to dinner") can show change in several target behaviors of immediate concern. These checklists—which the child helper can fashion—can be used daily or weekly (see Exhibit 7). Such an individually tailored scale was developed to assess the effectiveness of self-control training with John, a ten-year-old boy who was especially explosive when he received academic assignments that he viewed as difficult, even though they fit with his achievement test scores (Spirito, Finch, Smith, and Cooley, 1981). The teacher identified the sequence of events that typically resulted in classroom assaults, and from that sequence a scale was made:

0 = Willingly accepts assignment and completes it without negative comments, verbal abuse, or physical abuse.
1 = Speaks out in class to comment on the work, e.g., "I can't do this," "I'm not doing this work," or "Why did you give me such a hard assignment?"
2 = Speaks out in class to say assignment is too difficult, and moves on to another assignment.
3 = Verbally reports angry feelings, e.g., "This stuff is getting me mad." Shows signs of physical behaviors accompanying anger, e.g., legs shaking.
4 = Begins to loudly yell and/or curse at the school material, other students, and/or teachers.
5 = Slams book on desk, hits book or desk with hand. Throws book or other objects across the room or at the other students or teacher.
6 = Starts to cry.

Any changes in John's performance during the treatment period were rated on this scale. Such scales—more than such self-report inventories as the Children's Inventory of Anger (Finch and Eastman, 1983) or a simple count of yelling or book throwing— are useful for identifying progress because they give the child control over each component of the sequence to aggression.

Exhibit 7. Sample Weekly Personalized Aggression Checklist.

Mark the number of times each behavior occurs each day.

	Mon	Tues	Wed	Thurs	Fri	Sat	Sun
Ignores my request							
Yells at me							
Yells at sibling							
Threatens me							
Swears at me							
Swears at sibling							
Slams door							
Slams fist on table							
Slams fist into wall							
Threatens to run away							

All in all, identifying aggressive children is not difficult. Farrington (1978) found remarkable agreement between youth's self-reports of aggression and the ratings of different teachers made at four-year intervals beginning when the child was eight. Despite cultural differences and differing interpretations of the intent of some acts, aggressive children and youth make themselves known. Still, youth, and even their parents, may argue that their aggression is needed to defend against other's aggression. This contention may reflect the youth's underestimation of the level of his or her aggressive behavior and a miscomprehension of the norms of aggressive behavior. Thorough assessment must validate or invalidate this assumption, however, and is central to justifying the child helper's labeling of the child's behavior as creating more problems than other coping strategies.

Fred Fitt: Assessment

The consultant had a sense of Fred's problem from Fred's caregiver's perspective, so he now asked to talk to Fred. He was concerned that Fred would not talk, but he found him likeable.

Fred did not speak at length, but neither did he seem particularly depressed or hostile. Fred knew that his aggressive behavior was creating a problem for himself and his sister but thought that backing down would create greater problems in the long run. Fred was no less willing to discuss the types of incidents that were followed by fighting (which Fred called "doing business'). Fred acknowledged that he had had many talks with the group-home parents about these problems and said that he was doing the best he could to stop himself; until others left him alone, however, he said, he could not stop his aggression.

Partly to increase Fred's interest in changing his style of "doing business," the consultant asked Fred's sister, Annette, to join them. The threesome discussed placement alternatives given the group-home parents' current views on allowing Fred to stay in the home and the chance that they would change their views if Fred's behavior was more controlled. Although Fred knew that his behavior was jeopardizing his stay, he was so angered by again hearing that he might be sent away that he threatened to promptly leave the meeting and the home. Annette asked Fred to stay and to work on not getting so angry. Encouraged by the consultant, Annette poignantly described how important it was for her to stay in the home and for her to stay with Fred. Fred calmed down and listened. Knowing that a large goal was often very motivating at first but needed other subgoals to support it, the consultant queried Fred and Annette about other incentives for Fred's work on changing his behavior. They agreed that Fred would work for points toward a joint visit to their aunt and uncle's home. They also agreed to try working together on the problem. Their first tasks were to jointly list the times in the last two weeks that Fred had lost his temper and to pick the kind of situation where it seemed most important for Fred to improve. The social worker agreed to arrange a meeting between Fred and Annette and the Sharps the following week. He also agreed to call Fred's vice-principal and inform her that he would be working with Fred on an anger-control program.

Intervention

Social and cognitive strategies to reduce aggression are mature and well tested. When properly used, these techniques are effective against the powerful counterforce of aggressive behavior. Perhaps the greatest threat to their success is the common tendency of caregivers to inconsistently apply techniques for reducing aggression or to apply primarily punitive consequences for aggression without teaching or rewarding alternative behaviors. Interventions that address the physical contributors to aggression also deserve consideration.

Social Interventions

Aggression is a "social" behavior. Aggresssive behavior makes enemies yet yields social rewards of compliance and control. Aggressive social behavior warrants vigorous social interventions. Reducing the social gain of aggression and building alternative strategies for obtaining social rewards are the starting point for most interventions.

Rewards for Nonaggression. Rewarding nonaggressive behavior must be part of every program to reduce aggression. Caregiver and peer attention partially sustains children's aggressive behavior. That attention to positive behavior can have salutory effects on aggressive behavior is evinced by clinical-research reports showing that attending only to children's nonaggressive behavior can help reduce their aggressive behavior (see, for example, Frankel, Moss, Schofield, and Simmons, 1976; Grieger, Kauffman, and Grieger, 1976). More often, though, attention alone will not have significant impact on aggression. Roberts, Hatzenbuehler, and Bean (1981) found that attention for compliant behavior had little effect alone or in combination with time out for reducing aggressive behavior. Other rewards and penalties are needed. The addition of tangible rewards for compliant behavior is a more powerful adjunct to time out (Kazdin and Frame, 1983). Response cost and reprimands should also be a consequence for most aggressive acts. Patterson (1975, 1976b) provides much guidance to child helpers and caregivers who want to develop reward and penalty systems to reduce the aggressive behavior of children.

To facilitate the greatest possible reduction in the use of aggressive behavior, rewards for nonaggressive behavior should be delivered in all possible situations. Abikoff and Gittelman (1984) showed that an incentive system based on Patterson's work that included such rewards as money, television, time with a parent, and special treats plus the loss of privileges and the use of time out was effective in normalizing the aggressive behavior of twenty-eight hyperactive children aged six to twelve. The program taught parents to provide social approval and consistent consequences for behavior at home and also linked school and home so that parents could provide consequences for their children for behavior at school as well. A therapist also modeled and role played alternative behaviors for the child and worked with parents to help them develop a mind-set that supported the use of these techniques. After eight weeks, the frequency of the children's aggressive behavior had decreased from significantly higher than their classmates' to a rate that was virtually the same as their peers'.

A school social worker implemented a similar home-school communication program to reduce the incidents of physical aggression of nine educably mentally retarded children ages four to six from an average of twenty-one per child per day before the training to ten per child per day after five days of the program to fewer than three per day per child by the twentieth day of the program (Goff and Demetral, 1983). Children received brightly colored cards and praise for not hitting, kicking, choking, spitting, or biting during four- to eight-minute periods during the school day. If they obtained the criterion number of cards, they could bring them home and exchange them for privileges. (The criterion number of cards needed was increased as the children's performance improved.) The school social worker taught the parents about the use of the procedure in one meeting and through telephone consultation. Parents complied with the program more than 90 percent of the time (with the exception of one parent who was highly disorganized and complied about half of the time). Parents also reported that they had increased their use of positive consequences at home and that their children were less aggressive there as well.

Ignoring. Ignoring was once thought to be a key tool in a child helper's kit for reducing aggressive behavior. The author's experience and other research reports (for example, Wahler and Fox, 1981) suggest, however, that ignoring aggressive behavior—even when combined with rewards for positive behaviors—is a slow and impractical intervention for many caregivers. Although some aggressive behavior should and must be ignored during the initial stages of interventions with children showing a very high rate of aggressive behavior, aggressive behavior may have too many rewarding consequences for some children to resist, even though they receive less attention from adults or peers.

Time Out. As previously described (see Chapter Five), time out removes the child from opportunities for reward and, when effective, reduces the likelihood of the recurrence of the behavior that preceded and caused the time out. In work with young aggressors, time out is an invaluable strategy, and it deserves to be among the first approaches implemented in families with aggressive children or caregivers. Time out punishes the aggressive behavior and also gives the caregiver and child a "breather" that reduces further aggression. Caregivers and older children, once they see the value of time out for reducing further penalties and preparing them to earn rewards, may even learn to impose time out on themselves.

The unavoidable question remains: how does a caregiver get an aggressive child to accept his or her first time out? Rehearsing the time-out procedure with the child is a reasonable but often insufficient procedure. Roberts (1984) gave noncompliant children aged six to nine extensive description of time out and the opportunity to observe a parent and child actor engage in the following time-out sequences: compliance and praise, noncompliance and time out, yelling in time out (which was ignored), quiet sitting in time out and subsequent release from time out, and escape from time out and subsequent spanking and return to time out. Roberts found that these children still had to experience time out before it led them to play more compliantly (one child made fourteen escape attempts before completing an acceptable time out).

Caregivers may need good self-management skills and child helper support to implement time out, although some children accept time out without undue fuss. A Signal Seat, a time-out chair that emits a sound whenever the child leaves it without permission, was designed to help families quickly implement time-out procedures at home. Parents who read a self-instruction manual on positive reinforcement and time out, listened to a twenty-minute audiotape, and used the Signal Seat reported less use of spanking, less noncompliance, more positive attitudes about their child, and fewer and less significant problem behaviors when compared with parents given the same training but no Signal Seat and no training group (Hamilton and Mac-Quiddy, 1984).

Establishing time out may require that child helpers or caregivers provide physical guidance to move the child into the time-out seat. With very aggressive children, time out may initially have to be conducted in a child-proofed bathroom or a time-out room. Such a setting may be more infuriating and more punishing than a quiet chair, and the child helper should anticipate more of a fight in moving a child into time out (the child helper should anticipate quicker results as well). At first, just getting a child to stay in time out is a victory; the child's inappropriate behavior (for example, cursing, hollering, crying) in the time-out chair or bathroom may have to be ignored. Helping the child to complete the time out is of primary importance. If the child's behavior is still out of control when the signal indicates the end of the time-out period, then the timer should be reset for two minutes. (After time out is established, the timer can be reset to the full time-out period whenever inappropriate behavior occurs.) If the child will not comply with time out at all or causes the timer to be reset more than three times, then the child should be told that the prearranged privilege has been lost. When a child will not stay in the quiet chair and must be moved to a separate time-out room, efforts should be made to return the child to an open setting at an early opportunity, because when time out occurs completely away from family or classmates, the child cannot observe the pleasures of returning to free play and has less incentive to complete time out. Also, time out in an open setting requires additional self-management skills—the final goal of time out.

Because time out is so valuable, it should not be wasted. Professionals should prepare other child helpers or caregivers sufficiently so that they have a successful first experience. Preparation for handling possible trouble situations in implementing time out includes discussion and role play of (1) using time out in front of people who are not familiar with its use and may think it unkind (implement the time out and then describe how it keeps the peace in the family), (2) deciding which behaviors are to be followed with time out (only those that are specified to the child in advance), and (3) what to do if a child says he or she likes time out (ignore the child, but check to be sure that the child's non-time-out environment is rewarding).

Once time out is established, consistency becomes paramount. This is no small feat given the varied settings—the supermarket, dinner table, doctor's office, classroom, and car, for example—of child and caregiver interactions. Effective alternative time-out procedures include marking on the child's hand at the time of the behavior deserving time out the number of minutes in time out the child has earned and giving time out at a later time, drawing a chalk line around the child to signal time out, and putting a ribbon on the child to show that time out has been earned and must be taken at home. Bus-stop benches, the grass at a park, and even the sidewalk can provide suitable time-out settings for children and youth. Although implementing time out in these settings may be awkward, the value of providing the same consequences in all settings is worth the strain.

Some children, like Denise, whose story follows, have great difficulty staying calm during time out. An organizing task such as a sheet of routine math problems may keep such children from becoming agitated and distracted and avoid additional consequences that again prevent opportunities for social interaction. Although time out can often be administered in unrestricted settings and in a quiet chair, Luiselli and Greenidge (1982) found that reducing the hitting behavior of Denise, a severely retarded, legally blind, deaf child, required a more restrictive time-out procedure. Denise habitually raised her arms over her head and brought them down fiercely on the shoulders and heads of children and adults. Before the use of time out—despite positive attention for appropriate and nonaggressive behavior—Denise was hitting in this way about eight times per day. Time out was originally conducted in a chair in a barren corner of the room. Denise typically knocked over the chair and left the area; her aggressive behavior did, however, decrease to about four times a day. After four days the investigators attempted a more restrictive time out and placed Denise in a space created by a recess in the school wall and covered by a tumbling mat so that she could see but not leave the space. After an initial increase in aggression, her rate dropped to about three aggressive responses per day. This procedure was also abandoned because of difficulties in keeping the mat in place—and the subsequent rewarding attention she received from teachers—as well as the disrupting effect of Denise's time-out behavior on her peers. Finally, she was placed in a time-out room measuring seven by seven feet with lighting, ventilation, and a peephole through which Denise was observed every minute that she was in time out. This version of time out was instituted with the consent of Denise's parents and all program supervisors and directors. During the thirty-two days in which the time-out room was used, only nine aggressive responses were recorded, meaning that on 84 percent of the days, Denise did not attack anyone. Follow-up during the next three months revealed only two assaults during that time.

Reprimands. Time out, although invaluable, is not the punishment of first choice. Alone and with understandable and doable definitions of "what to do" and rewards for improved "doing," effective reprimands should be tried first. (If reprimands are not effective, time out may enhance their effectiveness.) Hall and colleagues (1972) helped a teacher in a classroom for the trainably mentally retarded improve her use of verbal reprimands with a seven-year-old deaf girl, Andrea. Andrea habitually bit or pinched herself, her peers, the teacher, and visitors to the classroom. She was so disruptive—she averaged seventy-two biting and pinching episodes per school day—that she had no opportunity to learn or to make friends. The teacher began reprimanding her after each incident by pointing at her with an outstretched arm and shouting, "No!". After eighteen days, the average number of biting and pinching episodes had dropped to five per day. When the teacher stopped reprimanding, the incidence of these episodes rose to thirty per day. The procedure, although punitive, improved Andrea's interaction with peers who no longer feared her painful greetings. Sawin and Parke's (1979) research warns, however, that inconsistent use of reprimands and consequences may encourage aggression. They found that the incidence of aggressive behavior remained high during periods when reprimands were applied consistently when those periods were preceded by periods when consequences were applied inconsistently. Consistently applied reprimands were most effective when they followed consistently applied ignoring or negative consequences. (If reprimands are not effective, the addition of time out may enhance their effectiveness.)

Response Cost for Verbal Aggression. Many of the records of children referred to residential care describe the children as aggressive, which basically means that they use coercive language (for example, "If you do that, I'll kill you"). Assuming that such threatening language is itself a problem for youth and their caregivers—even if it is not followed by aggressive acts—Phillips, Fixsen, Phillips, and Wolf (1979) instituted a response-cost program to reduce aggressive language. First, following careful definition of *aggressive language* as "stated or threatened destruction or damage to any object, person, or animal," youth were reprimanded for its use (for example, "That's not the way to talk"). These reprimands had minimal effect. Fines of twenty points were next used and had far greater impact, reducing aggressive responses from an average of ten per child per three-hour period to less than one per child per three-hour period. Dropping the fines led to increases in aggressive behavior, though not to the level before the fines. Instituting fifty-point fines eliminated the aggressive language in that setting. No assessment was made of the relationship between these decreased levels of aggressive talking and levels of aggressive actions.

Enhancing Child and Family-Management Skills. Caregivers need more than lectures on the management of aggressive behavior (DiGiuseppe, 1983); they also need support for the consistent application of social consequences for aggressive behavior. Griest and colleagues (1982) developed an intervention to boost parents' skills and support for parents in deference to evidence that parents' perceptions of their children, personal adjustment, marital satisfaction, and extrafamiliar relationships are associated with child behavior (Williams and Forehand, 1984). All the parents of troubled children in their study were given parent training, with half the parents also given additional parent-enhancement-skill training (consisting of discussion, information, demonstration, role playing, and homework) to improve their overall parenting behavior. Parents given extra training maintained their increased use of positive rewards and contingent positive attention better than parents who received only parent training; the children of parents given parent-enhancement-skill training were also less aggressive.

Cohen, Keyworth, Kleiner, and Libert (1971) employed a school-home communication system, tenacity, and ingenuity to reduce the aggressiveness of youth ejected from other public schools. One such youth was referred to the principal of his previous school thirty-six times for fighting, cursing, spitting, and throwing objects during the year prior to his expulsion. A contract was developed with the boy, his mother, and the minister of the family's church during a brief parent meeting. The focus was on increasing the boy's prosocial skills; he was to be rewarded by his mother with money for time spent in the campus work building and for time spent reading. The opportunity to work at the neighborhood grocery store could also be earned for not fighting on the bus or in school for one week. This basic contract was modified by phone, by mail, and during visits by a staff member who rode the school bus. Contract modifications included a clause indicating that the youth would be referred to pupil personnel services for possible transfer if he was suspended again. The boy's number of suspensions fell from one every twenty days to zero following this agreement. The authors describe the merits of contracting to improve academic and aggressive behavior:

Parents who have entered into contracts with their children at the Learning Center may or may not be able to explain what a reinforcer is, but they tend to know how to identify and use one. Thus, without heavy emphasis on the theoretical aspects of behavior modification, parents have learned some of the very practical applications of the techniques by participating in building contingency contracts. Most important, perhaps, the contracts serve to control some of the parent's behavior. For many of the students at the Learning Center, the outcomes of past interactions with their parents have been unpredictable, punitive, and mutually debilitating. These kinds of interactions have created the conditions under which mistrust and aggression in the family thrive. . . . The soft data, in the form of feedback received during parent meetings, indicated that the contracting procedures might also be useful in beginning to rebuild trust and love between parents and their heretofore prodigal children [pp. 304–305].

The Barb: Desensitization to Anger-Inducing Situations. Few problems plague caregivers as much as youth who find an insult under every stone. Although the anger is often partially feigned, the youths involved often fool themselves into greater anger and, sometimes, tragedy. Hull and Hull (1983) found that male juvenile offenders, when compared to female offenders and nonoffenders and male nonoffenders, were not hampered by deficits in assertiveness skills but, rather, by an excess of aggressive behavior. Female offenders were not significantly different from male nonoffenders or female nonoffenders in aggressiveness or assertiveness. Hull and Hull also found that offenders had difficulty responding to authority figures who gave them negative evaluations and recommended that specific situations of this sort be used in training. Their suggestion supports the use of the *barb* technique.

The barb technique (Kaufman and Wagner, 1972) was developed to help youth learn to control their impulsive aggression. Now more than a decade old, the strategy and its applications are still valid. The technique begins with information about and demonstration of appropriate responses to interpersonal situations—or *barbs*—that incited aggressive outbursts. These are often role played. Next, the child helper discusses appropriate responses to those situations; these, depending on the culture, include (1) eye-to-eye contact, (2) neutral to pleasant facial expression, (3) moderate tone of voice, (4) a verbal response that includes a plan and may provide some positive consequences, and (5) follow-through on the plan. The responses are role played and critiqued by the child helper and youth. Incentives for using one or more of these responses in the school or home, rather than the more habitual threat or attack, are next agreed upon.

Practice begins within the youth's social ecology with the child helper who instigated the program giving the youth barbs with warnings; for example, "Fred, here comes a barb: what will it cost you to have left your books at school?" This warning is gradually reduced to "Fred, a barb's coming: you're fined 50 points for not bringing books home," to "Fred, here goes," to "Fred," and then to no warning. When the youth has mastered the prosocial reaction to the child helper, the program is extended to favorite and then to disliked caregivers. Requirements for the use of components of the prosocial response are also gradually raised. Later, other administrators and caregivers can be added to the brigade of barb tossers (the youth is not always informed of their participation).

Social-Skills Training. Clinical researchers working with youth have paid little heed to research showing the value of social-skills training with adults who have anger-control problems (see, for example, Foy, Eisler, and Pinkston, 1975; Frederiksen, Jenkins, Foy, and Eisler, 1976). Elder, Edelstein, and Narick (1979) and Bornstein, Bellack, and Hersen (1980) have contributed significant but small studies. Four physically aggressive adolescents residing in a psychiatric hospital for an average of five years each were treated with social-skills training by Elder, Edelstein, and Narick (1979). A social worker and intern led an on-ward social-skills training program four days a week, forty-five minutes per day, for two weeks to improve the youths' skills in making socially skilled interruptions and responding to nega-

tive communication. The youths role played various scenes constructed from situations characterized by the youths as troublesome. The youths improved their handling of these social-skill
areas and also reduced their token-economy fines for aggressive
behavior, their weekly seclusion rates, and their extragroup (for
example, in the lunchroom and dayroom) aggressive behavior.
Three of the four youth were soon released, and they maintained
their community placements through the nine-month follow-up
period. The intensity of the training experience is noteworthy.
Weekly social-skills training sessions (even if these are conducted
for more weeks) may not be sufficient to teach skills that last,
are generalized to other settings, and influence other areas of
performance. Massed practice may be needed.

Bornstein, Bellack, and Hersen's (1980) work included
four inpatients aged eight to twelve. Social-skills training occurred
in groups. A difficult situation was presented to a student in
the group, his or her response was obtained, therapist feedback
on the response was given and discussed with the child to ensure understanding, and the response was modeled by the therapist and practiced again until criteria for the target behavior
were reached. The social-skills training addressed eye contact,
hostile tone, requests for new behavior, and overall assertiveness.
Overall, the effects of the treatment were promising, as three
of four youths showed improvements in the target behavior that
were maintained for at least six months. The newly learned skills
were not, though, generalized to extratreatment situations. The
authors suggest that the difficulties in getting youth to use the
skills were attributable to the brevity of the training (only three
weeks), the teaching of responses that the boys did not think
would work because they were not tough enough, the failure
to address the boys' idea that responses had to be tough, and
the failure to identify responses that were useful and acceptable.
They also admit that the format was considered boring by the
youth and that only a very effective group leader saved the day.

The authors' concerns deserve further reflection. Socially
appropriate responses proffered by clinicians must be checked
against the youngsters' realities. Assertive responses that are
more acceptable and effective than the child helper's can be

identified by youth. Humor and sarcasm—although not conventionally considered to be assertive responses—can serve youth who are trying to avoid aggressive responses to perceived threats. Gaining peer feedback on the effectiveness of responses is also needed to ensure that trainees understand how they will be perceived. One useful strategy for this is to provide all group members with a supply of judges' cards (like those used in the Olympics) for use in rating role players. After each performance, the cards are passed to the role player. At the end of the session, the points on the cards are counted to identify and reward social successes for the day. So that impressing the judges will not become the overriding goal, the group leader should also ask group members for explanations of their ratings (this is especially important with raters who give extreme ratings or who give the same rating regardless of performance). This stimulates discussion and provides additional feedback to the performers.

Peers. Peers may encourage either disruptive and aggressive behavior (Christy, 1975) or more prosocial behavior (see Parsons and Heward, 1979). Youth may prefer peer-operated treatment programs over adult-managed programs as shown by Phillips, Phillips, Fixsen, and Wolf (1974), who found that peer and adult-directed administration of daily task completion in a group home were equally effective. Smith and Fowler (1984) used peer pressure to help behaviorally disturbed, developmentally delayed, underachieving kindergarteners. Children could earn up to three points for their activities during transition times if they (1) helped their team clean up their designated area, (2) went to the restroom as a team, and (3) waited quietly without fighting upon return. Children who earned all three points could vote on which recess activity the class would do. Children with two points could participate in the activity, but children with one point had to remain outside and clean other areas of the classroom. To be sure that all children had an opportunity to earn all three points, daily briefing sessions were held to remind children of the rules and allow them to role play the transition activities. At first the decision on the number of points earned was made by the classroom teacher. In a second stage of the program, a child who had earned three points the preceding day became the team captain and assumed the role of the coach and point giver (the teacher did not correct the monitors if they misawarded points). The same program was also tried in a summer compensatory education classroom. In this case, the children were the first to lead the groups (that is, no teacher-managed program preceded the child-managed program). The results again showed the powerful influence of peer monitoring, even though the monitors were less likely to withhold points from children who did not complete assigned activities. Throughout both programs the teacher was available to intervene during disputes over points—there were only three times when students thought they deserved more points, and each was resolved for the monitor. Fowler and Smith describe a phenomenon which this author has also witnessed: children who are designated team captains for a specific time period often assume the role for the whole day. Indeed, peer opportunities to prompt, evaluate, and reward the performance of others improve their self-monitoring over time. By acting as a monitor, with the accompanying speech and responsibilities, they develop their abilities to talk themselves through responsible behavior and reward themselves for it (children also reported that they were "being good" in order to be team captain).

Using their Structured Learning Approach, Goldstein and colleagues (1978) have employed peers as group leaders in social-skills training programs for aggressive adolescents. Youth are shown difficult situations and appropriate responses to those situations. These responses include use of negotiation, assertiveness, self-control, perspective-taking, and empathy skills. Adolescents are then given the opportunity and encouragement to role play the responses and get help in generalizing the skills to other settings. The use of peer leaders has been encouraging. Peer leaders were just as able to teach negotiation skills as adults were. Further, adolescents who anticipated that they would later be peer leaders acquired skills more quickly than did other youth.

Grieger, Kauffman, and Grieger (1976) reduced rates of aggressive behavior in a kindergarten class by encouraging children to report the cooperative or friendly actions of their classmates. Reports were made by children to the class during a group-sharing time. Children identified as having committed friendly acts also received a badge with a happy face. Aggressive acts fell from an average of forty to an average of fewer than ten per day under this procedure. After the teacher ceased to use this procedure and the rate of aggressive acts returned to the level before the intervention, the reporting time was reinstituted (although this time without the happy faces); the rate of aggressive acts in the classroom again declined markedly. This study shows the ability of peers to identify and reward each other's nonaggressive behavior and, in so doing, decrease the rates of aggressive behavior. Although these students were not selected for this class because they were aggressive, their high preintervention rates of aggression suggest that this approach deserves more use with aggressive children. Certainly, teachers will appreciate bringing a bit of utopia into their classrooms.

Cognitive Interventions

Like their social counterparts, cognitive interventions for aggression are most effective when they are long lasting and include occasional refresher courses (Camp and Ray, 1984). Cognitive interventions show promise when combined with social contingencies for angry or aggressive behavior. The primary uses of cognitive training in social interventions are to increase children's ability to control their impulses, to help children obtain available rewards for nonaggressive behavior, and to help caregivers consistently apply behavioral treatments.

Self-Instruction Training. The best-articulated and best-tested efforts to teach aggressive children self-management are those of Bonnie Camp and her colleagues (reviewed in Camp and Ray, 1984). The Think Aloud program (Camp and Bash, 1981) is designed to teach aggressive boys self-management and interpersonal problem-solving skills. The program manual provides material for forty half-hour sessions in which children are taught to use self-talk to guide social problem solving. The program includes activities to increase coping skills, to generate alternative responses, to understand cause and effect, to evaluate possible actions, and to understand the feelings of others (that is, social perspective taking). The research to date suggests that programs like this—particularly when augmented with booster sessions—can help improve the performance of highly aggressive elementary school children. Yet, although self-management training is quite promising for aiding older children and youth with impulse-control problems (see, for example, Kendall and Braswell, 1985), the evidence of the power of this technique to reduce aggression, which is only in part a result of impulse-control problems, is not convincing enough to argue for self-instruction training without other strategies for increasing nonaggressive interactions. Only Forman (1980) has compared self-management and response-cost procedures, and she found that both were more effective than no intervention, but that response cost was more powerful.

In some cases cognitive intervention alone is sufficient. Pfeiffer (1977) used self-instruction training with a high school boy who physically assaulted his girlfriend and verbally attacked his girlfriend and parents. Working with the youth alone, Pfeiffer taught him to understand his behavior using learning concepts, to identify and role play a series of provocative situations, and to use a self-management technique. (Initial efforts to involve the youth in reading about these principles as homework failed; the counselor did not despair, however, and instead began each session with a brief lesson on the relevant content.) The technique involved response inhibition in which the boy refrained from instantaneous reactions to provocative cues, cognitive repetition of self-control statements that identified how badly the boy would feel if he acted out his aggressive impulse, and self-praise for successfully refraining from aggression. As confirmed by the boy's girlfriend, family, and teacher at six and twelve months after treatment, the program completely eliminated the boy's physical aggression and reduced his verbal aggression by 80 percent.

Schlicter and Horan (1981) used stress-inoculation training with twenty-seven institutionalized juvenile offenders with serious anger-control problems. Their procedure involved stress inoculation and exposure to provocative role-play situations. The stress inoculation component was comprised of education and discussion in which the youths defined anger, analyzed recent anger episodes, reviewed their responses during those episodes, and identified alternative coping responses. The youths each also described and ranked six situations to which they typically responded with aggression. First, for the least provocative situation, each youth played the provocator, and the child helpers demonstrated cognitive and social coping strategies. Then the roles were reversed, and the youth practiced coping with the provocation until he had mastered it. This was continued through the sixth and most difficult situation. This strategy improved the youths' scores on role plays of other provocative situations and on the Anger Inventory (Novaco, 1975). On these measures, youth exposed to the stress inoculation improved more than youth given no treatment or youth simply taught relaxation training and exposed to provocation from the therapist without rehearsal of coping responses. No differences were observed by youth workers in the youths' behavior in the unit, partly, the authors reasonably propose, because of difficulties in coordinating a reliable observation system among staff. This procedure does appear useful in giving youth mastery over situations that previously had been troubling. The results show that the skills were learned and can be used if the social situation rewards their use. If the overall program also develops systematic incentive systems for encouraging coping responses to provocations—which did not occur in the project just described—youth with additional self-management skills should fare well.

Schrader and colleagues (1977) developed an anger-control program for adolescent drug abusers in a day-treatment program. Youth were identified by teachers for the anger-control program on the basis of their aggression toward teachers or peers. The six older adolescents involved were observed in their classrooms before they started training to identify their natural rates of verbal aggression and disruptive behavior. Youths' exposure to the program was staggered to identify differences in their performance that were attributable to the counseling sessions rather than to some other factor. The program consisted of five one-hour individual counseling sessions that included (1) a functional analysis of anger, in which the cognitive and social antecedents and consequences of anger were reviewed, a discussion of self-talk, and homework monitoring self-talk during anger-provoking situations; (2) review of self-talk and homework assignments and an introduction to relaxation and imagery exercises; (3) review of homework, self-instruction training involving substituting calming self-talk during anger-provoking situations, and practice combining relaxation and self-control statements; (4) role playing of anger-inducing situations and a general review; and (5) continued practice in self-management, introduction of self-praise for staying calm, and a final review. Following the treatment, five out of six students showed less verbal aggression and disruptive behavior than they had shown before. Homework assignments encouraged youth to practice skills learned in each session. The gains were stable at a three-month follow-up for four of the five youths who had made initial progress. Observations of behavior in the unit also showed that five of the six youth showed significant initial improvement, with only one youth losing those gains by three months after treatment. Before anger-control training, the youths averaged 17.25 incidences of verbal abuse and disruptive behavior per youth per week. During treatment, the rate fell to 4.4 incidences; by the three-month follow-up the rate was 3.9. Treatments were begun at different times, and the data clearly shows that the drops in incidence correspond to entry into the self-management training program. These findings, along with those of Schlichter and Horan (1981) and Snyder and White (1979), call for wider use of self-instruction with aggressive youth.

The case of John, the boy with the anger-control problem whose case was partially described earlier, provides several insights into the use of self-management training with children in schools (Spirito, Finch, Smith, and Cooley, 1981). At the outset of the treatment program, John was, on the average, scoring between a four (yelling and cursing) and a five (slamming or throwing books) on his daily individual rating scale. Interviews with John and his teacher indicated that the aggressive responses resulted from John's rising anxiety about receiving negative evaluations from the teacher. The psychologist met with John twice weekly for thirty minutes for four weeks to complete a training program involving information, practice, and application. John first learned that many people get scared or mad when they have to do work and that they may tell themselves that the teacher will think they are dumb or that they are going to lose control and hit something. John also learned that some people talk to themselves differently and tell themselves that the teacher will not think they are dumb and that they will learn from the task. In the second phase, John watched a video of his psychologist role playing a boy working on a problem and first talking aloud to himself in ways that get him upset and then in ways that calm him. John then practiced developing his own self-statements to keep calm; he was rewarded with food and praise. He also learned to recognize when his anger was growing, to calm himself with deep breathing, and to use rewarding self-statements when he used his self-management techniques. John's self-talk was first spoken out loud and then whispered and then just thought. In the application phase, John worked on schoolwork given by his teacher. The psychologist used a modified barb technique; he stood over John and said, "You can't get that one?" and "That's wrong." John was helped to talk himself through the assignment and past the barbs. John's classroom behavior began to improve within ten days after the training program began. In the month after training was completed, John willingly accepted classroom assignments 65 percent of the time compared to none of the time before treatment. John's aggressive outbursts (those scored as at least a 5 on the scale) dropped from one every two and a half days to one in twenty-eight days. John's teacher reported him to be the best-controlled child in the classroom by the end of the follow-up period. (The authors also note that John completed this sequence while his father asked John's mother for a divorce and John's mother attempted suicide.)

Feindler, Marriott, and Iwata (1984) included social- and cognitive-skills training in a program for troubled youth with multiple school suspensions (40 percent had police records). Students were selected for participation in the program because of the high rates of classroom or community disruption recorded on their school records. The training occurred during ten biweekly fifty-minute sessions, and students were divided into three groups of six youths (eighteen students also served as a control group). Group members learned behavioral control, social problem solving, and cognitive self-control. The behavioral-control efforts gave students skills and a rationale for suppressing verbal and nonverbal aggressive responses. This component included using self-monitoring to identify the parts of the anger cycle: (1) antecedent anger cues, (2) aggressive responses, and (3) consequent events. Students then learned to insert a brief time delay between the provoking event and their reaction. They also learned noncombative verbal strategies for handling conflict, including fogging (partially agreeing with the other person), broken record (repeating your request in a calm voice), and minimal effective responses (paraphrasing and encouraging more discussion with head nods and brief verbalizations such as "Uh huh"). The social problem solving involved specifying problems, identifying alternative responses, listing consequences of each response, implementing alternatives, and evaluating outcomes. Cognitive skills included self-instruction ("I'm going to ignore this and stay cool"), reinterpretation of provocative stimuli, self-evaluation of performance during and after conflict situations, and thinking ahead. Role play with actual provocative peers and authority figures and use of the barb technique allowed youth to practice their social and cognitive skills and helped them generalize them to situations outside of the class. Youth given the training received significantly fewer fines for aggressive verbal and physical behavior than the control group. (These differences were in addition to changes resulting from the ongoing token economy, which was not effective in reducing the number of fines for the control group.) The number of expulsions for severely assaultive behavior was halved for group members but was not significantly less than for the control group. This suggests that the token economy also contributed to improvements in all youths.

Caregiver Self-Control Training. Fleischman, Horne, and Arthur (1983) described procedures for helping caregivers reduce the aggressive behavior of children by boosting caregivers' use of positive techniques until the rewards from changes in children's behavior itself rewards caregivers' continued use of positive techniques. Wells, Griest, and Forehand (1980) taught mothers in parent-training groups to identify personal rewards and to administer these rewards daily after providing positive attention for their children's appropriate behavior and using time out for each instance of their noncompliant behavior. Mothers in this self-control training program entered into a contract with the therapist stating their agreement to practice these parenting skills with their children daily. Other mothers received only parent-skill training. Results of this strategy were positive but perplexing. No observable differences between the behavior of the mothers in each group were found. The behavior of children of mothers who learned to use self-control strategies improved more, however, than that of children of mothers given only parent-skill training. The limited self-control training procedure may have been just sufficient to change the mothers' behaviors to alter the children's behaviors but not enough to be observed. These findings suggest that the inclusion of sufficient self-control training for caregivers is worthwhile.

Physical Interventions

Physical contributors to aggression are just now beginning to be understood. Recent evidence (Pines, 1985) suggests that biological characteristics may greatly increase the likelihood of aggression even when social and cognitive contributors to aggression are minimal.

Exercise. The research of numerous investigators (for example, Milburn, 1980) has debunked the myth that engaging in physical exercise, watching or participating in aggressive sports, or verbally expressing anger or aggression decreases physical aggression. Just the opposite is often true. This not-so-new news has not, unfortunately, reached many juvenile detention facilities and group homes, where boxing and weight training are still promoted. Ill-advised caregivers are at times encouraged to express their anger to relieve "pent-up" emotions or to watch aggressive films to vicariously relieve their aggressive "urges." This is most unfortunate. Expression of anger may be a useful motivational strategy for people who are anxious or fearful and are, therefore, unable to defend their rights. Expression of anger is not necessary, however, for most children or adolescents. Biaggio (1980) showed that people who tended not to express their anger were not crippled by anxiety and worries but, instead, were characterized by high self-acceptance, social maturity, and dependability. This and related arguments (see, for example, Gaylin and Macklin, 1982) should further dissuade child helpers and caregivers from teaching aggressive children or youth to express anger as a coping strategy.

Medication. Campbell, Anderson, and Green (1983) reviewed ways that drug therapy can be a useful adjunct to social and cognitive treatments of aggression. They observed that stimulants such as Ritalin and Dexedrine are not effective in reducing aggression, although more recent research indicates that stimulants can markedly reduce the aggressive behavior of hyperactive children (Amery, Minichiello, and Brown, 1984). Haloperidol (Haldol) is effective in reducing aggression and temper tantrums of children in inpatient units but requires doses high enough to cause sedation and to have adverse effects on thinking (Werry and Aman, 1975). Lithium also effectively reduces aggressiveness (Platt and others, 1981), sometimes in children hospitalized in inpatient facilities who have not been helped by other traditional methods. Lithium has fewer untoward effects, including less interference with cognition (Platt, Campbell, Green, and Grega, 1984), if optimal doses are maintained. The use of lithium is under study at this time, and administration of the drug requires careful monitoring; thus, it is premature to advocate the widespread use of lithium.

Fred Fitt: Intervention

As agreed, a week later, after phone contact with all parties, the social work consultant met with Fred, Annette, and Mrs. Sharp (Mr. Sharp could not attend) to plan an intervention. Fred and Annette presented their list of incidents that resulted in angry behavior by Fred—there were sixteen during the two-week period—and they nominated Fred's response to reprimands or lost privileges in the home as the top problem. Mrs. Sharp agreed that this was the top problem and encouraged work on it, but she also expressed much concern about Fred's reaction to other youths' use of his belongings.

A plan was developed for both problems. First, an overarching incentive system was established. The consultant checked the list to determine how often Fred had reacted to either of these two kinds of situations in the two weeks that were being used as the baseline and found eight aggressive reactions to privilege losses and five to other youth. All agreed that these counts fairly represented Fred's current level, and these marks were used to judge Fred's progress. Fred was to earn ten points if he could reduce either of these rates by a least one per week and if he could reduce the overall rate of thirteen per week by at least two. For any week in which he reduced his overall rate by two from the previous week, he had the opportunity to take someone in the group home, besides Annette, for ice cream. When Fred had earned 100 points from role playing, handling barbs, and reducing the number of anger incidents, he earned an overnight visit with his aunt and uncle (given their permission). If Fred did not reduce his incidents of anger by at least one per week during the next two weeks and by at least five per week (that is, reduce them to less than one per every two days) by the end of the month, he would not remain in the Sharps' home.

Next, a specific plan was made for each problem. To improve his response to reprimands and privilege losses, Fred would work on the barb technique with Mrs. Sharp (who would get consultation from the social worker) and with Annette. Mrs. Sharp would help Fred to prepare for barbs by writing down some of the reprimands he could expect, and Annette would use these on Fred during their walks to school. Mrs. Sharp would also involve Mr. Sharp, the weekend relief workers, and other youths as appropriate.

For Fred's anger about others using his possessions, two techniques were agreed upon. The first was to call a resident meeting to discuss the problem; outline a temporary, two-month-long policy of stricter consequences for unauthorized use of others' belongings; and ask each youth to identify one item of clothing or one record, tape, tool, or magazine to place in a loan bank for loan, with permission, to anyone else for one day. Borrowable items were listed on a sign-up sheet in the kitchen. (Each night the items would be returned to their owners before they were loaned again.) Second, Fred would spend half an hour each week talking about the things he said to himself when someone borrowed his belongings. He would focus on his thoughts when belongings were legitimately borrowed from the loan bank. One week he would talk to Annette about his thoughts and also write down some thoughts, and the second week he would go over his thoughts in his individual meeting with Mr. Sharp. Fred also agreed to put increasingly more favored items in the loan bank.

The intervention was a mixed success. The barb technique was most successful. Fred found rehearsal of handling barbs funny at times and tedious at others. On occasion he appeared to have the rehearsals so under control that it was not clear that they were arousing enough anger to test his anger-management ability. He showed less anger in other house situations, however, and attributed that to his practice with barbs. The transition from using barbs with Mrs. Sharp and Annette to using them with Mr. Sharp and with other staff went more smoothly than expected because Fred expected commands and rules from the staff. Having peers use barbs went less well, as Fred was not able to accept taunts from peers that he had handled easily with adults. Moreover, some residents were unable to use the barbs carefully. To ease the transition, the entire house played "please pass the peas" at dinner each night. During this game, each youth and staff member read a humorous but insulting card (prepared by the house staff) to another diner; the insulted individual was required to look the insulter in the eye and simply say, "Please pass the peas." The cards were rotated each night.

The cognitive assessment of self-statements about loaning possessions was minimally effective since Fred had basically stated everything he said to himself by the end of the first session with Annette. He tended to perseverate on "they're jerks and they'll ruin it," or "I've only got one, what if they lose it,'' or ''they'll lose it just to get me mad.'' Gradually, during his meetings with Mr. Sharp, Fred began to employ such self-management statements as ''I can do without it for a while.'' Fred never did like loaning his belongings but began to accept the requirement and responsibility of sharing with others.

The loan bank required some modifications before it worked smoothly—for example, the point losses for taking something that was not in the bank or damaging a loan item had to be increased—but it became a house project and took some of the focus off Fred. After reassurance from house staff that Fred's behavior was increasingly under control, his aunt and uncle agreed to have him and his sister visit for a weekend upon Fred's garnering of 200 points. By nine months after treatment, Fred was still in school, and he and Annette were starting regular weekend visits in preparation for living with their aunt and uncle.

The Role of Social Support

Living with and helping aggressive children are exhausting and perilous. With younger children, the contagion of aggression can teach caregivers and child helpers to become vindictive and assaultive. With youth, the additional risk is that the child's aggression will be turned toward the adult during the adult's efforts to confront or control the youth's behavior. The threats—spoken and unspoken—of living with aggressive children hang like a shadow over caregivers and peers. The arrangement of social support is key to changing aggressive behavior. Whether the support comes from a self-help group such as Toughlove (York and York, 1980), which helps parents of adolescents set limits and stick to them, or from a derivative of the Foster Extended Family (Barsh, Moore, and Hamerlynck, 1983), which provides respite for foster parents of handicapped children, or from finally engaging a father in caregiving and behavior changing, a support network must be in place. Child helpers are a part of that network. Parent training in groups can also provide support (Barth, Blythe, Schinke, and Schilling, 1983). Involving caregivers in identifying their social-support resources and in diminishing the disruptiveness of other demands while they struggle to change their own behaviors and the behaviors of their children is well worth the effort.

{\u00a0}

School
Attendance Problems

School nonattendance is a lingering, widespread problem that is disadvantageous to children, families, schools, and communities. Nonattendance during adolescence is popularly and statistically associated with poor achievement (Kooker, 1976), being held back from promotion (Birman and Natriello, 1978), dropping out of school (Yudin, Ring, Nowakiwska, and Heinemann, 1973), and breaking the law (Morris, 1979). The long-term effects of early nonattendance on later attendance are less commonly known. Epidemiological findings show that nonattendance in grades one through seven is predictive of high nonattendance in later years (Berganza and Anders, 1978). Students with many absences in the early years have accelerating rates of absences over time, and students with good attendance records at the start of their school careers typically have even better attendance over time. By sixth grade, absence rates are sturdy predictors of high school dropout (Lloyd, 1976). Retrospective data suggests that early nonattenders may learn avoidance strategies that persist into adulthood and find expression as adult anxiety, agoraphobia, and breakdowns in social-role participation (Berg, Marks, McGuire, and Lipsedge, 1974; Kandel, Raveis, and Kandel, 1984; Tyrer and Tyrer, 1974).

Children's nonattendance may also impair family life. For many parents nonattendance means extra costs from lost work time or child-care expenses. Battling with children refusing to attend school is also highly stressful. Abusing parents indicate that getting their child to go to school is difficult and a precipitant to aggravation and aggression (Coltoff and Luks, 1978). In such cases, overlooking nonattendance may be negatively reinforcing for parents as it takes away the stress and feelings of failure from unskilled and fruitless attempts to enforce attendance. Still, many parents use every way they know to encourage their nonattending child to go to school.

The costs of nonattendance to schools far overshadow the gains of not having extra and often difficult children to teach. Although disregarding the nonattendance of some more difficult students may ease a teacher's burden, nonattendance is a bane to schools. Teachers report greater dissatisfaction with classes with high absentee rates, in part because of class disruptions from helping sporadic attenders catch up and keep up. More dramatic disruption of school activities may also arise from vandals, who are usually frequent nonattenders. Low average daily attendance rates disrupt school budgets too, since attendance rates usually determine state aid; for example, every percent of increase in attendance increased revenues to the Houston schools by more than $1 million per year (Peirce, 1983). The loss of revenues may even result in fewer teaching jobs. Finally, and perhaps most basic, school and social service personnel and most parents believe in the importance of attending school and the norms learned at school; nonattendance violates these norms and the benefits of adhering to them.

Nonattendance rates vary dramatically by school and district. Weather and illness account for a 6 to 7 percent rate, depending on a school's location and the age of the children enrolled. Yet a California state project to improve attendance found initial nonattendance rates ranging up to 96 percent (Berry, 1983). Nationally, as many as two million students are out of school each day. For some groups—for example, migrant children and teenage mothers—attendance figures are very poor. School dropout rates for Hispanic youth, which usually correlate with increasing periods of nonattendance, exceeded 50 percent in some areas of the United States in 1979 (Cisneros, 1979). For Native Americans, dropout rates range from 40 to 90 percent (Steinberg, Blinde, and Chan, 1984).

Who Are the Nonattenders?

Nonattenders are a varied lot. Ricardo is five years old and does not want to attend kindergarten anymore. Three weeks was long enough, and now he cries and fights every morning until his mother gives up, runs for the vanpool, and leaves Ricardo home in his grandmother's care. Judy is a sixteen-year-old and has a learning disability. She rarely attends school for a whole day or on Monday or Friday. Instead, she prefers to drink with her boyfriend or frequent the shopping malls with friends. On the surface, Ricardo and Judy share only their preference for not attending school. According to classic distinctions between *school phobia* and *truancy*, Ricardo is phobic and Judy is truant. Yet, the distinction is more apparent than real. Not surprisingly, emotional, cognitive, and social factors contribute to both school phobia and truancy (Croghan, 1981; Grala and McCauley, 1976; Lazarus, Davison, and Polefka, 1965). Ricardo is anxious about separation from his grandmother and about school achievement but also is excessively critical of his own performance and does not understand social expectations. Judy surely enjoys the pleasures of nonattendance but (as will be shown in more detail) gets few rewards from attending class and lacks self-management strategies for dealing with the many frustrations of school.

School nonattendance is a useful umbrella term for these overlapping behaviors and is apt for the majority of students who have a mixture of phobic and truant characteristics. Here, *school phobic* will be reserved for younger children, whose nonattendance appears to be controlled primarily by anxiety and through avoidance strategies. Estimates of the incidence of such phobias range from 3 per 1,000 elementary school children (Leton, 1962) to 17 per 1,000 (Kennedy, 1965). Factors associated with school phobia are:

1. Rapid onset of nonattendance following a school or family transition.
2. Child is a good, perhaps overanxious, student.
3. Child finds school and community more punishing than staying home.

4. Family is aware of nonattendance.
5. Nonattendance is continuous.
6. Child is unassertive and afraid to separate from parent or home.
7. Child is younger.
8. Child is anxious, upset, even nauseous when faced with attending school.

Truant more correctly describes youth who refuse to attend school primarily because extramural social rewards are greater than those available at school. The size of this truant subgroup of nonattenders is difficult to estimate, but these youth likely are the bulk of older nonattenders (Ruby and Law, 1982). Factors associated with truancy are:

1. Gradual development of nonattendance after history of absences.
2. Child is poor and uninterested student.
3. Child finds community more rewarding than school or home.
4. Family is unaware of truancy.
5. Nonattendance is sporadic.
6. Child is independent.
7. Child is older.
8. Child is apathetic and unperturbed when faced with attending school.

Of course, none of these three labels cover the child who remains out of school because of his roles in the family economy, including babysitter, crop picker, storekeeper, and primary bread winner, nor do these categories include the more than 250,000 nonattenders kept from school because of expenses, discrimination, or suspension or expulsion (Children's Defense Fund, 1974).

Judy Jarlow: Background of a Case Study

Judy became known to Mr. Holzberg, a pupil personnel services counselor, from an individual educational plan (IEP) meeting following her entry into junior high. Because of a longstanding learning disability and discontinuous schooling during a series of foster-care placements, Judy was three years behind her expected grade level. She had one hour of specialized reading instruction daily and monthly meetings with Mr. Holzberg to discuss her adjustment to the school. She lived with her new foster parents and their daughter Kate, a recent high school graduate. Judy met with her guidance counselor, Mr. Holzberg, as scheduled during the first three months of school and told him that everything was going fine. He suspected at the third meeting, however, that she had been drinking and came to his office from outside school rather than from a class. He told Judy his conclusions, and she denied them. After the meeting, he checked on Judy's attendance for the prior two months and noted a pattern of Monday absences and then, increasingly, Monday and Wednesday or Monday and Friday absences. Mr. Holzberg decided to take action and call Judy for a special meeting to find out more about the contributors to her nonattendance.

Contributors to Nonattendance

Nonattendance arises from a set of social, cognitive, and physical characteristics. These precursors of nonattendance often gain gradual expression. Older children may show progressive development of nonattendance by first missing a least-favored class or perhaps cutting school on the days that the physical education class meets. Some older children also have physical reactions, such as sleeping or eating disturbances. Younger children may begin having trouble going to bed or getting up because both are associated with school attendance. Physical reactions like enuresis or nightmares may increase or reemerge. In summary, school refusal seems sudden only when a long trail of social, cognitive, and physical indicators has been obscured or overlooked.

Social Contributors

Children and youth partially base their decisions about attendance on their appraisal of the pleasures and penalties of passing time in or out of school.

Home. Staying home can be very entertaining, and children may find more familiar social and material rewards at home than at school. Most younger children expect parent and teacher disapprobation of their efforts to stay home. Anticipation of such penalties may encourage attendance or, like most penalties, foster use of such escape tactics as leaving for school but then cutting some or all classes and forging an absence note. Schools are slowly developing programs to reduce the success of such escape strategies, including no-excuse policies (Malbon and Nuttall, 1982; McCulloch, 1974) and computerized attendance systems that identify children who cut classes so their parents can be notified.

School. Many children and youth find school unrewarding. Children commonly attempt to stay home because of particularly discomforting events like gym class, chorus, and tests or the occurrence of episodes of violence or ridicule. Fears about school are nurtured by time spent away from school. Phobic episodes are greatest after a vacation, illness, or weekend (Gordon and Young, 1976; McDonald and Shepperd, 1976). They also increase at times of change in the social and academic structure of the school, particularly during transitions to elementary and junior high school. The rewards and punishments a child expects to receive from the academic and social activities of school may explain more about nonattendance than the satisfactions of home or community. Alternative schools, student-centered instruction, and innovative course offerings are based on the notion that increasing the rewards of the school day increases students' motivation to attend school (Brokinsky, 1980). Basic education, whatever its virtues, is unlikely to provide young people prone to school refusal with attractive alternatives.

Schools can provide rewarding experiences in other ways. Mayer, Butterworth, Nafpaktitis, and Sulzer-Azaroff (1983) increased school attendance in grades seven through twelve in eight public schools by training teachers to more often use constructive discipline techniques and provide attention, praise, and privileges for desired student performance. In an equally ambitious and successful project, Felner, Ginter, and Primavera (1982) restructured students' classes by assigning all students in each homeroom to the same sections of required classes to provide a consistent and rewarding peer and teacher support group. Project students reported more positive school relationships and showed significant attendance, grade point average, and self-esteem increases when compared to a control group. The Houston Independent School District distributed a total of $250,000 in Astroworld amusement park tickets to children with perfect attendance records and straight A's and to students in the class in each school with the best yearly attendance record. The increases in attendance also earned the district $4.5 million in state revenues (Peirce, 1983). A well-controlled study of characteristics of a wide range of schools suggests some of the educationally rewarding experiences offered by schools with high attendance: frequent homework, high expectations for student achievement (regardless of children's abilities), children's work displayed on classroom walls, a school curriculum planned by grade rather than by classroom, more total teaching time, and fewer auxiliary activities (Rutter, Maugham, Mortimore, and Ouston, 1979). The age of the school buildings, size of the school, staff size, and class size had no direct effect on attendance. Clearly, increasing the rewards for school attendance is possible and more affirming than increasing the costs of nonattendance.

Community. Expected pleasures or penalties from "hanging out" in the community also influence attendance. Pleasure may be obtained from the friendships of other nonattenders, the challenge of not getting caught for cutting school or for petty crimes committed while in the community, legal and illegal money-making opportunities, and the privacy of adult-free settings. School rewards must compete with these community rewards.

Countering these incentives for staying in the community rather than the school are the penalties for nonattendance. Although truancy has been legally decriminalized along with other status offenses in most states, truants may nonetheless be liable to arrest and incarceration (Mulvey and Hicks, 1982), and in any case, other law violations committed while out of school may result in police action. In addition, school suspension and expulsion may follow chronic nonattendance. At a more personal level, students cut off from friends and school activities may feel isolated, and few students are free of anxiety about the long-term effects of abridged educations. Some districts have begun prosecuting parents for their children's nonattendance (Hanson and Hoeft, n.d.). The effectiveness of this policy in improving attendance is attributed to inceased pressure on children by parents. Although just how this pressure is exerted is not known; threats, loss of privileges, and assaults may be part of parents' efforts to promote attendance.

Perceptions of the rewards and punishments of the home, school, and community contribute to school nonattendance and characterize different types of attenders, as shown in Table 8. Previously considered distinctions between school phobics and school truants can be further clarified by considering the pattern of rewards and punishments that they experience. Whereas these labels are somewhat roughly hewn, they can guide an initial assessment and interventive efforts. School phobics tend to find home rewarding and school and community punishing. Phobic refusers are children whose experience of school is so unpleasant that they remain home even though home is not especially rewarding. A child who eagerly attends school will find school rewarding, have less of an attraction to staying home, and not enjoy spending time in the community during school hours because of the loss of access to school and concern about penalties for nonattendance. An uninterested attender is a child who has little attachment to school but finds no other more attractive alternative. Such children are at risk of becoming nonattenders should home or the community become more attractive (perhaps when mother goes back to work and leaves the home vacant or when they reach driving age and can find other community activities). A truant refuser is a child who often cuts school because the experience is very negative, even though the rewards of other activities are minimal. A classic truant, as previously discussed, is one who finds the adventures of the community to be most rewarding and the experience of school most penalizing.

Cognitive Contributors

Children's beliefs about school and self partially account for their nonattendance. As discussed in Chapter Two, these

Table 8. Social Contributors to School Nonattendance.

Type of Attender	Staying at Home	Going to School	Hanging Out in Community
Classic School Phobic	Rewarding	Punishing	Punishing
Phobic Refuser	Neutral	Punishing	Punishing
Eager Attender	Neutral	Rewarding	Punishing
Uninterested Attender	Punishing	Neutral	Punishing
Truant Refuser	Neutral	Punishing	Neutral
Classic Truant	Punishing	Punishing	Rewarding

beliefs contribute to the appraisal of social rewards and punishments. Beliefs about (1) the value of the rewards, (2) the availability of the rewards, (3) the criteria for the rewards, and (4) the likelihood of meeting the criteria for the rewards all affect the child's decision to attend school.

The Reward's Value. Rewards are personal. One student's mohair sweater is another student's hairshirt. Pleasing authority figures by high attendance may have less reward value for some than the pleasures of making one's own decisions and exercising one's own liberties (Brehm, 1966). The often-touted association of school attendance, graduation, and employment is not tangible to most youth and may have little effect on the reward value of attendance. When dropouts do have a clear sense of what their educational curricula will be, they are more likely to return to school (Borus and Carpenter, 1983). Youth's inability to personalize the concepts of "graduation" and "employment" robs these long-term outcomes of their reward value. Studies of development (for example, see Keating, 1980) and practices (Gilchrist, Schinke, and Blythe, 1979) suggest that immediate rewards have more value for youth than long-term rewards. Also predictive of reward value are youths' cognitive appraisals of the value of a reward to others of high status and of the cost of the effort needed to obtain the reward.

Assessment can help identify beliefs that work against attendance for each child. Direct queries like, "Do you wonder what use it is to go to school?'' may be useful. Less direct approaches, such as asking children about their three wishes, their notion of their future, and the education of other family members, may also yield assessment information. In the face of youths' predictable lack of cooperation, however, the child helper will have to make some assumptions about needed cognitive competencies.

Availability of Reward. No matter how valuable it is, the reward that appears to be unobtainable does not inspire effort. Indeed, cognitive consistency theory (for example, see Feldman, 1966) argues that an unobtainable outcome eventually becomes an undesired outcome—"I didn't want it anyway," the person will say. Students with siblings or friends as models of school failure may assume that steady attendance, achievement, and school completion are unobtainable. Students with low achievement may perceive improvement to be beyond their reach. Students who conclude that life's benefits are distributed capriciously or, worse, by dictates of malevolent and unfair forces do not easily grasp the idea that changes in their actions can lead to changes in outcome.

Criteria for Reward. Some students may value the rewards of school attendance or success and assess those rewards as generally available for deserving students but not believe that they themselves are deserving. These students may not correctly identify the criteria for success. School-phobic children, for example, may set their standards for success so high that a minor mistake is very humiliating and crushes thoughts of school attendance. Such overanxious children are likely to have strict criteria for self-praise (if they praise themselves at all) and to assume that their parents, peers, and teachers are equally critical. These children may fail to monitor their successes and to use self-talk that focuses on paths to improvement rather than on past mistakes (see, for instance, Marlatt and Gordon, 1980; Kendall, 1981).

Likelihood of Meeting the External Criteria. Perhaps most frustrating to child helpers are students who possess the skills needed to obtain the rewards of school success but not the belief in their own efficacy needed to ensure goal-oriented activity. These students may see themselves as incapable of reaching the goal. The failure to develop a positive image of themselves may deprive students of the motivation needed to sustain attendance in the face of anxieties or the appraisal of home or community as a safe and fail-proof setting.

As suggested by Bandura's (1977) work, teaching these students the academic and social skills needed to succeed in the school setting may not, in and of itself, increase students' assessment of themselves as competent and able students. Without the "cognitive click" (Mahoney, 1980), when the child recognizes his or her own improved performance, such students may continue to feel discomfort in school, a forerunner of school refusal. A sense of one's own efficacy helps spur persistent and high-quality school performance (Schunk, 1983). Changes in school attendance, especially for youth with school-phobic tendencies, may accompany changes in mind-set and in appraisals of the value of, accessibility of, and criteria for obtaining the rewards of school.

Physical Contributors

School phobia is frequently expressed as a physical malady. As such, the school nurse or family physician is often the first professional with an opportunity for assessment. Anxiety about school may generate complaints about stomachaches and headaches, skeletal pain, fever, and "just not feeling good." These physical complaints plus fatigue from sleep-disrupting nighttime worrying, wheezing, trembling, pallor, hyperventilation, coughing, tics, and especially vomiting may follow the onset of phobic reactions. The *school-phobic triad* involves (1) vague physical symptoms, (2) no physical or laboratory evidence of illness, and (3) school nonattendance (Schmitt, 1971).

Physical problems may also contribute to difficulties in school that set up school refusal. Uncorrected visual problems—near-sightedness as well as eye-hand coordination—may frustrate learning attempts. Alternately, some students respond to such correctives as glasses or eye patches with despair. Bladder and bowel control problems may cause fear of humiliation for younger students. Seizure disorders or disfiguring physical handicaps may have similar outcomes.

Assessment

Assessment should provide an understanding of social, cognitive, and physical contributors to nonattendance. Even though initial efforts to return a child to school may be more similar than different regardless of the cause of nonattendance, a functional analysis of the nonattendance can give guidance to child helpers' continued efforts to support children's school-adjustment efforts. Distinguishing between children primarily motivated by negative reactions to school attendance and those primarily motivated by positive incentives in the home or community may provide crucial assistance to child helpers. Even more than with other cognitive and social interventions, however, child helpers may have to act without a frim grasp of all the contributors to a child's nonattendance. Nevertheless, data accumulated from interactions resulting from efforts to return a child to full school attendance can help guide the child helper.

Ecologically sound assessments generally begin by identifying the perspectives of the child, teacher, family, and, when physical symptoms exist, health care providers. Assessment of older nonattenders like Judy typically involve a brief interview with the referrer and a longer interview with the youth.

With school-phobic children younger than ten years old, the interview that follows the referral may or may not include the child, since the mission of the assessment is to identify family and school contributors to nonattendance. Medical problems must be ruled out. Given a clear case of school phobia, assessment will focus on impediments to the child's rapid return to school and on locating and encouraging caregivers who can most staunchly support the return to school. Following time-honored procedures (see Kennedy, 1965; Lassers, Nordan, and Bladholm, 1973), discussion with the phobic child about reasons for not going to school should be minimized. Rapid return is the primary goal; analysis of possible contributors follows only if school adjustment is incomplete. The lure of delaying return until assessment is complete is attractive but dangerous—phobic children only become more anxious if allowed to remain at home.

The assessment of older school refusers must be more comprehensive and address the full range of physical, cognitive, and social contributors. Interviewing the youth is often helpful—particularly to pique the youth's interest in increased attendance and to identify supportive others who might assist the change process. For the truly phobic adolescent, a not-so-common individual, the assessment should identify images or events associated with the onset of anxiety. This review of images and events can profitably begin with the earliest-remembered anxiety attack, as shown by Croghan's (1981) amelioration of a high school senior's phobia that began after a humiliating experience in sixth grade. Because many older school refusers have anxiety about school, the interviewer can ascertain the events of the day and ask youths to assess their comfort level during each event.

Judy Jarlow: Assessment

After Judy missed Mr. Holzberg's scheduled meeting, he saw her leaving the cafeteria and suggested that they meet then. In his office, he rescheduled a meeting that he had on his calendar for the following hour to provide time for a thorough assessment. His goal was to identify social, cognitive, and physical contributors to Judy's increasing nonattendance. Judy's goal was, essentially, to maintain her current belief and action patterns—seemingly the path of least resistance.

Mr. Holzberg began the assessment interview by briefly discussing his concerns about Judy's absences based on the school's record. He asked whether Judy shared his concerns about her change in attendance. She affirmed that her nonattendance was a problem but said that she was "getting it straight." (Mr. Holzberg didn't expect wholehearted recognition of the problem but acknowledged that they shared the concern.) He surprised and amused her by arguing, however, that nonattendance had its advantages, too. Together they listed the benefits of staying out of school. She brought the discussion around to the costs of nonattendance, and they generated a range of problems that nonattendance presented for Judy, dividing them according to their short- and long-term costs.

Among the problems with short-term costs, Judy identified problems with her math teacher and math grade and with her foster mother after her foster mother was called by the attendance office. Judy also expressed her wish to see her birth mother, who lived out of town. Mr. Holzberg agreed to work on these problems with Judy in exchange for renewed efforts at regular attendance and sobriety at school.

Referring back to the list of costs and benefits, Mr. Holzberg identified key social contributors to nonattendance and prompted further discussion of Judy's social network. He learned about her relationship with her boyfriend Jake, her admiration for her foster sister, her still-fragile relationship with her foster parents, and her relationships with her homeroom and math teachers and with two girls she knew from Ala-teen (the adolescent version of Al-anon, which she attended when living with her birth mother). In the little time remaining, he inquired about any problems Judy had with fatigue or illness and about her definition of success in school and her expectancies for reversing her slide into nonattendance. She offered to try not to miss any Monday classes or math classes until they could meet again in two weeks to agree on a plan for action.

Treatments

Child helpers confront a seeming paradox in work with nonattenders, especially nonattenders with more phobic characteristics, in that some research and theory supports exposure to the feared situation as the best approach to reducing phobias (for example, see Bandura, 1977; Kennedy, 1965), and some suggests that exposure to punishing environments increases avoidance of those environments (for example, see Parke, 1975). The former findings argue that rapidly returning the child to school demonstrates that school is less punishing than anticipated, and the latter suggest that the return should follow environmental or cognitive changes that reduce the punishing characteristics of school attendance.

The paradox can be partly resolved by employing treatments in which the child is rapidly returned to school, punishing qualities of the environment are assessed and then reduced, and the child's opportunities for continued avoidance are limited. With the young phobic child, for example, fears are often larger than life and are most humanely and successfully dispelled by rapid return to school. The classroom environment should be checked to ensure the absence of serious risks to the child and then quickly programmed for the child's return (for example, by forewarning the teacher of such expected protest behavior as crying or vomiting and by sending along a change of clothes). Adjustments to improve the child-school fit may follow later (Hsia, 1984). Success rates with younger children treated in this way are high (Kennedy, 1965). The older truant, on the other hand, often will return to school only after marked changes in the environment of the school, the consequences of attendance, or cognitive appraisals of school. These young people may need a fresh start and a carefully restructured educational reentry program. Restructuring may initially require tutoring, a shortened school day, supportive liaison work with sometimes hostile teachers, or a special classroom placement (Cretekos, 1977). Young people whose attendance is already sporadic and who have well-developed sources of home or community reinforcement require the most system intervention and have the least chance of returning to school full time. As described earlier, many children have features of both phobics and truants and require a full array of interventions. The following discussion provides alternative interventions for the child helper.

Social Treatments

Social interventions can involve family members, caretakers, peers, and school personnel and can facilitate young people's efforts to return to steady attendance.

Working with the Family. The return to school of the young phobic requires the support of adult family members and school personnel. When involving the child in the meeting will not create undue stress, this should be done. The conference should review such contributors to nonattendance as parental concerns about the child's welfare and means for coping with the anxiety and guilt arising from the child's protest behavior. Even if they are exaggerated, sound reasons for school avoidance from the child's perspective—like family crises, upcoming performances, recent school failure, or threatened violence—should be reviewed. This review should not, however, impede rapid return. The conference should conclude with a plan for the child's return (forceably, if necessary) to school the very next day and several contingency plans to bolster parents' sense of power—or, as Hsia writes, "to motivate them to stage a showdown" (1984, p. 364). The conference should also plan to ensure that school staff do not inadvertently undo the plan by sending the child home. Although return should be rapid, child helpers can coach family members in elements of a graduated return, such as talking to the child about returning to school the next day while the child is relaxed and doing something enjoyable. Although such a discussion may raise a child's anxiety and prompt some counteractions, it will at least provide the child and parent with the opportunity to cognitively rehearse the events of the next day.

At times the school or parent will stand firm against returning a child until he or she is willing to go. In such cases, child helpers can call on other strategies. In one strategy for aiding school-phobic children, the child helper or the child's parent or sibling gradually exposes the child to the school via after-school visits to the school, talks with staff, attendance of only favorite classes, home visits by classmates or teachers, and having homework brought to the home. Even though such gradual approaches often work, the child who is more quickly returned to school and well rewarded for efforts toward active classroom participation more rapidly gives up gross somatic and verbal protests.

The return to school should not, however, mark the end to the intervention. Since school-refusing children are generally vulnerable to school stresses, follow-up should be used to check for persisting contributors to nonattendance, such as fear of failure, poor social skills, family crises, and mismatch between teacher expectations and a child's real or perceived capabilities. Some children may need more extensive treatment, which should include the parent and be guided by the rapidly growing literature on treating children's fears and anxieties. Coolidge, Willer, Tessman, and Waldfoger (1960), among others, conclude that school-refusing, and especially school-phobic, children may have difficulty making friendships and playing comfortably with peers. These children may benefit from friendship groups and social-skills training (Cartledge and Milburn, 1980).

Children with sporadic attendance may require less intensive interventions. Providing parents with information that the school is concerned about their child's nonattendance or simply that their child was not at school that day can promote attendance. For children and youth missing whole days or partial days of school without their parents' knowledge, note systems can provide families with daily reports of their children's attendance (Barth, 1980). Such notes have been regularly employed by group homes with predelinquent and delinquent youth (see, for example, Thoresen and others, 1979), and they can also be used by families (Blechman, Taylor, and Schrader, 1981) and even whole classrooms (Lahey and others, 1977). The "best" way to operate such systems is not yet known (Barth, 1979), but it is known that a range of procedures with various types of family involvement and incentives have been successful. Essentially, home-school systems involve providing families with knowledge of their child's school attendance or performance. Families, which typically control more incentives than schools, can use this information to encourage school attendance. Variations of home-school communication procedures, beginning with the least intrusive procedures and moving to the most intrusive, are listed in Table 9.

School notes for informing families can range from simple assessments each day of school performances of concern to class-by-class accounts of attendance, using a form such as the one shown in Exhibit 8. A few guidelines apply to all note systems.

Table 9. Variations of the Home-School Communication System.

Family Involvement	Reward
Family is sent brief letter home via school note system.	Family praises child upon bringing home signed note from school.
Family receives phone call from school or child helper describing family's role.	Family provides something special when child brings home signed note from school.
Family attends school conference to go over reward system.	Family provides specified daily privileges contingent on school attendance.
Family and child participate in ongoing family contracting game.	Family provides specified privileges and response costs contingent on school attendance.
Family implements full program, including troubleshooting by contacting school personnel when the system breaks down.	Family institutes and then phases out point system and token economy for school attendance.

First, notes should carry only the information the families need. If the family has agreed to provide only praise or privileges, then the notes need go home only on days of satisfactory performance. For token-economy-point systems with both privileges and response costs, notes must be completed and sent home every day. If no note or an incomplete note comes home, the parents are told to assume the worst and require the full response cost.

Second, the notes should be tamper proof. Guidelines for the notes and the notes themselves should be as simple as possible, and ink should be used by attendance staff and teachers. For older children, the temptation to fill in the blanks to signify attendance or to forge marks indicating attendance will be lessened if teachers initial their marks and add a handwritten note to the card if they suspect tampering. Third, implementation should become the child's and family's responsibility. Completing school notes takes only a moment of a teacher's time, but it is still an added effort on behalf of a child with apparent disregard for school. The teacher's image of the child often improves

Exhibit 8. Sample School Note for a Junior High School Student.

(Student's Name)   (Date)

Class	On Time[a]		Behavior[b]			Work[b]			Teacher
English	0	1	1	2	3	1	2	3	_____
Social Studies	0	1	1	2	3	1	2	3	_____
Physical Ed.	0	1	1	2	3	1	2	3	_____
Science	0	1	1	2	3	1	2	3	_____
Lunch	0	1	1	2	3	1	2	3	_____
Art	0	1	1	2	3	1	2	3	_____
Spanish	0	1	1	2	3	1	2	3	_____
Mathematics	0	1	1	2	3	1	2	3	_____

[a] 0 indicates not on time, 1 indicates on time.

[b] 1 indicates poor performance, 2 indicates adequate performance, 3 indicates excellent performance. Bonuses and notes to parents may be written on back.

when the child or youth assumes responsibility for getting the teacher's signature each day. The child is then doubly rewarded for a successful day. Incentives delivered at home should aid the child's efforts to obtain the teacher's signature. Daily notes can also carry messages about homework assignments, work completion, or in-class behavior. Teachers may find notes a valuable way to reach parents. These guidelines and a careful reading of Atkeson and Forehand (1979), Barth (1979, 1980), and Schumaker, Hovell, and Sherman (1977) will help child helpers quickly use this method to aid school refusers.

Some high schools inform families of their child's daily attendance by recording coded information on a telephone answering machine. This strategy has fostered increased attendance (Bittle, 1977). Using a more selective but time-consuming approach, Parker and McCoy (1977) called the parents of frequently absent elementary school children to praise them for taking responsibility when their children attended school. This method improved the children's attendance significantly, even more than did the principal's praise of the children at school.

Increasing direct contact with families of nonattending children can also promote change. One school district had a litany of problems that are familiar to most schools with low attendance rates, including absences accumulating without home contact, identified nonattenders receiving no follow-up counseling, parents not informed of their children's excessive absences, and few curriculum or program adjustments to encourage better attendance (Bauer and others, 1977). An attendance promotion program was developed involving (1) a phone call home after three days of nonattendance, (2) a letter home notifying parents that the child was out of school for five days and asking if the school could be of help to the family, (3) a letter requesting a conference after the child missed ten days of school, and (4) a subsequent home visit. Elementary school students in all cases returned by step 2, while older youth often required more intervention. The program developers recommend the omission of the ten-day letter and an earlier home visit. This visit might provide the opportunity for instituting a home-school communication system or recommending additional reentry adjustments.

Child helpers can also help reduce nonattendance by helping families reduce the disruptions that preempt attendance. "Family business" was ranked as the fourth leading cause of nonmedical absences by one sample of teachers, parents, and educators (Robinson, 1979). Knowledge of helping networks and family day-care providers can minimize families' reliance on children to care for sick siblings. Assistance in obtaining financial, social, and mental health services may also provide families in need with those extra resources that can help keep a child in school.

Working with the Schools. Child helpers willing and able to conduct inservice training and consulting with school personnel can inform them of several promising approaches to reducing nonattendance. In one school-wide program involving ten classrooms and 212 children, Barber and Kagey (1977) increased attendance in grades one through three. Children were permitted to attend part or all of a school-wide party and gained access to "fun rooms" depending on the number of days they came to school. To record daily attendance, students designated as

Attendance-Star Stickers placed a star next to each attending child's name each day. Monthly attendance increased to 275 days during the first four months of the program compared to 180 days during the same period the previous year. In comparison to other schools in the district, the experimental school's attendance ranking changed from next to last to first; this resulted in an increase of $2,000 in state allotments.

Peer influences and activities can also help reduce nonattendance in school-wide programs. Morgan (1975) used the *triangle method* to help ninety-two excessively absent (more than five days a month) Latino elementary school children improve attendance. First, each frequently absent child was teamed up with two regularly attending neighborhood friends. When all three children attended school on any given day, the group earned points toward early recess. Attendance on days the problem child typically missed earned bonus points. Encouraged by the praise and persuasion of peers, absentees' school attendance improved. The success of this method compared favorably with that of teacher praise of the frequently absent child. The triangle method's apparent advantage is its promotion of social interaction and improvement of the social position of low-status, nonattending children. It also stresses the value of attendance to those who already attend.

Cross-age tutoring may improve the attendance of some otherwise infrequent attenders (Maher and Barbrack, 1982). Socially maladjusted and infrequently attending inner-city students paired as cross-aged tutors with younger, educably mentally retarded children showed significant improvement in attendance during and after the tutoring program. This improvement sharply contrasts with the results of peer tutoring and participation in group counseling; when these strategies were used, attendance declined. The author's experience using older elementary school special education students as cross-age tutors suggests the feasibility of this approach for elementary school children as well. A thorough orientation to cross-age tutoring and well-defined and structured tutoring activities—reading or math flash cards and speed tests, for example—should enhance such projects' success.

Child helpers can also consult with teachers on classroom and policy issues and may influence attendance. Efforts to encourage the school and teacher characteristics associated with good attendance may help. Encouraging more teacher interest in attendance and supervising teacher efforts to bring one well-liked but nonattending child back to the fold will facilitate future efforts. Supporting activities that attract parents to school may also have positive side effects on attendance.

Any discussion of school-wide activities to promote attendance would be incomplete without mention of the importance of providing students and their families with maximum opportunity for involvement in a spectrum of school decisions and activities. Schools should be available for evening and weekend use by the community; schools should cooperate with community agencies; school advisory councils should include members of various ages, social status, and races; students should be involved in developing codes of conduct; and businesses should contribute to attendance-incentive programs (Steele, 1978). School-wide programs can become community-wide programs. Child helpers need not be school district employees to develop attendance programs—many of the programs just described were operated by outside professionals.

Working with the Community. The community is the source of many rewards and, as such, a potential competitor with the school. Even though out-of-school activities often occur in adult-free spaces, child helpers can exert some control over community rewards. These efforts may, in conjunction with family and school efforts, boost attendance. For example, nonattenders often spend the day in shopping malls, pool or video halls, parks, and restaurants. Outreach to operators and attendants may lead to policies that discourage youths from patronizing these settings during school hours. Video arcades, concerned about their public image, have been quick to limit daytime use by students. Fast-food restaurants have even provided coupons to schools for distribution to youth with improved attendance records ("High Schools Under Fire," 1977). One pool hall manager, after discussion with a youth worker, denied a frequent player access to the hall at any time unless the youth presented a completed school note (Tharp and Wetzel, 1969). The author persuaded another pool hall manager who did not want to limit access to the hall to provide a bonus game each time a low-attending youth attended all of his classes. Every full week's attendance earned another youth a free jazz class at the YWCA.

Community members can also help encourage attendance at a broader level. Meetings with community groups, church leaders, Little League coaches, and retailers can inform the community at large of the seriousness of the truancy problem. Community members can be encouraged to speak with youth, call parents when a personal relationship exists, and when needed, follow up with a phone call to the school.

Cognitive Treatment

As outlined earlier, youths' beliefs about the value of school, the availability of school success or pleasure, the level of performance needed to achieve success, and the likelihood of their achieving successful performance influence attendance. Offering youths the opportunity to explore these beliefs in an unstructured interview may provide the impetus for change. Structured skill-building exercises may also stimulate cognitive change. Changing young people's beliefs about themselves and school and the fit between them is often a slow and uncertain process. Successful school experiences may be the most reliable modifiers of beliefs. Those experiences may occur most readily and have their fullest impact on a youth's beliefs with assistance from specific cognitive-change strategies.

Child helpers can foster reestimates of school's value by stimulating students to think of potential and current pleasures. Social-network mapping can encourage thinking about schoolmates who might offer conversation, help with classes, or company during lunch. Projecting network maps for six months in the future given steady attendance and then given leaving school can show the isolation that awaits school dropouts. Many young people forget that school friendships and activities can be a source of fun. Identifying youths' favorite people—movie, television, and music stars; athletes; fashion models; aunts and uncles—

may remind youths that many of them finished high school. Phone calls or letters to some of those people may prompt replies that encourage attendance.

Students may believe that school success will not accrue to them regardless of their effort or skill. Older youth especially often judge themselves to be victims of teachers' arbitrariness or prejudice. These beliefs are often stubborn. Antidotes to such belief systems are not always successful, but some cognitive strategies have promise.

Since teachers differ, a teacher-by-teacher analysis may help students clarify which teachers they believe ''have it in for them'' and why, and which teachers they think of as fair. This procedure suggests to the student teachers with whom effort and skill will pay off, and teachers with whom extra attention may be required. The child helper can encourage students to identify students similar to themselves—that is, those of the same race, with similarly cut hair, or with a history of trouble—who are achieving success. This may help make success seem more possible and advance a discussion of the coping strategies that others use to manage in a sometimes hostile environment. Cognitive rehearsal of successful interactions in such environments may also forward reentry into the classroom.

Phobic children may be particularly prone to hold unrealistic standards and to assume equally harsh judgment from peers and teachers (Gordon and Young, 1976; Kelly, 1973). Skills for monitoring success and for self-reinforcement (components of self-management, as discussed in Chapter Five) can help counter these debilitating standards. Covert extinction (see Chapter Five) has been found in one case study to rapidly reduce an adolescent boy's incapacitating anxiety attacks arising, in part, from fear of ridicule by peers and continued school failure (Smith and Sharpe, 1970). The successful cognitive procedure (coupled with an end to daytime television when the child chose to stay home) involved presenting imaginary scenes from school that evoke maximum discomfort. This is the *implosive* variation of covert extinction. In this procedure the scenes represent such ''worst fantasies come true'' as a sadistic principal, impossible-to-answer test items, and taunting peers. On the first day the fantasies caused great anxiety, weeping, and chest pains; by the second day the youth attended his most dreaded class; by day four he was back in school to stay. The risks of such a procedure—principally, that the child's fears will be exacerbated rather than extinguished—suggest that this technique should be used only as a last resort (Graziano, DeGiovanni, and Garcia, 1979).

More gradual exposure to the most anxiety-producing images has frequently been used with phobic youth (Morris and Kratochwill, 1983). Although the procedure, known as *systematic desensitization*, lacks conclusive experimental support, numerous case studies (for example, Lazarus, 1960; Croghan, 1981) and some controlled tests (for example, Van Hasselt and others, 1979) suggest the efficacy of desensitization with school phobia.

The technique is essentially cognitive and involves repeated exposure to fear-inducing scenes related to school. Studies of the desensitization of adults (see Mahoney and Arnkoff, 1978) and youth (Van Hasselt and others, 1979) suggest that relaxation training is not essential to the procedure. Still, relaxation skills may benefit a fearful child. Several descriptions of relaxation training with children are available for the child helper's use (for example, Koeppen, 1974; Ollendick and Cerny, 1981). Relaxed conversation or play prior to the presentation of scenes may also assist the covert extinction process. A sample script for a girl afraid of criticism follows here. The scenes are based on the girl's reports of school and the child helper's hunches about fearful scenes. Each is recast into a positive experience. The first four items provide a positive orientation to the procedure and to school attendance. The last two items provide the opportunity for some overlearning and comic relief.

- You are calm and relaxed as you vividly imagine the school playground at your elementary school. You remember how much you enjoyed playing outside with your friends. This memory leaves you feeling successful and peaceful.
- You are calm and relaxed as you vividly imagine yourself sitting in the sun on the grounds of Roosevelt Junior High. You are talking with Jill and feeling successful and peaceful.
- You are calm and relaxed as you vividly imagine waving

hello to your math teacher on the way to school. You feel successful and peaceful.

- You are calm and relaxed as you vividly imagine yourself talking to Jill in the cafeteria before school. You feel successful and peaceful.
- You are calm and relaxed as you vividly imagine sitting in math class and not getting called on. You feel successful and peaceful.
- You are calm and relaxed as you vividly imagine that your math teacher calls on you and you give the correct answer. You feel successful and peaceful.
- You are calm and relaxed as you vividly imagine that your math teacher calls on you and you give the wrong answer. Your teacher calls on someone else. You remind yourself that you can do better next time. You feel successful and peaceful.
- You are calm and relaxed as you vividly imagine that your math teacher calls you to the board to solve a problem. You give the wrong answer. Your teacher calls on someone else. You remind yourself that you can do better next time. You feel successful and peaceful.
- You are calm and relaxed as you vividly imagine that your math teacher calls you to the board to solve a problem. You give the wrong answer. Your teacher scowls at you and tells you to work harder. You remind yourself that you can do better next time. You feel successful and peaceful.
- You are calm and relaxed as you vividly imagine that your math teacher calls you to the board to solve a problem. You give the wrong answer. Your teacher scowls again and the other kids laugh. You remind yourself that you are the best judge of how much you are learning. You feel successful and peaceful.
- You are calm and relaxed as you vividly imagine that your math teacher calls you to the board to solve a problem. You give the wrong answer. Your teacher scowls again and the other kids laugh. One of them shouts that you are stupid, and then they all jump on their desks and point to you. You

remind yourself that you are the best judge of how much you are learning. You feel successful and peaceful.

- You are calm and relaxed as you vividly imagine that your math teacher calls you to the board to solve a problem. You give the wrong answer. Your teacher scowls again and the other kids laugh. The teacher shouts that your answer is the funniest thing she's ever seen, and the class begins to sing, "It's the funniest thing we've ever seen." You join in the singing. You remind yourself that you are the best judge of how much you are learning. You feel successful and peaceful.

The child helper ends each session with discussion of what might really happen and what kind of self-talk might keep the girl calm and relaxed.

In lieu of slavish reliance on external standards and rewards, children and youth can learn to assess their own performance and reward a job well done. Self-monitoring and rewarding require the specification of desired behavior. For each school-refusing child, these behaviors will be different but will at first include precursors to staying in school rather than any special academic or interpersonal performance. An external reward system can initially provide a focus for such self-praise statements as "I'm doing okay. I'm staying at school. I'll get to stay up late tonight." Later, the monitoring might include in-school performance and shift to a personal standard: "I answered that question right. I'm fitting in okay now."

Covert modeling (Cautela, 1976) is an appealing and useful technique for increasing students' sense that they can meet the criteria for school success. With the child helper providing demonstrations, young people can practice visualizing other people or themselves achieving short- and long-term goals and obtaining their fair rewards; for example: "You see yourself walking home after school. A boy comes up and says something funny. You laugh and think that you made it through a tough day, and you feel successful and hopeful." For children and youth without a vision of a happy outcome to any school-related efforts, such images may offer a welcome alternative.

Physical Treatment

Overwhelming fatigue or anxiety can contribute to school refusal and may respond to physical treatment. Other often-cited illnesses, such as sore throat or fever, can be checked by a physician and then monitored at home. Parents can then be counseled to disregard children's claims about those symptoms, be assured that they will not infect other children, and be told to ignore further questions or complaints about the "illness."

Insomnia is one common complaint of nonattenders (Schmitt, 1971) and may stem from nighttime worries or, after the child has begun to stay home, from daytime sleeping that depletes the need for nighttime sleep. Vigorous exercise, caffeine-free drinks, and a no-naps policy should help lessen this contributor to refusal (Piccione and Barth, 1983). The anxious or depressed child may still feel fatigued but more manageably so.

More severe physical symptoms of anxiety may require direct treatment. Low doses of minor tranquilizers have been used to facilitate the initial return to school (Lazarus, Davison, and Polefka, 1965). Imipramine has also been administered successfully in high doses (Gittelman-Klein and Klein, 1973) but seems ineffective in lower doses that carry less risk of side effects. Any of these drugs should be used only if earlier efforts at returning the child to school are unsuccessful and if cognitive anxiety-reduction techniques fail. Because school phobia is not a medical problem, drug treatments are generally not indicated.

Judy Jarlow: Intervention

Change for Judy began with her tacit agreement to talk about her nonattendance, to identify her social network, and to make an effort to increase her attendance. Still, Mr. Holzberg knew that initial commitments are flimsy. In the two weeks before their next meeting, he called Judy's social worker, Mr. Tsai, to inform him of the new direction of his work with Judy and her interest in seeing her birth mother. Mr. Tsai responded that he was not optimistic; he was not meeting with Judy at all anymore, and his monthly contact with her and her foster parents was by phone. Still, he agreed to meet with Mr. Holzberg and Judy (should her interest endure).

Mr. Holzberg also spoke with Judy's homeroom, social studies, and math teachers to learn more about their relationships with Judy, Judy's performance, and their willingness to act as mediators. All three were frustrated with Judy but willing to pull together packets of missed classwork and to participate in a home-note system, which they had used with some of Mr. Holzberg's other counselees. Mr. Holzberg left a meeting reminder for Judy with her homeroom teacher. Finally, he checked on Judy's attendance during the past two weeks.

Prior to his meeting with Judy, Mr. Holzberg identified his goals: he hoped to review old business, start the home-school note system, identify tasks, and explore social and cognitive threats to change. When Judy arrived, Mr. Holzberg asked her about her attendance. Her report matched the attendance report—no absences on Mondays, two missed math classes, and one Friday absence. He reaffirmed his commitment to helping her with her problems and told her of his contacts with her social studies and math teachers. He asked if anything else important had changed since the last meeting. After some discussion, Judy and Mr. Holzberg agreed to arrange a once-a-week math tutorial with a twelfth grader Judy admired, to hold off for two more weeks setting up a meeting with her birth mother, and to organize a system by which she could earn privileges for better attendance and math grades. Judy agreed to continue monitoring her attendance and to request make-up work from her teachers.

Further discussion explored possible incentives for improved attendance. Mr. Holzberg suggested that Judy's foster-sister Kate might be willing to spend some extra social time with Judy during the weekend following a week of perfect attendance. Judy agreed to ask Kate if she would take her to the mall, go with her for soft ice cream, or wake Judy when she comes home from a date to tell Judy about it. Each reward would be contingent on a week's complete attendance. Judy also agreed to ask Kate (Judy did not want to involve her foster parents) to oversee Judy's response cost of a one-hour-earlier bedtime for any daily classes not checked on her school note. Mr. Holzberg recommended that Judy propose a two-week trial to Kate and that she give Kate his phone number for questions. He agreed to call Judy's foster parents to explain the system and to provide her with a two weeks' supply of notes. Judy agreed to have each teacher sign the note each day.

Last, Mr. Holzberg inquired about ways Judy's resolve to attend each class might break down. Judy said that Jeff gave her rides to school and sometimes suggested they go elsewhere or take a two-period lunch. Judy did not think she could resist the temptation to go with Jeff, but said she hoped Mr. Holzberg would not be mad because Jeff was almost her boyfriend and she wanted to keep him. She decided to tell him on Saturday that she had to get to school every day for these two weeks and try to get him to take her seriously. Mr. Holzberg and Judy role played ways to say this seriously. One plan was to ask Jeff to pick up other friends, too. Judy also mentioned two other ways to get to school and agreed to ask Jeff to be part of the program and to meet with her and Mr. Holzberg in two weeks.

Mr. Holzberg sent Judy out with a list of each of their tasks, a supply of home notes, and much encouragement. Although she was sober today, he regretted not talking to her about her drinking. He made a note to talk about that next time, to set up the tutoring, and to call Judy's foster parents.

Mr. Holzberg met with Judy biweekly for the next three months. Her decline in attendance stopped during this time (although she continued to miss school more often than the average student). Whereas she had missed an average of six days of school per month in the two months prior to counseling aimed at increasing her attendance, she now missed an average of three days per month. Several parts of the plan had apparently contributed to this change. Judy met with her math, social studies, and homeroom teachers to find out what she had to do. They agreed to provide her with past assignments and to notify Mr. Holzberg of her attendance each week. Judy also arranged to have the reward of a special event with Kate, her foster sister, each week that she had perfect attendance. For the first three weeks, Judy daily brought home notes (as shown in Exhibit 8) with each teacher's signature on them. When Judy began to tire of this, Kate suggested that she obtain notes weekly. She continued this for six weeks and then arranged to have Kate call the attendance office on Friday to confirm Judy's attendance. (Judy saved Kate the trouble if she had skipped a class by telling her in advance.) The treats differed each week. Most often they involved eating out at convenience restaurants, going out for ice cream, or watching television together. Kate and Judy planned the next week's treat at the end of the current week's treat. When Judy missed the weekly treat because of imperfect attendance, she and Kate still planned the next week's activity.

Success was less rapid with Judy's tutor. Both were present for the first two weeks, but the tutor left school early to travel to a sports event on the third week, and Kate was absent on the fourth week. Mr. Holzberg talked with the tutor after learning about this from Judy and identified a time following Judy's drawing class when the tutor had no other commitments and when Judy was most often at school. Judy still missed two of the next four meetings. After some questioning about other problems in meeting with her tutor, Judy indicated that she was embarrassed about her reading skills. Mr. Holzberg attempted to ascertain whether the tutor had made any demeaning remarks or in any way contributed to Judy's embarrassment, but Judy said that that was not the problem. Together, Judy and Mr. Holzberg reviewed the self-statements that Judy had about her reading and eventually arrived at some humorous self-statements that she could use when she made a mistake or thought that she was reading "silly stuff." She also talked to the tutor about reading some books that the tutor liked to allay Judy's concerns that the tutoring was a chore for her tutor.

Least successful were efforts to help Judy assert herself with Jeff. Picking up their friends en route to school was successful for a while because, in Judy's words, "There is always one of us with somebody to see at school, so we all go." Jeff wearied of this within a month, however, and just he and Judy began riding to school together again. Judy missed three days of school in two weeks. Mr. Holzberg and Judy again rehearsed what she would tell Jeff about her need to be at school every day. She did tell him, and he seemed to understand, but each of her absences in the ensuing weeks occurred when she rode with Jeff.

Mr. Holzberg talked to Judy about her drinking, and she expressed some concern about it. Her birth mother was a heavy drinker, and Judy did not want to have the same troubles. She agreed to go back to Ala-teen because, although she did not think that she was an alcoholic herself, she admitted to needing some reminders about what drinking can do to your life. An old friend in Ala-teen made this a pleasant proposition for Judy. Judy seemed to have little interest in seeing her birth mother as she became busier and more successful with Jeff, her tutor, Kate, Ala-teen, and school.

During the last month of school, Mr. Holzberg and Judy resumed their original schedule of monthly meetings. They discussed Judy's summer plans and any changes that might transpire and influence her commitment to returning to school in the fall. They reviewed their successes of the year and considered Judy's plans for next year. They concluded the meeting with some optimism that Judy would continue to stay enrolled in school during the next year.

Adaptations for Highly Troubled Families

Children with prolonged histories of school refusal and families with few resources present the greatest challenge to child helpers. Children with mentally ill or substance-abusing parents need allies within their social networks. They may benefit from staying with nearby relatives or friends during the school week. Teachers or school staff living nearby may agree to provide transportation to school each morning. Meetings of members of the child's social network may bring about feasible plans for a return to steady attendance.

One county has shown the effectiveness of providing highly troubled families with multiple services and powerful incentives to motivate their children to attend school. This comprehensive program followed the county's frustration with falling attendance rates, consequent increased crime and dropout rates, and increased truancy rates following juvenile court adjudication (Hanson and Hoeft, n.d.). The program, based on the research of Grala and McCauley (1976), combines counseling and legal consequences and has four levels of service involving: (1) the local school, (2) a truancy prevention office, (3) the community social services office, and (4) adult court. At each level, service providers are held accountable for specified activities. The school in which a truant child is enrolled must hold a conference to discuss the child, meet with the child's parents, and assign a counselor or social worker to the case. If these efforts are unsuccessful, the school administrator enlists the help of the truancy prevention office. This office assigns a youth outreach worker to the child and family within twenty-four hours and informs the parents that they will be subject to legal action unless they get their child to school. If the youth outreach worker reports insignificant improvements in attendance or notes complex family problems, he or she refers the family to the community social services office to obtain community resources that might reduce family constraints on the child's attendance. If the child remains out of school, the family is requested by certified mail to attend a meeting at the truancy prevention office's courthouse quarters. There, contracts are developed requiring parent and child to take specified actions (for example, parents may be required to bring the child to school each day, phone the school to verify that the child is in attendance, and obtain a physical exam for the child) to end the nonatttendance. The parents are also served with a formal legal warning that they are contributing to the delinquency of a minor. If inadequate attendance persists—the outcome with 10 percent of the families—the case is referred to the adult court. To date the project has rendered guilty verdicts in 96 percent of all cases; penalties include $25 to $500 fines and even thirty-day jail terms for parents.

The results after five years support this program. Dropout rates decreased more than 25 percent, absence rates of the truant students fell by 38 percent (compared to a 42 percent increase for the control group), and savings to the district exceeded $200,000 per year over the program cost. Although this program may not be suitable for all school districts, the integration of resource provision and community sanctions is in keeping with other child welfare programs designed to provide families with sufficient but not unlimited resources and time to adapt their performance to community standards (Ten Broeck and Barth, in press). Child helpers concerned with attendance may initially find such programs disquieting and then recognize their justifiable helpfulness. According to Ziesemer's (1984) research, children often find such programs beneficial. More than half of the children who went to truancy court found the experience helpful for such reasons as "It got my mom to get help for drinking," "It got me a new foster home," and "I'm in a support group for incest victims" (p. 177).

Conclusion

The school attendance of children and youth is an easy-to-determine and important measure of the performance of a child's social ecology. Few indicators are so predictive of a child and his or her family's ability to participate in and benefit from the key reward-bearing institutions of our society. Schools that provide supportive services and incentives for attendance provide a great service to children, their families, and society. Unfortunately, many school staff and administrators seem to have few expectations that they can develop and implement programs that will increase school attendance. Child helpers with confidence that their efforts can help to increase attendance can use feasible and cost-saving procedures for boosting average daily attendance in schools.

8

Underachievement
in School

Impulsive, hyperactive, unpopular, noncompliant, learning disabled, reluctant learner, inattentive, and *antiachieving* are terms that describe children who learn less than their ''intelligence'' promises. *Underachievement* is used here as a convenient term to indicate poorer-than-expected academic outcomes resulting from a range of cognitive and social conditions. Underachievement is the difference between what *could be* learned and what *is* learned and may result from impulsivity, hyperactivity with or without attention deficit disorders, visual-perceptual disabilities, or other specified or unspecified social and cognitive deficits. Each can keep children from performing as well in one area as they do in others. As many have argued (for example, Hallahan and Kauffman, 1977; Lambert and Sandoval, 1980), children who do not learn have more in common than their labels imply. After years of research to identify the differences between groups of children—for example, between children who are learning disabled and those who are hyperactive—who do not learn well, the grouping of all these children into a single category of ''underachievers'' may seem audacious and indiscriminate. Proscriptive educators, who believe in thoroughly assessing a child's deficit before planning a deficit-specific intervention, need not, however, be dismayed. The methods described in this chapter provide a framework for facilitating greater achievement, teaching and maintaining self-management, and involving parents. The

257

specific remedial tasks of correcting oral language problems, perceptual disorders, and other learning handicaps can follow.

Common Causes of Underachievement

Before entirely leaving behind the various reasons for underachievement, the three most common—learning disabilities, impulsivity, and attention deficit disorders—will be considered.

Learning Disabilities. Severe visual-perceptual difficulties (for instance, inverting letters), motor problems (for instance, not being able to kick a soccer ball), language disabilities (for instance, not being able to say words even though you can spell them from dictation or when looking at a picture), and auditory disabilities (for instance, not being able to isolate the sounds in the word *duck)* are forms of learning disabilities. Children with specific learning disabilities may have learning and behavioral signs in common with children with developmental disabilities (which are more definitively distinguished by some form of biological block to learning) but can generally be distinguished because they process concrete information better and because their scores on specific learning tasks are less consistently low.

Attempts to distinguish between children with specific learning disabilities and children who are simply underachievers have generally not, on the other hand, been successful (Epps, McGue, and Ysseldyke, 1982; Warner, Schumaker, Alley, and Deshler, 1980). Although children labeled as learning disabled may have a specific learning disability, they often have more general impairments that are undistinguishable from those of other low achievers. Consistent with that finding, Kavale and Glass's (1982) meta-analysis of available research in this area found little evidence that perceptual-motor training succeeds in remediating the problems of learning disabled children.

Impulsivity. Impulsivity is the choice of less rewarding immediate goals over more rewarding and long-term alternatives (Ainslie, 1975). For some children, delaying gratification is extraordinarily difficult. Kogan (1983) concludes that cognitive style (that is, reflectiveness or impulsivity) has a dramatic relationship to success on school tasks, though it is more or less handicapping or beneficial, depending on the task or circumstance. Generally, reflective children make fewer reading errors, do more detailed visual scanning when solving a visual-discrimination problem, and are more apprehensive about making errors than are impulsive children. Impulsive and reflective children also differ on the way they respond to difficult problems. Although both groups of children slow down when problems become more difficult, impulsive children speed up (and consequently miss more items) when problems are most difficult (Lawry, Welsh, and Jeffrey, 1983). Older children are typically less impulsive than their younger counterparts (Salkind and Nelson, 1980), but the enduring costs of impulsiveness to a young child's learning and school success can be great.

Attention Deficit Disorder. The term *hyperkinesis* is dead and resting somewhere along with such other discarded diagnostic labels as *imbecile*. The DSM-III replaced the diagnostic category *hyperkinetic reaction* with *attention deficit disorder* (ADD). This change emphasizes the attention problems of these children rather than their excessive motor activity. (To account for motor behavior, ADD can be specified as with or without hyperactivity.) Although many ADD children are impulsive, not all impulsive children have ADD. Parents and teachers rate as many as 50 percent of all school-age boys as overactive, restless, distractible, or inattentive (see discussion in Whalen, 1983). This means that many nondisabled children may benefit from techniques described in this chapter, and that a high activity level alone is not a trait that distinguishes ADD. Although the strict definitions of ADD, learning disabled, and underachiever differ, auditory and visual inattention is considered a critical element of all problems (Hallahan, Lloyd, Kauffman, and Loper, 1983).

ADD does not live up to the expectation of many caregivers: "Be patient and the child will outgrow it." Children who are hyperactive in adolescence continue to experience such problems as impulsivity and distractability and describe themselves as more defensive, less confident, less smart, and more socially immature than their peers; "they are dissatisfied with their own behavior, morality, and relationships and they show more evidence of pathology" (Waddell, 1984, p. 54). Children and caregivers may interpret the label of *ADD* or *hyperactivity* as indicating a problem beyond their control, a mental handicap, and even a deformity. The result may be a treatment strategy that relies too heavily on the interdependent notions that the child is the victim of a sickness and should not be held responsible for his or her underachievement; the child will outgrow the problem, and patience is the only answer; and the problem is a medical problem, and only pills will make a difference. Child helpers must beat the drum to emphasize that children and caregivers can work together to provide an environment and skills that will lead to the greatest achievement possible. "It's not my fault I'm hyper" (or "It's not the child's fault he or she is hyper") cannot remain unchallenged.

Although children should not be blamed for difficulties in learning that are beyond their control, the expectation that social and academic performance will be to the level of ability must be maintained with appropriate interventions and incentives. Patience is certainly a virtue for every caregiver and child, but waiting for a child to outgrow his or her problems costs that child many opportunities to develop independently and successfully. For some disabilities such as dyslexia (the reversal and miscoding of letters and numbers), time does not eliminate the problem but only provides the opportunity to learn coping strategies. For problems like ADD, time may help children reduce their levels of stimulation, but the slowing effects may not show until the late twenties. Pills can help some children who are underachievers, but the reliance on medication to the exclusion of cognitive and social changes is inappropriate. Even if they are taking medication, children should take it with the understanding that it provides them with a strategy for managing their behavior so that they can learn; children should also learn other strategies and that the use of these strategies is under their own control.

Gary Anthony: Background of a Case Study

Gary Anthony is a fifteen-year-old youth. He is the youngest of three children; his two sisters, aged twenty-one and nineteen, attend local colleges. Gary attends an adolescent day-treatment program located in a public school. He spent his early years in mainstream classes (he was left back once and was about to be left back when he was switched into a class for children with educational handicaps) and spent the years from ages twelve to fourteen in group care because of his aggressive school behavior, incipient substance misuse, and uncontrollable behavior at home (such as staying out all night and threatening his mother). He was diagnosed as seriously emotionally disturbed (SED). Gary returned to his parents' home after making substantial progress in his behavior during eighteen months in a structured group home and six months of weekend, and then extended, visits with his parents. At the time of his return, he was enrolled in the day-treatment program for SED children.

Gary's parents are of black and Latino background. His father is an auto mechanic, and his mother is a telephone operator. His conflict with his parents has been mitigated by his time away from home and his exposure to consistent rules and consequences. Gary works with his father on the family cars and, at times, helps him work on other cars that Mr. Anthony fixes during the weekends. Mr. and Mrs. Anthony have given up the idea that their son will go to college and hope that he will become a mechanic or auto worker. They have learned a significant amount about looking for and acknowledging Gary's strengths and weaknesses during individual, couple, and family counseling with the liaison counselor from the group home.

Assessment

Comprehensive assessment of underachievement includes evaluation of teachers' ratings, children's academic achievement and intelligence test (IQ) scores, and interviews with caregivers. Much effort has been invested in determining the appropriateness of comparing intelligence test scores and academic achievement. Psychometricians argue that subtracting achievement scores from aptitude scores is not a sufficient procedure for identifying underachievement. (Instead, they propose procedures that are more precise but also more complicated than useful for most practitioners.) Scholars who are attentive to cultural barriers to achievement and the failure of standardized aptitude tests to fairly assess children from minority cultural backgrounds also rebel against standard psychometric assessment procedures (see, for example, Mercer, 1984). Reynolds (1983), alternately, reviewed the psychometric evidence for the cross-cultural validity of intelligence, aptitude, and personality tests and found "a considerable body of literature currently exists failing to substantiate cultural bias against native born American ethnic minorities with regard to the use of well-constructed, adequately standardized intelligence and aptitude tests" (p. 336). This author agrees with Reynolds's contention: "Despite the existing evidence, we do not expect the furor over the cultural test bias hypothesis to be resolved soon" (p. 336).

As a consequence of this furor, by law, no child in the United States can be placed in a special education class or program on the basis of IQ tests alone, and some school districts (such as the San Francisco Unified School District) do not even include IQ scores in special education assessments. This seems like the right decision, because any child who performs slightly below chronological age on achievement tests no matter what the reason—whether because of special learning disability, educational deprivation, impulsivity, or aggressiveness—may need educational services with characteristics of special education. Whether in or out of special education, delivery of appropriate educational programming and counseling requires assessment of (1) social and cognitive contributors to the problem, (2) task-achievement skills needed for future goal attainment, and (3) instructional and motivational factors that may lead to success.

Social and Cognitive Contributors. Underachievement may result from social and cognitive barriers to maximum—or even reasonable—use of a child's aptitude. The key social influences on achievement involve the child's relationship with teachers, peers, and family. Assessment strategies for evaluating social performance have been discussed earlier (see Chapter Three). The most commonly used and recently updated and restandardized instrument in the schools is the Vineland Social Maturity Scale (Doll, 1965; Sparrow, Balla, and Chicchetti, 1984). Social maturity can be scaled from one year through adolescence. The test's domains are broad and cover the range of social functioning from self-help skills to socialization skills to maladaptive behavior. The instrument can be completed by teachers (it takes about twenty minutes) or given by child helpers to parents in an interview about the child. The data from teachers and parents can be directly compared to isolate areas in which the child performs significantly better at home than at school or the reverse. Other conclusions can be drawn about a child's daily living skills at home, school, and in the community; about the child's socialization, including the child's interpersonal relationships and use of play and leisure time; and the child's responsibility and sensitivity. The latest version of the scale includes ideas for program planning and identifies prerequisite skills so that educational plans to address deficits in any domain can be developed. Easy-to-interpret forms to report assessment findings to caregivers are also included.

Unfortunately, neither the Vineland nor any other scale indicates a child's responsiveness to the social incentives provided in the classroom. Because most school teachers have limited skills and opportunities for providing positive social incentives for children's performance—for example, praise is less common than reprimands in many classes—children must respond to the incentives that are operating. Child helpers may be able to evaluate a child's responsiveness to a teacher in a way that the teacher cannot.

Cognitive impairments are an obvious element in the achievement problems of children, although they are not as easily assessable or identifiable as social problems are. Because this chapter cannot review all of the cognitive deficits of memory, attention, hearing, and visualization that may impair achievement, the assessment of these problems must receive scant mention. Certainly, however, child helpers should see that comprehensive psychological, neurological, speech, and hearing assessments are conducted for a child who performs poorly or unevenly. A thorough assessment provides useful ideas about the learning channels—visual, auditory, or motoric—that the child will find most dependable so that appropriate instructional activities can be developed.

Attitudes about oneself are an additional cognitive contributor to success. Although the evidence is not unmixed, academic achievement apparently is related to children's belief that they have little control over their behavior and success (Stipek and Weisz, 1981). Schunk (1983) found that increasing children's personal mastery by showing them models who performed successfully and who attributed this success to their own efforts led to greater achievement and task persistence. Zimmerman and Ringle (1981) reported that task persistence and expectations for success of black and Latino elementary school children increased following their witnessing of a model making confident rather than pessimistic comments while working on a puzzling task.

Assessment strategies for this possible contributor to academic performance are not satisfactory. Measures of locus of control or internal responsibility are not highly regarded by psychometricians and are probably unduly laborious for the information they yield. Observation of children as they complete a test battery may be equally informative. Statements such as "I hope I'm lucky" and "I can't do well on these tests even if I try very hard" and limited perseverance may indicate that a child has not previously been rewarded for his or her efforts and does not expect to be so rewarded in the future.

Task-Achievement Skills. A thorough analysis of the social, cognitive, and academic deficits that contribute to underachievement is important to the development of a useful intervention plan. Lloyd, Epstein, and Cullinan (1981) have pioneered the area of skill-attack strategies. In this approach—applicable to spelling, reading, and math—students' possession of the preskills required for successfully solving academic problems is assessed, and then students are taught rules for sequencing the use of those skills. Many child helpers cannot take the time to conduct such detailed analyses, but they should be aware that such strategies are available and are likely to benefit children with learning difficulties.

Instruction and Motivation. A child's academic behavior must be assessed in relationship to the learning environment. The teacher's instructional styles and strategies are major contributors to the child's success. Child helpers can learn about classroom management and individual instruction techniques by observing in the classroom or during consultation with the teacher. Classroom observations can be revealing. Many teachers use unsound instructional and motivational systems that rely heavily on verbal punishment. (This is, unfortunately, not just a stereotype; see Thomas, Presland, Grant, and Glynn, 1978.) Underachieving children may also be grouped with other unsuccessful children not given opportunities to display their successes in class and may be taught by teachers who do not receive adequate support and encouragement. Modeling correct examples, requiring children to correct their responses and then providing rewards, and providing opportunities for children to respond—for example, to read aloud—are also associated with increased learning rates and are often underused (see, for example, Greenwood, Delquadri, and Hall, 1984; Pany and Jenkins, 1978; Stromer, 1977). Observation of teachers' uses of these approaches can lead to change.

Gary Anthony: Assessment

Gary's classroom behavior was exceptionally disruptive. Teacher observation indicated that he was out of his seat an average of six times per hour and that he did not complete seat work without monitoring. He was inclined to instigate fights between students who were upset with each other. His school attendance was good, although he was late starting his work three of five mornings and after lunch nearly every day.

Gary's educational testing showed that his verbal IQ on the Wechsler-R was 89, and his performance IQ was 82. His reading level was third grade and two months, his math level was second grade and four months, and his spelling level was second grade and three months. Gary refused to complete some tests (for example, the Developmental Test of Visual-Motor Integration), was subject to minor personal and environmental distractions, and tended to give up on unfamiliar or not immediately obvious problems.

On the recommendation of Mr. Anthony, who complained that all the tests ever did was tell them what Gary could *not* do and never told them what he *could* do, the school social worker engaged a vocational rehabilitation counselor from Easter Seals to assess Gary's vocational skills. The assessor observed the following about Gary. He lacked confidence and was critical of his work, especially his reading ("I am stupid in reading"). He at times asked for help before attempting a task that he could complete and, at other times, expressed resentment at the interviewer for making suggestions ("I know, I know"). He succeeded on fairly complicated mechanical tasks and was able to follow complex instructions on mechanical and clerical tasks. He did not understand enough math to use a ruler. He was unable to complete a standard job application form. The evaluation indicated that Gary might be capable of moderately complicated gross assembly, fairly simple tool operation, lock or burglar alarm assembly, work in auto body repair, or painting. With improvement in self-management and work-related academic skills—like reading instructions and performing measurements—Gary had possibilities for more varied and better paid work. Gary's learning environment generally supported his efforts. An individual token economy and group incentives rewarded his academic and social successes, and he had daily opportunities to read with the teacher and an aide. Observation by the school social worker indicated that his interest in reading seemed to be piqued by topical materials and that he was less attentive during rote learning. She also noted that he made few attempts to seek help when he seemed unable to progress in arithmetic and that his help-seeking behavior deserved more support.

Group Incentive Systems

Learning, even for high achievers, can be painstaking, tiring, and unsettling. High achievers persevere because they have sufficient personal, social, and material incentives. Underachieving children need rewards that are at least as sweet.

Group incentives are useful for motivating student achievement (Slavin, 1981; Wodarski, 1981). With various strategies, group rewards encourage student performance by providing students with a group norm for comparison and with the opportunity to contribute to the well-being of others through their own achievement. Group reward systems can be classified as dependent, independent, and interdependent.

In the *dependent* model of group rewards, group or subgroup rewards can depend on the performance of one or two individuals. Harold and Maude fight often and loudly. Under a dependent group reward system, if Harold and Maude do not fight on any given day, everyone receives a specified additional benefit (for example, an extra five minutes of break). If Harold and Maude do not fight during the entire week, all class members receive, for example, 10 percent bonuses on their points for a field trip. Dependent group reward systems may be particularly useful when a few group members perform below their abilities and below the norms of the group and when their behavior otherwise disrupts or annoys the group. Children who become rejected by the group—as signified by the group's low expectations of them ("what a nerd, he can't do anything")— can be given the opportunity to gain bonuses for the group through improved performance. Dependent reward systems combine well with lotteries. Tickets for the lottery might be earned on days on which Harold and Maude do not fight, and the lottery would be held when they do not fight for a week. Dependent reward systems should not be used with a response cost for the entire group; this is a sure recipe for scapegoating.

Independent rewards or benefits are provided only for members of the group who meet the standard group criterion. In such reward systems, each group member's individual benefits are independent but are shaped by group norms. For example, Sundance achieved 80 percent correct responses on his in-class math assignment (the class standard) and gained full recreational privileges at lunch, but Butch completed less than 80 percent of his problems correctly and so lost lunch privileges (even though his problems were more difficult than Sundance's). Independent rewards can also use rates of behavior for comparison. Thus Butch, on the other hand, by week's end reduced his "talk outs" (defined as talking to teacher or peers without permission; talking, singing, or humming to oneself; or making statements not related to class discussion) from eight per day to six (more than a 10 percent decrease), but Sundance did not reduce his talk outs from his previous week's rate of five per day. Although Butch had more talk outs than Sundance, he showed more progress and so earned more points. Independent rewards are most useful when the heterogeneity of the class precludes a single acceptable standard for performance, but when a percentage or rate of successful behavior can be identified. Like all reward systems, and perhaps a bit more so than most, independent reward systems require commitment and courage to define behavior and set standards. When this is done, however, then all group members, regardless of their performance level, are working toward the same goal.

Under the *interdependent* model, rewards or benefits are made available if *all* group members meet the criterion. So, when all students meet the criterion for each day and they all qualify, for example, to go on a field trip, the entire group goes. To raise the level of expectation and performance, students can earn points toward a bonus privilege after criterion levels are achieved. Thus, if the bonus tally reaches 100 points, the class as a whole can receive a special privilege (like an ice cream stop on the way back from the trip). The interdependent system can also include response costs. For example, if the sum of all students' talk outs during a day is less than ten, then the entire class obtains the privilege of listening to music at lunch, but if it is over twenty, then the entire class might lose that privilege and the opportunity to eat lunch away from their desks. Or if the sum of all "topic changes" (defined as switching from the current topic to another topic without explaining the relationship between topics or saying that one would like to make a topic change) in a group discussion is less than four, then the last ten minutes can be spent discussing any topic. Lotteries can also be added to interdependent systems. Lottery tickets can be earned daily for appropriate behavior, but the drawing is only held (or the grand prize only awarded) when all students meet the criteria.

The interdependent approach easily incorporates the use of teams. The class is split into teams, and the team with the fewest talk outs (or most points or whatever) gets a reward like choosing the music for lunch time or beginning a break earlier.

The Good Behavior Game introduced by Barrish, Saunders, and Wolf (1969) is an example of an interdependent group incentive system. It has since been used in many programs and is now being tested on a large scale in the Baltimore Unified School District. In the game, students are divided into teams, and any student's disruptive behavior (for example, talking, whispering, or leaving one's seat without permission) results in a check against his or her team. Checks are placed on a chalkboard in the classroom. Either one or both teams can win. The game and its rules are carefully explained to the class. Students are informed that they are going to play a game each day and that the class will be divided into teams. Any team that receives fewer than five marks receives the privilege of wearing victory tags, and a star is placed by each member's name on the winners' chart. If both teams win, all students earn a privilege. If only one team wins, only that team earns the privilege. Out-of-seat behavior and talking out decreased from about 82 and 96 percent, respectively, to 9 and 19 percent during the Good Behavior Game. In Barrish, Saunders, and Wolf's original test, the game was won by both teams in 82 percent of class periods.

The interdependent reward system is versatile and enjoyable. The competitiveness of youth can be put to good use. In addition to greater achievement, group cohesiveness can be enhanced by team effort. It is important for this reason to change groups frequently so that no divisive rivalries develop. Some youth who do not join the team or who consistently perform below standard and penalize the team can also create conflict. These youth may also need an individual incentive system that includes bonuses for improved performance and response costs for failure to meet team scoring levels. The criteria for awarding points should also include good behaviors (in keeping with the game's name) and not just the absence of bad behaviors. As the school year progresses the procedure should also progress, beginning with awarding points frequently after short games (for example, games lasting fifteen minutes) and later awarding them after an hour, a half-day, a day, a half-week, and, at maximum, a week.

Response Cost

To promote greater academic achievement and more attention to work tasks, Witt and Elliott (1982) developed an easy-
to-implement response cost lottery system. Their work was with
underachieving fourth graders who had been referred for removal from their regular education classroom and possible placement in a classroom for behavior-disordered children. The teacher
first explained the procedure to the children, described the rules
that they had to adhere to in order to make progress in their
academic work, and described rewards that could be obtained
by the lottery winner, including extra recess time and pencils.
Slips of paper were placed on the boys' desks during the study
time. A slip was taken away for violating each rule. The boys
placed the slips of paper remaining after one-half hour in a box
for a Friday lottery and one winner was then drawn. The youths'
on-task and academic behavior increased from 10 percent to
73 percent and their academic accuracy increased from 27 percent to 90 percent during the response cost phases. The beauty
of this system—in addition to its success—is that inappropriate
behavior cost students access to additional rewards but did not
limit their opportunities to interact with other children at recess.

Suspension from school for nonattendance or underachievement is a response cost that seriously limits the child's
opportunity to learn. (Designing a more counterproductive response to the behavior of underachievers than at-home suspension would require a significant effort.) Alternatives are available. After learning that 50 percent of all suspended children
were ninth graders and newcomers to the school, and recognizing
that out-of-school suspensions lessened their attachment to the
school and were not working (most of them were recidivists),
Sweeney-Rader, Snyder, Goldstein, and Rosenwald (1980) developed an alternative version of in-school suspension that included counseling services and family treatment. An improved
school orientation program was developed to improve the transition from junior high schools to the high schools. The in-school
suspension program usually lasted from one to five days and pri-

marily included suspended youth (92 percent) but also included a few self- or teacher-referred youth.

The content of the program emphasized responsibility and decision making. In-school suspension staff held meetings with parents to help them develop effective ways of setting limits and communicating with their children and with school personnel. They also provided follow-up services to students for the remainder of the academic year. This included contact with caregivers and teachers to monitor attendance, academic achievement, and general problems. Absenteeism, referrals for second suspensions, and incidents involving a need for discipline all dropped after participation in the program. Parents' and students' satisfaction rose.

Although often helpful, response cost is neither necessary nor sufficient for behavior change and sometimes may hinder it. Hogan and Johnson (1985) found that although using response cost as part of a token economy was initially effective in improving classroom behavior of emotionally disturbed youth, removing the response cost was greeted with better achievement (and much pleasure) by students. Rosenbaum and Baker (1984) found that hyperactive and nonhyperactive children learned an academic task with equal facility under conditions of positive reinforcement for success, but hyperactive children's performance deteriorated more than nonhyperactive children's when they were given no feedback or only negative feedback, and they also used less effective self-control strategies and made more negative comments about the task. The findings argue that a positive approach to teaching underachieving children is likely to meet with better success and that child helpers must help these children develop skill in managing under circumstances—like those found in many classrooms—that provide limited positive feedback.

Social and Academic Skill Training

Academics is just part of underachieving children's trouble. Underachieving children are also more frequently nominated as "liked least" by their peers and as conduct problems by their teachers than are other youth (see, for example, King and Young, 1982). Coie and Krehbiel (1984) compared approaches to helping socially rejected, underachieving, fourth-grade black children. Children were given either social-skills training with a focus on helping them improve their relationships to other children, academic-skills training with an emphasis on improving their seat work, or no additional counseling or tutoring. Academic skills were taught twice weekly during school in forty-five-minute sessions. Social skills were taught to individual children in pairs with other nonrejected children in the class and then in after-school groups. Ladd's (1981) program was used. (Undergraduate and graduate students, respectively, provided the training.) A year after the program ended, children exposed to academic skills had significantly better reading skills than their counterparts *and* also improved social standing. Probably because of their greater attention to their work, they bothered other children less and so became significantly better liked. Children given social-skills training had social-preference ratings that were significantly higher than those of children not in any program and not significantly less than those of children taught academic skills. The evident potential of academic tutoring to improve the social relationships of disliked children deserves attention.

Direct Instruction

Child helpers should know that, despite the merits of student-initiated learning programs for high-achieving children, education to correct educational deficiencies is most effective when it is highly methodical. Becker, Engelman, Carnine, and Rhine's (1981) direct-instruction approach has been controversial but has had unrivalled success in reaching disadvantaged and underachieving children in the elementary years through Project Follow-Through. Approaches that minimize the distractions of self-exploration and avoid premature efforts to teach conceptual understanding until basic skills are mastered are especially valuable for learning complex new skills. More indirect methods of discovery, even in the name of helping them to really understand, will often not be as good a friend to underachieving children as direct instruction.

Self-Instruction

Many underachieving children have "a production deficiency—they do poorly because they fail to produce verbal mediators at the right place and the right time. When given specific instruction to use the strategy, they perform competently" (Hallahan, Lloyd, Kauffman, and Loper, 1983, p. 114). Self-instruction training can augment children's ability to attend and to achieve academically.

Self-Recording of Attending Behavior. Self-instruction strategies can be quite simple. Kneedler and Hallahan (1981) thoroughly tested the use of self-recording of behaviors. In their study, audiotape tones sounded to remind eight- to eleven-year-old students to ask themselves whether they were on task and then to record their answers. The procedure involved use of an audiotape with random tones from ten to ninety seconds long (they averaged forty-five seconds) and a card with "Was I paying attention?" written across the top. The card had a place for checking *yes* or *no*, depending on how the child answered the question: "Was I paying attention when I heard the tone?" Children can be trained to use the procedure in twenty minutes by helping them identify what proper attending is and then modeling and rehearsing the procedure. Brief instructions on following days are also helpful. A script for introducing self-recording (adapted from Hallahan, Lloyd, and Stoller, 1982, p. 12) follows.

> Johnny, you know that paying attention to your work is hard for you. You've heard teachers tell you, "Pay attention," "Get to work," "What are you supposed to be doing?" and things like that. Well, today I'm going to describe a plan that will help you help yourself pay attention better. First, this is what I mean by paying attention. [Teacher models immediate and sustained attention to task.] And this is what I mean by not paying attention.

[Teacher models attentive and inattentive behaviors and requires the student to categorize them.] Now, can you show me what you look like when you are paying attention? [Teacher watches child.] Well done. Can you show me what you do when you do not pay attention? Yes, that does look like you are not paying attention. Okay, now let me show you what we're going to do. While you're working, this tape recorder will be turned on. Every once in a while, you'll hear a little sound like this. [Teacher plays tone on tape.] When you hear that sound, you will quietly ask yourself, "Was I paying attention?" If you answer "yes," you will put a check in this box. If you answer "no," you will put a check in this box. Then you will go right back to work. When you hear the sound again, ask the question, answer it, mark your answer, and go back to work. Now, let me show you how it works. [Teacher models entire procedure.] Johnny, I bet you can do this. Tell me what you're going to do every time you hear a tone. Let's try it. I'll start the tape and watch you work on these problems. [Teacher observes student's use of the entire procedure, praises its correct use, and gradually withdraws his or her presence.]

The conclusions from the researchers' evaluations are: (1) the procedure works best with pupils who are distracted from their work but who otherwise have the competencies to complete it, (2) self-recording results in increased on-task behavior and more academic productivity (although not necessarily more accuracy), (3) back-up rewards are not necessary to the success of this procedure, (4) the beeps and the recording are necessary to the initial learning, (5) teachers and other pupils are not bothered by the procedure, (6) having the child assess his or her own attentional behavior is more effective than having someone else assess it, and (7) increased attending skills generalize to other subjects and last after the tape player is removed.

Christie, Hiss, and Lozanoff (1984) employed a similar procedure to help regular classroom teachers of hyperactive children use self-management training. Three third- and fourth-grade boys and their three teachers participated in the program. The boys were, on the average, one-half year behind grade level in academic performance. Each child was videotaped during the classroom academic work period (in concurrence with Hallahan and Kneedler, 1981, the authors later concluded that taping each child individually is unnecessary, and the children can all learn from a single instructional tape), shown the tape, and taught to classify their behavior as *on task* or *off task*; the latter includes such inappropriate behavior as inattention, aggression, emotional outbursts, making disruptive noise, seeking attention, and talking out of turn. The training required six one-hour sessions over six weeks (the authors, after noting how quickly the children learned to accurately observe themselves, suggest that the training period could be shortened). In their own classrooms, teachers signaled children when they wanted them to record their own behavior for fifteen minutes. (Teachers at first also recorded the children's behavior during these periods and found a high level of agreement between their assessment and the children's.) Children had tape recorders nearby that periodically beeped to remind them to observe and record their behavior. No praise or punishment was given for children's performance during these times. On-task behavior occurred about 33 percent more often during the periods when self-recording was done than it did during periods without self-recording. Although changes in achievement were not assessed, such an increase in attention might add as much as two hours per day to the time a child has available to learn.

The author found a modification of this procedure to be useful. In a day-treatment classroom, all youth were taught to self-record on-task and off-task behavior with individual tape players and tones. A tape with random beeps (that were distinguishable from the tones) set on one-, three-, and five-minute intervals served to remind all the students in the class to observe their behavior without requiring that they record it. The tape had a second benefit: it served as a classroom monitor at times.

When it beeped during such off-task behavior as an emotional outburst, it at times stopped the participants in their tracks and they, sometimes with jack-o-lantern grins, returned to their business.

Academic Tasks. Leon and Pepe (1983) helped educable mentally handicapped (EMH) and learning disabled (LD) students aged nine to twelve improve their math scores with self-instruction training. EMH and LD teachers were taught self-instruction training during a one-day workshop. Teachers learned to teach students self-instruction using the following five steps:

1. The teacher works the problem saying the self-instruction out loud.
2. The teacher and student work the problem together saying the self-instructions out loud.
3. The student works the problem saying the self-instructions out loud.
4. The student works the problem saying the self-instructions in a whisper.
5. The student works the problem using cognitive self-instruction.

The results were promising. Not only did the students who were taught self-instruction during the daily fifteen-minute training sessions accomplish more arithmetic modules than children not so trained (105 versus 62), but they passed far more modules requiring similar but more difficult computational tasks (70 versus 22 for the other students), which shows generalization of the skills learned using self-instruction training.

Self-instruction can also be applied to reading. Students can learn to figure out words they do not know by asking themselves four questions. After the student asks, "How do I figure that word out?" he or she asks: (1) "Can I blend each individual sound together?" (2) "Can I find out what the word means from reading the other words in the sentence?" (3) "Does the word belong to a word family that I know (like *kiss* and *sis* and *miss*)?" (4) "Does the word have two words in it that I know (like *someone*)?" (Children with more experience with this method can learn to compare clues to be sure that they agree with each other.) Once the child has an idea of what the word might be, the child asks, "Is that a real word?" and then "Does it make sense here?" If it makes sense, the child should learn to say, "Yes, that makes sense; I figured it out myself." If it does not make sense, then the child is taught to breath deeply and to say, "So what, I'll just try to figure it out again."

Child helpers will do well to remember that simply paying attention, staying in one's seat, and not fighting do not necessarily lead to improved academic performance. Swanson's (1981) work points out the importance of identifying and motivating children to work on the subgoals but not neglecting the final and logical goal of academic achievement. Swanson used self-recording, tokens, and free time made contingent on achieving the desired outcome in three experiments on reading comprehension. The first study showed that self-recording and tokens helped reduce errors of children reading out loud but did not improve their reading comprehension. In the second study, making free time contingent on silent reading and self-recording increased independent silent reading but did not affect reading comprehension. Only when reading comprehension was identified as the desired goal did the contingent free-time and self-recording procedures lead to its increase.

Cameron and Robinson (1980) taught underachieving, hyperactive, seven- and eight-year-old children self-management skills to improve their on-task behavior and math accuracy. The self-instruction training was provided individually and out of the classrooom in twelve half-hour sessions over three weeks using an approach similar to that described earlier in Chapter Five and by Meichenbaum and Goodman (1971) and Kendall and Braswell (1985). To encourage the transfer of newly learned skills to the classroom, students first learned to carefully match and sequence shapes and then applied these visual analysis skills to math problems. By the third session, students learned to use an answer guide to check their work and to award themselves points for correct answers. This procedure was extended to the classroom as students checked their math problems in class, totaled the number of points earned, and brought their worksheets to their tutorial sessions. After the twelve sessions, each student was given an individual recording poster and a box of rocket stickers. Children recorded their daily count of correct math problems; if all were correct, the rockets could land on the lunar surface of their posters. Teachers gave the students exclusive responsibility for using these posters, and use them they did. During the self-responsibility stage, students' math accuracy continued to improve or, at worst, remained the same. In addition, the skills generalized to reading, and the children's reading scores also improved. Increased academic ability from self-instruction is not always so dramatic. Success with learning disabled children has, however, also been reported in Andre and Anderson's (1979) study of reading improvement and Kosiewicz, Hallahan, Lloyd, and Graves's (1982) work with handwriting.

Sewell, Chandler, and Smith (1983) found that black youth with a more developed idea that they (rather than their teachers) were responsible for their successes were the most successful problem solvers. These findings argue for vigilance by child helpers against assuming too much responsibility for youth's success and for efforts to strengthen youth's self-evaluation and self-reinforcement skills.

Correspondence Training. If child helpers can help children learn to do what they say they will, child helpers can breathe a sigh of relief. Mounting evidence suggests that children— even cognitively impaired and nonverbal children—can learn to make their behavior correspond to what they say or show they will do (Israel, 1978; Whitman, Burgio, and Johnston, 1984). The procedure is strikingly simple. Children are asked to say or, in the case of nonverbal children, show what behavior they will perform. Such behaviors are usually not complicated and may include attending, remaining quiet, staying in one's seat, and handwriting. If children then do what they say they will do, they are rewarded; if they do not, they are not rewarded. Over time, the correspondence between saying or showing and doing is strengthened. The final step is to say or show themselves what behavior they will do and to follow through. Although this is a new area of research and practice, the outcomes seem quite encouraging. Correspondence training has been shown to reliably increase on-task behavior during training, during a period without rewards, and across new situations (Whitman and others, 1982); what is not known is how successfully this approach increases achievement.

Peer Tutors

Learning by teaching complements learning by listening. A meta-analysis of sixty-five tutoring programs (Cohen, Kulik, and Kulik, 1982) and two recent reviews (Jenkins and Jenkins, 1985; Kalfus, 1984) point to the potential of peer tutors to learn and to teach. Epstein (1978) found that both tutors and tutees in an experimental group of learning disabled, primary-grade children achieved reading scores that were significantly higher than those obtained by other children. Epstein's program included a thorough pretutoring orientation for the students, easy-to-follow instructions for the students, programmed materials to reduce errors, and tutors selected on the basis of their skill. Holliday and Edwards (1978) argue that peer tutoring may work well with black students because it parallels cultural practices that stress the responsibility of older children for their younger siblings. In these researchers' work, fourth- and sixth-grade tutors worked with low-achieving third-grade students once each week over a seven-month period. The third graders' average gains in vocabulary and comprehension levels were twenty-four and sixteen months, respectively. Dineen, Clark, and Risley (1977) helped three underachieving nine- and ten-year-old children teach each other spelling words by rotating as the tutor, tutee, or nonparticipant. As tutors and as tutees, these children learned more than they had before and than they did in the nonparticipant role. Such successes do depend on appropriate recruitment, training, and supervision of peer tutors (Jenkins and Jenkins, 1985).

Peer tutoring must complement and not compete with the class's management. Peer tutoring is most successful in classrooms that reward cooperative peer behavior, that provide clear and orderly learning objectives, and that have compatible learning and behavior-management systems (Gerber and Kauffman,

1981). Development of these classroom characteristics should precede implementation of a formal peer tutoring program.

Careful selection of tutors and tutees is important to operating an effective peer tutoring program. Because research (for example, Feshbach, 1976) indicates that peers may initially be quite disapproving of poor performers but will become more positive and develop a greater liking for the tutee after some success (Ehly and Larsen, 1977), it is vital to inform tutors to encourage tutees by noting their successes but to pay little heed to their mistakes. At first, then, the tutor's role should be reviewing material with which the tutee is likely to be successful. Simply saying "The correct answer is _____" and going on to the next word or problem is usually sufficient. Keeping a record of correct and incorrect responses is important for monitoring progress, providing the teacher with information about what is and is not learned, and signaling improvement. In time, the tutor can become more precise in correcting the erring tutee. For example, Rosenbaum's (1973) spelling procedure has the tutor cross out the letters after the last correctly spelled word and to request that the tutee try again; if the second try is unsuccessful, the tutor writes in the correct letters and goes on to the following word. Going back over the missed words a second time can provide additional learning opportunities when the tutor-tutee dyad are ready to take on the responsibilities of remediation. As always, good work by the tutor or tutee should gain recognition from classmates, teachers, and caregivers. Peer tutoring can be arranged formally, as previously described, or encouraged as part of normal interpersonal teaching in the classroom. Jenkins and Jenkins (1985) provide many useful strategies for recruitment, training, supervising, and keeping peer tutors. Child helpers should also be acquainted with Joseph Lancaster's (1803) system of peer-mediated instruction, which he developed in the nineteenth century and spread throughout the Western world; the system was based on much planning and good sense and no research.

Medication

Medication is a villain to many child helpers. Many child helpers have observed or, perhaps more often, been warned about such side effects of medication as permanent tics, stunted growth, the development of an external locus of control, and appetite and sleep loss. Improper use of stimulant medication is, indeed, easy to find. One of the most common and fundamental misuses of drugs results from the failure to carefully monitor whether dosages increase the desired behavior (or increase undesired behavior) and to stop, change, or continue the use of drugs as appropriate. As Rapport (1984) points out, however, "the misuse of a treatment does not negate its potential value, i.e., *abuses non tollet usum*. Pejorative reviews regarding the efficacy of psychostimulant treatment are premature and . . . further, they tend to promote a behavioral elitism which rarely facilitates our ultimate purposes" (p. 134). Hyperactive children have the right to get the medical help they need *and* to be taught healthy coping strategies so as to have the best possible memories of childhood, to avoid unnecessarily strained relationships with their parents, to avoid special school placements when possible, and to have success in social relationships. (In addition, nonhyperactive children have the right to be free from aggresssion by nonmedicated, hyperactive peers.) An interview with Lisa, age eleven, as reported in Whalen (1983, p. 188), describes one positive response to Ritalin:

Interviewer: This is an "imagination" question. Let's say you stopped taking Ritalin altogether.

Child: Oh wow, I'd stay home from school!

Interviewer: How come?

Child: Because I know what would be happening if I didn't. I wouldn't get my work done at all.

Interviewer: What about your friends?

Child: Nobody would like me then, if I didn't take it. They'd think in their minds, "Gosh, she doesn't even want to play. What a baby!"

Interviewer: Pretend that a friend of yours was about to start taking Ritalin and she asked you what you thought. . . .

Child: They'd ask me, like "what does it *do*?" I'd just tell them, "Well, it helps you concentrate, get more friends, and you want to join in the games more. And you'd be invited more places."

Medication can be a hyperactive child's ally. Humphries, Swanson, Kinsbourne, and Yiu (1979) found that twelve hyperactive children who were given methylphenidate (Ritalin) far outperformed twelve hyperactive children who were given placebos on difficult tasks (completing mazes) that required patience and persistence. The children without medication started out succeeding at about the same rate as those with medication, but they could not sustain their success. Varley (1983) has shown that ADD adolescents had significantly better school and home performance while using Ritalin and that those children who had responded well to Ritalin before puberty but had been removed from the drug responded well again; in short, no excitatory effects or other evidence of a switching or paradoxical mechanism was found. (Mild appetite suppression was found and should be monitored in adolescents vulnerable to eating disorders.) Taking a longer-term view, Waddell (1984) found minimal differences between adolescents who had and had not been treated with medication. Hechtman, Weiss, and Perlman (1984) found that young adults who had been treated with medication for at least three years performed about as well as nonmedicated hyperactive peers on school and work and had about the same frequency of personality disorders (they had significantly poorer performance than nonhyperactive counterparts, however); they had less delinquency, better social skills and self-concepts, more positive views of their childhood, and fewer car accidents than nonmedicated hyperactive counterparts. As youth, the medicated children also did significantly less stealing than nonmedicated hyperactive youth.

The benefits of stimulant medication were demonstrable for Martin, a fourteen-year-old youth recommended for assignment to state juvenile prison because of a long history of assault and a recent attack on a counselor with a weed picker (Barth and Sullivan, 1984). Martin would have been sent away except for a judge who thought that he was too young to go to prison and ordered a social history. The author interviewed the boy and his grandmother and reviewed his case records to learn that in the six years since his first arrest at age eight, he had averaged only *one* police contact or runaway episode during each of the three years that he had followed his prescribed Ritalin regimen and *six* arrests or runaways during each of the three years without Ritalin.

To evaluate the impact of Ritalin on Martin, a no treatment-treatment evaluation was conducted during his stay in juvenile hall. He was started on Ritalin after his first court review. Unit records showed that at the time of his first court review, he had been on the lowest step of the juvenile hall ward program and had five fights during six weeks of detention. After beginning Ritalin, data on its effects were collected from unit staff who had unanimously opposed his reprieve. Martin climbed one step per week in the program, the maximum possible, and had no fights in four weeks. This documented change confirmed the record of the past years and his grandmother's assessment that "that child has always had a nervous condition." Following a second review, Martin was discharged to a group home rather than to the youth authority. One year later he was still there and ready for discharge.

Other medications show less impressive results. Garfinkel, Wender, Sloman, and O'Neill (1983) found that Ritalin was significantly better in improving the academic and social classroom behavior of adolescents than were tricyclic antidepressants (TCAs). They did find some sleep and mood deterioration as a result of the stimulant medication and better sleep and mood from the use of TCAs. Given the greater known side effects of TCAs, however, child helpers should be sure that an adolescent with ADD is given a chance to succeed with cognitive- and social-skill training and then using stimulant medication, the least intrusive of the two medications.

Medication and Skill Training. Medication and skill training may be a useful combination. Horn, Chatoor, and Conners (1983) found that a combination of Dexedrine and self-management training increased the on-task behavior (as measured by classroom observers) and lowered the distractibility and hyperactivity (as rated by the teacher) of a nine-year-old hyperactive psychiatric patient. When used alone, stimulant medication was more effective in increasing attention and reducing impulsive responses. Neither treatment was effective in improving the

boy's spelling and math performance; this required direct reinforcement. As the authors point out, this finding is consistent
with other investigations of the combined benefits of skills and
pills (see, for example, Wells, Conners, Imber, and Delamater,
1981) and with findings by other investigators of no additive
gain for stimulant medication and external reinforcement. Combining medication with external reinforcement may teach children that they have no responsibility for their change and that
"it is not up to you." Adding self-management training teaches
the child that "all of it is up to you—partly by taking your
stimulant medication and partly by talking yourself into slowing down and staying calm."

     Side Effects. Along with the well-documented benefits of
stimulant medication, child helpers must be knowledgeable about
the side effects of various drugs, because this knowledge, first
and foremost, will help protect children, and it will help child
helpers to inform concerned caregivers. Caregivers often do not
consistently provide stimulant medications to their children. In
Firestone's (1982) study of hyperactive children and families,
26 percent refused stimulant treatment altogether, 20 percent
of those who did place their children on medication had stopped
using it by the end of five months, and another 25 percent
stopped before the end of one year. Only 10 percent of the
families consulted with professionals before terminating stimulant medication. This high termination rate occurred despite
little complaint about side effects, recognition of improvements
in behavior, and parents' reports that their children were still
quite troublesome.

     Caregivers' concerns about side effects may have con-
tributed to the discontinuation. For example, a common concern of caregivers is that a child's growth will be stunted. Temporarily stunted growth is not uncommon, but the effects do
not last. Children who have taken stimulant medication grow
to the same size as those who have not (Hechtman, Weiss, and
Perlman, 1984). A frequent misconception is that the effects of
stimulant medications are such that if their child is not medically
hyperactive, the medication will not work and may be hazard-
ous. In fact, stimulants can also help normal children to con-

centrate and stay on task (Rapoport and others, 1980). Caregivers may also be concerned that stimulant use will contribute to later drug abuse. The stimulants do not make children "high"; they simply make children more attentive. Several investigations have found that hyperactive children are overrepresented among drug abusers (for example, see Eyre, Rounsaville, and Kleber, 1982); this relationship appears to be independent of whether or not the child was given stimulant medication as a child. Caregivers may also believe that a neurological exam and brain-wave test are essential to identify the need for medication; these are less reliable sources of information than teachers' and caregivers' reports before and during medication trials. Drug holidays—that is, time off of medication—are not, despite popular conceptions, necessary. More important is ensuring that a child experiences success, whether it is on a Saturday or summer vacation. Youngsters on Dexedrine may look pale and have circles under their eyes, but they are not necessarily having adverse reactions. Last, the failure of the medication to "work" or its making a child act like a "zombie"—indications that the dose is insufficient or too great—may discourage caregivers. The size of effective doses is not closely related to the size of the child. While no dose of Ritalin should exceed 1 milligram per kilogram (2.2 pounds) of the child's weight, the dose should be titrated by increasing 5 milligrams at a time until behavior improves or until negative side effects (for example, headaches and irritability) are noted.

Collaboration with Caregivers

During the high school years, children are in school for 13 percent of their waking hours; parents, at least nominally, are in charge of their psychosocial and educational development during the rest. In a review (Walberg, 1984) of twenty-nine controlled studies of school characteristics and children's achievement, 91 percent of the comparisons favored children in programs designed to improve the learning environment in the home over children not participating in such programs. The average effects of these programs were twice as great as the effects of social class on predicting children's achievement. Parent roles include supervising homework, providing an audience for a child's work, supporting school programs, and advocating better schools.

Yet most parents have little contact with schools. Becker and Epstein (1982) report from their study of over 3,000 teachers that only 41 percent loan books to parents, 24 percent encourage parents to play informal games with their children, 66 percent encourage parents to read aloud or listen to reading, and 2 percent encourage parent-led discussions of television shows. Related research found that 96 percent of parents reported never having received a home visit, 36 percent never went to a teacher conference, 60 percent never received a phone call from a teacher, and 36 percent never received a handwritten note from a teacher. Parents who did receive some home-school communication gave their children's teachers a higher rating. More experienced teachers initiated more communication with families.

Home-School Notes. The plain and powerful procedure (previously discussed in Chapter Seven) for communicating with caregivers known as the home-school note (Barth, 1979, 1980) can also increase achievement. Drew and others (1982) developed a home-school communication system to enable parents to better reward their children's academic achievement. Two third-grade boys achieving well below their ability levels and their parents and teachers were involved. The parents were contacted by the school counselor and asked to identify some rewards that they could offer daily for improved academic performance as indicated by a positive school note. The parents decided to reward the children with outdoor play upon their return home. Initially, the boys had to complete their math problems with at least 76 percent accuracy (indicating a C performance). Their completion rates rose from a combined pre–school-note level of 24 percent to 96 percent after the home-school note procedure was implemented, and accuracy rates rose from 16 percent to 84 percent. Careful monitoring of the operation of the school-note system by the counselor in the early stages of intervention kept one parent from not following through on her agreement that her son would stay indoors if he did not complete his work, even though he threatened, sulked, and sneaked about.

Polster, Lynch, and Pinkston (1981) describe a successful program to reach and help underachieving youth through a home-based reward system. They contacted parents and arranged for an adequately lighted, quiet study area for students, with a chair and clear writing surface, and parental rewards for successful school performance as indicated by daily teachers' notes home. In one case, parents had already tried to reward their child, Louis, by paying him for higher grades, but he was still two years below grade level, despite his apparently average learning ability. The family agreed to make several changes in this unmotivating procedure: they allowed Louis to watch television only after his homework was completed (Louis admitted that he watched television but did not get much pleasure from it); they provided the study area for Louis; and they rewarded Louis for his performance weekly. Louis improved his semester grade-point average from a D – to a C +.

Parents and Tutors. Hewison and Tizard (1980) have shown that a critical factor in a child's reading ability is whether or not the child is read to at home. In the Belfield Reading Project, school staff visited parents, advised them how to promote their elementary school children's reading skills, and helped schools organize a system in which reading books were regularly sent home with children. The Belfield project began the involvement process with a letter to parents from the principal and an invitation to discuss the program at an evening meeting. The plan was simple. Each child came home at night with a special plastic folder containing a school reading book and a card filled in by the class teacher with suggested reading for that night (see Exhibit 9). Parents listened to their child read, initialed the box, wrote any comments on their side of the card, and returned the book and folder the next day. Teachers, parents, and students were enthusiastic about the project, and students learned to read significantly better when regularly read to by parents. After two years, more than half of the children in the program were reading at or above their chronological age; only one-third of the children in comparison classes were at age level (Tizard, Schofield, and Hewison, 1982). The child helper's role in facilitating such programs should not be underestimated. Advocating or raising funds for more books and folders, consulting with teachers about

Exhibit 9. Sample of One Week's Completed Reading Card.

One Week's Reading Card

John Bennett   Week ending 4 / 6 /1981
(Child's name)

_____IN_____ (Teacher) Belfield Community School

Suggested Reading	Comments
	Please initial if you hear your child read
Weekend Page 15, 16, 17 _JB_	Good.
Monday Evening Page 19 _JB_	John is reading very well at the moment.
Tuesday Evening _JB_ Yes, he is trying hard. From that on 22 to the end of it.	Struggled with course and counted.
Wednesday Evening _JB_ good try p. 24 & 25	Good.
Thursday Evening _JB_ very nice reading 28 & 29	Good.

Source: Adapted from Jackson and Hannon, 1981, p. 11. Used by permission.

the program, meeting with parents individually or in groups, talking with parents of slow readers about their child, and helping less affluent families to share reading materials are but a few ways that parent involvement in reading can be promoted by the child helper.

Efforts to help parents become involved in assisting their underachieving children must be carefully orchestrated. Parents are generally willing to help students on assignments that are short, that guarantee success, and that have practical and meaningful instructions about what to do (Epstein and Becker, 1982). Homework is often desired by parents because it promises more achievement. The effectiveness of homework is limited, however, by the availability of an appropriate and consistent place to study and incentives (especially teachers' comments) for accurate and timely completion of homework (Strother, 1984).

Child helpers can also encourage teachers to reach out to more parents. This effort can be aided by recognition that teachers often believe (1) that parents care but cannot do much to help the school or their children in actual learning, (2) that parents care but should not help with school learning because they will make problems worse or should spend their time with their children differently, and (3) that teacher involvement programs take considerable staff time.

Parent Training

Underachievers can also get help outside the school. A comparison of Parent Training (PT) programs based on social learning principles, Parent Effectiveness Training (PET), and no treatment at all showed that parents of six- to ten-year-old hyperactive children reported less hyperactivity, decreases in severity of their children's problems, and less frequent occurrence of their children's problems after exposure to either of the training programs. In addition, parents who learned PT methods for parenting rated their children as more improved than did PET parents, were more willing to recommend the program, viewed the program as more relevant to them, and were less likely to drop out. The improvements were clinically significant, as 50 percent of the children in the PT group received normal ratings of impulsivity after the training (none of the children were so rated before the training), and specific problems occurred with 40 percent less frequency. These outcomes are noteworthy in that no individualized instruction—phone calls, individual problem solving during sessions, or home visits, for example—were included; this was strictly an educational approach, yet it was still effective.

Parenting an underachieving child is disappointing, aggravating, and often lonely. Mash and Johnston (1983) found that the self-esteem of parents of hyperactive children was lower than that of parents of normal children. Mothers of young hyperactive children reported much stress, depression, self-blame, and social isolation. When parents' self-esteem was low, their perception of their children's problems was greater. Fathers were less troubled by their children's difficulties than were mothers. When fathers did believe that their children had significant problems, the mothers' self-esteem was even lower. The authors suggest that helping fathers support mothers and help reduce mothers' social isolation and despair may be more useful than trying to teach fathers alternative child-management strategies (which they may be unlikely to use because of their limited contact with their children).

Bard and Fisher (1983) identified several beliefs that may be held by caregivers and that may contribute to children's underachievement. These are: (1) things will turn out okay whether my child works or not; (2) everything should be entertaining or enjoyable for my child; (3) it is demeaning, dishonorable, and destructive to cooperate with authority in any way; (4) nothing about school will ever benefit my child. Parents' support for these beliefs is assessed, and their ability to participate in helping to refute these beliefs is reviewed.

Parents who receive concrete recommendations from child helpers about how they can assist their child often are grateful. For example, in addition to telling a parent that a child has a dyslexia, child helpers should tell parents to "be sure that Sam carries your phone number with him on a card and that you put a green band on the left side of the card, a red band after the phone number, and a sun at the top of the card so he can read it correctly"; or to "buy Sally a simple pocket calculator with big numbers for doing her math." The child helper should also address parents' needs for support, informing parents of their legal rights and of self-help groups (such as the Association for Retarded Citizens and the Special Education Resource Network) that might assist them in obtaining additional services for their child and that might provide other information, companionship, and understanding.

Gary Anthony: Intervention

The individual educational program developed for Gary by the school team, the Anthonys, and Gary was detailed and included many subgoals, but it did not specify the larger goal of Gary's education. This was done in family meetings led by the school district's social worker. As a result of these meetings, the treatment team, the Anthonys, and Gary agreed that intervention had four goals: (1) to help Gary improve his self-management skills so that he could function independently, (2) to help Gary improve his prevocational academic skills, (3) to encourage Gary's vocational-skill training, and (4) to provide support for the family during their reunification.

Self-management was taught by using a tape player and self-recording procedure for on-task behavior. A classroom token economy in which points were awarded for good behavior and academic accomplishment during ten daily work periods (with the reward of a biweekly outing) and the use of the Good Behavior Game (with the rewards of extended lunch period and music during lunch) helped Gary maintain appropriate social behavior. Most difficult to change was Gary's subtle instigation of fights between other boys. This pattern was identified by the classroom teacher and was first confronted during a class problem-solving meeting. Gary's strategies for instigating trouble were so varied, however, that a definition of his behavior was difficult to develop. Finally, an understanding was reached that if Gary was close to a fight, he would suffer the same consequences as the fighters, and if Gary discussed a previous fight between two classmates—which was one form of instigation—he would be penalized one-half of his behavior points during that work period. This program had a modest positive effect on Gary's behavior.

Academic skills were taught in two ways. First, the objectives for improving Gary's reading and math skills were carefully assessed. The prevocational skills for completing job applications, reading the instructions for parts assembly, measuring (using both the metric and the customary systems), and keeping a bank account were given particular attention. Whenever possible, exercises that applied to these goals were used. Second, Gary developed a contract to complete academic tasks at home. These were typically math and reading review exercises from the previous school week. The contract is shown in Exhibit 10. The contract was similar to one that Gary had with his group-home parents and which was used during some parts of his transition from group care. The homework was corrected every morning by the teacher's aide.

Vocational-skill training was arranged for three afternoons per week through a regional job training program in a nearby auto body repair shop. This provided Gary with much satisfaction and additional incentives to achieve in math and reading. Family counseling was continued biweekly. One meeting was in the Anthonys' home and included discussion of a range of family and school issues and troubleshooting about the contract. The second meeting was at the school with other parents from the SED program.

Consultation

The professional child helper often assumes the role of consultant to teachers. Many school consultants do not do their job properly, at least according to their consultees. Kadushin (1977) found that consultants most often focus on personal characteristics of consultees, but consultees want sessions to focus on specific problems. Indeed, Alpert's (1976) review shows that consultation directed at changing the teachers' personal coping styles does not help teachers improve their classroom performance.

Exhibit 10. Sample Parent-Child Contract to Increase Academic Achievement.

Goal: Gary will improve his performance on homework.

Gary's Tasks:

Gary will do 1 hour of homework each night.

  A. On days when Gary is finished with school at 3:30, he will:
      1. Have a snack and take dogs out (until 4:00 P.M.).
      2. Have time to himself.
      3. Study from 7:00 to 8:00 P.M.
  B. On days when Gary finishes school at 2:00, he will:
      1. Have snack and take dogs out (until 2:30 P.M.).
      2. Study from 2:30 to 3:30 P.M.
      3. Have time to himself.

Consequences: If followed, Gary will improve his grades and earn more money every two weeks. If not followed, as indicated by a weekly teacher's report, Gary will lose special weekend privileges.

Mom and Dad's Tasks:

  A. Mom or Dad will ask Gary one time and only one time per night if he wants help with his homework.
  B. Dad will not remind Gary about the contract.
  C. Dad will not watch television while Gary is studying.

Signed: Gary _____

          Mom _____

          Dad _____

Modifications:

  A. Gary will not make trips to refrigerator.
  B. Gary will not talk on phone (if a friend calls, Gary will ask the friend to call after he is finished with homework and hang up).
  C. There will be no punishment or rewards for grades.
  D. A missing assignment or missing signature from the teacher's progress report is cause for loss of weekend privileges.
  E. Any subject in which Gary receives a test score lower than 60 must be studied for an extra 15 minutes per day during the following week.

Signed: Gary _____

          Mom _____

          Dad _____

Medway and Forman's (1980) findings also show that consultation that focuses on changes in teacher and student behavior is better liked by teachers and more effective in changing student behavior. These and other findings indicate that the key ingredient in consultation may be problem identification; once that is done, problem resolution typically follows.

Teachers more often ask school psychologists to administer tests and school social workers to work with families than they ask either to provide consultation (Piersel and Gutkin, 1983), in part because they attribute a child's underachievement to the student's internal characteristics and home environment rather than to teaching or classroom factors (Gutkin and Ajchenbaum, 1984). Somewhat contrary to what might be expected, then, teachers with less control over a child's behavior are less inclined to seek and accept consultation. The consultant must, therefore, find opportunities to reach out to inexperienced and less-skilled teachers, recognize their successes, concur that learner and home characteristics limit learning, and then lay out minimally intrusive intervention strategies for teachers.

Consultants must not only consider what will be effective but what classroom teachers will find acceptable (Witt and Elliott, 1985). Acceptable interventions like assertive discipline, perceptual-motor training, and diet treatment for hyperactivity are widely adopted, despite the absence of research indicating their effectiveness (Cairns, 1983; Kavale and Glass, 1982). As previously discussed, stimulant drug treatment for hyperactivity is, contrarily, both highly effective for hyperactive youth and often shunned by human service professionals. Algozzine, Ysseldyke, Christenson, and Thurlow (1982; also cited in Witt and Elliott, 1985) surveyed teachers' preferred interventions for underachieving children with multiple behavior problems. In order of preference, teachers preferred (1) an intervention that they could participate in, (2) having the child work with another child helper, and (3) having the child transferred to another classroom. These findings are somewhat counterintuitive—given the notion that teachers are often eager to dump the responsibility for difficult children—and suggest that pride and autonomy are teacher characteristics that should not be underestimated. The language with which interventions are suggested is also important to teachers; as Witt and Elliott (1985) point out, if teachers talk about a student's lack of responsibility, then "more responsibility" should be defined, and the intervention should be planned to increase responsibility rather than to increase on-task or compliant behavior. Consultants can shape teachers' thinking, but they should start with the teachers' ideas and descriptions. Above all, the amount of time required by an intervention contributes to its acceptability by teachers.

9

Stealing

Stealing troubles the caregivers and communities of many troubled children and youth. Russo and Shyne's (1980) survey of group-care facilities indicates that stealing is a problem in 97 percent of the facilities surveyed and that in 5 percent of the facilities, a majority of residents steal. In Rowe, Cain, Hundleby, and Keane's (1984) study, foster parents reported that 36 percent of their children had a problem with stealing. Among ten- to eleven-year-olds, 33 percent of foster children were thieves; this far exceeds the 3 percent found in birth homes in the Isle of Wight study by Rutter, Tizard, and Whitmore (1970) and the 1 percent rate in a California study (Macfarlane, Allen, and Honzik, 1954). Children who steal are, therefore, often in settings where child helpers can serve them. Youth under seventeen accounted for 20 percent of all personal robberies and 24 percent of personal larcency (purse snatchings and pickpocketing) between 1975 and 1980 (Laub, 1983). Losses to shoplifters total more than $13 million daily, with youth representing 50 percent of all shoplifters (Heinstein, 1974; also cited in McNees and others, 1980). Eighteen percent of arrests for property crimes in 1977 were of children less than fifteen years of age (Flanagan, Hindelang, and Gottfredson, 1980). The problems that stealers create are not only for others. As a result of compulsive stealing, youth may experience significant guilt and anxiety and alienate peers, family members, and significant community adults. Youths arrested for stealing risk further increases in their criminal behavior as a result of exposure to the juvenile justice system (Sarri, 1980).

The Families and Careers of Children Who Steal

Children learn much of what they know from their parents. Few families of stealers, however, encourage or demonstrate stealing. Upon a child's apprehension for theft, many parents are surprised to find that their young children steal or that they steal so often. This surprise may be sincere even though parents have watched their children disregard the property rights of siblings, friends, and themselves from an early age. Normative studies of stealing suggest that the most stealing occurs for boys and girls at age three (when 18 percent of all girls' parents report stealing as a problem and 12 percent of boys' parents), and then stealing diminishes quickly for girls and more gradually for boys, rebounds at about age eight, and typically becomes a minimal problem by age eleven. Achenbach and Edelbrock (1981) found that for boys, stealing at home begins to rise at about age eight or nine until by age twelve or thirteen about 9 percent steal; this rate remains roughly steady until age sixteen.

Most children and youth, especially males, steal some time. Few boys never steal (Belson, 1976). Youth who continue to steal start early (Mitchell and Rosa, 1981; Loeber, 1982). Of children whose parents stated that they had stolen at several different times, 66.7 percent later committed a criminal theft. Moore, Chamberlain, and Mukai (1979) found that preadolescent stealers—whose parents had described at least four stealing incidents in the previous four months—were arrested in five of six cases by the age of seventeen. Only one of three young stealers in their study escaped a future of chronic offending. Other investigators agree that early and cross-situational stealing is a strong predictor of serious later delinquency (Loeber and Dishion, 1983). Children who steal in more than one setting are at greatest risk of continuing to steal and of becoming criminals (Loeber, 1982). Mitchell and Rosa (1981) found that when only parents identified a child as a stealer, 14 percent became recidivists, but when only the teacher identified the child as a stealer, 46 percent became recidivists. Clearly, by the time a teacher identifies a child as a stealer, stealing is well established. Even more telling is if both parent and teacher identify a child as a stealer; 71 percent of children who were identified as stealers both at home and at school did not stop stealing and were apprehended even after an initial arrest. The evidence overwhelmingly argues that efforts to stop stealing should begin early and include assessments and interventions across a child's varied social settings. Child helpers must recognize that their desire to save face for a child by not discussing the child's stealing with neighbors, relatives, and teachers may prevent the coordinated and early intervention that a child needs. By the time others learn that stealing is occurring, the time for intervention may be past.

The Path to Stealing. When the likelihood of suffering negative consequences as a result of stealing is small, children quickly suspect that the odds of successful stealing are in their favor. As their stealing progresses and no negative side effects ensue, their hunch is confirmed. West and Farrington (1977) determined that only 1.5 percent of youths who bought stolen goods and only 8.3 percent of shoplifters were caught and convicted. However, more than one out of three youths who stole cars and almost two out of three who broke into and entered buildings were apprehended. As detailed in Rutter and Giller (1984), Great Britain's clear-up rate (that is, the proportion of recorded offenses for which a person has been arrested, summoned, or cautioned) for robbery, theft, handling stolen goods, and burglary is only about 33 percent.

Successful lying furthers the likelihood of escaping punishment for stealing. Since lying helps youths avoid the penalties of stealing, stealing and lying go hand in hand (Patterson, 1982). Families often fail to punish stealing, only occasionally punish lying, and too often fail to reward honesty; they then wonder why stealing does not stop and lying increases. A child who is rewarded for telling the truth will not be much of a stealer. The likelihood of negative consequences must be increased for stealing treatments to succeed.

Families of Stealers. Patterson's (1982) investigations of stealing using children in clinics and their parents show that parents of stealers are less involved with their children than are parents of young aggressors; the latter parents may be hostile and punitive but involved. Engaging in stealing (and other co-

vert delinquent acts, such as substance abuse) is closely tied
to the failure of parents to notice and respond to their child's
stealing. The longer the stealing continues and the more settings in which it occurs, the less straightforward will be the treatment. Children who steal are often allowed to wander and are
not required to account for their whereabouts or activities or
to abide by curfews or set mealtimes. Partly because of their
parents' longstanding neglect of them, adolescent stealers are
more difficult than socially aggresssive children to treat. Teaching and motivating parents to supervise their children and to
apply appropriate consequences are critical to success (Loeber,
1982; McCord, 1978).

Even though the research on family contributors to delinquency encompasses more than just stealing, some delinquency
studies do distinguish between stealers and other delinquents,
and others provide information relevant to understanding the
families of stealers. Gove and Crutchfield (1982) found that the
degree to which a child cares what the parent thinks of his or
her behavior is more strongly associated with delinquency (including stealing) than are the conventionally accepted correlates
of delinquency, which include socieoeconomic status, race, and
parents' marital relationship. Congruent with the notion that
wandering is strongly related to stealing, not knowing one's
child's friends is also strongly associated with delinquency. Overall, ineffectual family functioning, far more than family makeup
or class, is associated with delinquency. These findings agree to
an impressive extent with those of Loeber and Dishion's (1983)
review of predictors of male delinquency; they too found that
family management was the best predictor of delinquency. Males
who steal, like aggressive boys, attempt to coerce family and
peers more than nonproblem boys do (Patterson, 1982), but their
parents do not reciprocate the coercive behavior as much as other
parents (Reid and Hendriks, 1973; Loeber, Weissman, and
Reid, 1983). The limits of family factors for distinguishing stealers must also be recognized since peer and economic factors also
influence stealing. Neuhring (1976) compared family and personality profiles of repeat auto thiefs, non-auto thiefs, and other
criminals whose auto thefts were incidental to their crimes; he
found no differences.

Anthony Delano: Background of a Case Study

Anthony Delano became known to Mr. Fernandez in Mr. Fernandez's role as consultant to a group home. Twelve-year-old Anthony entered group care after release from juvenile detention. He had stolen a motorcycle and was thereafter arrested and incarcerated. Since this was his fourth arrest, the juvenile court determined that a community placement was needed. A brief stay in foster care resulted in his running away. He was returned to juvenile hall after stealing a jacket from a department store. From there he moved to the group home.

Anthony was a thief of longstanding. Anthony's mother recalled that he had stolen since he was a small boy. She reported that beginning at age four he often brought home—by stuffing them into his socks—small "souvenirs" from visits to his cousins. She told him that he should not do that but, because she did not want to make him look bad in front of her sister or make herself seem like an inadequate parent, she never took those "souvenirs" away or made him return them. (When the cousins paid return visits, she even hid them.) Anthony often borrowed things from his twin brother without asking and that was a great cause for fighting. Ms. Delano also reported finding many things in the garage that she did not remember purchasing but claimed that she could not be sure since the garage was always in chaos. When she asked Anthony about them, he told her he did not know about them.

By the time Anthony was six, his mother suspected that he was stealing money from her wallet but was never quite sure since she was a waitress and kept a lot of cash around. The school did not report his stealing, and because Ms. Delano did not want to aggravate his reputation for being a difficult child, she did not mention his stealing. Since his behavior was generally impulsive and unmanageable, Ms. Delano's concerns usually focused on Anthony's poor work and fighting and how his hyperactivity might be controlled. Ritalin seemed to control his stealing somewhat, but Anthony's grandmother did not like its use and convinced Anthony not to take it. Financially strapped, Anthony's "habit" of finding jackets and shirts and even a bicycle were both a concern and a relief for his mother. She learned not to ask him questions, because he became quite upset and would yell such things as "It's my jacket. So what. Don't I need a jacket? My friend didn't need it no more. What's the problem?" Ms. Delano did not know what to say or do.

From conversations with Anthony's brother Paul, Ms. Delano believed that Anthony usually stole alone. Although he had one breaking-and-entering charge from a runaway incident with a group-home mate, this seemed the exception. Paul told Ms. Delano that Anthony often stole from stores, garages, and backyards when he was out at night. He took food, clothes, and beer. In the afternoons he stole from friends' homes.

Assessment

Interventions with stealers require assessment of the child and of family and school management, social settings, physical settings, cognitive styles, and incentives. As with other interventions described in these pages, programs for reducing problem behavior of children and youth will meet with greater success if modified in accord with characteristics of the child, family, problem, and setting.

The Child. Although stealers are not known for their candor, a thorough assessment that includes specific questions about the circumstances of thefts is possible. By the time most stealers are working with child helpers, they will admit that stealing is a problem and that they wish to stop stealing. This does not ensure, of course, that they will comfortably and completely describe their stealing behavior to child helpers. Thorough assessments will, therefore, require dogged pursuit of detail.

To encourage disclosure, Henderson (1982) suggests that the interviewer reward all replies by the stealer that comply with the interviewer's expectations for information and that concede that the child helper's description of the stealing event is correct; for example, "So, as I understand it—please correct me if I get anything wrong—you steal about twice a week (Pause). Okay, and you steal mainly from garages (Pause). I see, with friends (Pause). All right, and usually after dark (Pause)." Still,

engaging the child in describing the stealing is more important
than gaining confessions of the full range of his or her illicit activities. Such assessments of stealers will be time consuming but
often worthwhile.

The Family and School. Assessment of family and school
management of stealing is foremost in importance for helping
young stealers. Young stealers will not change unless their environments change. The rewards of stealing—excitement, a sense
of mastery, and new material belongings—must be counteracted
with punitive consequences for stealing. Assessment must consider the key elements of family and school management: rules,
monitoring, and consequences.

Many families do not have articulated or understood rules
for children. Such families are not only likely to have more aggressive children, they are more likely to have children who steal
(Patterson, 1982). Children must know the time to be home,
their household responsibilities, how the possessions of other
family members should be regarded, and what will happen if
these conditions are not met. Child helpers should ask caregivers
and children about their understanding of the rules with regard
to these issues. Definitions of stealing should also be ascertained
from all family members. How families recognize and reward
adherence to rules also needs to be known.

If rules are developed but not used, however, they soon
become meaningless, and children learn to not take rules seriously. Rules cannot be used unless caregivers observe children's
behavior. Monitoring requires that caregivers know where the
child should be according to the rules, whether his or her responsibilities have been fulfilled, and whether he or she has unfamiliar
possessions. Monitoring of prosocial behavior—"How did school
go today?" for example—is also essential to provide examples
of appropriate problem-solving behavior and to ensure that
children receive praise for success. (Families of delinquents often
fail to check on a child's progress at school, according to Wadsworth, 1979.) Families and school teachers should be queried
about their ability to monitor young stealers. For example, does
the teacher take a cigarette break or talk with other teachers
at an end of the playground where children cannot be observed

entering and leaving the school, or is the child regularly left at home without parental supervision?

Finally, rules without consequences do not shape lives. More than half of all stealers are social aggressors (Patterson, 1982). Many caregivers do not administer the negative consequences that should follow stealing because they find confronting children who are very likely to counterattack to be a dreadful chore. Reprimands and removal of privileges typically result in hostile outbursts, so caregivers must have considerable instruction, encouragement, and monitoring to build their child-management skills. Child helpers should assess the response of children to caregivers' past efforts to reduce stealing and identify the ability of caregivers to reprimand, use time out, and withdraw privileges. Child helpers should make sure there is agreement among all of a child's caregivers about appropriate consequences. This assessment will inform child helpers of how much effort must be directed at reducing social aggression before a stealing reduction program can succeed. As always, the ability of caregivers to have rewarding interchanges with the child must also be reviewed. If a simple inquiry about the child's whereabouts or a positive comment about the child's success in following the rules is greeted with hostility, this, too, will influence planning.

Social Setting. Knowledge of the stealer's social setting provides much information needed to develop a useful intervention. Whether the stealer works alone, with one friend, with a group of friends, or with an organized group influences the continuance of stealing. Stealers who work alone are most likely to find cognitive and social rewards in stealing that can be replaced through structured interventions. Finding alternative benefits to replace the camaraderie that accompanies friendships based on stealing or that counter the rewards and pressures of group stealing is more difficult. When possible, child helpers should endeavor to isolate stealers from friends and groups or, if that is not feasible, as in the case of brothers who steal together, should treat them together. It should be noted that the strategies described in this chapter do not necessarily apply to gangs or organized thievery.

Physical Setting. Where and from whom a youth steals must be known before intervention plans are developed. Is the youth equally likely to steal from a store, a school, other people's homes, and family; or is the youth more likely to steal in one setting or another? Assessment of thefts should include questions about the whereabouts of the owners of the property at the time of the theft. What is stolen in each setting also warrants assessment. For example, stealers who take items of value to others but not to the stealers themselves may be stealing for revenge or maliciousness (Lambert, 1976). Alternative ways of expressing anger can be developed in addition to standard social and cognitive treatments.

Cognitive Approach. Children who steal differ in the degree to which they plan their thefts. Henderson (1982) described a youth who had problems falling asleep and would thoroughly plan a theft during his efforts to sleep. Other youth act more spontaneously after entering into situations that offer the opportunity to steal; for instance, youth who are unsupervised in friends' homes may steal, even though their original intention was simply to kill time. In between the planful and spontaneous stealers are youth who develop plans so that they can take advantage of a stealing opportunity, but who do not plan or engineer the opportunity.

Interventions differ according to which cognitive approach a youth takes. Planful youth should be queried about when they make their plans. In the case of the sleepless stealer, relaxation exercises enabled him to sleep more easily, with the result that he spent less time planning thefts. For other planners, cognitive rewards or punishments may be most effective. For youth who steal only when the opportunity arises, interventions should emphasize reducing wandering and associated opportunities for stealing. These interventions will receive more discussion later in this chapter.

Incentives. Motives for stealing may be deduced from how children and youth typically dispose of their stolen items (Henderson, 1982). Are items thrown away or lost, consumed (spent, eaten, used, or sold), given away (to friends, family, or girlfriend or boyfriend), or hidden?

Youth who steal for revenge or to wantonly strike out against peers or authority may steal items with no apparent worth to them and subsequently toss or give them away. Malicious stealing is often associated with boredom; a sense that the home, school, or care facility is unfair; and poor supervision of high-temptation areas. Malicious stealing of another child's prized items or money requires efforts to encourage the victim to more closely supervise possessions, to avoid talking about possessions, and to lend possessions judiciously. For these mischievous or malicious stealers, intervention may require working with organizations or persons against whom the stealer seeks revenge. Group incentive programs and overcorrection are often indicated as well.

Probably the most common incentives for stealing are the pleasures that accompany or follow consuming or selling stolen items. Youth who rely on stealing to extend their budgets require alternative means to acquire material goods. Stealing may also bolster a youth's sense of competence, so analysis of the cognitive association between stolen possessions and self-worth is needed. The latter analysis is even more true for youth who steal primarily to provide friends and lovers with presents. Interventions with these youths may be facilitated by the cooperation of those on whom they bestow their largesse. In some cases these significant others may have come to rely on the stolen items and may provide abudant social and sexual rewards for stealers. Social-skills training may help youth develop constructive dialogues with friends, family, and lovers and find alternatives to giving material goods for maintaining those relationships.

Youth often experience physical pleasures from stealing, including a heightened level of arousal in general (stealing for kicks) or sexual arousal. Straightforward questions about "rushes," body sensations, and "sex drives" that accompany or follow stealing may help youth begin to recognize these motivators. For youth who find thinking about stealing to be sexually arousing and use these thoughts while masturbating (Moler, 1977), the intervention should include reprogramming of masturbation around appropriate sexual experiences (Henderson, 1982).

Youth who hide what they steal may be compulsive stealers who do not steal for gain and are instead humiliated by their failure to control their actions. These youth are typically sensitive to social evaluations of their actions. These youth may steal mementos of people or places (for example, of a foster home that they are leaving). Interventions with such stealers may also require networking with significant people in the environments from which the child steals along with discussion of acceptable items to take as mementos and alternative mementos like photo albums and life books.

Anthony Delano: Assessment

Mr. Fernandez's interview with Anthony yielded much useful information. Anthony's greatest wish was to be treated fairly and to have the chance to do things like his brother could without everybody watching over him. He reported that he did want to go home but wanted to go to a different school when he went back to his community. He believed that his reputation was so bad that no one would give him a chance.

Anthony admitted to stealing "small things," but he said that he knew the guy who owned the motorcycle and did not steal it, that the store security guard was just trying to get him mad by picking on him, and that he had just forgotten that he did not have enough money to pay for the jacket he had tried on. Anthony had difficulty saying whether he planned his thefts or committed them spontaneously. He at first argued the latter in his effort to convince Mr. Fernandez that he was a "gee whiz, I just got excited and mixed up" kind of stealer. Later he described knowing which homes were the easiest to hit. Anthony did not give much of his loot away, nor did he hide it. He used most of it and traded or sold some. He enjoyed showing off his new acquisitions and was clearly a proud stealer.

The assessment interview also identified incentives that could be used to help Anthony change his ways. Anthony enjoyed free time, snacks, television, and the use of his bicycle. Enjoyable forms of free time reported by Anthony included "hanging out" near a local convenience store and at a video arcade, going to the homes of friends, break dancing on the campus of the local community college, and going to dances. He also identified several activities—break dancing, soccer, and motorcross racing—that he could do to keep busy and out of trouble.

Mr. Fernandez assessed family management in an interview with Anthony, Paul, Ms. Delano, and Anthony's grandmother. The family agreed that since Ms. Delano had started working, the family was not as close. Ms. Delano worked from 3 to 10 P.M., and the grandmother could not get Anthony and Paul to sit down and eat dinner together. Ms. Delano did not insist on family mealtimes; the boys fed themselves from food she prepared ahead. Family rules existed for going to school, not swearing at Grandma, and not smoking in the house. Disapproval and threatened grounding were the consequences most often used when these rules were broken.

Intervention

Stealing begins and is sustained for many reasons. Renshaw (1977) has chronicled twenty-three different reasons that stealing may occur, including biological factors (for example, genetic factors such as the presence of XYY chromosomes), sociological factors (for example, peer pressure), unconscious factors (for example, seeking punishment for guilt or defending against depression), and conscious factors (for example, the desire to feel powerful). Caregivers may explain away a child's stealing using these or other reasons and so fail to act to stop the stealing. A family described by Reid and Patterson (1976) believed in still another reason—"possession by the devil"; Stumphauzer (1976) cited a family that blamed stealing on "a sickness." Such beliefs are not uncommon, since many stealers are committed to their course of action from a very early age. They seem to know how to steal without example or instruction. One seven-year-old stealer in the author's practice informed school cafeteria staff that be would be charging his lunch for the school year and proceeded to spend each day's lunch money on snacks and cigarettes. At school's end, his mother was sent an invoice for the lunch money he owed. (The child, unfortunately, was beaten for his crime and was not required to make restitution to his parents or school.) The same youth, now eleven and on probation, while en route from a gas station with a full gas can to fill up his mother's out-of-gas car, stole money from a pedestrian by threatening to pour gasoline on her and light it. The boy's parents could not understand where he had learned to do such things and thought he was "born to steal."

Stealing interventions must counter the attractions of material rewards, peer and self-congratulation, and excitement as well as the stealing habit itself. Treatments that enlist several methods may be most effective, although evidence suggests that younger, more prosocial, and less experienced stealers can be helped with interventions that rely on one approach that counteracts the stealers' dominant reasons for stealing (see, for example, Brooks and Snow, 1972; Matson, Coleman, DiLorenzo, and Vucelic, 1981; Stumphauzer, 1976; Wetzel, 1971). For older and more committed stealers, a combination of family management and specific antistealing interventions is often necessary—and, at times, insufficient.

Labeling and Consequences. Labeling is the linchpin of stealing treatment. Labeling means calling stealing what it is. Patterson (1982, p. 265) describes "substantial empirical evidence that many embezzlers, auto thiefs, check forgers, and persons involved in assaults or rape *do not* view themselves as criminal or delinquent." They do not label their activities as crimes. For example, "one child during an intake interview, was asked whether he had ever stolen anything. He answered that he had not. When asked whether he found things and brought them home, he answered, 'Yes, he finds things all the time'" (Patterson, Reid, Jones, and Conger, 1975, p. 136). Stealers may not, at the outset, accept the appropriate label. Elliott, Ageton, and Canter (1979) report that delinquent children who were caught and labeled as delinquent suffered no loss in self-esteem. Only those who were also counseled had lowered self-esteem. Apparently, the counseling led them to correctly label their criminal activities.

Children learn that their behavior is stealing and that it is serious when caregivers and child helpers repeatedly tell them

and show them. Adherence to a rigorous definition of stealing is indispensible. A clear definition helps parents stop arguing with their children about whether they were stealing and
helps stealers label their behavior more accurately. Slang that
blurs the interpretation of the act of stealing—"borrowed,"
or "souvenired," for example—should be corrected. Careful
adherence to a definition of stealing and the application of predetermined consequences for *all* stealing should lessen or end
possession of items (1) that "my friend did not want anymore,"
(2) that "I found on the way home from school," (3) that "the
lady at the store gave me because I did some errands for her
and she likes me," and (4) that "my friend left over here when
he stopped over (and you weren't home)—I'll be sure to try
to return them to him (but he doesn't go to my school anymore, so I'm not sure I can)." Stealing of consumables may
not decrease, but the bringing home of goods is likely to lessen
as labeling and consequences become consistent. Guidelines
to help parents recognize and define stealing are shown in
Exhibit 11.

The difficulties in labeling stealing should not be underestimated. Even Reid and Patterson (1976), who strongly stress
the importance of calling stealing *stealing*, report that one boy's
progress during their stealing intervention program was successful and that "although the stealing had not stopped completely
at the time of this report, one of the two events reported in follow-
up was *marginal* (one involving stealing an empty milk bottle;
the other involved his taking another boy's jacket)" (p. 139,
emphasis added). Although the authors do not deny that these
actions were stealing, as many parents might, their use of *marginal* to describe the stealing demonstrates the powerful tendency
to take some stealing incidences less seriously than others and
illustrates how easily parents can progress from taking an event
without utmost seriousness to forgiving it entirely.

A child who is punished for stealing by caregivers when
they are not certain that the child is guilty of stealing may be
unfairly treated and may complain bitterly. Caregivers are likely
to sympathize and, in respect for the child's rights, drop or
reduce the charges and consequences. Adler (1981) argues that

Exhibit 11. Handout to Help Caregivers Define Stealing.

1. The most important part of working to decrease stealing is defining stealing as stealing. Stealing is the child's taking, or being in possession of, anything that does not clearly belong to him or her. The parents (or teachers) are the only judges. They may label an act as stealing by observing it, by having it reported to them, or by noticing that something is missing. There is no arguing about guilt or innocence. It is the child's job to be sure that he or she is not accused. The value of the object is irrelevant. Trading and borrowing are not permissible. Any "purchases" that the child brings home must be accompanied by a receipt; otherwise they must be returned and consequences instituted.

2. Once the behavior of stealing has been labeled, then consequences must be applied. Caregivers should avoid discussions, shaming, or counseling.

3. *Every* stealing event must be so labeled and consequences given.

4. Caregivers should avoid using excessive detective tactics (such as searches); they should just keep their eyes open and investigate the origins of new property.

5. Consequences for stealing should be extra chores or other work and loss of privileges for the day of the stealing, and basic privileges only on the following weekend. There should be no other consequences such as humiliation or beating. Special privileges can be earned again on the following day.

6. *Remember*: Stealing goes hand in hand with a child's wandering and caregivers' not knowing the whereabouts of their child. Check-in times are recommended if stealing is a problem.

7. Do not tempt the child. Keep items like those that the child has stolen in the past away from the child. For example, avoid leaving a wallet or cigarette pack in view or unwatched.

8. Stealing may occur no matter how many possessions a child has, so giving a child everything is not a successful approach to ending stealing. The child should, however, have some way of earning his or her own money so that he or she may have a choice of things to buy.

"when there is a stealing incident and the culprit is identified *beyond a reasonable doubt*, disciplinary action is necessary" (p. 165; emphasis added). Reliance on this guideline, however, will severely curtail caregivers' opportunities to help young stealers. Knowing beyond a reasonable doubt that stealing occurred requires catching a child with an item of known origins and finding that the accused child can provide no reasonable explanation for the article's appearance in his or her possession. In practice, this rarely happens. To help stealers, caregivers must operate on their convictions when they have a "preponderance of evidence" rather than evidence that goes "beyond a reasonable doubt.'' The suspicion of stealing is all the proof that is needed. The result may be some unfairness, but that is a lesser evil than the result of too rigorous standards, which is ineffectiveness. Child helpers must dare to be wrong. It is the child's responsibility to avoid giving child helpers reason to err. Group consequences are another viable solution when culprits are not known; examples of effective group consequences will be discussed later in this chapter.

Loss of privileges and extra chores are feasible and appropriate consequences for stealing. For each stealing event, two hours of work (such as chores, writing or arithmetic practice, or a reading assignment) is fitting. All basic privileges—that is, phone, television, and snacks—should be suspended until the work is completed. Special privileges—movies and going out to play with friends, for example—should not be reinstated until after the next weekend. If the theft occurs on a weekend, full privileges can be earned back for the following weekend days (see Chapter Eleven for additional discussion of consequences involving working, writing, reading, or sitting in time out during free time following a serious lapse in behavior). Restitution and overcorrection (discussed later in this chapter) should also follow a theft.

A procedure to label and provide consequences for stealing helped Steve, a seven-year-old in a classroom for children with severe learning and behavior problems, become a reformed stealer (Rosen and Rosen, 1983). All of Steve's belongings were marked with green stick-on circles by his teacher every school morning. At the day's end, Steve's possessions without stickers were counted as stolen. Before consequences for stealing were provided, Steve stole an average of six items per day. After his teacher began to provide praise and points toward purchases at the classroom store for every fifteen minutes that Steve did not have any stolen goods (and took away points and gave a reprimand when he did have possessions that were not his), his stealing declined to one item every three days. This apparently effective stealing reduction strategy was then removed for a week to test the durability of the improvement; Steve returned to stealing five items per day. When the incentives were reinstated,

Steve's stealing again returned to less than one event every three days; this system continued for four weeks. During the following twelve days, the checkpoint intervals were extended from fifteen minutes to two hours, and Steve stole only one item. At this time, the program was discontinued. Monitoring of Steve's stealing continued, however; he stole only three items during the next month. Stealing was clearly a well-established but still tractable behavior pattern for Steve. No substitution of other inappropriate behavior was noted either; in fact, Steve's disruptive behavior (verbal and physical aggression, teasing, leaving an assigned area, and property destruction) decreased by half. The results also generalized to other places. Steve's parents reported that household items no longer disappeared, and his teachers reported that during two occasions when classmates stole food from the cafeteria, Steve did not.

Restitution and Overcorrection. The Bible suggests restitution (now known as *overcorrection*) of five oxen for every one stolen and four sheep for every sheep stolen, and the stealer who has nothing should be sold. Although translators of the Old Testament would have been more accurate if they had used *overcorrection* to describe this ancient procedure and although their penalties are a bit harsh, the concept is sound. Restitution still is often used—at least in a partial way—with youth who steal. Of the group-care facilities surveyed by Russo and Shyne (1980), 54 percent reported using "reparations" in response to "usual" stealing.

It is not clear whether overcorrection is used as often. Overcorrection is not simply vindictive; it shows promise with children who steal. In early work, Azrin and Wesolowski (1974) used overcorrection to reduce the twenty thefts per day among thirty-four residents of an institution. The residents were not children—their mean age was thirty-four—but they had, on the average, the IQ of fifteen-year-olds. Building on previous work with one resident thief (Azrin and Armstrong, 1973), they instituted an overcorrection procedure requiring a thief to return an item of identical worth in addition to returning the stolen item. This overcorrection, or theft reversal, procedure reduced thefts by 50 percent on the first day, by 75 percent on the second day, and by 100 percent on the fourth day.

Matson, Coleman, Lorenzo, and Vucelic (1981) helped two boys at a psychiatric institute to overcome their stealing with restitution and overcorrection. Because the procedure required room searches, the children and their parents were asked for informed consent after an explanation of the procedure was given. To assess the stealing, an inventory of each child's belongings was made—only paper items and clothing were excluded because they were not objects of stealing for these boys. (The authors agree that the assessment procedure was feasible because children's ability to hide stolen goods in an inpatient unit was less than in a community setting.) The procedure involved returning stolen items (when possible), apologizing to the victim, and five minutes of cleaning chores for every item stolen. This latter overcorrection procedure was used rather than the ''theft reversal'' procedure because giving back consumable items was impossible, and the children did not have funds to purchase items similar to those they stole.

Children responded negatively to the work procedure at first, and the staff was reluctant to implement it. For both staff and children, compliance increased as the program continued. Changes in stealing behavior were noted during the treatment and four and sixteen weeks after the boys' discharge from the unit. During the twelve days before the procedure was instituted, the boys each stole an average of eighteen items per day. By the end of treatment, their theft rate was less than one item per day between them. Follow-up found them in residential community-based treatment settings and continuing their low rates of stealing.

Three nine- and ten-year-old children housed in the same inpatient unit were treated by the same authors using overcorrection and reinforcement. The overcorrection procedure was as just described, and the reinforcement program involved giving the subject a reinforcer judged to be of considerable value by the subject and staff. If no stolen items were discovered during room check at 7:00, the subject received the reinforcer. If stolen items were found, the child was informed of this at 7:00, and no reinforcer was provided. A careful case evaluation showed the reinforcement procedure to be less effective than the overcorrection procedure, which reduced stealing from an average of twelve stolen items per day per child to a rate of none per day by the end of forty days; this rate was maintained until two months after the program's finish.

Some form of restitution for stealing is always possible, even when the stolen item has been consumed. Aside from the previously described consequences for stealing, the child should be required to meet the person who was victimized (for example, the store owner or neighbor), apologize, and return the object or whole or partial remuneration for it. If the child has stolen from a store, the caregiver should ask if the child can speak to the store supervisor. In a face-to-face meeting the child should apologize and return the merchandise or, if it has been consumed, damaged, or lost, ask how he can repay the theft (for example, by returning the item, working at the store, or staying out of the store for some fixed amount of time). If a child steals from another family member, then an overcorrection of twice the cost of the goods is appropriate. The overcorrection payment should be made over time to be sure that the child who stole is not prevented from participating in all social events that require some money. Because families of children who steal are notably poor at monitoring their children, child helpers should insure that the full restitution is completed. Children should also have the opportunity to earn income from chores that exceed what is typically expected—for example, washing the car, digging out a stump, or cutting down weeds.

Perhaps the worst time for child helpers who work with children who steal is when a child on probation steals something from a store or citizen. Because probation officers often have grossly oversized caseloads and can provide little help, reporting the theft is noxious, and the temptation is strong to continue implementing the behavior-change program and not involve the law. In such cases, however, home consequences are not sufficient. Reporting the theft is essential for a child to learn that stealing will not be ignored or protected. (Many overburdened juvenile justice programs are willing to tolerate some theft and will consider leaving the child in the community if a child and his or her family can show reasonable efforts toward improvement.)

Individual Incentive Systems. Social incentives can help eliminate stealing. Wetzel (1971) described the case of Mike, a ten-
year-old resident of a home for mildly disturbed children. Mike's
records showed stealing, destructive behavior, and firesetting
from the first grade. His behavior was unchanged by such labels
as "psychopath" and "passive-aggressive personality, aggressive
type, severe" or by services from a child guidance clinic, special
education, juvenile detention, and foster care; he continued to
steal at home and school, became a court ward, and entered
a residential facility at age eight. Because of his continued stealing, his relationships with others remained poor. Mike reported
that he could not control the stealing, even though he knew that
it was wrong. Well-intentioned but futile efforts to help Mike
included reframing his behavior as "attention seeking," providing a loving foster mother, spankings, social isolation, and
stern confrontations.

As a consultant, Wetzel suggested that Mike receive rewards for not stealing and lose privileges for stealing. Staff could
not identify any items that would be motivating enough to Mike
to change his stealing behavior. A look at his free-time activities
indicated that Mike (who was Mexican-American) had good rapport with a Spanish-speaking Chicana cook, Maria. Through an
interpreter, Wetzel asked her if she could serve as mediator, and
she agreed to help Mike. She began by strengthening her bond
with Mike by increasing her contact with him. Maria invited
Mike into the kitchen to help prepare Mexican meals and to go
with her to her home and church and on shopping trips. Mike
taught Maria new English words, and their mutual fondness grew.

Child-care workers were instructed to record every stealing
episode and to report the incident to Maria. When she learned
of a stealing incident she informed Mike, "I'm sorry that you
took so and so's such and such because now I can't let you come
home with me tonight." She was told to accept no excuses and,
instead, to walk away and resume their friendly exchanges the
following day. Mike's stealing behavior decreased steadily over
the months. Several stealing episodes were followed by loss of
his privilege to see Maria. These were followed by long stints
without stealing. Other stealing incidents were justified by staff

as "typical of the kids" or "minor" or "still better than before"; these were followed by more incidents. The consultant's recognition that new child-care staff must understand and implement the intervention resulted in more consistent treatment of Mike's stealing. As his stealing behavior decreased, Mike was rewarded with social praise by staff. Mike's verbal acknowledgments of his reduced stealing were heavily praised by staff and peers. As he stole less, his peer relationships improved, and his interest in spending time with Maria waned. His bedwetting also decreased during the four-month intervention.

Jackson (1984) suggests that rewarding alternative behaviors can be an effective foil to stealing. She describes several applications of a procedure that involves the child with the forbidden object rather than removing or punishing the child. A child in residential care who continued to steal food and money despite reprimands, beatings, and expulsions from school was made the money-collecting monitor who kept his classmates' money for their weekly swim. The boy kept careful records and was rewarded when everything tallied up just right. His reported stealing ceased. The same techniques worked with children reported to steal lunches—they were made lunch monitors—and with a child who stole from the pantry and was finally given a key to help ensure that nothing was again found missing. These children, too, were rewarded for their success. This technique—although not formally evaluated—seems applicable whenever responsibility for preserving or stealing items can be limited to a single child.

Application of Stealing-Reduction Programs in Group Settings. McNees and colleagues (1980) reduced youths' shoplifting in a convenience store by more than half with a clever system using the then-popular "Jaws" motif. To achieve the difficult goal of accurately counting stealing, items that were most commonly stolen were tagged, the tags were pulled off by the cashier at purchase, and the tags were then compared to the total number of items removed from the shelves to ascertain the number of stolen items.

Children were invited by poster to "Help stop 'Jaws' the shoplifting shark." Cashiers gave each child a cardboard shark's tooth every time they reported that they had remembered to pay for everything; five shark's teeth could be exchanged for a small prize from a treasure box. A graphic of a fisherman and ''Jaws'' showed the fisherman closer to hooking Jaws after each day that the shoplifting rate decreased. Children could cash in their teeth for two surprises during a two-day period when Jaws was hooked. After this period, Jaws would drop to the bottom of the ocean and would again only move up toward the fisherman on days when the rate improved. The program was accompanied by a marked but temporary reduction in shoplifting; the average weekly rate of thirty-two items stolen per week fell to fifteen during the duration of the program but then rebounded to forty-four after the program was terminated.

Even though the decrease in stealing was not permanent, the program clearly worked. The promise of this creative effort is obvious for settings like group homes, community centers, and emergency shelter-care facilities that cannot be fully supervised, have children with a limited attachment to the institution, and can roughly determine theft rates. The latter is most difficult for community-based treatment programs. In the best of several imperfect procedures, children or staff who have had something stolen report this to the setting supervisor. The supervisor then notes that the item has been stolen, offers a brief period of amnesty, and asks for news of the item. If it is not forthcoming, then the theft is recorded. Because stealing rates are lower for institutions than for stores, child-helping agencies or homes should use a weekly tally of stealing or require a string of no-theft days before bonus privileges are given. The risk that theft victims will be pressured not to report can be lessened by keeping the lengths of the periods leading to rewards short.

Classroom stealing is also troubling, costly, and reversible. To make the tracking of stolen objects easier, Switzer, Deal, and Bailey (1977) ''planted'' items in second-grade classrooms with stealing problems. Unlike ''sting'' operations, this program rewarded the use of self-control by providing group rewards if the planted items were not stolen. Teachers had reported that items such as money, pencils, pens, and toys were often missing two or three times in a single day. To assess classroom stealing rates, ten items, including erasers, a nickel, and magic markers, were placed around the room for ninety minutes daily. Items were placed on the teacher's desk, on the bookcase, near the water fountain, or at other classroom tables. Because similar items were frequently stolen, the planting of these items did not unduly incite the children to steal. The use of these items did, however, allow the consultants to assess whether their interventions were effective.

First, an antistealing lecture was given every five days in three classes, but it had no effect on stealing. In each class in succession, a group program was begun that rewarded the entire class with praise and ten minutes of free time after their snack period for not stealing or for returning any stolen items during a brief amnesty period when the teacher left the room. The failure to return a stolen item resulted in a quiet snack period and no free time.

Stealing decreased from a rate of 464 items during 194 classroom days of lectures or no intervention (an average of 2.4 items per day) to just 5 items during the remaining 50 classroom days of the school year (a rate of 0.1 items, or twenty-four times less per day). Hidden audiotaping of students' activities when the teacher left the room revealed no peer pressure to return items; instead, the tapes captured students' reframing of the problem as one of finding the lost items. Pre- and post-intervention sociograms showed no marked shift in children's friendship preferences. Teachers also indicated that stealing of nonplanted items decreased during the intervention. The use of group contingencies was shown to be effective and may have been the only appropriate intervention because even at the end of the study (and after at least 469 items were stolen), teachers still did not know who was responsible for the stealing. To implement this procedure in homes, classrooms, or residential units, a reliable theft-detection procedure must be developed. This is obviously more difficult in more fluid settings, although records of the cash in the kitchen drawer, liquor in the cabinet, and cigarette lighters in the purse can be maintained.

A ten-year-old boy, Jim, was stealing at school during recess and lunch by wandering back into his unoccupied classroom (Brooks and Snow, 1972). He was found with stolen items on his person and often traded them with friends for other desirable items. Jim's classroom behavior was also disruptive, and his academic achievement commensurately low. The teacher developed and explained a group contingency program to Jim and his classmates. Jim would receive points for completing his work, remaining in class for a full forty-five-minute period, or staying with the group when it left the class for an activity. When he earned ten points, the entire class would receive fifteen minutes of extra free time. If Jim did not complete his work, left class early, or left the group, the class would lose one minute from the next scheduled play period. Jim was also given ten cents for each ten points he earned. During the first week, Jim earned free time for his class each day and received much peer support for his efforts. His stealing stopped. The teacher terminated the program after one week, but the improvements reportedly persisted the remainder of the school year.

Cognitive Treatments. Just the thought of the consequences that might follow stealing—most prominently, guilt, capture, humiliation, and punishment—keeps most people from stealing. Cognitive treatments endeavor to increase the discomfort from the thought of stealing and the relief and satisfaction from not stealing. There are several cognitive strategies that can be used to help decrease stealing behavior.

A twelve-year-old compulsive stealer learned to use *cognitive self-reinforcement* to control her stealing during individual and family treatment (Stumphauzer, 1976). She had strong family and school support but had been stealing at home, in school, and in the community since age seven. She was increasingly isolated as a result of parental surveillance and, without the rewards of peer interaction, ever more dependent on the attention that her stealing garnered her. Prior to beginning the intervention, the child was given a medical examination, and her parents and teachers recorded her stealing behavior.

The young stealer first learned to imagine herself in situations where she was likely to steal and paying attention to items besides those that she usually stole. She learned to follow this shift in attention with self-reward statements like "I'm proud of myself" and "I'm trustworthy—I keep my hands to myself, they are not gummy, and my mind is on learning at school." After she had learned this strategy well, she began to practice it during actual forays into those high-temptation situations and to count her stealing episodes. As her stealing decreased, she began to cognitively reward herself for her reduced stealing as well as for her use of stealing-reduction strategies. With the additional assistance of a family contract that promised her praise, money, special activities, and a favorite Sunday meal as incentives for a week of not stealing, she quit stealing. The stealing had not recurred by the time of an eighteen-month follow-up assessment. Her likelihood of renewed stealing is remote, given the expansion in her prosocial peer network and her family's increased attention to other family concerns.

Stealing sequences were followed by imaginary punishment, or *cognitive self-punishment*, for a young man with a ten-year history of biweekly stealing. The youthful thief imagined stealing an item from a store, imagined that he was wearing an alarm that would sound as he got ready to steal, and then imagined getting caught by the manager (Guidry, 1975). He practiced these visualizations as he wandered the aisles of stores. To back up these negative consequences, he also imagined a series of negative consequences that might follow stealing, including being caught, the police being called, having handcuffs put on, being shoved into a police car and taken to the county jail, standing before a judge, and having his parents find out about his theft. The boy imagined these punishments every time he got in or out of his car. He was seen by a child helper weekly for a month and then monthly for three months. Stealing behavior dropped to zero during treatment; after ten months he attributed his lack of stealing to his "sense of responsibility that I didn't feel before" and the feeling that he might get caught (p. 169). During those ten months he had taken two items when he was sure that he would not get caught.

Cautela (1967) also used cognitive self-punishment with juvenile car thieves and burglars. In the treatment for car thieves, for example, the youths are asked what cars they prefer to steal and under what conditions. A vignette is then constructed from

that information. The self-punishing image of nausea is introduced after the thought of stealing; leaving the scene without
stealing is rewarded with a feeling of relief. A typical scene is
as follows: "You are walking down a street. You notice a real
sharp sports car. You walk toward it with the idea of stealing
it. As you're walking toward it you start to get a funny feeling
in your stomach. You feel sick to your stomach and you have
a slight pain in your gut. As you keep walking, you really start
to feel sick, and food starts coming up in your mouth. You're
just about to reach for the handle of the door and you can't
hold it any longer. You vomit all over your hand, the car door,
the upholstery inside, all over your clothes. The smell starts to
get to you and you keep puking from it. It's all over the place.
It's dripping from your mouth. You turn around and run away
and then you start to feel better" (p. 463). Cautela indicates
that most juvenile offenders cooperate well with this procedure.
Although its overall efficacy is untested, the procedure seems
reasonable.

Evidence suggests that stealers have inadequate *self-instruction* skills. Delinquent youth show less likelihood than nondelinquent youth of choosing a small immediate reward over a larger
but delayed reward (Unikel and Blanchard, 1973). Delinquent
youth spend more time than nondelinquent youth thinking about
immediate goals rather than planning for longer-range goals
(Landau, 1975). Delinquent youth, including stealers, are more
likely to rely on external controls than self-control (Beck and
Ollendick, 1976), and this tendency—even within the delinquent
subgroup—is associated with the rate of offending before and
after treatment (Ollendick, Elliott, and Matson, 1980).

Delinquent youth can apply self-instruction training. They
can, for example, improve their academic performance by learning to set goals for themselves (Ayllon and Milan, 1979; Gagne,
1975). Other self-instruction programs have resulted in improved
vocational training (Seymour and Stokes, 1976) and room cleaning (Wood and Flynn, 1978). In Seymour and Stokes's study,
older adolescent females in a maximum-security institution were
taught to self-monitor and record their appropriate behavior,
and the staff rewarded these behaviors with tokens and privileges

that had not helped improve the young women's behavior when it was monitored by the staff. Their behavior improved significantly with the use of self-monitoring.

Little has been reported about the use of self-instruction training with stealers. Haines, Jackson, and Davidson (1983) compared the effectiveness of general moral development training with a Direct Instruction Program (DIP) to prepare preadolescents to refrain from stealing. During six sessions, the children were taught to apply a resistance response chain. They learned to identify Temptation Problem Situations (TPS), to observe their initial reaction of over-excitement and of focusing on the desired object, and to apply a three-step process of self-control in order to bolster the decision not to steal. Perhaps most important, they were taught to identify even remotely feasible alternatives to stealing that still resulted in obtaining the desired object. Although not tested on a group of known stealers, this program suggests that preadolescents can learn stealing-resistance strategies if these are carefully developed to match their cognitive styles.

Combined Treatments. Henderson (1982) developed an Individualized Combined Treatment (ICT) method to help ten boys who wanted to stop stealing. All youthful participants had to first state that they wanted to stop stealing. (Henderson reports that few youths were unable to say this.) Next, a definition of stealing ("taking or having in your possession anything that does not belong to you") was agreed on. During the assessment interview, characteristics of the stealing and disposal of stolen items were discussed. Relaxation and self-control training were included in the combined program, as were positive external incentives for not stealing. Procedures were learned during daily sessions for one week. After one week, sessions led by the child helper became increasingly less common, and self-relaxation sessions became more common. After relaxation training provided a youth with an inner experience that sharply differed from the arousal state associated with stealing, the youth learned to imagine himself in a high-temptation situation and to use calming cues and then visualize walking away without stealing. To extend this self-control training to the external environment, child-helping adults informed youths who completed the self-instruction component that they would arrange stealing oportunities for them in their school and residence and would then provide bonuses for not stealing. These "traps" were made increasingly less obvious and the items increasingly easy to take without being caught.

To provide external incentives for not stealing, some record of not stealing must be maintained. Obtaining such a record is no small feat, but not impossible. Henderson's approach was to provide every stealer in treatment with a notebook or "stealing diary." Two types of entries were made in the diary: one, by an adult (usually a parent or teacher), when any length of time elapsed in which the stealer was not observed to have stolen; and the other by adults at both ends of any journey—signatures and time of departure and arrival were noted. In the latter case, if the time logged in is similar to the measured time for the journey, these minutes are also logged as nonstealing time. (Over the treatment period, the youth becomes increasingly responsible for keeping the diary.) All nonstealing time is rewarded with back-up privileges and prizes. Identifying back-up privileges is a key feature of the ICT program. Rewards that substitute for the losses incurred by the cessation of stealing are ideal. If peer attention is the incentive for stealing, then day trips with peers (and adult supervisors) to an amusement park may substitute. If thrills were the stealing incentive, then opportunities to ride motor scooters may be well received by youths.

The ten youths treated with the ICT approach had been stealing from six months to eight years and had been in as many as nine previous treatment programs and as few as zero. After ICT, only two youths reported stealing a total of three times during the first year after treatment and not for the two years after that. Considering that these two youths had a total of thirteen years of pretreatment stealing, these changes are marked and suggest that Henderson's method may be useful for other child helpers working with stealers.

Anthony Delano: Intervention

Ms. Delano, Anthony, Paul, and Grandma learned to define stealing. Each received a written definition of stealing and read it together. Likely difficulties in applying the definition were reviewed. Anthony said that it was not right to think that everything he did was wrong and to ask questions later. Mr. Fernandez told him that he looked forward to the time when Anthony stopped stealing; until then he would have to avoid activities that looked like stealing and situations that might tempt him to steal. All possible alibis for having stolen items were reviewed so Anthony would know that his mother was prepared to dismiss them.

Anthony's access to afternoon and evening free time, snacks, television, and his bicycle were redefined as privileges and made contingent on implementing the antistealing plan. Anthony was initially furious about this change. He accused his mother of becoming his probation officer, said that he did not want "to live in no penitentiary, no matter what the address," and threatened to run away. He learned to accept the conditions slowly, and only because his mother was determined to restrict his legitimate and illegitimate use of privileges: his bicycle was locked up with a lock that he could not remove, a record was kept of the ice cream bars in the refrigerator, and if Anthony watched television when Ms. Delano was out, then Anthony would lose evening privileges. Grandma was the monitor of television watching until 8:00, when she went to bed.

Controlling access to free time—and, hence, reducing wandering—was difficult. Even though Ms. Delano was not home when Anthony came home from school, Anthony was expected to check in immediately after school. He was told to call Ms. Delano at work when he arrived home and, if she were not available, to leave a message. To ensure that he was not calling from a pay phone booth or calling from home and then running back out into the community, Ms. Delano called him once or twice between 3:30 and 5:00. If he did not answer the phone—no matter what excuse he gave—then he was considered to be away from home. He had to earn permission to visit friends' houses (and when he did, he had to provide a phone number at which he could be reached) or to go to dances. He was not permitted to "hang out." In short, Anthony got the messages that (1) he should inform his mother of his whereabouts at all times, (2) his mother should be able to determine that he was where he said he was at all times, (3) wandering and stealing went hand in hand and were the rationale for so closely monitoring his behavior, and (4) free time is a privilege.

Anthony's participation in the stealing-reduction program also had benefits. First, exceptional school and home performance for any period of time might merit additional bonuses and opportunities for more desirable free-time experiences such as motorcross racing or going to dances. Trips to a local speedway to race child-sized cars and trips to a favorite pizza parlor were also available following weeks with no curfew violations and with positive reports from teachers.

Stealing was the second target of intervention. Because Anthony's behavior was generally unprincipled, the likelihood that he was a compulsive stealer was small. (In any case, if child helpers cannot tell what kind of stealer they have on their hands, then they should treat the stealing with an incentive system.) With much coaching and the help of the photocopied guidelines provided earlier in this chapter, Ms. Delano defined stealing for Anthony. Stealing occurred when packs of cigarettes were missing, money was gone (Ms. Delano opened her first checking account so that she could deposit her cash in a bank machine on the way home), or anything that did not belong to Anthony showed up at home. Week after week Ms. Delano (and Mr. Fernandez) told Anthony that the suspicion of stealing was sufficient to institute the penalty; Anthony did not have to be found guilty beyond a reasonable doubt.

All stealing incidents were treated the same: (1) Anthony was required to complete reading, writing, and working tasks for the remainder of the day; (2) he was restricted to home for the first weekend after the theft and, depending on his behavior the following week, might be restricted to home the next weekend as well; (3) if the theft was from a family member, then Anthony was required to work off double the cost of the theft by completing the chores of other family members (for these occasions only, Anthony's work was valued at the minimum wage); and (4) Anthony's theft of property from the community—no matter how small—was reported in a letter to his probation officer that Ms. Delano and Anthony both signed.

Anthony also rehearsed cognitions that supported his efforts to stop stealing. Once a week—usually just prior to the Sunday family meeting with the child helper—he wrote an edition of the *Free Press* (an example is shown in Exhibit 12). At first, Mr. Fernandez made a special effort to work with Anthony on the *Free Press*, then the responsibility for providing assistance switched to Ms. Delano; finally Anthony earned $1.00 a week from his mother for writing the *Free Press* by himself.

Exhibit 12. Sample of *The Free Press*: A Self-Management Technique for Young Stealers on Probation.

THE FREE PRESS
                                               Volume I

Something that I like about having my freedom and living at home is:

Something I did this week that will help me stay free and at home is:

Something I can do next week that will help me stay free and at home is:

Author _____

Editor _____

Date _____

The questions to which Anthony wrote self-instruction responses varied over time but began with those shown in Exhibit 12. His responses also varied, especially after changes in the responses were required for him to earn points toward privileges. Anthony initially resented the question about what he liked about his freedom. He would answer, "It's better than juvenile hall." Later he began to identify specific aspects of community living that he enjoyed (such as going dancing or riding his bicycle).

His responses to what he did and what he planned to do tended to be general (for example, "I went to school" or "I could go by the rules"). After six weeks, his mother became the "editor" of the *Free Press* and their collaboration led to discussions of Anthony's successes and plans. Ms. Delano was skillful at identifying signs of progress and adding her comments to his.

    The success of the intervention was not absolute. Anthony responded well to the requirement to be at home and reduced his stealing to not at all in the first month, two times in the second month, and only one time each in the third and fourth months. He whined frequently about the injustice of it all, however, and so after a while his mother initiated a change in the consequences so that he was given additional penalties for whining. This adaptation of the program was her first and suggested that she was carefully monitoring and responding to Anthony's performance— she had previously not noted or responded to either his threats or his complaints. Her change was very gratifying to Mr. Fernandez. Unfortunately, lost in his reverie about ways to further encourage Ms. Delano's independent management of the program, he failed to insist that Anthony also be able to achieve benefits for cooperating with his mother's requests and fulfilling his responsibilities. This seemingly simple change in the program, along with the end of school, unsettled Anthony, and he ran away. Recalling earlier discussions about running away, Anthony's mother responded appropriately and did not chase him. She called friends to no avail and, after twenty-four hours, she called the police. Anthony called a few hours later from a "friend's house" near his previous group home and complained about how he was taken for granted and all he got was more and more chores to do. Following the plan rehearsed by phone with Mr. Fernandez, she told Anthony that she loved him and wanted him at home; she reminded Anthony that there would be consequences from running away but that they would be manageable; and she told him that when those consequences were completed, she and he would review the situation and discuss ways to reward him for better behavior. He said that he was not sure he wanted to come home anyway and hung up. He was home later that night.

Anthony reduced his stealing at home and, to a lesser extent, in the community. Three months after the six-month intervention stopped, he was caught shoplifting athletic socks in a department store. His mother restarted the antistealing program. Because the judge was impressed with the progress Anthony had made and his mother's increased ability to manage his behavior, his probation was extended, but he was allowed to remain at home. One year later, according to his mother's report, she was letting him stay out more, but he had not brought any stolen items home. His probation was terminated.

Many stealers profess that they wish to stop stealing. Although these claims may not be wholeheartedly genuine, they represent a beginning point for treatment. Henderson (1981, p. 232) notes that, "to the surprise of adults, most young thieves are adamant that they want to stop." He claims to have met only one stealer during his seven years of work in juvenile corrections who reported that he did not want to stop stealing. Henderson's success and the success of others argue that a willingness to engage in treatment is more important than an initially sincere wish to stop stealing.

Caveats are still, however, in order. Patterson's (1982) conclusions after more than a decade's work with stealers suggest that stealers are more difficult to help than other youthful offenders. When families are unwilling or unable to restructure their family management, then the power of treatment is limited. Individual interventions with the stealer (as used by Henderson) or interventions in group settings remain viable courses for child helpers, but are less likely to succeed than are comprehensive efforts to change the social ecology of the stealer that begin with the family.

10

Firesetting

Humankind's exaltation of fire dates back to long before the beginning of civilization. Fires have long fascinated and thrilled their creators and observers. Recognition that firesetting is a serious personal problem also dates back many years (Pilgrim, 1884–1885). Firesetting is now a major reason for hospitalization of children and youth and was involved in the hospitalization of nearly half of the children reviewed by Jayaprakash, Jung, and Panitch (1984) during a single year. The social and economic problems arising from firesetting are no less significant. Juveniles start between 75 and 90 percent of all arson fires according to a spokesman for the National Fire Academy ("Juveniles and Fire," 1984). Wooden (1985) reports that 14 percent of all fires are set in schools and that arson, at a cost of roughly $240 million per year, is the most expensive crime inflicted on schools. The costs to victims and firesetters are also great; an eight-year-old boy with learning disabilities played with a fire that raced out of control and took another human life. The boy was vilified in newspaper editorials and placed in foster care. His life was scarred.

Many children play with fire. More than a few set them. Kafry (1978) found that 45 percent of the children in kindergarten, second, and fourth grades had played with matches, and 21 percent had started fires. Of children who repeatedly played with fire, four out of five eventually set a fire. Baizerman and Emshoff (1984) suggest that firesetting is a typical act of curiosity for children ages three to five and of risk taking for children eleven to thirteen. Nevertheless, all firesetting is of concern. The younger children are when they first begin fire play,

329

the more serious their firesetting may become. Stewart and Culver (1982) found that children who set fires in order to kill someone (for example, who set their parents' bed on fire or say that they want to burn the house down and kill everyone) had set more fires than most children before the fire of murderous intent and started setting fires earlier. Like stealing, playing with fire is more common among males than females.

Background on Firesetting

Firesetting is often linked to other forms of misbehavior. Patterson's (1982) investigation of firesetters indicates that at least 78 percent had also been liars and stealers. More than 90 percent of thirty-six firesetters identified in clinic case records were also stealers. Older firesetters are particularly likely to have progressed from aggression and disobedience to lying and stealing and then to firesetting. Temper tantrums, fighting, and destroying others' property were also associated with firesetting by Gruber, Heck, and Mintzer (1981). Children who are more noncompliant and lie and steal more than other firesetters are more likely to continue as firesetters after treatment (Stewart and Culver, 1982). Kuhnley, Hendren, and Quinlan (1982) also found firesetting associated with cruelty to animals. Learning disabled or hyperactive children also set fires with uncommon frequency (fire may provide sensory gratification for children with sensory defects; Heath, Hardesty, Goldfine, and Walker, 1983). The notion of the otherwise well-mannered child setting a fire for want of other external responses to a grievous loss (for example, the loss of a parent because of divorce) clearly has its place, but it may be a small one.

Firesetters have an unusually large percentage of absent fathers or of nonbiological fathers living with them (Gruber, Heck, and Mintzer, 1981); only 5 percent of firesetters were living with both parents at the time of their admission for treatment in a study done by Stewart and Culver (1982). Ritvo, Shanok, and Lewis (1983) also found that significantly fewer firesetters had a biological mother in the home (42.9 percent) than did a group of aggressive inpatient youth who were not firesetters (81.8 percent). (Both groups had low percentages of biological fathers in the homes—24 percent for firesetters and 40 percent for nonfiresetters.) Physical abuse by caretakers was more common among firesetters than among other hospitalized children in Jayaprakash, Jung, and Panitch's (1984) study.

Learning to Set Fires. Firesetting is learned from family, peer, or media models. Quite pedestrian examples of fires in family life include those associated with cigarettes, gas heaters, stoves, fireplaces, and birthday candles. Some children learn about the power of heat or fire during punishment with heat or fire—for example, a hot spatula on the buttocks or a cigarette burn (Baizerman and Emshoff, 1984). Firesetters may learn about fire from parents who work in fire-related industries, including forestry, fire departments, and steel works (Macht and Mack, 1968). Wooden and Berkey's (1984) research suggests that a minority of firefighters (about 9 percent in their study) are childhood firesetters who grew up to be firefighters, continue to have difficulty with social responsibilities and conflict (for example, they have a high divorce rate), and have children who have set fires. A recent case in which the son of a local county fire commissioner was convicted for setting murderous brush fires is but one of many accounts of a child who learned fire play from firefighters.

Children and youth report a range of motives for setting fires, including enjoyment of the fire and excitement, revenge against parents or foster home, enjoyment in seeing the fire engines, revenge against authority, and desire to be a hero (by putting the fire out later); fires are also set in the process of stealing (Lewis and Yarnell, 1951).

Since most children observe fire use and play with fire, of greatest concern are characteristics that differentiate children who do and do not become firesetters. Children who learn inappropriate fire play may have received no clear rules about appropriate fire play, no rewards for appropriate fire play, and no sanctions for improper fire play and may have opportunities for unsupervised fire play.

Types of Firesetting. Fineman's (1980) analysis and Wooden's (1985) study of more than 100 children apprehended for arson distinguished four groups of firesetters. The first and youngest group (children younger than ten) consists of curious youngsters who accidentally start fires during developmentally typical play with matches. These children comprise 60 percent of firesetters and are at low risk of recidivism. These children, usually boys, set fires near home, do not collect fire tools, and try to put out the fire if it gets out of control. The second, somewhat older group (children aged seven to ten) consists of upset children who use fire to cope with their distress. Problem firesetters in this group collect firesetting material, may set fires with peers, set fires near home, have trouble at school, and have recently experienced changes in their environment or family makeup. Fires are often preceded by anger over lost opportunities or privileges. These firesetters may show some regret for starting fires. The third class of firesetter is between the ages of eleven and fourteen; collects fire tools; sets fires in or near home; has difficulties in relationships at home; and sets fires alone, with peers, or in groups. In this high-risk group, many use fire against authority—one fourteen-year-old boy with a history of setting fires set his junior high school on fire as a graduation protest, for example. The fourth and smallest group is an extreme-risk group of severely disturbed youth. Such youth comprise about 0.3 percent of all firesetters. These youth (like the mass murderer "Son of Sam," who also set more than 200 fires) show serious thought disorders and delusions.

Danny Diamond: Background of a Case Study

Danny Diamond lived with his foster mother and three other foster children. Danny was placed in this foster home after surviving serious abuse that included multiple-fractured legs. At age seven, he had one leg that was crooked and caused him to limp, was reading at a prekindergarten level, frequently screamed and yelled, and seldom stayed seated for more than a minute at a time. Because of his behavior, he was not in any school program from age five to seven until his welfare worker found him a school placement in a nonpublic special education program. At school, Danny frequently stole from other children, the teacher, and unguarded classrooms. He yelled regularly and fought in a limited, hit-and-run fashion with other children. His eagerness to learn was apparent, despite his bizarre verbalizations and uncontrolled behavior.

At the first quarterly parent-teacher conference, Danny's foster mother, Ms. Chassen, reported delight in his progress but expressed concern because Danny was waking up in the middle of the night, taking clothes out of the hall closet, putting them on top of the gas stove, lighting them on fire, and running through the house yelling. She did not want to return him to the department of social services because she loved him and knew that he risked being institutionalized, but she did not know how long she could put up with this behavior. The teacher told Ms. Chassen that she would like to meet the next day with her and the school social worker, Danny's public child-welfare worker, and Danny to develop a plan for stopping Danny's stealing. Ms. Chassen confirmed this meeting with the school social worker on the phone at that time but could not reach the child-welfare worker. She was informed by the worker's supervisor that the child-welfare worker would make every effort to meet the following afternoon. The supervisor also asked whether, in the meantime, there was anything she could do to ensure that Danny did not burn down Ms. Chassen's home. Ms. Chassen said that Danny did not light fires if she let him sleep with her and agreed to do so that night. Ms. Chassen also agreed to bring her teenage son to the meeting to look after Danny during times that the adults met without him.

Assessment

Assessment must focus on immediate risk of conflagrations and identify possible treatment strategies and resources. To construct an accurate picture of firesetting behavior, interviews should be conducted with the parents alone, the child alone, and the parents and child together.

Parents. A guide to interviewing parents (developed for parents of seven- to fourteen-year-old children but markedly the same as the interview guide for parents of younger children) is shown in Exhibit 13. A child's firesetting history is impor-

Exhibit 13. Questions to Ask Caregivers to Distinguish
High-Risk Firesetters Ages 7–12.

1. Was this the child's first fire? Yes____ No____ If "no," how many others were set? ____

2. What was set on fire? _____

3. What materials were used to start the fire? Matches____ Lighter____ Flares____ Other____

4. How did the child get the material to start the fire? Found it easily____ Went out of his/her way to acquire it____ From another child____

5. Is the child curious about fire? Mildly____ Moderately____ Extremely____

6. Do you think the child was pressured or coerced into firesetting behavior by peers? Yes____ No____

7. Do you believe that the fire in question was an accident? Yes____ No____

8. Do you think that the child was attempting to do harm or destroy property by setting the fire? Yes____ No____

9. Was the child part of a group or with another child when the fire was set? Yes____ No____

10. Do you believe that the child planned to set the fire? Yes____ No____

11. Did the child lie about his/her involvement in the fire? Yes____ No____

12. Do you think the fire was set because the child was incapable of understanding what he/she was doing? Yes____ No____

13. Has the child previously used matches or fires properly? Yes____ No____

14. Did the child panic when the fire got out of control? Yes____ No____

15. Did the child attempt to get help? Yes____ No____

16. Was anyone with the child when the fire was set? Yes____ No____ If yes, who? _____

17. Is there any indication that the fire was preceded by family difficulties or family arguments? Yes____ No____

18. Is there any indication that the fire was started after the child became angry at another person or himself/herself? Yes____ No____

19. Is there any indication that the fire was set primarily to destroy something or someone? Yes____ No____

20. Is there any indication that the fire was set primarily because the child was told that he/she could not use fire? Yes____ No____

21. Is there any indication that the child sees magical qualities in fire? Yes____ No____

22. Does the child deny interest in the fire, even though information to the contrary is available? Yes____ No____

23. Does the fire appear to be a cry for help? Yes____ No____

24. Does the fire seem thrilling or funny to the child? Yes____ No____

25. Does the child usually do what you say? Yes____ No____

Source: Adapted from Federal Emergency Management Agency, 1980.

tant to ascertain. Additional information about the firesetting implements and the ecological context of the firesetting will help determine its causes. Evidence that the fire was an accident, that the child sought help in attempting to control the fire, and that the fire was not set to destroy something suggests a less serious firesetting problem. Indications to the contrary and that the child found the fire thrilling or funny, is incapable of understanding what he or she was doing, believes that fires are magical or dreams about fires, was part of a group, or set the fire because he or she was told not to use fire, or that his or her behavior is generally beyond the caregivers' control, cue the interviewer to the seriousness of the problem.

If parents do not cooperate in the assessment interview, then the interviewer must reassert that the parents' cooperation will help keep the child from destroying property and endangering the family and that their comments will not be used against the family but only to help the child get needed help. They should also be told that they may be criminally and civilly responsible for any fires that the child sets and that they can be charged with child maltreatment and have the child removed from their care if they do nothing to reduce the risk that the child will endanger his or her own life and those of others.

Child. An assessment interview should include the child's perspective—no matter what the child's age. For older children the interview should consider, at minimum, the issues listed in Exhibit 14. The key questions should confirm the interviewee's history of firesetting, how much premeditation and effort were involved in starting the fire, the child's linkage to a peer group of firesetters, the child's explanation for setting the fire, and interpersonal motives for firesetting. Questions to rule out the likelihood that the child is a Class 4 (that is, psychotic) firesetter should also be asked. Family management practices that may be useful in intervention should be sought. The presence of physical or sexual abuse should also be ruled out or confirmed.

For children younger than seven, the important assessment content is similar with the exception that more time may be needed to develop rapport and determine the child's level of understanding. Rapport building can be helped with doll

Exhibit 14. Questions to Ask Children About Firesetting Behavior.

1. How many fires have you set? ____
2. How many different things have you set on fire?
   a. One____ More than one____
   b. What have you set on fire?
      Paper____
      Own property____
      Others' property____ Trash____ Leaves____
      Self, animals, other people____ Own room____
      Other____ (Explain) _____
3. How did you start the fire? _____
   _____
4. Where did you get the material to start the fire? _____
   Found it____ Went out of way to acquire it____ From another child____
5. Who was with you when you started the fire? _____
   Name _____
6. What do you think made you want to start the fire?
   a. Don't know____
   b. Another child told me to____
   c. To see it burn____
   d. To hurt someone____
   e. To destroy something____
7. Was the fire set after any of the following?
   a. Being angry at brother or sister____
   b. Family fight____
   c. Being angry at a friend____
   d. After getting "loaded"____
   e. After getting hit____
8. Did the fire or fires you have started make you happy or make you laugh? Yes____ No____
9. Do you dream about fires at night? Yes____ No____
10. Do you think about fires in the day? Yes____ No____
11. Can fire do magical things? Yes____ No____
12. Are you home without your mother or father a lot? Yes____ No____
13. Do you fight with your mother or father a lot? Yes____ No____
14. Do your parents punish you by hitting you when you do something wrong? Yes____ No____

Source: Adapted from Federal Emergency Management Agency, 1980.

and puppet play. These puppets and dolls can be used to test whether the three- or four-year-old child who does not talk during the interview even understands the interviewer; for example, the child may be asked to squeeze a puppet's nose or to put the dolls in a chair. Pictures of fire-damaged houses, cars, or wildlands and burned telephones, toys, books, or paper can be used to learn how much the child understands about firesetting. Relevant questions for youngsters include: What do you think this is? How did it get that way? If a fire could burn this toy, what else could it burn? Can a fire burn you? How can we use fire so that it does not burn?

Parent and Child. In the parent and child interview, the child helper interprets the findings from the individual interviews. The child helper clarifies the problem from the parents' and the child's perspectives, helps the family define firesetting and agree on penalties for it, specifies short- and long-term goals, ascertains beginning tasks to mitigate the threat of future fires (which almost always involves clearing the house of all fire tools and making contact with any additional treatment resources), reviews barriers to task accomplishment, and arranges future contacts.

School. Because firesetting children may believe that they have no alternative means of resolving their problems, assessment must identify stressful school problems and consider strategies for helping children resolve those problems. Interviews with the classroom teacher contribute to the picture of the sources of a child's stress and the child's need for improved child management, responses to dealing with frustration, and strategies for getting control over situations. Evidence of parental maltreatment should be confirmed. The child's interests, friends, and successes should also be identified as resources for treatment.

Danny Diamond: Assessment

The meeting began with everyone in the room. Ms. Chassen reported that Danny's fire play had been occurring about once a week for several months. The assessment focused on Danny's firesetting behavior and other accompanying competencies or deficits. The middle-of-the-night firesetting cued Danny's welfare worker to ask Danny—who conducted himself with unusual aplomb in the joint interview with his mother and the teacher—if he was happy with his sleep. That question did not clarify his sleeping situation, so she persevered and, following a series of more pointed questions, learned that Danny slept in a room with an older brother and with a younger brother who was having nightmares, and that he did not sleep well because the weather was too hot. His mother said she had great difficulty getting Danny to bed, and he was very difficult and moody in the morning. Since Danny was currently taking Ritalin at nine, twelve, and three o'clock, the school social worker recognized that Danny might also benefit from medication at bedtime—which is known to help some hyperactive children stay calm and to sleep (Chatoor and others, 1983)—but first determined to try other strategies that might help improve Danny's sleep.

The assessment of Danny's firesetting experiences was made more difficult because his foster mother and social worker did not know whether Danny had set fires in the past. Danny had many characteristics associated with children who set fires, including bedwetting, stealing, cruelty to animals, hyperactivity, recent change in family structure, parents who abused him, and physical disability. Danny was too awed by the large meeting and too used to dissembling under pressure to talk candidly about his firesetting history. When it was clear that Danny could not contribute further to the assessment, the school social worker suggested that he and his brother go to the playground; Danny left with reluctance. Since Danny was already involved with a clinical treatment team, the use of a structured assessment to determine his risk of future firesetting and need for referral was unnecessary. His generally rambunctious behavior and past firesetting suggested, however, that a full-scale intervention was needed.

Intervention

Like stealing and aggression, firesetting must be closely and unyieldingly labeled and punished. *Setting fires* is a more serious label than *fire play* and should be defined to include any fire-related behavior, no matter how remotely related. Even though small children may not understand the relationship between thoughts and behavior, they must learn that watching movies about fires and obsessively looking at pictures of fires are not permitted as they may lead to wanting to see a fire and wanting to set a fire. Child helpers and caregivers must become determined to restrict children's unsupervised access to fire-related materials. The message may need to be repeated frequently since the common "wisdom" of our times wrongly assures people that thoughts are harmless and thinking about things is a good substitute for doing them. However true this is for adults, there is little wisdom or accuracy in it for firesetting children.

Response Cost. Simple social learning procedures may be all that is needed for Class 1 and 2 firesetters. Carstens (1982) used the consequence of chores with a four-year-old firesetting boy. Several weeks prior to beginning treatment, the child was caught sneaking out of the house with matches. He told his mother that he was going to light the matches and throw them in a puddle. Perhaps holding an implicit belief that this would be cathartic and would help the child grow bored with fire, the mother watched the boy throw lighted matches into the puddle for an hour. She then informed him that he was never to light matches alone but that he should call her whenever he wanted to light matches under her supervision. Despite her reasoned and sympathetic response, he attempted to set fire to his bed with his mother's cigarette lighter the next day. The mother spanked the child and again discussed setting fires. After finding him lighting matches while sitting on the lawnmower, she called the fire department, which sent the fire chief to warn the child that he might kill himself and his family if he continued to play with fire. In the following two weeks, the boy left burnt matches and lighters in several places, including closets. After he attempted to set fire to his parents' bed (they were not in it), he was referred to a pediatrician and then to Carstens, a psychologist familiar with social and cognitive behavior-change procedures.

In the assessment interview, the parents reported that their son was also noncompliant, aggressive, a thief, and cruel to animals. The parents were taught to *label* firesetting as any behavior that involved touching firesetting tools or evidence that a match or lighter had been lighted (for example, finding a lighter out of place). If this occurred, the child was to complete one hour of work at home such as washing walls, cleaning between the kitchen tiles, and scrubbing the back porch. Three weeks later, the parents were also taught to use time out for dealing with the child's noncompliant and aggressive behavior. The family terminated treatment shortly thereafter, stating that they did not see the need for more. The threat of the work penalty (which was never carried out) had effectively ended firesetting, and the child ceased talking about or playing with fire. By the six-months follow-up interview, the boy had not set any other fires and was reportedly less aggressive. This procedure appeared to be effective with a young child without a long history of firesetting. Also noteworthy is the failure of the mother's informal satiation strategy (that is, watching her son throw matches into the puddle). Satiation of firesetting is not a proven technique and, because of the reinforcing properties of the flames, may be counterproductive. If satiation is to be used, it should be used as later reported in this chapter—when followed by negative practice, other penalties for fire play, and rewards for acting in ways that compete with fire play.

A well-balanced reward and response-cost system was used by Fleischman, Horne, and Arthur (1983) in work with a nine-year-old boy who was reported setting three fires in the previous half year. Except for his fire play, the boy was reported by his mother to be well behaved. This suggests that the boy's behavior was largely under the control of family rules and rewards. The treatment procedure was, therefore, like those used for other antisocial behaviors such as stealing and aggression—that is, it included defining firesetting, chores for any fire-related behavior, extra chores for not completing the earlier chores, and a reward system for behaviors that lowered the likelihood of firesetting. Sessions were also devoted to increasing the family's positive interactions and the boy's opportunities to assume responsibility at home and to build his self-confidence. The latter program involved points for reporting events that showed the boy's courage—raising his hand in class and jumping off the diving board, for example. Firesetting stopped after one additional instance of fire play and the application of the chore response cost.

Promoting Safe Fire Use. Like many other undesirable behaviors, firesetting has a positive counterpart: safe fire use. Holland's (1969) contribution to teaching safe fire play remains outstanding. Seven-year-old Robert was setting fires once or twice a week with matches he found at home or in the community when he was left unsupervised. Slapping, touching him with a smoldering object, and locking him in his room resulted in only brief respites from firesetting. The parents were referred to a couples counseling program, which had no effect on their son's dangerous behavior. In response, Holland, their counselor, met with the couple five times following group meetings (showing understanding that the child's behavior was affecting the marriage and not just the other way around). Because the mother did not believe that Robert could change, the father implemented the program.

First, the father proclaimed that any additional firesetting would result in the destruction of Robert's new and prized baseball glove. Second, he told Robert that any matches or match covers that he brought to his father would be greeted with a one- to ten-cent reward and praise. At first, empty matchbooks and then full books were left around the home to teach Robert to return rather than hoard matches. (Matches that have been wet and dried so they look like they will work but will not can also be used.) In time, Robert's mother also began to reward him. Robert's father also began to teach his boy safe and self-controlled fire use by sitting, on consecutive evenings, with Robert and a book of twenty matches between them. Every match that Robert refrained from lighting earned him one cent. On the first three nights he lighted ten, three, and zero matches and earned ten, seventeen, and twenty cents, respectively. On subsequent evenings, Robert's father varied the per match bounty from zero to ten cents and praise. After five weeks of treatment, Robert's two-year fascination with fire play, fire tools, and firesetting ended. The varied monetary rewards for turning in and not lighting matches were continued for a few months.

Stawar (1976) also employed Holland's strategy for teaching a child to turn in, rather than light, matches. Working with a seven-year-old boy who had set four fires during the preceding three months and had not been dissuaded by parental repri-

mands, lectures, or spankings, Stawar used cognitive preparation and social rewards for turning in matches. Employing what
he called "fable mod," he began by telling the boy a story of
a child who was playing and found some matches and proudly
brought them to his mother who told him how wonderful he
was and put the matches away and gave the boy his favorite
candy (which were penny candies). A variation of the story was
told to the boy several times, and then he was engaged in telling the story with the therapist. During and following the telling of the story, the boy was rewarded with praise and his be-
loved penny candies. The mother was then told that her son
was ready to participate in the program, given information about
setting books of matches about the home, and instructed to provide social and penny-candy rewards to the boy for retrieving
matches. During the following two weeks, the boy returned the
matches he found on nineteen out of twenty-four occasions (he
ignored or overlooked the matches the other five times) and set
no fires. The mother continued the program by telling the story
about the boy who found some matches and rewarding her son
for participating with her, and by rewarding the boy whenever
he found matches and brought them to her. By the seven-month
follow-up interview, the boy was no longer setting fires.

   Positive practice that involves lighting matches, putting
them out, and then cleaning up may also reduce firesetting. This
was Welsh's (1971) approach with a seven-year-old boy who
was noncompliant, troublesome at school, and a repeated firesetter. Following traditional procedure, the child was first seen
in traditional play therapy for six sessions while the social worker
met with the parents. After no progress had been made, the
therapist, with the misgivings of the therapist's supervisor, began
an overcorrection procedure. Four rules were used in lighting
matches: the match must be held over the ashtray at all times;
after the match was taken out of the book, the cover had to be
closed; only one match could be lighted at a time; and the burning match had to be held until the child felt heat on his fingertips, when the child must blow out the match. In the first session Welsh reports that the boy "happily began lighting matches,
going through one-and-one-half boxes (60 matches) in forty

minutes; some discomfort was shown toward the end of the session'' (p. 285). At the beginning of the second session the child continued to light the matches but soon wanted to play with toys. After lighting a few more matches, he was allowed to do so. In the third session, the boy protested having to play with matches and had to be commanded to sit at the table and light ten matches using the match-lighting rules. The child was then allowed to help his father burn trash at home because he was able to do it more appropriately. By the end of six months the firesetting behavior had not returned. The procedure was replicated with another boy who had set multiple fires, including one to his own bed. The child enjoyed the match play for three sessions and continued to seek fire-lighting opportunities at home. The fourth session was doubled in length to 100 minutes, and only during the last 10 minutes did the boy appear satiated and want to do something else. Three additional sessions were needed before he said that he would rather not light matches. Firesetting stopped during this month. After six months he still was not lighting matches.

Wolff (1984) also used satiation with a seven-year-old firesetter in a five-day-a-week residential program. The boy's weekend foster parents were enlisted to record the number of times that the boy engaged in fire play or firesetting (they were particularly motivated to participate in the assessment because they had previously had their house burned down). They continued to use the same consequences they had been employing for fire play, despite their negligible success in reducing the boy's fire play up to then.

The satiation procedure was the new wrinkle in the intervention. Wolff also had the boy light matches one match at a time with the match cover closed, blow out the match, and then place the burnt match in a metal pail with water. (Unlike Welsh, Wolff did not require the boy to keep the match lighted until he could feel the heat on his fingertips.) They followed this procedure twice a day for thirty minutes. Because reduction in match lighting was minimal after the first ten sessions, another ninety sessions of negative practice were completed. During those ten weeks (in which an average of more than two books of matches per session were used) the boy's match lighting during therapy sessions never did decrease. The boy did increasingly resist the match lighting, however, and by session fifty-two had to be forced to get started. By session seventy-four he was complaining that he wanted to stop the sessions. Far more significantly, however, the boy's fire play dropped to zero after six weeks (from a pretreatment rate of four incidents per week). The firesetting behavior had not recurred by the end of a two-year follow-up period, and the foster parents, with much relief, reported that the boy's attraction to fire was no longer a problem.

Social and Cognitive Strategies. Firesetting can kill. Thus, comprehensive programs are imperative. *Comprehensive* does not, however, mean *restrictive*. Comprehensive programs involve efforts toward both cognitive and social change based on sound theory and research. A classic intervention and a subsequent replication illustrate comprehensive social and cognitive methods.

Tony, aged eleven, burned down his group home (Mc-Grath, Marshall, and Prior, 1979). He had been sent to the group home after setting four other fires and receiving two convictions for firesetting. He had few interpersonal skills and considered himself victimized by other youth. Treatment was given by child-care workers during Tony's stay in a juvenile detention facility. Four hypotheses about Tony's firesetting were developed from interviews with Tony, the staff, and the referring psychiatrist and from group-home records. A treatment element was developed for each hypothesis, as shown in Table 10. The plan

Table 10. Treatments for Firesetting Behaviors.

Hypothesis	Treatment Element
1. Firesetting occurs following difficulties coping with stress.	1. Social-skills training.
2. Firesetting occurs following problems relating to peers.	2. Social-skills training.
3. The process of firesetting is rewarding.	3. Overcorrection.
4. Child does not fully recognize the dangers of firesetting.	4. Cognitive self-punishment and fire-safety project.

Source: Adapted from McGrath, Marshall, and Prior, 1979.

was accepted by the child's lawyer and the family court as an alternative to long-term institutional care.

In response to Tony's problems with his peers, child-care workers (supervised by the three researchers) conducted fourteen hour-long sessions involving modeling, role playing, and videotaping. Difficult situations like being teased or losing at cards were enacted, and alternative cognitive and social responses discussed and practiced. Positive practice and overcorrection diminished the pleasures of setting fires. Tony was required to light a sheet of paper in a metal container, extinguish the fire by dousing it with water, and scrub the container thoroughly. Throughout this procedure he repeated self-instructions about the dangers of fire and the need for safety (for example, "fires can kill people," and "this fire is safe because it can't spread and there is water to put it out"). This sequence was repeated three times per session for eleven sessions.

To increase Tony's understanding of the dangers of fire, he underwent five sessions of covert sensitization (Cautela, 1967). This procedure involved cognitive self-punishment followed by negative reinforcement for resisting the urge to set a fire. He listened to several five-minute audiotapes describing Tony setting a fire and the subsequent aversive consequences of the fire—for example, "the flames spread very quickly and you realize you are trapped. You scream for someone to let you out, but no one comes. The smoke is choking you, and the heat is burning your skin . . . " (McGrath, Marshall, and Prior, 1979, p. 70). Following these punishing tapes, a relief scene is presented that describes Tony beginning to set a fire and then deciding not to and finding other ways to cope with the situation.

Tony also undertook a fire-safety project. He visited the fire station and talked with the fire chief about the horrors of fire, went to the gutted group home, viewed three films on destruction caused by fire, and presented a project on fire safety to the fire chief for his evaluation and praise. These instructional activities occurred during sessions of three hours a week for six weeks; their completion was rewarded by the point system operating in the group home.

Tony showed an increased frequency of behaviors that reduced the likelihood of firesetting. He increasingly approached staff to help him work out stressful interpersonal problems and engaged in more conversation, sharing, and sportsmanship with his peers. Tony did not set any fires in the detention facility, but after the court ruled that Tony was not able to go home and that he would be placed in a group home, he set two small fires in flame-proof containers. In the following two years in the group home, Tony did not set any more fires. The comprehensive treatment apparently contributed to the reduction of firesetting and allowed Tony to stay in community settings and develop effective self-management, interpersonal, and academic skills.

Ten-year-old Jim received an even more comprehensive treatment than Tony (Koles and Jenson, 1985). Jim, like many firesetters, was in foster care. He had a seven-year history of firesetting that included burning down his family home and a more recent record of setting two fires per week for the last three months. He denied setting fires, despite frequent confrontations over fires set in the foster home. The staff from the day-treatment program that Jim attended built on McGrath, Marshall, and Prior's (1979) efforts and implemented a program that included (1) social and cognitive problem solving; (2) relaxation training; (3) fire-safety education; (4) the same overcorrection procedure as was used with Tony (the procedure was conducted by Jim's foster parents daily for three weeks); (5) response cost of three days of early bedtimes and no allowance in the event of fire play; and (6) (instead of the covert sensitization used with Tony) visits to the intensive-care burn unit at a university hospital, where Jim met a boy his age who had seriously burned himself. Progress was rapid, although not instantaneous. Jim set seven fires in the first three months of treatment (a decrease of two-thirds) but no further fires in the following year. The authors indicate that Jim's comments about and drawings of the visit to the burn unit indicate that this visit may have contributed greatly to his progress and required less time than the cognitive approach. Their successful replication and extension of previous work argue for continued use and testing of the elements of this program.

Community-Based Programs. The best-known community-based program for assisting young firesetters and their families is the Firehawk Children's Program ("Firehawk Children's Program," 1984). The program provides comprehensive fire-safety and fire-prevention training and pairs fatherless children who have been identified as firesetters with firefighter volunteers who act as long-term companions to the children. The program is now conducted by the National Firehawk Foundation, which has more than a hundred affiliates in twenty-six states. Initial pilot testing with 30 youths—culled from 160 referrals as "definite risks" because they had set an average of two to four fires—yielded a 100 percent reduction in firesetting by the time of a six-month follow-up.

The Firehawk program uses community resources—firefighters as well as professional consultants. The latter are especially important for families with recent economic or marital disruptions and youths with a range of behavior problems. The program uses the screening procedure previously described in this chapter (and more completely described in Federal Emergency Management Agency, 1980, 1984). Youths who are assessed as medium risk—especially, fatherless boys with a range of family and school problems—seem most appropriate for involvement with firefighters.

Because the child's level of development is critical to assessing the seriousness of the firesetting and to developing a reasonable intervention, different procedures are detailed for children under seven and for children between seven and fourteen. The first set of procedures (Federal Emergency Management Agency, 1980) addresses the needs of firefighters working with young children. The more recent work (Federal Emergency Management Agency, 1984) is a response to the need to have an expanded and more socioecologically based intervention for older children. The mission of the programs is to teach fire service personnel to assess the risk of recurrent firesetting, to help fire service personnel to better educate children who set fires out of curiosity (Class 1) and their families, to teach fire service personnel to set up a structured community program for children and adolescents who start fires, and to improve fire service personnel's referrals for mental health assistance.

Both programs emphasize the importance of a relationship between the firefighter and the child. The goal of this relationship is to promote opportunities for identifying the risk of future firesetting, provide education about fire safety, and develop contracts related to increasing behavior that can compete with firesetting (especially school attendance and achievement). The firefighter also encourages and aids families in obtaining referrals to professionals who are capable of helping families improve their family-management skills. The manuals discuss the importance of developing behavioral contracts, developing arrangements for the child to make restitution for property destroyed in fires, and helping parents improve their family-management skills. The core of the program is the relationship between the firemen and the fatherless boys. The manuals include information on contributors to firesetting behavior, developmental issues in firesetting, and interviewing skills that promote open communication between the firefighter-interviewer, parents, and child.

An example of how pairing with a firefighter may work is the case of Amos, a child who, at seven years old, had twice set fire to his own apartment building. Amos became involved with the local Firehawk program and was paired with a fire inspector. Amos was on medication for hyperactivity and had difficulty at school. He began spending eight to ten hours a week with the fire inspector at the firehouse, studying the equipment and learning what really happens when people set fires. This relationship apparently helped Amos, whose school behavior also improved as his firesetting ended (Mehren, 1984). One concern with this approach is that behavioral theory and findings regarding the link between firesetting and having a father in a fire-related occupation would suggest that visits to the firehouse may stimulate rather than suppress excitement about fire. Patterson (1982) suggests, therefore, that visits to fire stations be provided as a reward for reduced fire-related behavior and not as an incentive to reduce firesetting. In the absence of a structured Firehawk program, Patterson's approach seems well founded.

Links between mental health professionals and the firefighting community are also important for preventing fires. Firesetting can be contagious. Baizerman and Emshoff (1984) report that in a thirty-day period following a major fire in Minneapolis in 1982, there was a 400 percent increase in the number of fire-related deaths. When firefighters know of community fires, they should inform educational, social service, and mental health agencies to help them understand and counter the increased likelihood of firesetting among high-risk youth.

Danny Diamond: Intervention

Danny's teacher also began to help Danny develop more understanding of what fires could do. The entire class compiled a book entitled "Fires Are Not Funny: Tips to Stop Fires from Starting." Each child was also asked to bring in stories from the newspaper about fires. The teacher read one story from the newspaper about a family who had their house burned down and had no other place to go. Each student told what they would do if their house burned down and what they would miss the most that would be destroyed in the fire.

Danny also received assistance in gaining more peer acceptance and rewards. He was assigned a cross-age tutor from the high school (who was reading at the second-grade level and was, therefore, two years ahead of Danny) to help with his phonics flash cards. Danny greatly enjoyed the time tests using the flash cards that he completed with his tutor. With his social worker he began work on a life book, which he also worked on at school; in this book he included magazine clippings and hand-drawn pictures depicting places from his past and members of other foster families.

Danny's foster mother rewarded him for sleeping through the night with hugs, kisses, and—Danny's favorite—a special breakfast prayer. These were the only rewards that she was willing to give, as she was concerned about the other children feeling left out if Danny was given material rewards. Because sleeping through the night seemed to preclude Danny's firesetting, the social worker suggested to the teacher and Ms. Chassen that they develop a system by which Danny's other out-of-control behavior could be reduced. Because of Danny's history of deprivation and intense reaction to the loss of benefits or privileges, the use of response cost was reserved for the worst of behaviors—that is, fighting and getting up at night; the cost for such activities was loss of dessert at home and loss of recess at school. Tangible rewards at first provided strong incentives for Danny, and these were followed by the use of a checkerboard bank book. Danny earned squares for achievements in the classroom and at home. When the checkerboard was entirely colored, Danny was allowed to choose from a menu of privileges and prizes.

Other sleeping conditions were also changed. Three boys in a room was too many, but no easy alternatives were apparent. Instead, the social worker suggested some changes to reduce the younger brother's nightmares (that so disturbed Danny). A light was left on. The younger boy was also rewarded along with Danny for sleeping through the night. Danny's nighttime thirstiness was reduced along with his complaints about the heat by the coming of winter and by leaving the bedroom door open and swinging his bed out from the wall so he could catch a draft.

Lying behavior was also reduced. Preliminary attempts to help Danny distinguish between fact and fantasy by responding to the lies as "that sounds like the way you would like it to be, Danny, but that doesn't sound like the way it was" were cause for protests and tantrums by Danny. In time, his classroom teacher, social worker, and foster mother developed an agreement that they would all say "No, Danny" and shake their heads when he was lying. The classroom teacher also used response costs when Danny lied. She drew five boxes on a card on his desk. Each one was worth one peanut M&M (his favorite candy). For each lie he told, one box was crossed off. Each box that was unmarked at day's end was worth an M&M. The social worker was not in a position and Ms. Chassen was not willing to use response costs for lying. They simply asked for additional versions of the story until he told more of the truth.

In the year following intervention, Danny set no more fires, regularly slept through the night, and reduced his fighting behavior. Although the intervention for firesetting was but one of several efforts to get Danny's behavior under control, the overall result was an apparent end to firesetting.

Management of Firesetting

Caregivers are rightfully alarmed when they learn that they are caring for a firesetter. For this reason, these children and youth are often quickly moved from community settings into hospital settings. A hospital can be a setting for reducing firesetting behavior if the general family-management skills of the child's caregivers and problems of abuse and changing family makeup can be addressed, and if strategies such as response costs, rewards for safe behavior, restitution, and overcorrection can be instituted. Child helpers on hospital staffs or working with hospitals must, then, assess the child's environment as carefully as they assess the child. Return of a child who has been hospitalized to a less restrictive environment must be preceded by a specific and well-rehearsed supervision and intervention plan. The environment should be scoured for situations that might prompt firesetting—paper trash in containers without tops, the availability of caregivers' matches for lighting gas stoves (matches should be replaced with a chemist's flint), and the accessibility of flammable chemicals (such as turpentine or lighter fluid). When a Firehawk program is available and a youth is without a father figure or when father, child, and firefighter are willing to work together, these resources deserve consideration.

Siblings or fellow residents must be included in the treatment planning. Other children and youth can often recognize the seriousness of the threat to them of living with a youth with a history of firesetting. Channeling this recognition away from hostility toward the youth and toward a house-based plan for intervention is critical. This can be accomplished as it was in Danny's case by developing the firesetting child's social skills and providing opportunities for that child to contribute to the group's greater good through achieving group rewards by completing safety-related tasks or refraining from fire play.

Extra vigilance should be used whenever a child who has been a firesetter or who associates with a firesetter is told that he or she will be placed in another setting. Even though this change in setting may be one to which the child agrees, transitions create enough uncertainty to lead children to return to older, more familiar ways of solving their problems. When the placement is not agreeable to the youth—for example, as would be the case with a child who is sent from a group home to juvenile hall because of shoplifting—the risk of firesetting is markedly greater. A buddy system and extra vigilance may lessen that risk.

11

𝖄𝖄𝖄𝖄𝖄𝖄𝖄𝖄𝖄𝖄𝖄𝖄𝖄𝖄𝖄𝖄𝖄𝖄𝖄

Running Away

Running away removes young people from intolerable situations—at least momentarily. Runaways trade the certain limitations of home for the uncertain promise of a new locale. Runaways are "youth gone from home without parental permission for more than eight hours and/or gone from home with the specific intent of running away" (Brennan, Huizinga, and Elliott, 1978, p. 87). The *National Statistical Survey of Runaway Youth* (Opinion Research Corporation, 1976) estimated that nearly a quarter of a million youth run away each year. Running away may be harmless and even enlightening (Orten and Soll, 1980). Too often, however, runaways become involved in burglary, drug use and selling, alcoholism, vandalism, assault, and prostitution (Bracey, 1979; Baizerman, Thompson, Stafford-White, and An Old, Young Friend, 1979; Edelbrock, 1980).

Despite an ever more comprehensive and sophisticated understanding of why youth run away and where they go, the literature on preventing runaways, working with current runaways, and reducing repeat runaways is sparse. Current legislative guidelines for diverting runaways from the juvenile justice system have now been in place for more than a decade (Juvenile Justice and Delinquency Prevention Act, 1974). Although the current system appears to have preferable results and costs, experimental treatment-outcome studies are all but nonexistent. Treatments proposed in this chapter are based, therefore, on descriptive information about runaways, anecdotal reports of outcomes with runaways, weak experimental findings, outcome-evaluated procedures not specifically designed or tested for runaways, and the author's experience.

353

The Runaway Experience

The majority of runaway episodes are not well planned and reflect spontaneous impulsive behavior that takes youth to other parts of a community, to the homes of relatives, or to the basements or backyards of friends. Others end up sleeping in parked cars, under the bleachers at nearby schools, or at transportation depots (Roberts, 1981). A large majority of runaways are reasonably well protected and have safe accommodations at night. Serious sexual or violent victimization of runaways seems to occur in less than 3 percent of all cases. Most runaway episodes are brief, with about 60 percent lasting three days or less (Opinion Research Corporation, 1976). Children return home about 40 percent of the time on their own. When they do not, parents are most successful in finding them. However, about one in six runaways is gone more than a month, and 5 percent do not return within six months. A few runaways tap networks of other runaways—perhaps the most notorious example is Charles Manson, whose "family" found him through the runaway grapevine. Increasingly, runaways do not return to the long-term care of their birth families or substitute families (Beyer, 1980). Other runaways do not run from nuclear families but are refugees from previous escapes. These youth may be fleeing from their pimps, from group homes or unlocked mental health facilities, or from the vagaries of life as emancipated adolescents without skills to fully care for themselves (U.S. Department of Transportation, 1980).

Runaways may occur in any type of family structure—closed, random, or open (Kantor and Lehr, 1975)—when it is operating ineffectively. The *closed* family is highly structured, hierarchical, and rule governed, with the individual, and especially the adolescent, subordinate to the group. In their flawed versions, these families may not provide adequate rewards for individual family members or may restrict adolescents from obtaining satisfactions in the community. These families may encourage running away toward the promise of greater freedom and rewards. When such a family structure fails, it is more prone to physical punishment or sexual abuse (Groth, 1978; Sgroi, Blick, and Porter, 1982)—both associated with runaways (Opinion Research Corporation, 1976) and "throwaways" (children who are kicked out of the house by their parents; Donahue and Gullotta, 1983).

In the *random* family there is little attention to rules or structures and children wander and wonder. Adolescents in random families can determine their own living style and for this reason are often envied by their counterparts in closed families. For some families this minimal structure results from insufficient parental resources due to numerous children or single parenthood. Such families have more than their share of runaways (Opinion Research Corporation, 1976). In their flawed version, these families may fail to protect their children from sexual abuse by boyfriends and relatives; from physical, educational, and emotional neglect; and from the attractions of a wholly unstructured and often illegal life-style.

The *open* family balances order with flexibility and the rights of individuals with the family's group needs; this family structure seems to reduce running away. The *National Statistical Survey of Runaway Youth* (Opinion Research Corporation, 1976) concludes that parents of nonrunaway youth were different from parents of runaway youth largely in their communication and problem-solving patterns. Specifically, parents of nonrunaway youth were more likely to provide better supervision, provide help with schoolwork and related activities, remain open to discussion about problems, and express happiness with their child and appreciation of their child's behavior. Open family structures are not without flaws, however, and these families may be especially confused by problems whose solutions are not amenable to democratic problem-solving strategies. For example, these families may not cope well with a youth who is involved in a relationship centered around sexual passion and drug use. Their rational and open-minded approach may be no match for the visceral attractions of out-of-home experiences. These families may also have difficulty labeling their child's behavior for what it is and recognizing that their family problem reflects a difference in values rather than a misunderstanding.

Gender and culture may interact with family type to explain running away. Wolk and Brandon (1977) argue that girls run away to escape a closed family and its overprotection, whereas boys more often run because they have been unsupervised for too long and have developed impulsive and escapist behavior patterns. Traumatic decisions about pregnancies or sexual assaults may be cause for any child to run away, but these reasons certainly motivate more girls than boys. Subcultures with more nomadic traditions or where children are expected to leave home to find their economic niche encourage running away more than those with the expectation of continued participation in the family of origin.

　　　　Children and youth become runaways for many reasons. Seeking adventure and opportunity (à la Huck Finn) is still a reason (although a relatively rare one) for running away (Brennan, Huizinga, and Elliott, 1978). Brennan and his colleagues (Brennan, 1980; Brennan, Huizinga, and Elliott, 1978) identify two more common explanations for runaway behavior. Runaways may leave home because of interpersonal *strain* and conflict at home that result in alienation from family norms and values and attachment to the norms and values of peers at school or on the street. Runaways may also be youth with little commitment or ability to comply with home, school, and peer norms who run from *social control*. When the family is abusive, this is an adaptive response. Youth may, of course, also run away for a combination of reasons. Physical attacks may follow strain from a caregiver's unfulfilled expectations that a youthful family member use more self-control. Such runaways may need interventions that address all explanations for running away. Indeed, most families readily provide all of these explanations when queried about the reasons for a child's running away. For purposes of exposition and despite their overlap and interaction, these explanations will be considered separately.

　　　　The assumption that runaways have strong tendencies toward psychopathological or sociopathological behavior is contradicted by recent research. "The behavior of most runaways is a rational response to stress and frustration. . . . There is reason enough in the home and school environments to prompt even the most mentally healthy person to consider flight as a way of coping" (Brennan, Huizinga, and Elliott, 1978, p. 316).

Running from Family Strain. Strain among family members is cause for "escape" and for youths' attempts to find environments with less strife and more opportunities to achieve their perceived developmental needs. Strain may arise from disruptive family events. Sudden shifts in income due to parental unemployment may upset the family equilibrium and lead a child to decide that he or she is a family burden or that it is unappealing to stay home. Children may run because of fear or upset due to divorce, separation, or a new parental figure in the home. Studying a group of suburban runaways and a comparison group of nonrunaways, Roberts (1981) found that runaways were often confronted with a recent change in parental structure (either by having a parent move out or a new parent move in). The resulting addition or shifting of roles may cause family strain. For example, Donna, at age fifteen, was required to babysit for her younger siblings nightly while her parents were at Alcoholics Anonymous and Overeaters Anonymous. Donna described her reason for running away (Roberts, 1981, pp. 22–23): "My parents haven't been getting along and they have been taking it out on me. I had this party to go to and at the last minute she (mother) told me I couldn't go. I was being punished for not cleaning up the kitchen and had to stay in the whole weekend. I felt like they were keeping me in a cage, and I couldn't get off the block and it all got to me and I took off."

Alternately, strain may arise from too little parenting. Parents who are preoccupied with work problems, alcohol abuse, relationship conflicts, and poverty may neglect their children. The children of parents who make too few demands—for example, who allow children to fix their own meals at their own times—may begin to wander (Patterson, 1975). Consistent with other findings that parents of troubled children fail to track their children's behavior or quickly and appropriately define that behavior as deviant (Patterson, 1982), almost half of the parents of runaways in studies by Brennan, Huizinga, and Elliott (1978) did not consider that their child had run away, even though the youth was gone overnight without permission. This wandering often leads to stealing (Patterson, 1982) and the self-injurious use of other survival skills. The child may join with other children or youth who are also on their own and, essentially, engage in daily episodes of running away. In their limited understanding, such youths may assume that they have learned to meet their own developmental needs. This is often the case among young women who run away to prostitution (Bracey, 1979).

Running from Family Control. Running away is typically associated with excessive efforts to exercise parental control. Parental expectations for the performance of their runaway children are often portrayed as unrealistic and strict (see, for example, Blood and D'Angelo, 1974; Stierlin, 1974). It should be kept in mind, however, that many of these reports originated in an era when the police and child helpers were the villains and the runaway was romanticized. Current perspectives on adolescents' reports of overstrict parents recognize that strict punishment and seemingly excessive parental control may be encouraged by the youth's unacceptable and intractable behavior. Runaways are often involved in delinquent behavior before, during, and after running away. Getting caught selling drugs or shoplifting and the feared or actual consequences from parents are common precipitants to running away (Roberts, 1981). Olson, Leibow, Mannino, and Shore (1980) show that the family conflicts of adolescence that precipitated running away were themselves preceded by parent-child control problems from the earliest years. Runaways were more likely to exhibit troublesome, unresponsive, and antisocial behavior accompanied by parental irritation, punishment, and parental favoritism of other siblings. Gottlieb and Chafetz (1977) also find that interpersonal confrontations leading to runaway behavior often are preceded by long histories of disagreements, fighting, and threats (despite sincere though unsuccessful attempts to minimize hurt and find compromises).

Running from control is common and is increasing among children in group care (Adler, 1981; Russo and Shyne, 1980). Running away is often threatened, attempted, or accomplished after weekend privileges are not earned, peers are punished, or moves to other residences are proposed or arranged. Since group-care settings are often designed to teach a child to control his or her own behavior by first modeling external controls, conflicts about control are all but endemic.

Running from Abuse. According to the *Standards Relating to*

Noncriminal Misbehavior (1982) developed by the Juvenile Justice Standards Project of the Institute of Judicial Administration and the American Bar Association, running away can often be "the most rational, mature, and adaptive response to an intolerable situation" (p. 28). Never is this more true than when youth run from familial assault or molestation. Precise estimates are unavailable; however, according to researchers Lourie, Campiglia, James, and Dewitt (1979), anywhere from 8 percent to 30 percent of all runaways report sexual or physical abuse. Physical abuse or the threat of physical abuse triggered about one quarter of the runaway events reported by suburban adolescents (Roberts, 1981). Abuse is also a reason for getting kicked out of the house. Refusal to continue incestuous relationships with father figures may precipitate this rejection, as may an adolescent's threats to report abuse or an adolescent's physical counterattacks against parents. Reconciliation of families may still be the goal of treatment, but it is subordinate to ensuring the child's protection. Reporting laws must be followed in cases of abuse. These make gaining parental involvement difficult but provide the child helper's intervention efforts with the support of the legal system and its sanctions.

Ned Hemmali: Background of a Case Study

Fourteen-year-old Ned Hemmali came to the Oasis, a short-stay shelter for runaways in a medium-size metropolitan city. He was referred to the Oasis by counselors who determined from discussions with Ned and from telephone contact with his mother and uncle that an immediate return home would not work since Ned was not willing to return without some changes in his home life. He said he would only return if his mother moved to a new apartment. Ned arrived on a bus, and Ms. Whitecloud, a counselor at the Oasis, and another youth in temporary care met him at the depot. The conversation on the ride back was small talk.

Talking to Ned confirmed the assessment that Ned was unyielding about going home and that he and his family would need assistance to be reconciled. Ned explained his side of his story in the initial interview. His stepfather recently deserted his family, and Ned, his younger sister, and his mother moved in with his aunt and uncle, their son, and Ned's grandmother. Ned did not think that this arrangement would work from the outset, but he was not consulted about the decision. His mother explained that they could not live alone on her income and no savings and that this was just a temporary situation. That was nine months ago. Ned shared a room with his cousin and his sister and was governed by the uncle's rules. He continued at the same school but no longer walked to school, instead taking the city bus. He found it less and less attractive to go to school and began to cut one day a week to go back to his previous neighborhood and "kill time" or go to the stores or to the park. His absences went unnoticed for a month but were then reported to his uncle and mother by the school attendance officer. The result was a warning from school and a one-month grounding at home. Ned found the punishment unfair—especially because the house was so noisy and there was no escape from his grand-mother, cousin, and sister. They argued about his cutting classes and about who was to blame for the situation. After he was caught sneaking out of the apartment, his curfew was extended by two weeks, and his uncle threatened to beat him if he ever disobeyed again. Ned then ran away.

Assessment

Assessment of runaway behavior may occur at the point of initial contact between child helpers and runaway youth or at the point that future running away is threatened or impending. Assessment must consider not only the causes but also the current patterns of the runaway behavior. The child helper needs to know whether the running is new and amenable to change or habitual and well-entrenched. Assessment must also consider family resources and behavior patterns associated with running. Brennan (1980) distinguishes between Class 1 runaways, who are not highly delinquent or alienated, and Class 2 runaways, who are delinquent and alienated (see Table 11). Families of Class 1 runaways differ little from those of nonrunaways. In both cases, communication training, family therapy, school counseling, and social-skills training may be needed (Adams, 1980).

Table 11. Assessing Runaway and Family Types.

Runaway Type	Family Type		
	Random	*Open*	*Closed*
Class 1 Not delinquent, abused, or alienated			
A. Walkaways	Natural helping; service referral	Brief family counseling; limit setting	Communication training
B. Fugitives	Social-support mobilization; brief family counseling; natural helping	School intervention; communication	Marital and family treatment
Class 2 Delinquent, abused, or alienated			
A. Second-degree runaway	Intensive in-home services	Early return from shelter	Probation or child welfare intervention
	Stay at shelter with possible emancipation program to follow	Contracting and problem solving	Encourage independent living
B. Third-degree runaway	Provide independent living program and social services as needed	Arrange for family support of independent living with relatives in community	Provide youth and family with suggestion that future contact may be wanted

Social-support networking can complement such services in re-building runaways' attachments to their families, neighborhood, school, and community. For youths escaping from over-con-trolling parents, networking with other parents may provide the family with information on reasonable norms, positive models of negotiation, and a boost to family morale (Rueveni, 1979).

Class 1 runaways can be further distinguished by their personal skills (Orten and Soll, 1980). *Walkaways* are reasonably mature for their age, have age-appropriate self-control, and are considered well adjusted by peers. They may run for existen-tial reasons or because of a singular crisis in a relationship (such as upset about an abortion), or over-controlling parents. *Fugitives* are youth with fewer cognitive and social skills who may be socially isolated, unappealing to or rejected by parents, and im-pulsive. Such youth may run to gain attention or may impul-sively respond to an opportunity that arises while wandering in the community.

Alienated youth with more runaway experiences pose greater challenges to child helpers. Youth who have become alien-ated because of abuse, neglect, or delinquency (Class 2 runaways in Brennan's nomenclature) may not have reunification with their families as the foremost service goal. According to Orten and Soll (1980) this group is composed of second- and third-degree runaways. Second-degree runaways have some experience on the run but maintain an interest in returning home. They may have serious problems with their families but problems that are not a threat to the child's well-being. Third-degree runaways are more seasoned youth who have become skilled at street sur-vival and have few incentives to return home. These youth are usually older (sixteen to eighteen); have been pushed out of their homes; have no parents because of death, abandonment, or court termination of parental rights; are living with relatives or are in foster care when they run away; and are engaged in substance abuse (Berkeley Planning Associates, 1982). Youth with these characteristics are unfortunately not uncommon. The large numbers of such youth in runaway youth programs encouraged Congress to modify its initial goal in establishing the Runaway Youth Act from reuniting youth with their families to reunification only if this is determined to be in the youth's best interest. The treatment goal for these youth is often independent living *and* improved family relationships, since youth with continued contact with their birth parents have more success making the transition to independent living (Barth, in press).

Ned Hemmali: Assessment

Through her questions, Ms. Whitecloud reconfirmed that Ned did not risk physical injury if he returned home and that the chances were slim that Ned would run from the current setting. She learned that his uncle had not hit him and that Ned did not fear that. She also found out that Ned did not develop an attachment to street life in the city. He panhandled and stayed in various places but did not connect with any one place or set of people and did not become involved in prostitution or any other income-producing trade. He called his mother from the runaway house. Because Ned was a nonabused, first-time runaway with a strong attachment to one parent figure, Ms. Whitecloud's expectation was that Ned would give reconciliation a chance.

Ms. Whitecloud told Ned when he called her from the runaway house prior to his arrival at the Oasis that he would have to participate in family counseling including all family members, that his maximum stay at the Oasis would be one month, and that he would be on a stepped privilege system. Upon arriving at the Oasis, Ned was instructed to immediately contact his family. He was allowed to decide whether he would like to arrange the first family meeting on that day (Friday) or wait until after the weekend. Because Ned wanted to get back into school early the following week and wanted his mother's help in starting back to school, he chose to ask his mother if she could meet that evening. She agreed to do so. Ms. Whitecloud queried Ned about his uncle's availability, and Ned said that he had not asked his uncle. After some pressure and encouragement, Ned again called, this time to check on his uncle's availability and willingness to come to counseling. His uncle agreed to come one time.

Before the family meeting, Ms. Whitecloud completed a more thorough assessment of Ned. She identified his school strengths and weaknesses and successes and failures and asked about his neighborhood and school friendship network. She learned that he had friends at school, but those friendships had deteriorated since he moved to the new neighborhood. He continued to have a good relationship with the metal-shop teacher. He had no career aspirations, although he thought being a motorcycle mechanic might be right for him. He had no experience with motorized vehicles but wanted to save for a motorbike. He had no religious affiliation or membership in any community activities. His stepfather's brother lived nearby, and he and Ned were still on good terms. His paternal grandmother was also nearby, but they had little contact in the last ten years. Ned finally acknowledged that his relationship with his mother had been strained for a "awhile" (Ms. Whitecloud had difficulty pinning down when the strain started, but it predated the time when his stepfather left and Ned's family moved.) Ned said that his mother asked him to do things that "no other kid has to do" and that he sometimes just did not do them. Ms. Whitecloud decided to explore these rule conflicts in greater depth in the family meeting and instead asked more about his commitment to and performance at school. He acknowledged that he had not had good attendance since he shifted to junior high two years ago. He reiterated his interest in attempting to return home, but only if he and his mother and sister found a different place to live.

Intervention

Intervention with runaways is a challenge. The goal of working with runaways is to change the child's social ecology to increase his or her safety and ability to maintain a stable living arrangement rather than to stop runaway behavior with surveillance and punishment. Intervention may have preventive, interventive, and rehabilitative goals. The preventive goal requires identifying indications of impending runaway behavior and increasing the skills of everyone in the youth's home to reduce thoughts and actions that encourage escape. The interventive goal includes responding to the runaway youth in a way that promotes a return home or entry into a service program, planning ahead to prevent the recurrence of running away, and counseling that addresses the reasons for running away. For Class 2 youth (and especially third-degree runaways) the rehabilitative goal is often to build the resources of the youth in his or her social ecology for maintaining a safe, stable, and independent living arrangement.

Prevention of Running Away

Can initial episodes of running away be prevented? Research suggests the availability of opportunities for primary prevention of running away. Parents typically have a sense that their child will run away (Brennan, Huizinga, and Elliott, 1978). In about 40 percent of all runaway cases, some help seems to have been sought before the runaway episode occurred. The most common sources of aid are family physicians, school counselors, and local clergy. Adolescent runaways identified the events that triggered their running away, including arguments with parents, insults by parents, unfair consequences (for example, constant grounding), truancy, recent school suspension or expulsion, and beatings by teachers or other youth (Brennan, Huizinga, and Elliott, 1978). Justice and Duncan (1976) identify four early warning signs of running away: excessive fighting, temper tantrums after early childhood, chronic truancy, and habitually not getting along with others. Nevertheless, initial runaway episodes cannot be prevented unless child helpers have information about family or school behavior and knowledge of the precursors to running away so they can suggest and implement intervention.

Running away is often preceded by aggressiveness, wandering, staying out late, and other behaviors that approximate longer runaway episodes, and child helpers can help caregivers institute programs for reducing these precursors to running away (see, for instance, Patterson, 1975; Thoresen and others, 1979; Kirigin and others, 1979). Fortunately, most initial episodes of running away are not highly dangerous to the child and usually end in the child returning to the family. The first runaway episode may bring the family's troubles to the awareness of child helpers and may motivate families to pursue new solutions to their problems, including counseling. Secondary prevention of running away is generally, then, more feasible.

Intervention with Running Away

Lessening the chance of future running away begins with the first contacts between child helpers and youth. Decisions about the treatment strategy must be made with the youth and caregivers or potential caregivers. These decisions are often shaped by the results of attempts at reunification. Infrequently, the decision will be made to forgo attempts at reunification and to move rapidly toward arranging an independent living program.

Initial Contact. Few runaways seek contact with child helpers. Less than 5 percent of Ostensen's (1981) sample of suburban runaways were self-referred to the runaway shelter. Most came via police departments, probation offices, or schools. As "aliens in their own land," runaways avoid people who are unappreciative and who threaten their independence. Even children kicked out of their homes by their parents frequently blame themselves for their status and harbor fears of future confrontations with parents and so shun formal services to avoid further rejection. Runaways thus keep their distance from adult service providers. Yet child helpers do meet runaways under many circumstances. Since most runaway episodes start and stop within a few-mile radius, runaways may only temporarily leave their schools; may be referred to family service agencies by parents of a runaway's friend; and most commonly may be brought by police officers, social service staff, or probation personnel to youth runaway shelters. The initial contact with and assessment of the runaway may prove pivotal in engaging the youth in a help-finding process that leads to successful reunification with family or placement in an independent living program.

The Traveller's Aid Society of Los Angeles has developed a "passive approach" to working with runaways. First, staff members do not approach youth and ask them if they need help; they wait until a youth is referred or comes for help. Then they do not ask confronting or probing questions and do not pressure the youth for information. At first they accept the youth's version of his or her problems. They attempt to provide assistance to the youth immediately and in the youth's presence; for instance, if a girl states that she wants a job so she can become self-sufficient, a staff member might call a local employment agency, regardless of how unrealistic the prospects of finding a job. Staff members next ask the youth if he or she wants them to contact family or youth services near the youth's home. If not, the youth may be asked if he or she would like to call "Peace of Mind," a service (with a toll-free number) that will take the youth's name and a message for his or her parents without revealing the child's whereabouts. Most youth served by Traveller's Aid Society of Los Angeles return home or to their prerunaway setting. Follow-up phone calls indicate that most youth returned home or referred to another agency follow through on the service (U.S. Department of Transportation, 1980). (Contrarily, both Brennan, 1980, and Brenton, 1978, report minimal follow-through on referrals to counseling services for youth returned home, suggesting that child helpers should employ their best connecting strategies.) The approach of Los Angeles's Traveller's Aid society is in keeping with the procedures of most runaway houses; in Rosenheim's (1977) words, "First things first: Initially house, nurture and comfort the runaway. Then, later confront what kind of special problem—if any—the runaway child has" (p. 14).

The child helper's assessment of a runaway youth must guide decisions regarding whether to encourage the youth to return home, find temporary refuge and counseling for the youth in a runaway shelter, report the youth to child protection services and request temporary foster care, or find alternative living arrangements for the youth. These nonexclusive decisions should be influenced by the youth's wishes and the services available. Notifying protective services is mandated in most states when a child reports abuse, although child helpers may, after reporting, discourage the involvement of public social service agencies, and, with their permission, provide immediate crisis intervention (Lourie, Campiglia, James, and Dewitt, 1979).

Returning Home. Treatment may occur when the child returns home. Parent and child should have had the encouragement and opportunity to discuss the likely outcome of the return home and practice the responses they hope to give. Some families are on their best behavior after a child returns, which may mislead them into assuming that the need for family change is past. Other families may store anger during the time apart and be more prone to assault. When retaliatory violence is likely—especially if there is a history of violence, if the response to the child's phone call home was angry, or if the child stole something valuable from caretakers to finance his or her run—a child helper should accompany the child home. If the child lives far away, a youth service bureau, mental health center, school guidance division, family service agency, or runaway house should be contacted to ensure that reentry services are provided. The referring child helper can then monitor the family contact with the service agency.

Preventing the recurrence of running away is facilitated by parents' or child helpers' opportunities to plan ahead. At the same time, prevention is made more difficult by the child's familiarity with running away and often well-developed and rehearsed plans for "next time." Since family change occurs slowly, most runaways find many of the prerunaway conditions unchanged and soon after returning home threaten to run away again. Caregivers should avoid such threats as "go ahead and run but don't expect to just waltz back in here whenever you please" or passive acquiescence—for example, "that's up to you, I can't keep you here." The ideal response, which still may not stop a youth from running away, reaffirms that caregivers want the child to stay; that they expect that new solutions can be found; that they hope the youth will at least delay making a decision awhile and will first listen to some music, visit relatives for a weekend, or allow a friend or housemate to be part of the discussion; and that the youth is always welcome home as long as he or she is willing to try to find solutions to problems in living there. Preventive responses to the threat of running away will be most effective if supported by open communication, reasonable and certain consequences for running and for returning home, and encouragement to stay. Some "horse trading" of rights and privileges and modification of rules may help forestall a run and are often worthwhile. Although it is important to be firm, consequences should not be immutable nor should responses to running away be totally dispassionate and stereotypic. Child helpers are unlikely, on the other hand, to further their long-range goals for youth if they allow the threat of running away to disrupt reasonable expectations for meeting responsibilities and if their fear of precipitating a run leaves them unable to enforce necessary family rules.

Child helpers should help parents develop strategies to implement if a child does again run. One such strategy is described in Exhibit 15. The basic logic behind the procedure is that running away should not be rewarded by a suspension of family and school responsibilities, but neither should returning home be punished with massive privilege loss or physical or verbal assaults. The procedure for reintegrating a child into a family after a runaway episode is that used by Achievement Place (Phillips, Phillips, Fixsen, and Wolf, 1974) and kindred group homes, like Learning House (Thoresen and others, 1979). This procedure is only part of the Achievement Place approach, but it was at least partly responsible for a decrease in runaways from an average of 7.3 percent a month to 1.5 percent a month in five years (Kirigin and others, 1979). The procedures leading to this decrease required lengthy development time and were most effective when the model was fully implemented (Maloney, Surber, Fixsen, and Phillips, 1980). The protocol works best if certain child-management structures already exist, but it can operate in their absence. The structures used at Learning House, which were based on those developed at Achievement Place, included a points for-privileges system (or token economy) and work-write-read-sit (WWRS) restrictions. Although these structures can be introduced upon the runaway's return, ideally they should be developed before the first runaway episode.

In the points-for-privileges system, a child is entitled to three full meals a day, cordial relationships, school and after-school

Exhibit 15. Handout to Guide Caregiver's Response to Running Away.

If your child runs away:

1. Avoid the mistake of chasing after your child. If you are worried about your child, call your child's friends and talk with them and their parents to ask for information.
2. If your child does not return home after enough time has passed to concern you, then call the authorities, and they will also look for your child. They may tell you that you have to wait, however, before you can file a missing persons report.
3. If your child returns by him/herself, praise your child's good judgment for doing so.
4. Get your child busy with schoolwork he/she missed or with some family chores that are not punishing.
5. Talk about the event later when you have resumed the typical patterns of family life or when you have a counselor available to help.
6. Suspend basic privileges temporarily. Your child can earn back privileges by working and cooperating beginning on the following day. If your child cooperates and has good behavior, then full privileges can be earned back in about a week (but after the next weekend).

clubs or sports, a reasonable bedtime, and complete opportunities for self-care and engagement in family responsibilities. On top of those activities are *basic privileges* (Schumaker, Hovell, and Sherman, 1977). These consist of snacks, desserts, telephone, television, radio, stereo, play in the yard, and staying up thirty minutes past bedtime. Youths earn basic privileges by cashing in points earned for a variety of prosocial behaviors demonstrated at school and home. These are not difficult to earn and, unless a child's behavior is uniformly bad, at least some are earned each day. Youth can earn *special privileges*, including allowance, movies, favorite meals, and overnight trips, only after they earn basic privileges.

The WWRS restriction is a form of time out that complements the privilege system. During WWRS restrictions, youth are expected to spend their free time working on household chores, writing homework or positive self-statements, reading, or sitting in time out. WWRS restrictions serve, in part, to keep youth occupied when they have fewer activities to engage in because basic privileges are suspended. They also help youth catch up on work they missed during poor-performance periods (or, in this context, during runaway episodes). Work-write-read-sit restrictions also distract youth from the loneliness, anger, and confusion that often follow the return from running away. According to the protocol, when second-time runaways return to their family or group home, they are greeted cordially, praised for returning on their own (if they did), and informed that they will be able to earn basic privileges the next day and special privileges after the weekend. Parents, foster parents, or group-home parents instruct the child about the duration and content of the WWRS restriction. Assuming good behavior, the restriction might be in place for several full afternoons and later for about an hour a day. Restrictions are applied for no longer than until the end of the next weekend.

The plan shown in Exhibit 15 is for a family that did not previously use a points-for-privileges system or WWRS restrictions. The instructions are worded accordingly and allow the family to choose the privileges that will be suspended as well as the content of the restriction activity required. The plan was written with the family's assistance while the child was out of the home. Preferably, plans are written with the parents and child together after an earlier runaway episode. The child helper working with the family should monitor the family's implementation of the plan (to ensure that it is not too punitive) and help the family problem solve to reduce the causes of running away. Children rarely run away from homes in which they feel appreciated, in which reasonable expectations are held and enforced, in which positive events are readily available, and in which problems are resolved fairly and easily. Working to reshape the ecology of the home into this mold is the best runaway prevention.

Running away is an agonizing experience for families and youth. The extent of the family's upset influences the family's ability to respond according to plan. Parents may be furious that they worried so when they find that their child was sleeping in a neighbor's basement at night and never in danger. Brenton (1978) suggests that the reaction to a runaway episode may be similar to the response to a failed suicide attempt. Both parent and child may experience humiliation from the episode and determine to show the other party that this event will not cause them to change their behavior. If parents are unable to implement the planned strategy, child helpers can help them review their appraisal of the situation, understand their experience, and view alternative perspectives (including the child's) on the event.

Communication Training

Problems in communication with parents are reported by over half of the youth in runaway shelters that were queried (Berkeley Planning Associates, 1982). Parents being "too strict" was reported on one-third of client records. The primary goal of communication training is to change closed families into open ones. Thus, this approach is probably best suited to families that are close-knit but undemocratic, punishing, and overbearing and that have discordant ideas on family rules, responsibilities, privileges, and consequences. Notably absent is the ability to express affection (for example, see Satir, 1967). Improving the ability to express affection is a goal of both family therapy and communication training. Resolving structural family problems is often a prerequisite, however, to creating a family environment in which appreciation, affection, and love can flower. Communication training may also assist open families when it is combined with assistance in setting limits. Intervention strategies for random families include communication training and limit setting but may focus most intently on establishing family rules and consequences for obedience to and disregard of those rules.

Brief Family Intervention

Brief family intervention, Ostensen's (1981) communication-based approach to working with runaways, involves three to six sessions aimed at restoring parents' confidence that they can competently raise their children. The strategy is well-articulated and was shown to lower recidivism among a group of twenty-eight youth who completed the counseling program, although the experimental design of the project was not rigorous. These twenty-eight youth had a recidivism rate (defined as running away within the three months following counseling) of 25 percent in contrast to the youths who began the counseling and quit, whose recidivism rate was 62 percent. Youths who completed counseling and were nonrecidivists were, on the average, Caucasian females fifteen years old, who attended school regularly, had no previous involvement with police or probation, and had not had school problems requiring suspension or expulsion. They had not run away before, were gone for only one night, traveled less than ten miles from home, and were referred for counseling by school counselors or by juvenile justice personnel. Of those youth who completed the counseling, nonrecidivists typically had *not* been placed in foster care during the counseling period. These were clearly Class 1 runaways, and most were from homes with at least modest material resources. The intervention was especially successful with open families with difficulty setting and enforcing limits.

The counseling model has five parts. First, parents are asked to identify a few specific goals for their child that are essential and attainable. A single goal is then agreed upon, and the initial counseling session addresses that goal. Second, parents are asked to identify beliefs about their child (for example, running away is a family trait or a result of early childhood trauma) that diminish their ability to set and enforce reasonable expectations for prosocial behavior. Third, parents are asked to chronicle what they have done to improve their child's performance. Counselors enlist the child in identifying such unsuccessful parental strategies for controlling the child as threats, rhetorical requests ("Could you just be good for a while?") and *why* questions ("Why do you treat me this way?"). Next, parents are asked to identify the prosocial behaviors that they have successfully encouraged in their child. Parents articulate their successes in obtaining such desired outcomes as church attendance, daily showers, and decent language. Parental strategies used to achieve these outcomes are reviewed, with the emphasis on the importance of structured, clear directives and certain, reasonable consequences for nonperformance. Finally, the child helper expresses understanding that, given the parents' beliefs about the reasons for the child's inability to meet parental expectations, they never demanded the problem behavior in the way they had demanded other successful behaviors. This approach is intended to diminish parents' sense of failure and bolster their appraisal of their own competence by providing a rationale for unsuccessful past perfomance and a strategy for successful future performance.

Training in Communication and Problem Solving

Skills-training procedures for helping families resolve conflict have a long pedigree. Among the many researchers who have reported on the successful use of skills training with families are Alexander and Parsons (1973); Kifer, Lewis, Green, and Phillips (1974); Weathers and Liberman (1975); Blechman, Olson, and Hellman (1976); Lysaght and Burchard (1975); Hall (1980); Gant and colleagues (1981); and Robin and his associates (Bright and Robin, 1981; Robin, 1979, 1980, 1982; Robin and others, 1977). The approach described here draws on the work of these investigators and on the author's application of their models in family counseling. The problems these researchers address range from delinquency to status offenses (which might include running away) and often involve families with "parent-child conflict." None of the studies explicitly sought to reduce running away. They all, however, addressed issues that are associated with running away, including fighting, arguing over rules, overprotection, wandering, and curfew violations. As Beyer, Holdt, Reid, and Quinalan (1973) state, these programs are well-suited to address the precursors of running away because they look for "solutions [that] lie in better communication between caregiver and child and a willingness by both sides to accept some responsibility for the problem" (p. 5).

Problem-solving and communication training may be delivered in any setting (for example, a foster home, a runaway shelter, an independent living arrangement, or at home), but since homework assignments are a crucial part of the package, it is ideally conducted in the environment in which the caretaker and adolescent will continue to operate. The training can be done with one or both parents and the adolescent, with other older children (if they will contribute to the family outcome more than they will diffuse the training), or with several families together. The latter approach is more difficult to arrange but has a number of advantages. First, families can learn by listening to other families' adaptive and maladaptive strategies for problem solving. Second, the child helper can match children with adults other than their own parents to help reduce tension and performance anxiety when having participants practice new skills. This procedure also helps remind families that their problems and strategies are shared. Finally, families can become an important source of support for each other. Adolescents may find friends, but more commonly from the author's experience, caregivers find support. As previously detailed, strengthening every family member's social-support network can contribute to the family's total well-being.

Family communication and problem-solving training (FCPST) involves six basic stages. The initial stages incorporate the preconditions necessary to influencing behavior change: (1) defining the situation (for example, engaging the adolescent and parents together as clients and establishing a task-focused relationship); (2) assessing the family and the ecology; (3) teaching communication skills; (4) choosing and defining the problems on which to work; (5) discussing, evaluating, choosing, and planning solutions; and (6) implementing solutions and troubleshooting.

Every step of the process is clearly labeled by the child helper on worksheets used during the family meetings. If a family member jumps ahead to suggestions for implementing changes before the family agrees on a plan, child helpers label their comments and return them to the current problem-solving activity: "Right, Ned, that probably would help you *solve this family problem* and that might be a good *task* for your uncle. We'll talk about *tasks* later. First, let's finish with the *plan*." Problem-solving terms such as *problem definition, solution, evaluating solutions, planning,* and *tasks* are used at every appropriate moment until the family becomes familiar with them and, hopefully, begins to use them to organize their independent problem-solving efforts.

Defining the Situation. Families that have recently experienced running away may have many concerns about the future of their family, about what other significant people think about them since the runaway event, and about what will happen next. Parents are frequently angry at each other and their adolescent for causing the disruption and confusion that follow running away. Adolescents are often withdrawn and expect that whatever they do will lead to parental attack or to additional censure. The reward and punishment contingencies in the family will have changed, since the runaway event signals the adolescent's ability to escape punishment and to find some rewards in the community. Conversely, the adolescent will at times recognize that the rewards of the community are not easily obtained and may require sexual behavior and risk taking that he or she does not like. Both adolescent and parents are uncertain that the effort required by a counseling program will be rewarded with changes that make the family situation tenable. If the usual procedures for conducting an assessment, giving structure to treatment, and working with parents discussed in Chapters Two and Three fail with a runaway and his or her family, the child helper should address the possibility that residual concerns from the running away incident are blocking the family's efforts to master the training content. The child helper may want to meet with family members individually for further assessment and to encourage prochange attitudes. Discussions should attempt to encourage the belief that this is an opportunity to remake family patterns to everyone's advantage. The child helper should communicate that he or she will be trying to teach the family a system for solving their problems on their own that has worked for many families with similar troubles. The problem-solving strategy will require some changes in the way that family decisions are made but can nevertheless be adapted to their kind of family.

Assessing the Family and the Ecology. In addition to ascertaining the family's readiness to participate in the training, the assessment should address the specific problems that contribute to the adolescent's escape behavior and provide a baseline against which the family can compare their functioning before and after skills training. A convenient procedure is to use a checklist of common problems that plague adolescents and parents, such as the one shown in Exhibit 16. Separately, adolescents and parents identify the problems in their relationships with each other. After completing these checklists, youth and parents are often relieved to realize that they do not have every possible problem. Child helpers can then use the information from the

Exhibit 16. Sample Family Checklist.

Please check the correct information below:

You are:
1. ____ Youth
2. ____ Mother
3. ____ Father

Below is a list of topics that sometimes get talked about at home. Please circle every topic about which you and your (mother/father) (son/daughter) had a difficult and upsetting discussion during the two weeks preceding the runaway incident. Please put a second circle around the two most important topics.

1. Telephone calls
2. Bedtime
3. Cleaning up bedroom
4. Homework
5. Using the television
6. Cleanliness (washing, showers, brushing teeth)
7. Choice of clothes
8. Making too much noise at home
9. Fighting with brothers and sisters
10. Cursing
11. Money
12. Going places without parents (shopping, hanging out, movies, etc.)
13. Drinking, smoking, drug use
14. Going on dates
15. Choice of friends
16. Not talking to rest of family
17. Coming home on time
18. Getting to school on time
19. Low grades or trouble in school
20. Lying
21. Helping out around the house
22. Talking back to parents
23. Messing up the house
24. Staying out late
25. Food choices

Source: Adapted from description of Issues Checklist in Robin and others, 1977.

assessment to construct relevant didactic examples and role plays for the skills training. Discussion about the issues identified in the assessment is postponed, however, until later in the intervention.

Teaching Communication Skills. Before families are ready to tackle their more difficult problems, they are taught communication skills for problem solving. This is likely to occur in the first session. To encourage families to communicate freely—which is no small accomplishment—warm-up exercises are used in which families (whose members have switched around if there is more than one family) are asked to discuss a topic like the future of computers, the latest threat to peace, or great music.

Families then comment on family members' speaking and listening skills. They identify the people who spoke the most and the least, who stayed on the topic, who interrupted, who were critical or unkind, and who were agreeable and praising. The child helper keeps a tight rein on the interaction, gives everyone a chance to talk, maintains an expectation for a minimum of one comment from everyone, and does not allow family members to interrupt or criticize each other. Following this critique of communication, families discuss the best times they remember and their hopes for their family. Debriefing follows these discussions as well.

The child helper uses examples from the previous exercise to introduce six communication skills that help problem solving: (1) praise, (2) paraphrase, (3) I-statements, (4) partial agreement, (5) staying on topic, and (6) asking for information. They also learn to identify and find alternatives for "interrupts" and "zaps" (or attacks). Skills are taught according to previously discussed procedures: the skill is defined, a rationale is provided, and examples are given. The examples should be as relevant as possible and should enlist both a parent and child as recipients of the skills taught. Definitions should be simple and provided to family members in a handout. Identifying the risks of using each skill will keep family members from ruling out the skill because they can easily think of examples when the skill would not work. For example, *praise* may be defined as follows: "Commenting positively on a family member's achievements or personal qualities is praise. Praise makes people feel and act positively. 'Mom, you know it makes me feel really good when you tell me that you think I'm a good kid' is praise. Praise can have risks, though; people may think that your praise is flattery or may not feel comfortable having nice things said to them." Family members must also be informed that the *receiver* is the one who defines praise, interrupts, and zaps. If a comment does not feel good to the receiver, no matter how it was intended, it is *not* praise. Alternately, if the receiver experiences the communication as an attack, no matter how it was intended, it is a *zap*.

Perhaps the most important communication skill that

families learn is giving and receiving appreciation and criticism. Parents and adolescents too rarely feel appreciated and too often feel upset by each other's comments. The use of these skills helps lessen those common family experiences of "Don't you ever have anything good to say?" and "I just give you one suggestion and you explode." Several principles for expressing appreciation are described to families. First, appreciation is usually expressed in words, although hugs, gifts, and favors can add a nice touch. When possible, appreciation should be given soon after your teenager or parent does something you like (but it is never too late). Third, appreciation should be a mixture of the *specific*—"I really like the way you helped out with your baby brother today; thanks"—and the *general*—"You're all right, you know, Mom." Family members are also told that since trying to change behavior is so challenging, appreciation must be expressed often at first—for example, "You've been home on time these last two nights. Thank you for that"—until the new behavior is routine. Family members are further encouraged not to mix appreciation and punishment—for example, "Thanks for not playing that rotten music so loud"—since only the negative part of a comment may be remembered. Finally, family members are prompted to express appreciation for what others do, even if it is not perfect, so long as it is *better* than before.

Receiving appreciation is the next topic reviewed. When family members fail to effectively receive appreciation, they lower the chance that appreciation will be expressed again. Some examples of failures to receive appreciation are given in the following vignettes:

Mother: "Your room looks great, Ned."
Son: "All you ever do is talk about my room. You just want me to spend my whole life cleaning it."

Ned: "Thanks for the ride to see Jonnie, that was a big help."
Uncle: "Well, I'm just glad that you have one friend who's not a criminal. I just wish you'd be more appreciative of the other things I do for you."

Family members are trained to listen hard for the appreciation in the other person's comment and to ferret out hidden appreciation; for example, "You're hardly eating a thing these days" may mean, in part, "You're really changing your behavior." Appreciative responses to minimal compliments are rehearsed: "Yeah, I have been trying to lose a few pounds. Thanks for noticing."

The common tendency to make light of appreciation is identified and discussed. Child helpers suggest that family members avoid such comments as "Anybody can do that" or "Well, I've done it like this before, and you never had anything good to say about it then" and instead rehearse to just say "thanks" or to smile or to return the compliment; "Well, you're doing pretty good, too, Dad."

Families then learn to give and receive criticism. Even though appreciation will, in the long run, help increase behavior that contributes to family functioning, families must have effective strategies for addressing each other's intolerable behavior. Family members are encouraged first to be sure that another member's behavior is indeed intolerable and are taught to reframe criticisms as *requests* for behavior change. Family members thus also are expected to have a clear and reasonable idea of how they would like the other person's behavior to change before criticizing the current behavior: "Your talking back is a problem for me. I want no more than one question about the instructions I give you, and then I expect you to follow them within the time limit I set." Family members are also taught to remember that their idea of what should be changed is just an idea and not an indisputable fact. They practice checking with the recipient of the criticism to get his or her idea on the matter: "I think you are talking back more than you used to, and I am concerned. What's your impression?"

Parents and adolescents practice using I-statements to show that they take responsibility for the thoughts and feelings leading to their request for behavior change. "I get very upset when I think about that black eye your boyfriend gave you" is an example. Child helpers may wish to introduce the idea of "suggestion sandwiches." These combine an appreciation statement, a suggestion for improvement, and another appreciation statement—for example, "Mom, you are usually great about giving me my privacy, but today I was very upset when you said you'd been looking through my room. I do appreciate being able to talk to you about stuff like this."

Receiving criticism is perhaps the most difficult skill of all. Even hearing other people's criticism is painful—*really* listening to it is even harder. To help family members receive criticism calmly and with comprehension, family members are coached to anticipate the criticism and *breathe deeply*, thinking "relax" and reminding themselves that they are strong enough to tolerate criticism. They then practice *paraphrasing* the criticism instead of reacting to it—for example, "So you think I've been nasty lately." Partially agreeing with the criticism may also help keep the discussion calm. Family members learn to use such responses as "I guess I have been kind of uptight lately" or "You've got a point." This calmness can improve later discussions. Child helpers demonstrate ways that problem-solving statements—especially asking for *more information*—can make the exchange more constructive—for example, "Could you tell me a little more about what makes you think I've been nasty?" Families that catch on quickly to giving and receiving criticism also learn to handle critical retorts to critical comments—for example, "When I tell you that I don't like your getting home late for dinner so often, you say I'm being nasty. Hmm—perhaps that seems nasty, but I still want to discuss your behavior until we figure out what we can do to change it."

Communication skills are taught by having family members practice them in interchanges with the child helper and then with each other. For example, family members may write down a praise statement about another family member—perhaps, "You work hard to make this a good family"—and the receiver of the praise may then be asked to turn that into an I-statement—perhaps, "I do try hard for my family." Practice is then extended to role-play situations. At first, detailed scripts, such as the one shown in Exhibit 17, are used to ensure that the role play includes sufficient opportunity to use communication skills and to depersonalize the content. Such role plays are provided to give family members the opportunity to practice keeping calm while problem solving. The child helper should first demonstrate communication skills in response to the adolescent or parent who reads the scripted lines. Each family member in turn plays both parts of each script to get ample practice, a shared experience, and hopefully, a shared perspective.

Exhibit 17. Sample Role Plays for Practice in Keeping Calm.

Curfew: Parent's Version

Your child returned home well after the time you set. You will play the parent and I will play your child. Your goal is to keep calm and try to have a level-headed discussion. I'll play your child; I just got home, and you walk in.

Teenager: Oh uh! Still up, huh?
Parent:
Teenager: Look! Why do you have to worry about me? I'm okay.
Parent:
Teenager: You're really like a cop sometimes.
Parent:
Teenager: Heh! Most parents aren't so strict. Maybe if you had some fun sometimes you'd understand.
Parent:
Teenager: I'm really sick of you and this house.
Parent:
Teenager: All right! But can we do it tomorrow?
Parent:

Curfew: Teenager's Version

You just came home and your parent is upset about how late it is. I will play the parent, and you will play the teenager. Your goal is to keep calm and try to have a level-headed talk. Now, I'm the parent walking in on you in the kitchen.

Parent: You're late again.
Teenager:
Parent: I've told you before not to stay out. You're really going to get it.
Teenager:
Parent: I don't know what happened to you. You're not fit for this family.
Teenager:
Parent: I'm ready to put you on restriction for a month.
Teenager:
Parent: I'm ready to kick your tail downtown.
Teenager:
Parent: All right! But I'm serious about this.

Choosing and Defining the Problem. The family must agree on a problem to tackle. The problem checklist may prompt discussion of one highly rated problem. If not, each person nominates one specific problem. If the problems do not overlap, and the family cannot agree on which problem to discuss first, then the child helper sets the order in which the family will discuss the problems.

After family members have begun to communicate more often, more calmly, and more affirmatively, they next learn to define problems. Developing a good definition of a family problem is often the key to solving problems. Families learn that good definitions tell two things: (1) what the other person is doing or saying that is bothersome, and (2) how this causes a problem for the person defining the problem—in other words, what the problem definer loses because of what the other person does. Further, families learn that good definitions are short, neutral, do not exaggerate, and do not blame any other person. The child helper provides practice sheets (such as the one shown in Exhibit 18), which families use to identify good and bad definitions and to learn to write better definitions.

Once the first problem to be addressed has been chosen, the most positive and articulate family member states (1) what he or she believes the problem to be, and (2) what he or she thinks may happen because of the problem. For example, Mrs. Hemmali might say that the problem for her is that Ned does not talk to his uncle, and she worries that one of them will explode. Other family members paraphrase what the first speaker said. The first speaker tells whether the paraphrases are correct, offers clarification if it is needed, and thanks others for careful listening. In sequence, each family member also describes what the other family member is doing to cause the problem and what he or she is losing as a result; each other family member paraphrases these comments, and the speaker gives feedback to the paraphrasers as to the accuracy of their paraphrases. One family member serves as recorder and writes down the problem on a worksheet such as the Problem-Solving Worksheet shown in Exhibit 19. This description should include some part of everybody's ideas about the problem. This procedure is lengthy

Exhibit 18. Sample Worksheet for Defining Family Problems.

Developing a good definition of a family problem is often the key to solving that problem. A good definition of the problem tells you two things: (1) what the other person is *doing or saying* that *bothers* you, and (2) what problem this causes for you. The definition is short, neutral, does not exaggerate, and does not blame the other person. Below are several definitions. Read each one. Then say whether it is good or bad. If it is bad, write a better definition.

A. *Daughter:* I hate you, dad. You just are a real pain. I'm missing out on all the fun because you make me come home by 9 P.M. on weekends.
　　1.　Is this a good definition of a coming-home-on-time problem?
　　2.　If you said no, write a better definition:

B. *Father:* Son, the real problem with you is that you don't respect your elders. Kids just don't know the meaning of respect today. When I was your age, I would never talk to my father the way you talk to me.
　　1.　Is this a good definition of a talking-back problem?
　　2.　If you said no, write a better definition:

C. *Son:* I get angry when you bug me ten times a day about taking out the trash and feeding the dogs. I'm old enough to do these things without being reminded.
　　1.　Is this a good definition for a problem with chores?
　　2.　If you said no, write a better definition:

D. Below, a mother and a daughter define their problem about playing the stereo too loud. Notice how each accuses and blames the other. This is a poor way to define a problem. Write a better definition for each person.

　　Mother:　You are ruining your ears with that loud stereo. You just don't have good taste in music. How can you stand all that loud noise? I can't, and, what's more, I won't stand for it.

　　Daughter:　Don't talk to me about taste in music. You sit around all day listening to 1940s junk music. No one listens to that stuff anymore. And get off my back about the loud stereo. I have to play it loud to enjoy it.

　　Mother:

　　Daughter:

Source: Adapted with permission of Arthur L. Robin from "Parent-Adolescent Conflict: A Skill-Training Approach." In D. P. Rathjen and J. P. Foreyt (eds.), *Developing Social Competence: Interventions for Children and Adults*, pp. 191–192. © 1980, Pergamon Press.

Exhibit 19. Sample Problem-Solving Worksheet.

What is the problem? The problem includes:

Possible solutions (Key: Bad = − , Okay = 0, Good = +)

	Youth	Parent A	Parent B

A. Current Solutions
   1.
   2.			

B. Ideal Solutions
   1.
   2.			

C. New Solutions
   1.
   2.
   3.			

D. Compromise Solution 1.			

Best Solution:

Source: Adapted with permission of Arthur L. Robin from "Parent-Adolescent Conflict: A Skill-Training Approach." In D. P. Rathjen and J. P. Foreyt (eds.), *Developing Social Competence: Interventions for Children and Adults,* p. 189. © 1980, Pergamon Press.

but gives each family member an opportunity to see the costs of the current situation for each other family member. This recognition is critical to arriving at solutions that address the real costs of the problem and which do not insult family members by exaggerating those costs.

Discussing, Evaluating, Choosing, and Planning Solutions. The family next generates solutions. Each person states what he or she thinks the family currently is doing to solve the problem. The recorder paraphrases the comment and writes it on the Problem-Solving Worksheet under the section titled "Current Solutions." Each person then states his or her ideal solution. The recorder paraphrases and then writes solutions on the worksheet. Family members also suggest new solutions, which the recorder lists on the worksheet. This is not brainstorming, which families do not (in the author's experience) generally enjoy, may result in inflammatory suggestions, and does not seem to produce many useful new solutions. This is an opportunity to offer solutions that have a reasonable possibility of improving on current solutions.

Family members take turns evaluating each idea. Each solution is assessed by each family member, in turn, who answers these questions: (1) Will this idea make my problem less? (2) Will this idea make others' problems less? (3) Does this idea have a good chance of working? (4) Can I give up what this solution requires? The child helper may provide flash cards with the evaluation questions. Family members each make an overall judgment of each idea and record " + " for good solutions, "0" for acceptable solutions, and " – " for poor solutions. Family members then select the best idea as the solution by looking for any ideas rated " + " by everyone or the idea with the most plusses and least minuses. If one idea stands out as the best, this is recorded at the bottom of the worksheet. If no idea clearly stands out as the best, family members reexamine the ideas rated highly by most individuals and negotiate by generating a list of two or three compromise solutions that combine several ideas, evaluating the compromise solutions, and agreeing on one of these. The compromise solution is then recorded.

Helping families to implement the solution of their choice requires some craft but above all requires patience and thoroughness in helping them to develop a feasible plan. If the solution to the problem involves an exchange of behavior changes and privileges, child helpers must help the family develop working definitions of those behavior changes and privileges; consider when family members will start to change their behavior, and when new behavior might lead to privileges; and review what they will do if one individual fails to change his or her behavior or deliver privileges. Child helpers must also identify the responsibilities and tasks of each family member in monitoring changes and privileges. When solutions involve obtaining more information—about driver's education or employment training programs, for example—then tasks must be assigned. If a solution requires that parents try to gain admittance for their child to a program of his or her choice, behavior changes and privileges must be identified, and tasks must be assigned. The child helper and the family should keep a record of the expected behavior changes and privileges and the task commitments.

Implementing and Troubleshooting. Even the best plans need changes. Child helpers should attempt to guarantee that there will be no surprises for families. To preempt dramatic failures, each family member, in turn and using I-statements, identifies one way that he or she could defeat the plan and describes what he or she will do to avoid undermining the plan. Family members agree on a time that they will meet at home to decide whether their plan is successful and for troubleshooting. This should culminate in the development of a new plan, new tasks, and additional rehearsal and practice. Family members should recognize each other's willingness to participate in the problem-solving process and end with some appreciation for other family members' problem-solving efforts and skills.

Troubleshooting continues as families begin to implement their solutions. Implementation requires steps common to all behavior change efforts: planning, task identification and assignment, rehearsal, and trying again and again. Families learn this process through demonstration and repetition.

Ned Hemmali: Intervention

The next day, Ned's family visited the Oasis to meet with Ms. Whitecloud and Ned. After brief salutations, Ms. Whitecloud met with Ned's mother and uncle to demonstrate that she was not colluding with Ned and recognized their perspective and concerns. She learned that Ned's conflict at home dated back to his earliest years and had intensified during the latter months of strain between Mrs. Hemmali and Ned's stepfather. Ned reportedly had protested rules or consequences from his earliest years, kept to himself at home, and did not talk much to his cousin or sister. Ned was apparently less cantankerous at school, but he did not care about his grades or academic courses. He had never been diagnosed or treated for hyperactivity. Ned's mother and uncle assumed that he used drugs and alcohol but no more than other kids. Ned's uncle thought that it was time for Ned to shape up and intended to change the situation to "let Ned know what he's going to be up against in the real world before he gets there and screws up." He said that he did not think that he would ever hit Ned, but he would not promise otherwise. Mrs. Hemmali confirmed that her brother often gets angry but said he had not hit any of the children. Ms. Whitecloud talked briefly with Mrs. Hemmali and her brother to determine the first mutually convenient time to meet with school officials about Ned's return to school.

After twenty minutes, Ned joined the discussion. Ms. Whitecloud's mission was to encourage change, to provide structure to the family's problem-solving efforts, to diffuse confrontation, and to introduce communication techniques. She informed the family that she knew that they would all prefer a workable living situation to seeing each other at the Oasis. She said that she wanted to help them solve the problems that led to this meeting—the smaller "hassles" that caused conflict in the home as well as the larger issue about the best living arrangement for all. They would start with the small problems first. She asked each family member to complete the Family Checklist (shown in Exhibit 16). (She does not always use this checklist but thought that more information about the family's daily interactions would help her identify their skill deficits and underscore her interest in having the family consider issues other than where the Hemmalis should live; this was Ned's issue alone, and she did not expect to lose him by ignoring it.)

Each family member read the items they circled on their checklists and indicated their two important topics. Mrs. Hemmali had the most items circled, even though she did not readily describe high conflict with her son. The most significant problems reported by Mrs. Hemmali were "low grades or trouble in school" and "staying out late." To Ned the two worst problems were "talking back to parents" (which he said is what his mother and uncle say he is doing every time he tries to stick up for himself) and "low grades or trouble in school." Ned's uncle identified the same problems as Ned. Ms. Whitecloud informed the family that they would have a chance to address these problems starting with the second session. In the meantime she asked them to think about the question: How would you know if the problem was better?

Ms. Whitecloud then switched the focus of the session to communication skills and explained the rationale for learning to paraphrase, give appreciation, and receive criticism. After she described each skill, she demonstrated it and then had each family member respond to her verbal prompts with the target skill. She gave Mrs. Hemmali and her brother the tasks of giving appreciation and criticism once each day and spending ten minutes each day paraphrasing each other's comments about the way they would like the family to function. She assigned Ned the same task and agreed to serve as his counterpart. (Ms. Whitecloud considered this less than ideal since Ned and his family were denied the opportunity to express appreciation to each other, but she figured that practicing the skill during the meeting would help them to later use it at home.)

In the next session two days later, Ms. Whitecloud reviewed the homework and went over the communication skills. She next introduced the overall problem-solving structure and explained that this would help them solve some of the problems that led to family conflict. She first provided instruction and practice (using the problem definition worksheet shown in Exhibit 18) in defining problems. Ned's family chose to try defining each of the problems circled on their checklists. First Mrs. Hemmali and then Ned and his uncle said exactly what each other family member did to cause each problem and what made this a problem for them. They then, in turn, paraphrased each other's definitions. The definitions of "school troubles" were notably the same, which Ned's uncle pointed out. They decided to work on two problems—school and talking back—with talking back first.

Mrs. Hemmali again led off the discussion by describing what she called talking back: "When my brother or I ask Ned to do something that he should know he's supposed to do and he doesn't do it and then we ask again and he tells us to leave him alone.'' She said that the cost of this for her is that the things she asks Ned to do are good for him, and she worries that he will not be as happy as he could be if he planned ahead more. Further, when Ned does not do his household chores, then she has to do them. Ned defined talking back as ''using swear words or telling an adult to get lost or something like that.'' He said the worst part of this for him was that he never knew what he could and could not say and when someone was going to come down on him. His uncle said that talking back to him was ''everything from when Ned doesn't do what we ask to when he doesn't even act like he heard me to when he tells us off.'' He said that he worried about Ned, but more recently Ned's behavior just sent him into a rage and upset the rest of his home life. He added that he had been extra tense at work and that his blood pressure was high.

Ms. Whitecloud asked the family to come to an agreement about what the problem really was so everyone would know when it happens. They reached an agreement that talking back was not just swear words, and it was more than Ned's just not doing what he is asked. With some coaching, the family defined talking back as Ned's letting his mother or uncle know (either verbally or nonverbally) that he won't do what is asked and not giving any reason or saying when he will do it. They agreed that a problem exists when there are more than two espisodes of talking back per day. Ned's uncle expressed his concern that this definition could reward Ned for giving excuses rather than complying with requests, but Ms. Whitecloud reminded him to appreciate the progress made in arriving at an agreement and informed him that this problem could be handled later if it arose.

Ways to decrease talking back were the next topic covered. This time Ned began by describing what they were now doing to decrease talking back. He said that his uncle threatened him, and he tried to avoid his uncle and, recently, his mother. Ned's uncle said that Ned's solution to talking back was to talk louder and to challenge him or Ned's mother every time they tried to get him to come home earlier or to do anything at home. Ned's uncle stated that he threatened Ned more, and he did not know what else to do. Mrs. Hemmali said that grounding was a reaction to talking back as well as to cutting school and was one of her solutions.

Alternative solutions were discussed and recorded. The family had little trouble agreeing on several things to do. First, Mrs. Hemmali reported that she had been talking to some friends at work, and they thought that Ned's groundings were for too long a time. She thought that they should switch to one night of grounding at a time if Ned exceeded the one talk back per day limit. Ned got upset at this, saying that he could never make any plans that way because they might get canceled at any time. He suggested that he start getting an allowance for the days that he did his chores and got home on time without any talk backs. Ned's uncle said that he thought they would just fight over the money. He could not think of anything that would work but liked Mrs. Hemmali's idea. Ms. Whitecloud offered the solution of making the next night the penalty night for a talk back so Ned would have more time to plan. She also instructed the Hemmalis to spend about fifteen minutes on the coming weekend, when Ned would be home, to think of something Ned could earn for not talking back and for coming in on time. She encouraged them not to make any firm contracts about this until their next meeting with her, but she believed that they could come to some agreement about what Ned could earn. Because time was short she briefly asked each family member what might go wrong this weekend and how each might contribute to this. She had no time to respond to their comments with any troubleshooting guidance but hoped that posing the question was helpful.

In future meetings, Ned and his family came to some agreements about curfew, about what Ned would earn for not talking back (the first reward was two tickets to a motorcycle show), and what household work Ned had to do each week to get an allowance. The family also agreed on a plan to increase Ned's school attendance. An unexcused absence was agreed to be worth a weekend at home without telephone privileges. A month with no unexcused absences was good for a weekend in his old neighborhood with a friend. No agreement was made about penalties for coming home late, but they did agree that

Ned's right to take driver's education would depend on whether he started coming in on time. This was a far-off consequence for Ned, Ms. Whitecloud informed him and his family, but they thought it a good idea.

By the end of three weeks, Ned was living at home and reenrolled in school. He and his family continued to come to the Oasis for counseling for six sessions during the next four weeks. The troubleshooting accomplished during these counseling sessions helped to keep them on track. They also completed tasks to encourage their continued use of communication skills. They held family meetings between sessions for thirty minutes to talk about the programs that are under way and to clarify any definitions that are not working satisfactorily. Each family member rated each meeting on the Family Meeting Checklist, shown in Exhibit 20. Judging from their evaluations, their reports on the meetings, and observations of their problem solving during their meetings, the Hemmalis seemed increasingly able to solve their problems arising during the implementation of their ongoing behavior-change plans. Ms. Whitecloud agreed to continue to call once a week for the next month and to provide consultation if they were stumped by a family problem.

As a first-time runaway with a resourceful family, Ned and his family had a good prognosis. Ned's uncle changed his behavior toward Ned by yelling and threatening less, but his personal goal of setting more limits for Ned was unchanged. The Oasis's routine follow-up at three months found him to be a satisfied customer. He reported that he still had problems getting Ned to talk and with back talk, but they were more manageable. Mrs. Hemmali reported that she was still looking for a way to move into a single-family dwelling with her own children, but the issue was not often discussed and was no longer the focus of Ned's harangues. She was also setting firmer limits and using more statements of appreciation. She reported that the most valuable part of the counseling was learning to deal with Ned's criticism without blaming herself, yielding her position, or getting "down." Ned was the least satisfied customer but thought that there was less yelling and threatening. He still thought that he could hardly say anything without it being called

Exhibit 20. Sample Family Meeting Checklist.

Name: _____   Person Described: _____

Item Description	Not at All	Some	A Lot
Gave good reasons	1	2	3
Considered more than one view	1	2	3
Joked in a nice way	1	2	3
Offered new alternatives	1	2	3
Said something nice or gave praise	1	2	3
Asked about others' thoughts	1	2	3
Suggested a compromise	1	2	3
Brought discussion back to topic	1	2	3
Said back what other said	1	2	3
Expressed disapproval with I-statement	1	2	3
Argued or talked back	3	2	1
Talked about others' mistakes or errors	3	2	1
Yelled or used loud, unpleasant voice	3	2	1
Tried to change subject	3	2	1
Interrupted	3	2	1
Threatened	3	2	1
Exaggerated	3	2	1
Kept silent	3	2	1
Nagged, griped, or complained	3	2	1
Accused or blamed someone	3	2	1

Note: A summary score (high is better) will indicate overall quality of perceived family interactions during family meetings.
Source: Adapted from Gant and others, 1981, p. 104.

"back talk" but thought that the situation with his uncle was better. He did not think that his uncle would abuse him. He still wished to return to his old neighborhood and home.

Independent Living

Rather than trying to reunify a runaway and his or her family, it is at times better to try to foster a stable and safe independent living situation. Youths from violent or exceptionally disorganized families; youths with well-developed street lives; and youths with adequate self-care, preemployment, and home-maintenance abilities may all benefit from independent living arrangements. Child-helping services aimed at emancipating youths focus on helping youths establish adult identities and gain the prerequisites for participation in the adult world. A driver's license and a social security number are but two of the many possessions that adolescents may need help obtaining. Problems securing housing, finding work, budgeting, living with roommates, and avoiding loneliness and substance abuse are larger problems that adolescents in independent living programs cite (Anderson and Simonitch, 1981; Simonitch and Anderson, 1979). Strategies for instruction in independent living should call on the technology of competency building and systematically provide information, rationales, demonstrations, practice, troubleshooting, and assistance in maintaining prosocial performances.

Child helpers may still want to include significant adults in counseling sessions when helping emancipate adolescents. Recognition of a youth's new status by birth or foster parents may result in offers of assistance or opportunities for future reconciliation. In an era of increasingly difficult entry requirements for work and greater costs for establishing a residence or enrolling in school, it is not unexpected that youth with continued contact with birth or foster parents or with some other nurturing and resourceful adults are more successful (Harrari, 1980). Child helpers should identify whether the youth has any relationship with a nonexploitive adult who could provide immediate aid or promise future resources. Outreach to grandmothers, birth parents, older siblings, and former and current foster parents may identify an adult ready to make a commitment to helping a youth in his or her pursuit of an independent life (Barth, in press).

12

◊◊◊◊◊◊◊◊◊◊◊◊◊◊◊◊◊◊◊◊◊◊◊

Suicidal Behavior

Suicide rates for adolescents have increased every five years since 1950 (Solomon and Murphy, 1984). Suicide is now the second leading cause of death for adolescents and claims more than 6,000 young lives each year. From 1960 to 1980, suicide rates for white adolescent males increased from 59 to 138 per million, for white adolescent females from 15 to 35 per million, for black adolescent males from 15 to 16 per million, and for black adolescent females from 15 to 19 per million (National Center for Health Statistics, 1981). Suicide attempts are the major reason for psychiatric hospitalizations for latency-age children. Almost 75 percent of fifty-eight adolescents consecutively admitted to an inpatient unit arrived following suicide attempts (Pfeffer, Conte, Plutchik, and Jerrett, 1980).

Because the probabilities of suicide are key to assessment and intervention, they deserve thorough understanding. Motto (1985) reports that youths who feared that they were losing their minds or would die of a disease were at the highest risk of completing suicide. Children and youth who repeat suicidal actions after hospitalization are likely to have recently lost a parent, or to suffer from drug or alcohol abuse (Hawton, 1982). Prior suicidal gestures, high depression levels, and parental alcoholism are strongly associated with repeat attempts, as are especially serious original attempts (McIntire, Angle, Wikoff, and Schlict, 1977).

Children with major depressive disorder (MDD) and those from families in which at least one member suffers from depression or alcoholism are especially likely to attempt suicide (Carlson and Cantwell, 1982). Having a mother who has attempted or considered suicide (Orbach, Gross, and Glaubman, 1981) is associated with adolescents' suicide attempts, especially among girls (Shaffer and Fischer, 1981; Tishler and McKenry, 1982). Adolescent girls who have experienced pregnancies and abortions may be particularly at risk of suicide (Tishler, 1981). School problems (Kosky, 1983) and feeling worried about doing poorly in school also distinguish suicidal youth from other psychiatric inpatients (Pfeffer, Conte, Plutchik, and Jerrett, 1980). The recent death of a family member—including a pet—may precipitate suicide attempts (Kosky, 1983; Pfeffer, Conte, Plutchik, and Jerrett, 1980). Physically abused children and children who have witnessed violence between parents have higher suicide-attempt rates than do other inpatients (Kosky, 1983). Parental alcohol or drug abuse is another strong risk factor. Children with learning disabilities are overrepresented among suicide attempters (Peck, 1985), as are children and youth who are prone to rages and assaults (Pfeffer, Conte, Plutchik, and Jerrett, 1980; Shafii, Carrigan, Wittinghill, and Derrick, 1985); homicidal threats, gestures, or attempts preceded two out of three suicide attempts in Cohen-Sandler, Berman, and King's (1982) sample. Youth report that their suicide attempts are designed to seek relief from stress and to show others how desperate they are (Hawton, 1982). Parent-child conflict is a contributor to many suicide actions; children who attempt suicide often report their parents to be hostile, indifferent, or controlling (McIntire and Angle, 1972). Conflict with a boyfriend or girlfriend and social isolation are also commonly cited by suicide attempters (Hawton and Osborn, 1985). Good interpersonal skills are, alternately, linked to reduced risk (Pfeffer, Conte, Plutchik, and Jerrett, 1980). For these reasons, Trautman and Shaffer (1984) argue for the use of parent-child communication and conflict-resolution training similar to that described in Chapter Eleven of this book.

Male and female and black and white youth use different methods to complete suicide. Black males often use jumping from high places, whereas white males more often use carbon monoxide poisoning (Frederick, 1984). Guns are used in a majority of suicides among both white and black female adolescents, although black males and white females are more likely to use hanging than their opposites. Latency-age boys attempt suicide more often than girls do, but the percentage of latency-age girls who complete suicides is as high as that of boys (Pfeffer, Conte, Plutchick, and Jerrett, 1980). Older age is associated with completed suicides in both races. Youth aged fifteen to nineteen have ten times the likelihood of completing suicide as do ten- to fourteen-year-olds (Cohen-Sandler, Berman, and King; 1982); the mean age of suicide attempters is about fifteen (Tishler and McKenry, 1982). Youthful suicides differ from adult suicides. Boys attempt suicide more frequently than girls, whereas women attempt suicide far more frequently than men (Sudak, Sterin, and Hauser, 1975). White and nonwhite youth have similar suicide rates, whereas white adults have a suicide rate two to three times that of nonwhites (Sudak, Ford, and Rushforth, 1984).

Suicide: Manipulation and Signal of Desperation

Suicide attempts are coercive. They also signal desperation. Attempters may be using suicide actions to raise the stakes in the interpersonal poker game until caregivers fold and give up control. One fifteen-year-old youth attempted suicide with aspirin after her parents grounded her for the weekend for coming home late and smelling of marijuana and alcohol. The social worker reviewed the fairness of the family's current expectations for her behavior and of the consequences for not meeting them. The therapist supported the father's belief that the expectation of curfew and sobriety was appropriate but also supported the mother's belief that other restrictions on the daughter—forbidding her to go to PG-rated movies and controlling what she watched on television and whom she had over to the house, for example—were excessive. After some additional negotiation and problem solving, maintaining curfew, maintaining sobriety, attending school, and doing chores were listed as the four fundamental responsibilities of this child, and consequences were articulated for each. Most other elements of parental control were removed. The girl made no further suicide gestures, even when she was grounded a month later for two curfew violations in one week.

McIntire, Angle, Wikoff, and Schlict (1977) describe the manipulative aspect of suicide acts in their work on "pharmacological brinkmanship," or the attempt to change an oppressive situation through self-poisoning. The authors report that each year about 100,000 children aged five to fifteen poison themselves; 46 percent of these poisonings cause symptoms, and 24 percent require hospitalization. Although these typically are not accidents, the lethality of these attempts is less than 0.01 percent. (For youth aged fifteen to twenty-four the lethality rate rises to about 0.5 percent.) McIntire, Angle, Wikoff, and Schlict (1977) argue that self-poisoning is associated with attempts to control significant others but is used by children and youth who do not expect to die but only to "go to the brink but not fall off" (p. 607). Liberman and Eckman's (1981) report of in-depth interviews with twenty-four frequent suicide attempters captures the use of suicide for interpersonal control: "they were neither weighing a decision to live or die, nor making a self-destructive act in response to a sudden change or acute crisis in their lives. Instead we found people who were largely devoid of social and emotional coping skills and who used suicidal threats and gestures as one of many maladaptive behaviors in a longstanding, manipulative life style of 'controlling' their social relationships" (p. 1130).

Although suicidal actions may have the aim of manipulation, they should be viewed as incompetent acts to influence behavior. Such a perspective encourages the application of assessment and intervention skills that strengthen alternative social and cognitive coping strategies. Wicks (1974) aptly warns professionals against basing their treatment on preventing suicide attempters from manipulating the system. Of prisoners, he writes, "This rigid approach to inmate behavior should now be reviewed. Unless correctional administrators become willing to discard the suicidal manipulator model and show interest instead in the reason underlying all self-injurious behavior, little will be learned about the mutilators and such destruction will continue" (p. 250). Morgan (1979) concurs, indicating that half of the patients who committed suicide after leaving his hospital had been discharged, despite their insistence that they could not manage without hospitalization, by staff who were attempting to counter possibly manipulative behavior.

In an attempt to distinguish between a suicide attempt and self-destructive behavior that looks like a suicide attempt but which was performed with the belief that the act would not be fatal, Kreitman and Philip (1969) introduced the term *parasuicide*. In a later study by Kreitman (1977), only 1 percent of the people committing parasuicidal acts later committed suicide. Still, 41 percent of those who committed suicide during that time had committed parasuicidal acts prior to their deaths. Although the use of the term *parasuicide* is increasing, Albanese (1983) correctly argues that parasuicidal actions and suicide attempts cannot now be adequately distinguished for the purposes of treatment and should instead both be considered expressions of self-injury that may (intentionally or not) be lethal. This is particularly true with adolescents for whom no clear pattern of nonlethal attempts can be confidently established. *Parasuicide* suggests that the attempt was manipulative. A more useful conceptualization views all suicide attempts as indications that young people's cognitive and social skills are inadequate for them to change themselves or their environments to achieve sufficient satisfaction with living. Suicidal actions of any kind may indicate that a youth feels that "his power is so eroded, his means of gaining attention or serious consideration of his plight so depleted, that all he has left to bargain with is his life" (Ross, 1981, p. 634). To emphasize their commonality, parasuicides, suicide gestures, and suicide attempts will here all be referred to as *suicidal actions*.

Jenna Jackson: Background of a Case Study

Jenna was a thirteen-year-old girl who was brought by her mother to the general hospital and then to psychiatric emergency services after she was found unconscious after taking her mother's sleeping pills. Jenna lived in a large apartment complex with her mother, her mother's boyfriend, and two younger sisters. Her mother's boyfriend had been living with them for about two years. Jenna was in her first year of junior high school.

Three months before the suicide attempt, Jenna had gone to school but had left early and returned home. She was asleep in bed when her mother's boyfriend awakened her and forced her to commit oral sex on him. He told her that if she said anything about this he would deny it; that he would inform her mother that she had skipped school and was using this as a way to avoid the punishment; that he would find an occasion to beat her; and that if she did not comply with his wishes, he would force her sisters to instead. She succumbed to his pressure and accepted the mandated silence.

Since the molestation, Jenna's attendance, which was never good, had been especially sporadic. She was informed that the next unexcused absence would result in a suspension, and a parent-teacher-student conference would be required before she would be reinstated. She was getting mostly D's and F's in school. She was not involved in extracurricular activities. Her closest friend recently became pregnant and was thrilled to be on her way to motherhood despite her age and even though the baby's father lived with another woman. Jenna's contact with and enjoyment of her friend decreased. Jenna had begun eating excessively.

Jenna stayed clear of the boyfriend as much as possible but returned home one day to see him hurriedly leaving her sister's room and her sister looking very confused. Jenna, suspecting that her sister had also been victimized, was upset and angry. She took her mother's pills. Her mother came home thirty minutes later, found Jenna, and brought her to the medical emergency room.

Assessment

The following are questions to ask to help assess suicide risk. First, is the child or the child's family characterized by one or more of the previously discussed risk factors? Second, have recent stressors or transitions increased the child's burden? Third, does the child have a history of major depressive disorder or suicide actions? Finally, does the child have a specific suicide plan and the means for implementing this plan?

Recent Stressors and Transitions. Rudyard Kipling, in an autobiographical story, described his suicide attempt at age six after he was taken from his home and parents in India and sent to live with a brutish family in England. Children who lose a parent to death or divorce and face the major life changes that result are at increased risk (Hawton and Osborn, 1985). Youth who are threatened with a move from one treatment program to another—especially to a more restrictive program—may attempt suicide to forestall this change. Whether concluding that youth are trying to control their destinies or are being "manipulative," child helpers should recognize that transitions are prime times for suicide actions. Assessment of the suicidal child or youth must always probe for the presence of recent sexual or physical abuse or neglect.

Assessment should include contact with available significant others—including peers, former therapists, and siblings—to obtain a complete history of the suicidal crisis and its precipitants. Although friends may feel honor bound not to disclose information about a youth, when they *are* willing to discuss the youth—often when the youth is in a medically risky period—friends are frequently best able to give detailed information about the child's life-style, and the existence of substance abuse and previous preoccupation with suicide.

Major Depressive Disorder. Almost 80 percent of the children who seriously intend or attempt suicide suffer from a major depressive disorder (MDD) (Carlson and Cantwell, 1982). The following criteria are used to diagnose MDD (from Spitzer, Endicott, and Robbins, 1978):

1. Dysphoric mood or pervasive loss of interest or pleasure
2. At least four of the following eight items of depressive syndrome:
   a. Poor appetite or weight loss; increased appetite or weight gain
   b. Sleep difficulty or sleeping too much
   c. Loss of energy; fatigue or tiredness

      d.   Psychomotor agitation or retardation
      e.   Loss of interest or pleasure in usual activities
      f.   Excessive or inappropriate guilt
      g.   Diminished ability to think or concentrate
      h.   Recurrent thoughts of death or suicide, or any suicidal behavior

3.   Dysphoric features that last at least two weeks
4.   Sought or was referred for help for impairment in functioning
5.   No signs that suggest schizophrenia
6.   Does not meet the criteria for schizophrenia, residual subtype.

Note that all six conditions must be present for a positive diagnosis of MDD.

      Because of the high risk of repeated and lethal suicide attempts for children and adolescents with MDD, a thorough assessment must be made. The Schedule for Affective Disorders and Schizophrenia for School-Age Children (K-SADS) was developed to record the symptoms of six- to eighteen-year-old children (Spitzer and Endicott, 1978). The K-SADS-E interview schedule generates DSM-III diagnoses and also reveals the presence of suicidal ideation, the number and severity of any previous suicide attempts, and the seriousness of the subject's suicidal intention. Gammon, John, and Weissman (1984) demonstrated the reliability of the K-SADS-E and showed that structured interviews were far more revealing than were unstructured interviews by experienced clinicians. The latter often focused on intrapsychic difficulties and personality dysfunction and failed to accurately identify suicidal behavior that occurred prior to hospitalization and suicidal ideation that occurred prior to and during hospitalization and missed treatable DSM-III affective disorders such as bipolar disorder. Six out of seventeen youths interviewed had bipolar depression, as identified by the K-SADS-E, but none were so diagnosed by clinicians; four of the adolescents had previously attempted suicide, but only two of these attempts were recorded in the medical record. Other researchers also complain that clinicians believe that psychotherapy to change the child's personality must precede any attempts to address the child's affective disorders and assume that suicidal behavior "must be treated with confrontation, clarification, interpretation, and the positive effects of a therapeutic relationship" (Freidman and others, 1984, p. 223). This is counter to their finding that half of seventy-six hospitalized adolescent suicide attempters had bipolar disorder. Suicidal youth may often need concurrent medical, cognitive, and social interventions, as affective disorders may contribute to disturbances in family management that persist after the recovery of a stable mood.

At greatest risk are youth with a history of prior and nearly lethal suicide attempts. These clients need the greatest supervision. Youth with one or more suicide attempts with a low likelihood of lethality or a single nearly lethal attempt are the next-highest risk category. Youth with a history of suicide actions of limited potential lethality (primarily self-poisoning or limited wrist cutting) and longstanding depression are also at significant risk but typically do not require constant supervision. Youth without a history of suicidal actions or depression who are responding to a crisis (for example, an arrest or the death of a significant person) are at least risk. Decision makers should, of course, err on the side of caution rather than on the side of carelessness.

Suicide Plans. At greatest risk is a youth with a comprehensive suicidal plan that includes a decision about the method of self-destruction (for example, using a gun, pills, or cutting), assurance of the availability of the proposed method, specific details about the setting and timing for the suicide, and a conviction about what will happen as a result of the suicide attempt. Consistent with the argument of Chapter Three, the more elements of a plan that a person has clearly in mind, the greater the likelihood that the person will accomplish the task. This is helpful for encouraging prosocial activities, but it is reason for grave concern when the client's identified objective is suicide.

Case Management

Child helpers must help staff and families make decisions about care of a child following a suicide attempt. Youth who have committed suicidal acts often end up in the general hospital emergency room. Options include returning the child home, referring the child to a community-based crisis residential program, or admitting the child into the psychiatric unit of the hospital. The goals of the interviewer are to (1) establish rapport with all members of the family, (2) determine the current risk of suicide, (3) identify precipitants of the suicide attempt that are still present and personal and ecological resources that might ameliorate the potential harm of those precipitants, (4) determine the best short-term disposition, (5) determine the most effective plan, and (6) identify tasks and responsibilities for implementing the plan.

As always, placement in the least-restrictive environment necessary and respect for the therapeutic elements of the child's social ecology are critical. The family and child's ability to use community resources should be weighed. Hospitalization is less desirable for a child who is enrolled in school than for an adolescent who is homeless and unattached to school or work. Although drug overdoses in response to a crisis do not typically require hospitalization (Hawton, 1982), the family's ability to support the child rather than to ventilate anger is an important determinant of the safety of returning a child home. Richman (1979) describes a case in which a young man's suicide attempt by poisoning was considered to disgrace the family and to be too upsetting for the grandmother to know about. The youth was discharged home anyway—in part because hospitalization was also considered stigmatizing—and, treated in individual therapy rather than in a family context, later killed himself. In all cases, release from the hospital back into the community environment must follow some evidence that the social and environmental contributors to the suicide attempt—and not just the youth's cognitive and physical contributors—have been substantially reduced.

The availability of supportive community resources for a youth must also be considered in determining the appropriateness of return home. Two studies comparing youth who were returned home following hospitalization for suicidal behavior found that youth who were returned home had a lower rate of repeated suicide gestures than adolescents who lived away from home (Barter, Swaback, and Todd, 1968; Cohen-Sandler, Berman, and King, 1982). (In the latter study, three of the four post-discharge suicide attempts did occur, however, during visits to parents.) This is not proof that this is a better treatment, since there is no assurance that the groups of children were similar before their differential discharges, but it does suggest that the risk of repeated suicide gestures continues to exist despite restrictive placements.

Return home should follow a careful assessment of the lethality of the home environment. Guns, lethal medications, and poisonous chemicals should be removed or locked away. Families should be told not to keep the child under constant surveillance but, instead, to encourage the child to resume positive peer and school involvement. A medical examination should be obtained, since adolescents who do attempt suicide have higher rates of medical illness than their peers (Garfinkel, Froese, and Hood, 1982). When in doubt, it is preferable to keep the child in the hospital; an unnecessary hospitalization is better than a needless death.

A schedule of prearranged post-hospitalization calls to be made regardless of the client's condition has the benefits of not requiring the client to ask for more help and presenting evidence that the world is orderly and that the future promises some desirable human contact. The prearranged calls should be scheduled for both the child helper and the youth to communicate the youth's responsibility to keep contact. Aftercare for suicide attempters ideally spans two years, as this is the period of highest risk (Pfeffer, 1981).

Out-of-Home Care. Youth under arrest are unusually likely to attempt suicide. One-half of black suicide attempters were recently in trouble with the law (Breed, 1970). Flaherty (1983) noted that juveniles held in adult jails commit suicide at a yearly rate approximately 150 times that of the general population, and the rate of suicides in juvenile detention is roughly nine times that of the general population. Flaherty also found that seventeen of the twenty-one adolescent suicides that took place in adult facilities occurred with the ''sight and sound'' separations between adults and juveniles in place, as is required by law. The National Study of Jail Suicides (Hayes, 1983) found that fifteen of the victims were juveniles; twelve of the suicides occurred when the youths were placed in isolation, and six of the youngsters died less than fourteen hours after incarceration. Alessi, McManus, Brickman, and Grapentine (1984) assessed seventy-one serious juvenile offenders and found that sixty-one percent of the youth had attempted suicide within the last year; youth with affective disorders made suicide attempts with the highest likelihood of success. Prisoners who make homicidal threats or threaten to destroy property are at highest risk. Assessment of suicide risk includes a thorough intake interview about suicide history and a check for any physical evidence of self-injury. Albanese (1983) found that 20 percent of the inmates who made suicide attempts had scars on their wrists or forearms at the time of intake.

When an individual is at high risk of suicide, he or she should not be isolated. Suicide attempts in jail most often happen when inmate activity is minimal (that is, from 4 to 5 P.M., 10 to 12 P.M., and 5 to 6 A.M.) and on the first day of admission (Albanese, 1983). The policy of a "suicide watch" should be avoided, as it has a high failure rate. A better procedure is to place high-risk individuals in a public place with other inmates. Plastic razor blades or electric razors should be routinely used for all inmates, whether suicidal or not. Above all, inmates should have the opportunity for substantial contact and activity with peers and staff.

Residential treatment failities obtain as many as 60 percent of their residents directly from hospitals (Fitzharris, 1985). As a major provider of services to suicidal youth, group-care facilities must have well-articulated policies and procedures for preventing suicide attempts and for responding to new attempts. Many youth understand that they will be rehospitalized if they take suicidal actions. For a few youth, this is not a wholly unappealing prospect. Some find the hospital nurturing (it even comes with electric razor), some find it a good way to meet people, some use it to communicate to their families that the residential setting is unsuitable and that they should be at home, and some use it to avoid school. As previously discussed, if hospitalization is needed, it should not be withheld in fear that a youth is being manipulative with any of these goals in mind. Other steps can be taken to be sure that youths do not learn to injure themselves in order to enjoy the benefits of hospitalization. First, other group-home members can be restricted from visiting or calling the hospitalized youth. Contact between staff and the child should center around mutually supportive efforts to develop a discharge contract. One local halfway house for adolescents had a youth who was told that she would have to spend forty-eight hours in juvenile hall for program violations (substance misuse and curfew violations). She ran away and made a suicide attempt. After a brief trip to the hospital, which indicated that the attempt had had low lethality potential, she was brought to juvenile hall in the ambulance to spend her assigned time.

Suicide Contracts. Suicide contracts are important but must, like other suicide interventions, be personal and not just tactical. The no-suicide contract (shown in Exhibit 21) should be separate from and in addition to the task agreement that is completed with other members of the social ecology who agree to change their behavior. The suicide contract is solely for the suicide attempter, although it may refer to actions with which other individuals will collaborate. The suicide contract should be explained slowly. The child or youth should recognize that his or her safety is of paramount interest to the child helper. As much as possible this contract should be negotiated and personalized so that the child does not feel powerless. The only nonnegotiable element is the agreement that the child will not attempt suicide in the next twenty-four hours. A child or youth who will not agree to a no-suicide contract should not be discharged. Given the shortage of hospital beds, this is not a simple matter. If hospital staff insist that the child should be released, then the head of the psychiatric emergency service should be asked to sign a paper stating that she or he believes that the child will not kill him- or herself within the next twenty-four hours.

Drye, Goulding, and Goulding (1973) present a simple and effective procedure for monitoring suicide risk. The clinician

Exhibit 21. Sample No-Suicide Contract.

---

1. I, Beverly Smith, agree that I will not kill myself either accidentally or on purpose, even if I cannot get hold of my counselor from now until Wednesday, the time of my next appointment.

2. I agree to give everything that I could use to kill myself, including my gun, my knife, my sleeping pills, my tranquilizers, and my aspirin, to my friend, Ro.

3. I agree that if I think that I might hurt myself I will call my counselor, Dr. Jackson, at 383-5632, the suicide hot line at 764-1122, or Ro at 322-6827, or I will talk to my mother.

Signed   Beverly Smith

Witnessed by   Carolyn Jackson

Day and date signed   7/29/85

Effective until   Wednesday   7/31/85
                    Day   Date

---

asks the young person to repeat the statement, "No matter what happens, I will not kill myself, accidently or on purpose, at any time and even if I can't get hold of you" and to report his or her response to that statement. Responses of "I'll try" or "I can't" are considered unacceptable, and the client is told that he or she must make the no-suicide decision. The length of time for this verbal contract is negotiable and only must be long enough to bridge the time between that meeting and the next contact with a helping professional who will renew the contract. The authors report that in 609 cases where this criterion was strictly applied no fatalities occurred. Use of suicide contracts in this way must be coordinated with other treatment staff. (The contract can also be written, as shown in Exhibit 21.)

More limited forms of no-suicide agreements involve asking clients who make frequent but low-risk suicide attempts to determine the level and type of suicide precautions—including assurances of readmission to the hospital upon verbal request—that they need (Zich, 1984). Such a strategy provides alternatives to suicidal actions intended to gain protection. Suicide-proofing of hospital wards—in which clients identify and eliminate possible threats to their safety and control—is another approach that relies on the competencies of clients and, in so doing, promotes their sense of self-management (Benensohn and Resnick, 1973).

Professional Self-Management. Work with suicidal children and youth can generate intense anxiety and loneliness. Child helpers often identify with caregivers' sense of responsibility for creating conditions that were associated with a suicide attempt or completion. Child helpers often hold the belief that childhood is supposed to be halcyonic; children's wish to escape life confronts them with the fact that growing up is hellish for some children. Anxiety also arises from the clinician's inability to forecast which child will complete suicide and to know what is the least necessary amount of surveillance and control. Clinicians' anxieties about suicide may influence their assessments of children and their families and their success in intervening in systematic and careful ways.

Like the client and the client's family, the child helper must have adequate support to help the suicidal child. The child helper becomes a significant part of the family lifeline and must have a lifeline of his or her own. The clinician should discuss her or his anxieties about the possibility of a completed suicide with colleagues or supervisors. Support from others will help child helpers avoid a sense of frustration from the demands of clients and their families and from the long, slow path to recovery and reintegration that some clients follow. Child helpers, professional or not, who work with suicidal youth must seek and secure adequate professional consultation.

Jenna Jackson: Assessment

Jenna's first interview was with the social worker, Ms. Keller, on the medical unit. From an earlier discussion with Jenna's mother, Ms. Keller knew that Jenna had no history of prior suicide attempts and no history of mood swings or mental illness. In her private assessment interview with Jenna she dispensed with the mental status exam and, instead, focused on the suicide attempt. When given the chance to describe what happened before the attempt, she summarily described herself as disgusted with school and home and everybody else getting pregnant like fools and her not having any future. She said that she was sorry that she had done it and that it had not worked out and that she did not see any point in talking about it. Unable to engage her with open-ended questions, Ms. Keller inquired of Jenna whether she wanted to stay in the hospital or to return home. Upon learning that she did not want to go home or stay in the hospital, Ms. Keller inquired more about the situation at home. Jenna finally conceded that her mother was okay but should stop getting on her about her weight and going to school and that she could not stand her mother's boyfriend. Only after saying that some young people who try to hurt themselves do that because they are trying to get away from someone who is hurting them at home did Jenna tell the social worker that the boyfriend had made her commit fellatio (not her words) and that she was so disgusted that she did it and that he was going to be around that she just wanted to "check out." The circumstances and further questioning indicated a very high likelihood that Jenna's story was accurate, and Ms. Keller told her that she would have to report him to the police and children's protective services.

After informing Jenna that she would do so, Ms. Keller called in Jenna's mother and asked Jenna to tell her what happened. Ms. Jackson initially denied that Jenna's story could be possible and wondered aloud if Jenna was not just blaming her problems on her boyfriend. Following this comment, Jenna refused to say any more to her mother. Ms. Keller assured Ms. Jackson that she believed this story and would have to report her suspicion of abuse to the police. She asked that Jenna not go home until a social worker and police officer had interviewed the boyfriend and felt assured that they could keep the boyfriend off the premises so that he would not have any opportunity to retaliate against Jenna. Jenna was not sure that he could be kept away, but she was willing to return home. Ms. Keller provided her with the number of children's services in case Jenna wanted to call.

Knowing that circumstances might change, Ms. Keller talked to Jenna about possible difficulties that faced her with regard to the prosecution of the boyfriend and returning home. She asked Jenna if she believed that she would again try to kill herself (Jenna said no) and if she would agree to sign a no-suicide contract to that effect (Jenna said it was not necessary but that she would). They agreed to meet at Jenna's house the next day, and Ms. Keller said that she would give Jenna a ride to the local mental health center to meet a psychologist whom she wanted Jenna to meet and to talk with. Jenna informed her that she did not want to talk with anyone. Ms. Keller convinced her to try a single meeting. Before leaving, she talked with Ms. Jackson about removing all lethal medicines, weapons, and chemicals from Jenna's access.

Interventions

Prevention and treatment of suicidal behavior involve careful attention to youths' social and cognitive activities as well as collaboration with caregivers. Depression is not a necessary condition for suicide, but the absence of interpersonal rewards and the failure to think positively about the future are linked to depression and also associated with suicidal acts. A social learning explanation of depression and suicide is so clear and simple that it is tempting to dismiss it as simpleminded. This approach argues that depression follows when individuals conclude that future acts have such a low likelihood of returning rewards that they are not worth undertaking. Under the influence of such a world view, activity and rewards continue to decline. Suicide becomes more sensible than struggling but failing to secure a minimum level of satisfaction. This lack of minimum satisfaction may result from interpersonal interactions that do not yield social pleasures or cognitive interpretations of experiences as more punishing than rewarding. The result may be an overwhelming experience of not being able to gain anything from any act short of homicide or suicide. Social and cognitive interventions, then, that address suicide should focus on building social and cognitive skills for gaining life's too-scarce rewards. Preliminary work in this area has been done using social-skills training with depressed women (Hersen, Bellack, and Himmelhoch, 1982) and cognitive and social-skills training with adolescent mothers (Barth, 1985) and others (Rehm and others, 1979).

Specific interventions with clients who take suicidal actions have not been adequately tested. In one of few such tests, Gibbons, Butler, Urwin, and Gibbons (1978) evaluated a task-centered social work service for adult clients who attempted suicide by poisoning themselves. Clients who received task-centered services were compared with those who had been referred back to their physician or to psychiatric care. With clients who received task-centered services, the contact lasted twelve weeks or less; ten was the mean number of interviews (including interviews with collateral resources). At the twelve-month follow-up, task-centered clients reported more services (almost half reported that they had had "a lot" of help compared to 15 percent for the conventional-treatment group) and more satisfaction. Clients given a task-centered approach reported significantly fewer social, material, and emotional problems than the conventional-service group. There were no significant differences, however, in the repetition of self-poisoning.

Social Consequences and Skills. In 1979, Clum, Patsiokas, and Luscomb lamented the paucity of research on treatments of suicide attempters. Since then, the literature has had few additions. One is a study by Liberman and Eckman (1981), which, although it does not focus on adolescent suicide attempters, provides a provocative look at a group of adult suicide attempters. The clients were nonpsychotic, not addicted to drugs, and had attempted suicide at least once in the preceding two years (there were seventy attempts among the twenty-four clients). Contending that suicidal behavior, like other behavior, is learned and maintained by its social consequences (as shown by Frederick and Resnik, 1971; Bostock and Williams, 1974), the authors designed a program to evaluate the usefulness of a package of behavioral techniques for dealing with the interpersonal and anxiety problems of inpatient suicide attempters. Social-skills training was chosen as the primary element in the program because the emotional distress of suicide attempters is aggravated by difficult social relationships; seventeen hours were devoted to social-skills training. Ten hours of relaxation training were included in the package to assist suicide attempters in times of distress, and five hours of training in communication and in developing and exchanging mutually acceptable responsibilities and privileges with family members were included to reduce the family strain that often precipitates suicide attempts. This program was compared with more conventional insight-oriented inpatient therapy that included, during a ten-day period, seventeen hours of individual therapy, ten hours of group therapy, and five hours of family therapy. Both groups were exposed to the token economy on the ward and developed aftercare plans.

Measures of depression and interview ratings of the type and frequency of suicidal threats and acts, the frequency and urgency of suicidal thoughts, and the nature and specificity of suicidal plans were significantly less for the group that received skill training than for the group that received insight therapy when patients were assessed three, six, nine, and twelve months after treatment. Apparently, suicide attempts, the chronic, impulsive strategy for responding to stress, can be reduced with proper training, family involvement, and assertive aftercare.

Cognitive Interventions. Self-management strategies can also combat depression and reduce the risk of suicide. Self-management strategies previously described (see Chapter Five) include setting specific goals, breaking those goals into smaller goals, rewarding the achievement of those goals (often by self-praise), and continuing positive self-talk when first attempts to attain goals fail. By making rewards seem attainable, self-management skills make rewards more available. A naturalistic study of women who managed to cope with depression shows that these women relied on the self-management strategy of generating concrete definitions of problems, whereas women who were unsuccessful in coping with depression used vague, global definitions (Doerfler and Richards, 1981). Other findings show that self-esteem is more influenced by the overuse of critical self-statements than by the underuse of positive self-statements. Others have shown favorable effects of teaching self-management techniques to depressed adults (Rehm and others, 1979). Effective self-management is not, of course, the sole contributor to goal achievement. Family, school, and community characteristics may constrain the ability of the most skilled young person to achieve goals. Such skills help, however, to contradict the experience of help-lessness and to promote positive adaptation to the demands of growth.

Social and Cognitive Skills. Cognitive- and social-skill deficits may contribute to the failure to solve interpersonal problems by means other than suicide. Nidiffer (1980) employed both cognitive- and social-skills training with a college student who had attempted suicide four times since he was eighteen years old. The youth, T. R., was unsure of his ability to continue to pay for school, was failing several subjects, was masturbating more than five times a day, and was obsessed about sexual mat-ters during 90 to 95 percent of his waking hours. He was reported to be unassertive by his girlfriend and the therapist, who also noted a high rate of negative self-statements, and he reported that his thoughts were confused and fragmented. At the begin-ning of his treatment he scored a 32 on the Beck Depression Inventory, or BDI (a score indicating severe depression), and described himself as having twelve of the problems listed on the Mooney Problem Checklist.

Intervention involved a problem analysis of depressive episodes and suicide attempts and structured positive self-talk. The chain of events that typically led to depression included fighting with his girlfriend and brooding over his financial situa-tion or grades, isolating himself, and brooding some more. To help reduce fighting with his girlfriend, T. R. identified typical sources of conflict, worked with the therapist to identify asser-tive responses that would not offend the girlfriend or leave T. R. upset, and practiced implementing those responses and evalu-ating their effectiveness. To reduce his brooding, T. R. planned a pleasant thirty-minute activity that he could use if he observed himself brooding and considering isolating himself. These events included playing the guitar (he played professionally) or going for a drive.

T. R. wrote ten positive self-statements about himself (for example, "I am a good guitar player" and "I'm a good-looking guy") that he read to himself and thought about for five seconds every time he urinated (this was a common event because it was habitually linked to his masturbation and, therefore, also helped him cease thinking obsessively about his sexuality). By the end of two months, T. R. was masturbating less than once a day, the number of problems he identified had fallen to three, and his BDI score was down to 17. At two- and four-year follow-up assessments his scores were similar, and he was fulfilling work and spousal roles successfully.

Physical Interventions with Wrist Cutting. Chronic suicide attempters may use suicide attempts, especially wrist cutting, to release tension. Despite the apparent pain of wrist slashing, this activity may be highly reinforcing for the tense individual. In an ingenious and promising intervention, Rosen and Thomas (1984) successfully substituted a self-induced, noninjurious muscular pain from exercise for the self-induced, injurious pain associated with superficial skin cutting for three wrist cutters with an average of seven years of wrist cutting per person.

The case of Carol, a twenty-year-old woman who had been cutting her wrists since she was thirteen years old, illustrates the procedure. Carol was in an inpatient setting; had received years of psychotherapy and psychopharmacology to no avail; and was in an exercise program including calisthenics, team sports, and swimming that had not allayed her wrist-cutting behavior. Her wrist cutting occurred following boredom, frustration, and even pleasure. She cut her wrist to "avoid feeling bad." She suffered from a mild nerve disorder in her right hand because of the cutting. She cut her wrists an average of three or four times per day.

The rationale of the program was first explained to Carol. Whenever she experienced an urge to cut herself, she was to perform repetitive push-ups, sit-ups, and leg lifts, despite the onset of pain. Since this was difficult to do in public places, Carol was instructed, when in public, to squeeze a hollow rubber ball past the point of discomfort in her wrists and forearms and until she could not continue whenever she felt the urge to cut herself. During the first week she did not cut herself at all, but she did rub her wrist repeatedly against a hard object. By the second week and through the follow-up at one and one-half years, she did not cut herself again. She continued to perform the ball-squeezing technique frequently throughout the day. (The other two clients studied also stopped cutting themselves and ultimately discontinued squeezing the ball, although one of them did continue to carry it with her.)

Elliot, Smith, and Wildman (1972) used relaxation training and systematic exposure to events that were related to the suicidal behavior of a fourteen-year-old girl who had repeatedly slashed her wrists. The client typically cut herself an average of three times a month when she thought about her difficult past (which included abuse and trips through foster care, juvenile justice, and psychiatric services). The girl learned to relax and control her tension when looking at pictures of herself socializing with a friend and to tense herself when looking at a piece of broken glass pointed at her wrist. Later, she learned to do this without the pictures or her therapist's prompting. In a second procedure, she and her therapist developed a list of anxiety-producing thoughts that typically led to suicidal behavior. These thoughts included not living at home with her family and handling sharp implements. She learned to relax while reviewing these thoughts. Her suicidal acts were reduced to 0.17 times per month with no attempts during the last seven months of follow-up.

Medical Interventions. Ambrosini, Rabinovich, and Puig-Antich (1984) argue that psychopharmacological treatment of prepubertal depression may be the initial treatment of choice. The efficacy of antidepressants for children with MDD has only recently been reported (Puig-Antich and others, 1979) and needs further investigation. Side effects of such drugs as imipramine are similar to those for adults—dry mouth, abdominal pain, nightmares, insomnia, tiredness, chest pain, and difficulty learning—so drug use must be carefully monitored. Trials of imipramine should be evaluated at the end of one month; nonresponders should be reassessed, and additional treatments should be given. Lithium has been used successfully with people who frequently repeat dangerous suicide attempts, but maintaining safe and therapeutic levels of the drug can only be accomplished by experienced inpatient staff (DeLong, 1978).

Social and Group Support. Whereas most professionals

understand that talking about suicide does not increase the likelihood of recurrence, fewer nonprofessionals do. They must quickly be helped to understand that talking about the circumstances surrounding the suicide attempt is necessary to plan actions that can lead to a future with less risk of suicide. Friends and family members will naturally not want to hold themselves responsible for past or future suicide attempts. The child helper must make it clear that the responsibility is not held by any individual, but that the youth, the clinician, the family, and the peer group will work together to reduce the likelihood of future suicidal actions.

Ross and Motto (1984) developed a group approach for working with adolescents at high risk for suicide. They advertised the "Peer Befriender Group" to local high schools, mental health centers, and youth service bureaus. Youths who were referred were interviewed by the group leaders, who described the group and discussed their common concerns about confidentiality, the role of the family, the role of the group leaders vis à vis the school, and what the youths' participation in the group meant regarding the youths' mental health (that is, this did not mean that they were crazy). They were told that no one would know that they were in the group; that the group leader would not even acknowledge them on the street without permission in advance; that they could tell their families as much or as little as they wanted about the group; that group participation would not be reflected on their school record; that participation in the group indicated that they wished to reduce the pain in their lives, not that they were crazy; and that the group was for learning new ways to handle problems and was not "therapy" (an onerous term for many people). Sixteen adolescents were invited to participate; ten kept their interview appointments, and eight (six with previous suicide attempts and two currently threatening suicide) joined the group. Group membership fluctuated, and members came and went; by the end of the thirty-five group sessions held over a period of twenty weeks, the average number of sessions each adolescent had attended was thirteen.

The group leader's role was active and at times task oriented. In addition to facilitating the group sessions and organizing the surrounding support network, the group leader visited group members who were hospitalized, met with youth authority personnel to explore options for a group member, accompanied a group member to report a rape and to her physical examination, and took in a group member who had been beaten by her brother and provided shelter for three days. The group leader's commitment to the group and willingness to participate in their extra-group activities contrast with the traditional approach to suicidal clients, which is to maintain a moat between the client's and the professional's life outside of the therapy setting.

After two suicide attempts during the first three weeks of the group, group members exchanged telephone numbers and began to call on each other and the group leaders frequently during times of trouble. Within-group sharing led to joint problem solving. For example, one group member convinced another that family therapy was worth trying because it had been very helpful to him. Concern about making too many demands on each other prompted the development of an extension to the group to provide additional support—these were the "Adolescent Befrienders." These were primarily young adult volunteers who worked on the suicide hot line. Each was paired with a group member and maintained frequent contact with that member. At the two-year follow-up, only two members had been hospitalized, and none had attempted or completed suicide. Group methods with adults at risk for suicide have also been effective (Billings, Rosen, Asirnos, and Motto, 1974; Frey, Motto, and Ritholz, 1983) and argue for greater use of this approach.

Jenna Jackson: Intervention

Ms. Keller first called and then took Jenna to meet the psychologist, Ms. Failla, at the local mental health clinic. Ms. Failla recognized the need to engage Jenna and decided not to give in to her temptation to spend the entire interview assessing Jenna's social and cognitive resources and began to identify courses of action. Ms. Failla discussed Jenna's school situation and agreed that a transfer to the local alternative high school, which had more flexible school rules and a more supportive pupil personnel services staff, would be desirable. This was accomplished within two weeks. Ms. Failla also encouraged Jenna to continue to go to Daughters and Sons United (D&SU), an incest support group to which Ms. Keller had referred her. In D&SU she was paired with a buddy—a fifteen-year-old girl from her apartment building who had been in the group for a year. At D&SU, molestation events were discussed, and self-protection strategies were rehearsed. Helping Jenna develop a daily and weekly schedule also contributed to a vision of a future with goals. This also countered her tendency to live in the past and to brood about her cowardice in not standing up to the boyfriend or about her treatment by others.

Jenna continued to work with Ms. Failla at the mental health clinic. Part of their work concerned Jenna's troubled thoughts about the molestation experience. She reported that she was unable to stop remembering the molestation scene and to stop blaming herself for going through with it and not reporting it to her mother or the police. She complained that she was having a harder time going out into public places like restaurants and on buses and into phone booths. She did not know what to do about that or why she felt that way. (She no longer feared her mother's ex-boyfriend because her mother told her that he had moved to another part of the city.) She said that she had tried everything and that even though the D&SU group helped her with some things, she was sick of these thoughts and did not think she would ever be able to escape them.

Discussions about the legitimate and adaptive reasons for Jenna's response not to fight off or report her molestation were not successful in reducing her obsessive thinking. Later, Ms. Failla taught Jenna to use a thought-stopping procedure and a simple relaxation procedure whenever she began to think about her past response in a self-critical way. This procedure involved saying ''stop'' to herself whenever she became aware of the presence of a disruptive thought, replacing that thought with another more positive thought (Jenna chose to think about being at a Diana Ross concert), and relaxing. At first she just practiced after she got out of the shower and when she went to bed, the two times when she most frequently thought obsessively about her experience. Later she used the procedure in all circumstances. Her obsessive thoughts continued to diminish, and she later discontinued the thought-stopping procedure.

Jenna did not make another suicide attempt during the following three years. She continued in the incest support group for about nine months, until she decided that she was not learning anything new. Fortunately, her mother became increasingly supportive of Jenna's charges against her boyfriend (especially when she learned that he also had molested Jenna's younger sister). The intervention could not protect Jenna from all unwanted events; at age sixteen, Jenna became a mother.

Suicide and the Schools

Ross (1980) reports on one youth who shot himself through the head at his desk to the amazement of his schoolmates and teacher. Subsequent questioning revealed that he had written "death" on the back of his hand, had asked a student and a teacher if you had to be crazy to shoot yourself, and told a friend that he was "going to heaven soon." Clearly, school staff needed greater awareness of indicators of suicide. One county's suicide awareness program reduced the yearly suicide rate for adolescents from twenty to two ("Teen Suicide . . . ," 1985).

Professionals in or involved with schools can assume many roles. They can distribute brochures about suicide—these are typically available from community mental health centers or suicide-prevention hot lines—lead discussion groups, and participate in radio shows and newspaper articles. Awareness training should inform teachers and students of their duty to warn caretakers or others, rather than protect a child's privacy, if they suspect a person to have suicidal thoughts. Teachers are also encouraged to ask students whom they are concerned about, "Are you thinking about killing yourself?"

If a child helper or teacher is the first person to whom a child has told his or her troubles, the child helper or teacher should ascertain whether the child would like help talking about this with his or her family. Child helpers' questions should show that they are willing to discuss the subject and do not reject the child for having these thoughts. If possible, child helpers should spend sufficient time with the student to allow the student to vent his or her feelings before trying to cope with or solve the problems. This will also help child helpers assess the suicide risk. While discussion with the family is not necessarily the best first course of action, some young people are relieved to have help in bringing this matter home. After such sharing, the family becomes the client, and helping efforts can focus on helping the entire family unit. If the student does not want to share the information with family, then at the least, a mental health professional with suicide-prevention experience should be asked to help provide consultation and services.

If students inform teachers or counselors that they have friends whom they are concerned about but will not tell, despite urging, the names of the friends, counselors should encourage the students to tell their troubled friends that they are concerned about them and to have the individuals at risk of suicide call them (the counselors) or some other professionals. It is important that students identify a time when they will speak with their suicidal friends and that counselors call them shortly after that time to find out if they have done so and if they can call the suicidal youths themselves.

Teachers may be concerned when a child who has made a suicide attempt returns to class. After welcoming the child back, teachers should continue to show interest in the child that is not unlike the interest they showed prior to the suicide attempt; that is, teachers who had assumed a supportive role before the attempt might ask to speak with the youth at an inconspicuous time after his or her return to school and express support and willingness to help again. Teachers who had not been close to the child prior to the attempt need not change their behavior, so long as they understand from faculty meetings that there is a plan among pupil personnel services and other teachers and staff to support this child. Consistency is important as well as warmth.

Peers should be prepared to respond to their friends using

four guidelines (Ross, n.d.). First, *listen:* let the friend tell of his or her situation and feelings. Do not give advice or feel obliged to find simple solutions; just listen and try to imagine the friend's experience. Second, *be honest:* when a friend's words or actions are scary, say so; if it is not clear what to do or say, say that. This is better than acting cheerful. Third, *share any related experiences:* at times everyone feels sad, hurt, or hopeless. Tell the friend that. Let the friend know that he or she is not alone. Fourth, *get help:* keeping a secret may mean losing a friend. Students can try to help friends think of helpful adults they can talk to, or failing this, they should talk to someone themselves and find out what to do next. Discussion groups can help youth identify responses to make if they feel suicidal or suspect that a friend is.

Post-Suicide Intervention

Families of children who have completed suicide often need services. Valente and Hatton (1981) developed a group-treatment program for parents who sought relief from their suffering following the death of their child. Parents described their isolation from friends and family, whom they perceived as rejecting and not able to understand their experience or allow them to mourn. Families were often encouraged to "forget about it" and "get back to normal" and not given the opportunity to discuss their loss or ways that this had disrupted their usual strategies for "getting back to normal." Reliance on religion as a coping strategy was disrupted for some families because "suicide is a sin." Parents also reported difficulties in continuing to make the difficult decisions involved in parenting their other adolescent children. They were often afraid to set limits, keep expectations high, and not blame themselves when their children erred. Child helpers should reach out to survivors.

A meeting between a child-helping professional—either a school-based counselor or social worker or a visitor from a community agency—and the dead youth's closest peer group after twenty-four hours and within forty-eight hours is a good starting point (Hill, 1984). This group may not just be composed of the youth's intimate friends but may also include students from the young person's homeroom or other classes who experience the suicide with unusual poignancy. A close friend or sibling can often provide the school counselor with information about the child's peer group. The group should, however, be kept to a manageable size. Students should be excused from classes and provided with a private setting for the one- to two-hour meeting.

The meeting's goals should be fourfold. First, as much as is possible, the meeting should begin with a discussion of what is known about the suicide itself. Second, as part of a diagnostic check on peers who may become more vulnerable to suicide as a result of contact with a completed suicide, students can be queried about the kind of person that the student was. Third, students can give their ideas about what caused the student to kill himself or herself, and what they did or did not do that caused this unhappiness and death. Finally, in response to students' explanations of the causes of suicide, the child helper should endeavor to explain that suicides are a result of many personal and environmental factors. Particularly key is aiding students who feel singularly responsible for the death. ("Hmm, so you had not called her in the week before she died and think that she would have been less likely to kill herself if you had been a better friend. But weren't there other times when you did not talk for a week and when she was okay, and isn't that common to some of your other friendships? I hope you will see that this suicide was not something you could expect or prevent by yourself.") Students may also feel that the inhumanity of a single teacher, the school, family life, or the world as a whole caused the suicide. The child helper can acknowledge that it must at times be difficult to stay at school, since it seems so tied with their friend's death and that, yes, growing up in this time offers many difficult challenges. Still, a single teacher or the school cannot know everything about a child's life, nor would most students want any more known about them than already is, and a school's power to harm or to help a child with individual problems is limited (Hill, 1984). A related question that may arise in discussing the completed suicide of a schoolchild is, "Well, he used to be in treatment. Why didn't that help him?" (The unstated question is "what is the use of telling professionals about suicidal kids if they can't stop them?'') In response, the child helper can appropriately express grief and disappointment and add that helping professionals cannot help all youth but do have a good record of helping youth go beyond the momentary crisis and continue living as they rebuild their confidence and success.

Students should also be given a brief review of some of the indicators of suicide that they might see in themselves or in their friends (as discussed earlier in this chapter) and told that the child helper or a colleague will always be available to discuss their concerns about suicide. Students should also be assured that their reports of suicidal risk of a peer will be kept in confidence, although action will be taken by the child helper to assess the seriousness of the risk.

A broader, school-wide response may be needed following a suicide that appears likely to trigger other attempts. Community involvement following two Westchester, N.Y., suicides in 1983 included teaching all students and teachers how to recognize signs of suicide and how to respond to and report a suicidal teenager, a community meeting, the opening of a crisis room, and a suicide watch program for teenagers thought to be at risk (for example, close friends of the dead youths).

Consultation with faculty is also, at times, sought or needed. Faculty typically want to know what could have been done to prevent the suicide, what are the signs of a person at risk for suicide, what response should be made to students who are upset about the suicide (for instance, how much discussion of it is good, and how much might contribute to contagion), and what response should be made when a student is suspected to be at risk for suicide. The discussion of the first two items can follow upon the discussions with the dead student's peers. Providing students with a specific discussion time in each class prior to the resumption of classwork is a generally acceptable response to teachers' concerns about how much to discuss the death. This response communicates a teacher's concern but also says that the business of life and of the school must go on. Teachers should be encouraged to report any student they deem a suicide risk to the counseling staff or to call the community services in much the way they report child abuse—based on suspicion of a problem, not on certainty about the problem. If carefully handled, no harm should come from unconfirmed suspicions. Unfortunately, little is now known (see *Medical World News*, 1984) about whether or not the contagion theory of adolescent suicide is valid, or if suicides that are related in time and place (such as those in Plano, Texas, in 1984) are the result of common external circumstances (for example, living in a competitive, transient boom town). In either case, ample discussion is not likely to increase the risk of suicidal acts and may increase the number of people likely to intervene.

13

Conclusion:
Issues in the Use of Social
and Cognitive Methods

Clients have a right to the best treatment, and social and cognitive methods for helping children and youth seem to work. Studies of the outcomes of the methods described in this book suggest that child helpers should be eagerly adopting such strategies. This, however, is not the case. Despite their reputation as progressive thinkers and actors, human service providers often ignore or reject innovation (Stolz, 1981). Adoption of social and cognitive methods will occur only gradually. Judging by the evidence, however, children will develop more competencies, spend more time in less restrictive placements, and share fewer pains and more joys with their caregivers when such techniques are added to child helpers' repertoires.

Some agencies from which child-helping efforts originate are ready to adopt new practices. The Homebuilders Program in Tacoma, Washington, for example, hires therapists after intensive screening *only if* they are willing to go beyond family systems theory and *especially if* they are competent in an intervention approach that Homebuilders does *not* currently use. Many organizations operate quite differently, seeking, instead, to reduce staff dissonance by hiring like-minded practitioners (for example, interns that they have trained). If the essence of such organizations and the essence of the social and cognitive methods described herein are at odds, the methods may never

426

be given a fair trial. They may be rapidly rejected; respectfully ignored; or adopted, adapted, and absorbed in such a way that they make little difference. This chapter considers issues and strategies for implementing social and cognitive techniques in an ethical manner in agencies with no or little history of using them.

Clinicians who will be implementing social and cognitive methods that are new to them and their agencies should start small by picking a problem that seems reasonably transient, perhaps with a younger child, and choosing a proven technique. Agency life works against such propitious introductions. Supervisors may be most amenable to trying new interventions when they recognize that old ones have failed. Social and cognitive interventions tend to be used as treatments of last resort. Child helpers cannot fairly test the efficacy of these methods if they only use them with children with whom all else has failed. Early intervention using social and cognitive methods, as when using any other methods, is most likely to succeed. Although an initial success is not essential to continued opportunities to use new methods—unless the professional has promised too much—such a success will buoy subsequent efforts. Such was the experience of a consultant trained in social and cognitive procedures who was asked by a psychodynamic inpatient treatment staff to help reverse the bizarre and frustrating behavior of an eleven-year-old who was perseverating and hallucinating despite medication and intensive one-to-one therapy (Lavigne and Novak, 1981). The consultant began and then successfully phased out an incentive system to encourage improved self-care and reduce the boy's aversion to staff and their aversion to him. The increased positive exchanges permitted the development of a therapeutic, psychodynamic relationship.

Using the guidance of this book to work on such problems as firesetting or suicide is a stiffer test. Undertaking changes in conventional practice with young people prone to suicide or acts of arson requires appropriate caution and adequate consultation. Much current practice with firesetters and suicidal youth deserves to continue and be built upon, especially the careful monitoring of risk, assurances of vigilance by members of all parts of a child's social ecology, and thorough assessment of progress. With this approach, child helpers can have more confidence about applying social and cognitive methods in noninstitutional settings. Welsh's (1971) pioneering work with having a child light matches in a therapy session was done without the enthusiasm of his supervisor; few supervisors today are likely to respond with more exuberance to a supervisee's suggestion that a child be encouraged to light matches in his or her office. Yet the procedure worked and has been replicated. The lesson that Wolff's (1984) work, also with a firesetter, teaches is the importance of using progess in the community as the key guide to treatment. Even though Wolff found no rapid satiation of firesetting in his sessions as Welsh had, the child's fire-related behavior in his foster home on weekends was extinguished within three weeks and remained so for the next twenty weeks. Wolff's thorough assessment encouraged him to maintain and extend his treatment approach, although the boy responded more slowly than expected. Such thoroughness is critical to successful experimentation with methods that are unfamiliar and not fully tested.

Those of us who have attempted to use a software program, assemble a gas barbeque, or grow glorious roses know that reading this book will not lead to instantaneous proficiency. The written words that describe these practices are intermingled with self-talk that may go something like, "That sounds reasonable, but I'm not sure it would work with Petey given his current behavior, home life, and my experience at this." Such self-talk is healthy skepticism; the merits of too many methods have been exaggerated. In many cases, the programs that have been tried have been with children of different ages, ethnic identities, and situations than those of concern to a given practitioner. For social and cognitive methods, this is indeed the era of generalization—the time to determine which of these "documented" methods will work again, will work with severely emotionally disturbed rather than moderately mentally retarded children, or will work with children living at home rather than in residential treatment programs. Child helpers who test the generalizability of these methods to the problems of a given agency or population take fewer risks than those who originally developed these innovations, but nevertheless they face an imposing task.

Communicating with Other Child Helpers

Recently, there have been some much-needed efforts to identify a unifying framework for treatment (for example, see Goldfried, 1982; Lindenbaum and Clark, 1983) that emphasizes the similarities between approaches. Understanding these similarities can promote effective collaboration and communication. One parallel is that traditional psychodynamic and behavioral models both assume that children learn to act as they do—and as we often wish they would not—during uncountable interactions between themselves and caregivers (Wachtel, 1977). These series of interactions give children and parents social and cognitive histories that influence their current interactions. The importance of these histories is often underrated by professionals with a heavy social-ecological emphasis and overrated by professionals with more traditional psychodynamic training.

Commonalities certainly exist between humanistic and social and cognitive approaches to child helping. In her famous book, *Dibs: In Search of Self*, Axline (1964), a client-centered child therapist, aids Dibs with reflections that show Dibs how he arrives at the actions and sounds that he makes. Over time, Dibs begins to control his behavior by talking. This is a humanistic version of self-instruction training as described in previous chapters of this book. (Indeed, Woolfolk, Woolfolk, and Wilson, 1977, showed that the very same film of a child receiving rewards for good behavior was rated more favorably by observers when the technique was labeled "humanistic" rather than "behavior modification.")

A survey by Forehand (1985) of graduates of a primarily behavioral clinical psychology program and eminent professionals in the behavior therapy community suggests the importance of training clinicians to demonstrate the effectiveness of behavioral methods rather than argue about their effectiveness or cite the literature, communicate behavioral principles in nonbehavioral terms, not espouse behavior therapy as a panacea, be tolerant of other orientations, and accept treatment strategies from other orientations so long as their effectiveness is demonstrable. Considerable humility about social and cognitive methods is warranted. Although research generally supports the effectiveness of these methods, their success is not without exception. Much evidence suggests that clinically, rather than simply statistically, significant changes are difficult to achieve using any methods. Modest effects may be more common as the difficulties of the children seen in treatment seem to be increasingly severe.

As previously described, the comprehensibility of social and cognitive procedures does appeal to caregivers and clients. Child helpers will be heard most clearly if they describe procedures in the language of the listener. Still, professionals interested in applying social and cognitive techniques must beware of the irony of the law of parsimony, which suggests that the simpler the explanation for behavior, the less acceptable it may be to professionals. With colleagues, theory may be ear catching; with clients, less theory may work better. Yet the child helper must avoid the danger of reframing ideas completely to accommodate the world views of the audience. The child helper who describes the value of negative consequences may not help the hard-nosed listener to understand that positive consequences must get priority. Or the clinician who hears about the successes of cognitive-skill training may assume that this justifies cognitive "treatments" that consist only of efforts to interpret the child's beliefs and feelings. Child helpers must be clear about what they are and are not saying.

Child helpers who gain enthusiasm for the concepts, techniques, and language of social and cognitive methods must be wary of offending other practitioners. Tact and tolerance of other approaches are essential to surviving in a world that is protective of its traditions. Minuchin (1982) writes, "Our field is full of decaying truths. . . . Belief systems are maintained because they have existed before. We proclaim loyalties to ideas we no longer believe in; or, at least, we do not know if we believe in them any longer" (p. 657). Such words are fine coming from an internationally renowned practitioner; for most clinicians, they would create enduring hostilities. Nicholas Hobbs (1981) had the stature and seniority to call insight an "epiphenomenon'' and suggest that insight is neither the cause nor the effect of behavior change. He may be right, but his comment, if uttered in most agencies, would alienate everyone, including the receptionist.

Adaptive Adoption

Few social and cognitive interventions require total adoption. Interventions to help children with problems of wetting and soiling (dry-bed training, for example) may require nearly complete adoption, but most other techniques can be used in part. For instance, parent-adolescent communication training may appropriately address only a few communication skills, may not include all family members, or may minimize role playing. Adaptation may or may not be for the best. Little research reveals completely which components of an intervention are essential to the intervention's success. Practitioners should recognize, at least, the ways that their adaptation of the intervention differs from the approach as it was originally tested. In this way, when the adaptation does not succeed, the missing components can be added in future cases. Rappaport, Seidman, and Davidson (1979) distinguish between *manifest* adoption and *true* adoption of new techniques. Manifest adoption involves replicating the form but not the essence of a program; in true adoption, the essence is replicated as well. A third form of adoption is *adaptive* adoption; here, the implementer recognizes the adaptations being made, suffers no delusion that the program is being delivered as it was designed, and proceeds with reasoned clinical judgment. This is often the ideal, so long as practitioners check on the quality of the adoption if the intervention is not succeeding. One recent attempt to develop a "job club" for substance-abusing adolescents met with minimal success until a review by the program supervisor indicated that the youth were only having one job interview per week rather than the one or more per day specified in the original program. This correction quickly improved the club's success. Evaluation will help practitioners recognize when an adaptation is maladaptive.

Getting and Giving Supervision

Most discussions of program implementation consider how program managers and supervisors can encourage staff to use innovative methods (for example, see Bernstein, 1982; Delamater, Conners, and Wells, 1984; Gambrill and Stein, 1984). An equally challenging question is how to encourage the use of innovative social- and cognitive-treatment strategies without the supervision of a trained professional. This question usually receives familiar answers: attend workshops; go to conferences; and most important, identify a capable supervisor in the community—even from outside of the agency—to oversee the work. For many practical reasons, usually tied to time and money, these answers do not readily lead to action. Probably less than 15 percent of the professionals treating children are trained in and committed to social and cognitive methods (Norcross and Prochaska, 1982; Tuma and Pratt, 1982), and their training is quite recent (see, for instance, Garfield and Kurtz, 1974). The supply of supervisors with appropriate training and experience is certainly limited. Also, because the context of practice is so critical to treatment outcomes, for-hire supervisors who may not understand the practice setting are less than ideal. Thus, obtaining adequate outside supervision is difficult. Schiller (1985) describes the improbability of finding a supervisor to help a person train to be a pediatric behavioral health psychologist, concluding that four supervisors are needed to cover issues related to development, children, pain, and evaluation. Other answers are necessary.

The challenge is clearly articulated in the "Specialty Guidelines for the Delivery of Services by School Psychologists" (American Psychological Association . . . , 1981). According to the American Psychological Association, "When extending services beyond the range of their usual practice, school psychologists obtain pertinent training or appropriate professional supervision" (p. 674). This assertion would surprise more than a few psychologists (as it would if made by other professional organizations about their members). School psychologists are pledged to "maintain current knowledge of scientific and professional developments'' (p. 674), to "develop innovative theories and procedures" (p. 675), and to "limit their practice to their demonstrated areas of professional competence" (p. 674). Accomplishing these noble developmental tasks of the professional—to be current and to explore new techniques while not going beyond one's skills and training—is an ever-present professional challenge that stymies many professionals and their supervisors.

Working with Supervisors

The author's experiences as a supervisee and as an instructor of students with supervisors who lack training in social and cognitive methods forcefully argue that practitioners can learn to use social and cognitive methods while working under good supervisors with other training. Perhaps the greatest loss is that the supervisor does not model effective practices. This is an important, although not essential, element of supervision and consultation (Barth and Gambrill, 1984; Morton and Kurtz, 1980). Such practice can still be arranged with supervisors. Supervisees need not be shy about expressing their desire to role play: "Would you be willing to let me try to explain how to use a point system with you playing the foster parent?"

Supervisors frequently believe that they are unprepared for their roles (Akin and Weil, 1981). This may make them open to new approaches that supervisees may contribute to the supervisorial experience. Because many supervisors do not operate with a coherent theoretical model and program behind them and often reach for new ideas to implement their programs, the flexibility of experienced staff and their willingness to change may be considerable. For these and other reasons, supervisors may be sensitive to a supervisee's different theoretical or practice approach. Hobbs (1982) argues that few mental health consultants who have collaborated with Project Re-Ed have attempted to impose incompatible theoretical notions or operational procedures on their consultees. Most report respect for an ecological perspective in which they were not formally schooled. Davis and Sandoval (1982) argue that consultants (and, by implication, supervisors) should help create situations that promote the opportunity for consultees (or clients) to make choices rather than insist on doing things their way.

A capable and interested supervisor can be a sustaining resource for any professional. Experienced supervisors should understand ethics and its application, the ecologies of organizations, and how the child helper may be viewed by others as he or she uses innovative social and cognitive methods. Supervisors can help supervisees recognize the perspectives of clients and colleagues and find language that communicates to all parties. Because psychodynamic, humanistic, and even parapsychological interpretations about what motivates behavior have been better disseminated through the media than have social and cognitive research, clients' and colleagues' explanations for problems in living may closely approximate those of supervisors.

The supervisor of a professional who intends to employ a strategy with which he or she is not familiar or comfortable must first ascertain that the approach fits within the structure and responsibilities of the agency. A new school psychologist who is interested in leading stress-management groups for teachers may be dissuaded from doing so by a supervisor who knows that stress-management groups previously were led by new personnel and were treated with scorn by seasoned teachers. Such an intervention might ultimately injure the psychologist's credibility and lessen future effectiveness in conducting assessments or classroom consultation. Supervisors may also have significant information about children's lives. No matter what their theoretical orientation, supervisors should understand the basic issues about the experiences of, for example, children entering foster care or special education classes or being adopted and how to lessen the disjunctiveness of these transitions. Supervisors are also valuable for giving second opinions on the circumstances affecting a child or family or the influences on a collaborating child helper's behavior.

Supervisors who are not familiar with social and cognitive methods may (1) be willing to embrace them; (2) need gradual information, education, and demonstration before accepting them; or (3) be unwilling to use or tolerate them under any circumstances. The latter kind of supervisor is increasingly scarce but hardly extinct and can cause much difficulty for the innovative child helper. If a better match with another supervisor is possible, transfer can be sought. If that is not possible, child helpers may have to work around their supervisors. Such efforts may include enlisting others to present social and cognitive approaches at staff meetings, seeking help from peers or other supervisors, minimizing discussion of cases involving social and cognitive interventions and gradually working to change supervisors' responses to innovation, and developing supportive networks and directories of like-minded professionals (see, for example, Jason and others, 1985). Above all, this must be done in a way that safeguards the rights of clients.

Before working around a supervisor, supervisees should determine the agency's policy about the responsibility of supervisors. In some agencies evey practitioner must report to a supervisor, but the practitioner is solely responsible for effective and ethical practice. In such cases, the supervisor's fundamental role may be consultative, even though the supervisor may assume an authoritative role. In other agencies, especially public child welfare services, the supervisor may be sued for malpractice for harm to a child in a supervisee's caseload. In such cases, supervisors have a greater responsibility to monitor and control supervisees' practices.

Not to be overlooked are the supervisee's sources of influence with the supervisor. The energy and efforts of inspired practitioners can exert great influence, especially when a supervisor devotes part of his or her time to private practice or administrative tasks. Child helpers thus can influence supervisors by continually taking on new tasks (for example, investigating journals to which the agency might subscribe).

Confronting the supervisor may be necessary if the alternative is to misserve or reduce the power or prestige of a client. Ethical practice at times requires that practitioners use all behaviors necessary, so long as they are more ethical than the unethical performance they are meant to correct (Patti and Resnick, 1972). At times, a child helper may have to draw on support from inside and outside the agency to attempt to reduce the supervisor's control. Such a tactic might include having a fellow practitioner send a letter to the child helper, to the child helper's supervisor, and to the agency head indicating respect for the practitioner's use of social and cognitive methods. At other times, change may involve direct confrontation of the supervisor's ability and right to limit the use of well-documented treatment methods that respect the rights and potentials of clients. Articulating the values of the profession and the tenets of social and cognitive methods certainly may gain the support of colleagues, clients, and administrators (Brager and Holloway, 1978). Avoiding being labeled a troublemaker by maintaining professional competence while not committing to agency norms will increase the chances of change (Falck and Barnes, 1975).

The legitimacy of using social and cognitive methods without experienced supervision must be considered. Important discussion (for example, Stein, 1975) has addressed the impropriety of giving brief workshops in social-learning methods and encouraging practitioners to use powerful behavior-change techniques without adequate supervision. The result threatens to be a misuse of techniques and possible injury to clients, to the reputation of the agency, or to the reputation of innovative social and cognitive practices. At least, such training might fail to ensure that positive consequences precede or accompany negative consequences, that clients are given maximum choice, and that the application of the technique is as designed. Certainly no one gains from misguided attempts to use social and cognitive techniques. Acknowledgment must be given, however, to efforts to do something other than "more of the same." New efforts to change one's own behavior and respond in new ways to children and their families will at first be less than complete. So long as no harm—even if not much greater good—results, then the learning experience that should follow will justify the exploratory attempts. Errors accompany learning. This learning experience must not risk the safety of a child—by leaving a child unsupervised or in a locked, windowless time-out room, for example—but can risk being ineffective so long as it is instructive. To take advantage of such instruction, supervisors and supervisees must accompany practice of innovative methods with efforts to evaluate practice.

Practitioners are ethically bound, however, to inform clients of practices that they may engage in without full supervision. The National Association of Social Workers' Code of Ethics (National Association of Social Workers, 1983), like the codes of most other professional organizations, requires that a "social worker should provide clients with accurate and complete information regarding the extent and nature of the services available to them" (p. 260). Practitioners have a responsibility to inform their clients when their experience with treatment methods is limited. Yet disclosure is often lacking out of concern that such honesty will alienate clients or undermine their commitment to the treatment regimen. Feiner and Couch (1985) argue that the evidence in support of these concerns is not in the least compelling. Professionals who are students of social and cognitive methods can describe their status while maintaining their clients' right to decide whether or not to continue in treatment and without damaging the chances of successful treatment. Such a description might proceed as follows:

Professional child helper: I would like to add something else to our work together. The rules and rewards you set up for Jonathon are very slowly reducing his fighting. Yet it sounds like you are very frustrated with him and are wondering if he will make it in your home. Is that right?

Foster mother: Yes, he is doing better, but I worry about the other kids.

Professional child helper: I want to teach you to use time out as a way to more quickly reduce Jonathon's fighting. Time out involves making a child sit quietly as a penalty for misbehaving and has helped many children to fight less. I have a book that describes how to use time out. (Child helper pulls out *Living with Children*

[Patterson, 1976b].) I have read this book and talked to people with experience using time out and think it makes sense to try it with Jonathon. I must tell you, though, that I have not used it before, but I have read a lot about it, and I have discussed the approach with a colleague who has used it with much success. We will figure it out together.

Foster mother: I don't know. There is no way that Jonathon is ever going to sit quietly just because I tell him to. I think he needs some good swats, but I know that I can't do that. Are you sure that this will do any good?

Professional child helper: I'm not positive, but time out has helped many children who don't change easily, even when they are given rewards, reminders, and love. I think we can use our heads to figure out how to make it work for Jonathon, too. After all, none of those other kids who were fighting a lot before time out were in a hurry to go sit down either (grins). This book and some other things I've read have ideas about how to get a child to take his first time out. What do you think? Want to try?

Foster mother: What if it doesn't work?

Professional child helper: I'd like to try it for one month. I'll meet with you or talk to you every week. We'll keep track of whether Jonathon's fighting gets better. Of course, you'll have to keep Jonathon here during that time (laughs).

Foster mother: Oh! So that's your plan (laughs). Yeah, I guess we can manage him until then.

                                    Was this book written by anyone who
                                    knows anything about the kind of kids
                                    you always bring me?
Professional child helper: I sure hope so (grins).

To teach himself and his client new skills, this professional relied
on a self-help manual that has shown its effectiveness when
delivered with a clinician's assistance (Walter and Gilmore, 1973)
and alone (Patterson and Reid, 1973). Although too few such
manuals exist (see the review by Glasgow and Rosen, 1985), a
number have been pilot tested and have proven to be useful.

     Table 12, following on the works of Heads (1978), groups
the procedures discussed in this book according to their level of
restrictiveness and hazardousness to children. The table also
shows corresponding safeguards. Supervisors who are not ex-
pert in social and cognitive techniques would in most cases be
capable of supervising the less restrictive procedures. Workshops,
site visits by trained consultants, and use of manuals developed
by authors cited in these pages should improve the use of these
techniques. Standard consent forms or verbal parent or guardian consent should also be obtained.

     Supervisors who are not expert in social and cognitive
techniques would in most cases not be capable of supervising
the use of the more restrictive procedures. Participation in workshops, site visits by trained consultants, and use of manuals
developed by authors cited in these pages would be *essential* to
the use of these techniques, as would be evidence of prior efforts
with less intrusive methods, a documented procedure, and a time-
limited plan followed by review (Repp and Deitz, 1978). Parents'
or guardians' and children's written consent that includes specific
descriptions of the procedures to be used should also be obtained
if the procedures will be performed without the parents' presence.

Ethics

     Children reach the age of majority at eighteen. Before that,
parents have a right to consent to treatment for the child. Yet,
recognizing that some children may be competent at earlier ages

Table 12. Social and Cognitive Procedures and
Corresponding Consent and Review Procedures.

Least Restrictive or Hazardous Procedures	Moderately Restrictive or Hazardous Procedures
Social rewards	Cognitive self-punishment
Peer or child helper modeling	Time out that excludes child from view or uses time-out room
Reprimands	
Token economy with material rewards and response cost	Token economy that includes loss of privileges
Token economy with positive privileges	Overcorrection
Brief time out within view	Positive practice
Ignoring noninjurious behavior	Contingent use of physical restraint
Response cost by temporary removal of nonessential possession	Satiation and negative practice
Relaxation training	Physical punishment
Self-management training	
Instruction in self-praise	
Communication-skills training	
Restitution	
Supervision or Expertise:	*Supervision or Expertise:*
Nontechnical supervision or expertise	Technical expertise, trained supervisor, or on-site consultant
Consent:	*Consent:*
Standard consent form or verbal consent	Specific approval of parent or guardian and agency

to decide about certain aspects of their fates, many states have a "mature minor" exception to the parental consent rule that gives the right of consent to any minor who can understand the consequences of treatment. (Recent court rulings deny a mature minor the right, for example, to refuse incarceration in a mental hospital.) The mature minor status should pique professionals to recognize, with however much disquiet, that the rights of mature minors, like those of adults, cannot be selectively limited to those situations in which society approves of the choices being made. Still, ethical treatment can include changing children against their initial expressed desire to change when the child does not understand the consequences of his or her actions, when the caregiver does, and when the consequences are significant to the child and society. For an older youth who judges his or her best interest differently than do the youth's parents, more safeguards are needed. At least, parent or guardian consent should be sought for controversial treatment decisions made at school or in out-of-home care.

Ethical practice does not require that parents' and children's wishes be fulfilled—only that they be understood. Child helpers are not likely to err on the side of giving youth too many choices. Many of us reason that a child may need to suffer the disappointment, frustration, and loss of pride that accompany limits on decision making about his or her future in order to have the opportunity to be capable and proud for the remainder of his or her life. Recognizing the limited ability of young people to use foresight to make decisions, what limits should be placed on adults' control over the lives of young people? Above all, arbitrary and abusive practices should be eliminated, and procedures that guard against capricious decision making should be applied. Effective practice is the best safeguard and will preempt many of the grueling dilemmas that child helpers and their clients might otherwise suffer.

References

Abikoff, H., and Gittelman, R. "Does Behavior Therapy Normalize the Classroom Behavior of Hyperactive Children?" *Archives of General Psychiatry*, 1984, *41*, 449-454.

Achenbach, T., and Edelbrock, C. "The Child Behavior Profile: II. Boys Aged 12-16 and Girls Aged 6-11 and 12-16." *Journal of Consulting and Clinical Psychology*, 1979, *47*, 223-233.

Achenbach, T. M., and Edelbrock, C. S. *Behavioral Problems and Competencies Reported by Parents of Normal and Disturbed Children Aged Four Through Sixteen*. Monographs of the Society for Research in Child Development, no. 46, Serial no. 188. Berkeley: University of California, 1981.

Acosta, F. X., Evans, L. A., Yamamoto, J., and Wilcox, S. A. "Helping Minority and Low-Income Psychotherapy Patients 'Tell It Like It Is.'" *Journal of Biocommunication*, 1980, *7*, 13-19.

Adams, G. R. "Runaway Youth Projects: Comments on Care Programs for Runaways and Throwaways." *Journal of Adolescence*, 1980, *3*, 321-334.

Adams, P. L. *A Primer of Child Psychotherapy*. (2nd ed.) Boston: Little, Brown, 1982.

Adler, J. *Fundamentals of Group Child Care: A Textbook and Instructional Guide for Child Care Workers*. Cambridge, Mass.: Ballinger, 1981.

443

Ainslie, G. "Specious Reward: A Behavioral Theory of Impulsiveness and Impulse Control." *Psychological Bulletin*, 1975, *82*, 463–496.

Akin, G., and Weil, M. "The Prior Question: How Do Supervisors Learn to Supervise?" *Social Casework*, 1981, *62*, 472–479.

Albanese, J. S. "Preventing Inmate Suicides: A Case Study." *Federal Probation*, 1983, *46*, 65–69.

Alessi, N. E., McManus, M., Brickman, A., and Grapentine, L. "Suicidal Behavior Among Serious Juvenile Offenders." *American Journal of Psychiatry*, 1984, *141*, 286–287.

Alexander, J. F., and Parsons, B. V. "Short-Term Behavioral Intervention with Delinquent Families: Impact on Family Process and Recidivism." *Journal of Abnormal Psychology*, 1973, *31*, 219–225.

Alexander, J., and Parsons, B. V. *Functional Family Therapy*. Monterey, Calif.: Brooks/Cole, 1982.

Algozzine, B., Ysseldyke, J. E., Christenson, S., and Thurlow, M. *Teachers' Intervention Choices for Children Exhibiting Different Behaviors in School*. Minneapolis: Institute for Research on Learning Disabilities, University of Minnesota, 1982.

Alpert, J. L. "Conceptual Bases of Mental Health Consultation in the Schools." *Professional Psychology*, 1976, *7*, 619–626.

Ambrosini, P. J., Rabinovich, H., and Puig-Antich, J. "Biological Factors and Pharmacologic Treatment in Major Depressive Disorder in Children and Adolescents." In H. S. Sudak, A. B. Ford, and N. B. Rushforth (eds.), *Suicide in the Young*. Boston: John Wright/PSG, 1984.

American Psychiatric Association. *Diagnostic and Statistical Manual of Mental Disorders*. (3rd ed.) Washington, D.C.: American Psychiatric Association, 1980.

American Psychological Association, Committee on Professional Standards. "Specialty Guidelines for the Delivery of Services by School Psychologists." *American Psychologist*, 1981, *36*, 670–681.

Amery, B., Minichiello, M. D., and Brown, G. L. "Aggression in Hyperactive Boys: Response to d-Amphetamine." *Journal of the American Academy of Child Psychiatry*, 1984, *23* (3), 291–294.

Anderson, J. L., and Simonitch, B. "Reactive Depression in Youths Experiencing Emancipation." *Child Welfare*, 1981, *60*, 383–390.

Andre, M. D. A., and Anderson, T. H. "The Development and Evaluation of a Self-Questioning Study Technique." *Reading Research Quarterly*, 1979, *14*, 605–623.

Arnold, J. H., and Clement, P. W. "Temporal Generalization of Self-Regulation Effects in Undercontrolled Children." *Child Behavior Therapy*, 1981, *2*, 43–68.

Atkeson, B. M., and Forehand, R. "Home-Based Reinforcement Programs Designed to Modify Classroom Behavior: A Review and Methodological Evaluation." *Psychological Bulletin*, 1979, *86*, 1298–1308.

Axline, V. *Dibs: In Search of Self*. New York: Ballentine, 1964.

Ayllon, T., and Milan, M. *Correctional Rehabilitation and Management: A Psychological Approach*. New York: Wiley, 1979.

Azrin, N. H., and Armstrong, P. M. "The 'Mini-Meal': A Method for Teaching Eating Skills to the Profoundly Retarded." *Mental Retardation*, 1973, *11*, 9–13.

Azrin, N. H., Thienos-Hontos, P., and Besalel-Azrin, V. "Elimination of Enuresis Without a Conditioning Apparatus: An Extension of Office Instruction of the Child and Parents." *Behavior Therapy*, 1979, *10*, 14–19.

Azrin, N. H., and Wesolowski, M. D. "Theft Reversal: An Overcorrection Procedure for Eliminating Stealing by Retarded Persons." *Journal of Applied Behavior Analysis*, 1974, *7*, 577–581.

Baer, D., and Wolf, M. "The Entry into Natural Communities of Reinforcement." In R. Ulrich, T. Stachnick, and J. Mabry (eds.), *Control of Human Behavior*. Glenview, Ill.: Scott, Foresman, 1970.

Baizerman, M., and Emshoff, B. "Juvenile Firesetting: Building a Community-Based Prevention Program." *Children Today*, 1984, *13*, 8–12.

Baizerman, M., Thompson, J., Stafford-White, K., and An Old, Young Friend. "Adolescent Prostitution." *Children Today*, 1979, *10*, 20–24.

Balaschak, B. A., and Mostofsky, D. I. "Seizure Disorders."

In E. J. Mash and L. G. Terdal (eds.), *Behavioral Assessment of Childhood Disorders*. New York: Guilford, 1981.

Balsam, P. D., and Bondy, A. S. "The Negative Side Effects of Reward." *Journal of Applied Behavior Analysis*, 1983, *16*, 283–296.

Bandura, A. "Social Learning Analysis of Aggression." In A. Bandura (ed.), *Analysis of Delinquency and Aggression*. Hillsdale, N.J.: Erlbaum, 1976.

Bandura, A. *Social Learning Theory*. Englewood Cliffs, N.J.: Prentice-Hall, 1977.

Barber, R. M., and Kagey, J. R. "Modification of School Attendance for an Elementary Population." *Journal of Applied Behavior Analysis*, 1977, *10*, 41–48.

Barbrack, C. R., and Maher, C. S. "Effects of Involving Conduct Problem Adolescents in the Setting of Counseling Goals." *Child and Family Behavior Therapy*, 1984, *6*, 33–43.

Bard, J. A., and Fisher, H. R. "A Rational-Emotive Approach to Academic Underachievement." In A. Ellis and M. E. Bernard (eds.), *Rational-Emotive Approaches to the Problems of Childhood*. New York: Plenum, 1983.

Barker, R. G., and Schoggen, P. *Qualities of Community Life: Methods of Measuring Environment and Behavior Applied to an American and an English Town*. San Francisco: Jossey-Bass, 1973.

Barkley, R. A. "Hyperactivity." In E. J. Mash and L. G. Terdal (eds.), *Behavioral Assessment of Childhood Disorders*. New York: Guilford, 1981.

Barlow, D. H., Hayes, S. C., and Nelson, R. O. *The Scientist Practitioner: Research and Accountability in Clinical and Educational Settings*. Elmsford, N.Y.: Pergamon Press, 1984.

Barrera, M., Jr., and Ainlay, S. L. "The Structure of Social Support: A Conceptual and Empirical Analysis." *Journal of Community Psychology*, 1983, *11*, 133–141.

Barrett, C. L., Hampe, I. E., and Miller, L. C. "Research on Child Psychotherapy." In S. L. Garfield and A. E. Bergin (eds.), *Handbook of Psychotherapy and Behavior Change: An Empirical Analysis*. (2nd ed.) New York: Wiley, 1978.

Barrish, H. H., Saunders, M., and Wolf, M. M. "Good Behavior Game: Effects of Individual Contingencies for Group Consequences on Disruptive Behavior in a Classroom." *Journal of Applied Behavior Analysis*, 1969, *2*, 119–124.

Barsh, E. T., Moore, J. A., and Hamerlynck, L. A. "The Foster Extended Family: A Support Network for Handicapped Foster Children." *Child Welfare*, 1983, *62*, 349–359.

Barter, J., Swaback, D., and Todd, D. "Adolescent Suicide Attempts: A Follow-Up Study of Hospitalized Patients." *Archives of General Psychiatry*, 1968, *19*, 523–527.

Barth, R. P. "Home-Based Reinforcement of School Behavior." *Review of Educational Research*, 1979, *49*, 436–458.

Barth, R. P. "Report Cards as a Home-Based Communication System." *Social Work in Education*, 1980, *2*, 44–58.

Barth, R. P. "Education for Practice-Research: Toward a Reorientation." *Journal of Education for Social Work*, 1981, *17*, 19–25.

Barth, R. P. "Social Support for Adolescents and Families." In J. K. Whittaker, J. Garbarino, and Associates, *Social Support Networks: Informal Helping in Human Services*. Hawthorne, N.Y.: Aldine, 1983.

Barth, R. P. "Reducing Nonattendance in Elementary Schools." *Social Work in Education*, 1984, *6*, 151–166.

Barth, R. P. "Beating the Blues: Cognitive-Behavioral Treatment for Depression in Child-Maltreating Young Mothers." *Clinical Social Work Journal*, 1985, *13*, 317–328.

Barth, R. P. "Emancipation Services: A Review of Programs for Adolescents Aging Out of Foster Care." *Social Work*, in press.

Barth, R. P., and Blythe, B. J. "The Relationship of Stress and Child Abuse." *Social Service Review*, 1983, *57*, 477–489.

Barth, R. P., Blythe, B. J., Schinke, S. P., and Schilling, R. F. "Self-Control Training with Maltreating Parents." *Child Welfare*, 1983, *62*, 313–324.

Barth, R. P., and Gambrill, E. D. "Learning to Interview: The Quality of Training Opportunities." *The Clinical Supervisor*, 1984, *2* (1), 3–14.

Barth, R. P., and Maxwell, J. S. "Preventing Depression and Dysfunction Among Adolescent Mothers." In L. D. Gilchrist and S. P. Schinke (eds.), *Preventing Social and Health Problems Through Life-Skills Training*. Seattle: University of Washington Press, 1985.

Barth, R. P., Schinke, S. P., and Maxwell, J. S. "Psychological

Correlates of Teenage Motherhood.'' *Journal of Youth and Adolescence*, 1983, *12*, 471–487.

Barth, R. P., Schinke, S. P., and Maxwell, J. S. "Coping-Skills Training for School Age Mothers.'' *Journal of Social Service Research*, 1985, *8*, 75–94.

Barth, R. P., and Sullivan, R. "Collecting Competent Data on Behalf of Children.'' *Social Work*, 1984, *30*, 130–137.

Bateson, G., Jackson, D. D., Haley, J., and Weakland, J. "Toward a Theory of Schizophrenia.'' *Behavioral Science*, 1956, *1*, 251–264.

Bauer, R. R., Giblings, M. C., Grady, J. J., James, P. A., and Schultz, E. L. "The Development of an Early Intervention System for the Reduction of Excused Absences in Elementary and Secondary Schools.'' *Resources in Education* (ERIC), 1977, *12*, 73.

Baum, W. M. "The Correlation-Based Law of Effect.'' *Journal of the Experimental Analysis of Behavior*, 1973, *20*, 137–153.

Baumrind, D. "New Directions in Socialization Research.'' Paper presented at the Society of Research in Child Development, San Francisco, 1979.

Beck, A. T., Rush, A., Shaw, B., and Emery, G. *Cognitive Therapy of Depression*. New York: Guilford, 1979.

Beck, S. J., and Ollendick, T. H. "Personal Space, Sex of Experimenter, and Locus of Control in Delinquent Adolescents.'' *Psychological Reports*, 1976, *38*, 383–387.

Becker, H. J., and Epstein, J. L. "Parent Involvement: A Survey of Teacher Practices.'' *The Elementary School Journal*, 1982, *83*, 85–102.

Becker, W. C., Engelman, S., Carnine, D. W., and Rhine, W. R. "Direct Instructional Model.'' In W. R. Rhine (ed.), *Making Schools More Effective: New Directions from Follow Through*. Orlando, Fla.: Academic Press, 1981.

Bell, R. Q., and Harper, L. V. "Child Effects on Adults.'' Hillsdale, N.J.: Erlbaum, 1977.

Belson, W. A. "Juvenile Stealing: Getting the Record Straight.'' *Bulletin of British Psychology and Sociology*, 1976, *29*, 113–116.

Benensohn, H. S., and Resnick, H. L. P. "Guidelines for 'Suicide-Proofing' a Psychiatric Unit." *American Journal of Psychotherapy*, 1973, *27*, 204–212.

Berg, I., Marks, I., McGuire, R., and Lipsedge, M. "School Phobia and Agoraphobia." *Psychological Bulletin*, 1974, *4*, 428–434.

Bergan, J. R., Kratochwill, T. R., and Luton, J. "Competency-Based Training in Behavioral Consultation." *Journal of School Psychology*, 1980, *18*, 91–97.

Berganza, C. E., and Anders, T. F. "An Epidemiological Approach to School Absenteeism." *Journal of the American Academy of Child Psychiatry*, 1978, *17*, 117–125.

Berkeley Planning Associates. "The National Runaway Youth Program: Client Services and Outcomes." Contract #105-80-C-089. For *Department of Health and Human Services*, Jan. 1982.

Berkowitz, B. P., and Graziano, A. M. "Training Parents as Behavior Therapists: A Review." *Behavior Research and Therapy*, 1972, *10*, 297–317.

Berkowitz, L. "The Case for Bottling Up Rage." *Psychology Today*, 1973, *7*, 24–31.

Bernal, M. E., Delfini, L. F., North, J. A., and Kreutzer, S. L. "Comparison of Boys' Behavior in Homes and Classrooms." In E. J. Mash, L. C. Handy, and L. A. Hamerlynck (eds.), *Behavior Modification and Families: Theory and Research*. Vol. 1. New York: Brunner/Mazel, 1976.

Bernal, M. E., Klinnert, M. D., and Schultz, L. A. "Outcome Evaluation of Behavioral Parent Training and Client-Centered Parent Counseling for Children with Conduct Problems." *Journal of Applied Behavior Analysis*, 1980, *13*, 677–691.

Bernard, M. E., Kratochwill, T. R., and Keefauver, L. W. "The Effects of Rational-Emotive Therapy and Self-Instructional Training on Chronic Hair Pulling." *Cognitive Therapy and Research*, 1983, *7*, 273–280.

Berney, T., Kovin, I., and Bhate, S. R. "School Phobia: A Therapeutic Trial with Clomipramine and Short-Term Outcome." *British Journal of Psychiatry*, 1981, *138*, 110–118.

Bernstein, G. S. "Training Behavior Change Agents: A Conceptual Review." *Behavior Therapy*, 1982, *13*, 1–23.

Berry, L. "School Attendance Improvement." Lecture given at the School of Social Welfare, University of California, Berkeley, Apr. 19, 1983.

Bertsche, A. V., and Horejsi, C. R. "Coordination of Client Services." *Social Work*, 1980, *25*, 94–98.

Bertsche, J. W., Clark, F. W., and Iversen, M. J. *Using Informal Resources in Child Protective Services: A Self-Instructional Guide.* Missoula: Department of Social Work, University of Montana, 1982.

Bettelheim, B. *The Empty Fortress: Infantile Autism and the Birth of the Self.* New York: Free Press, 1967.

Beyer, I. M., Holdt, S. A., Reid, T. A., and Quinalan, D. M. "Runaway Youths: Families in Conflict." Paper presented at the Annual Convention of the Eastern Psychological Association, Washington, D.C., May 1973.

Beyer, M. "Continuing Care for Runaways." *Journal of Family Issues*, 1980, *1*, 300–302.

Biaggio, M. K. "Anger Arousal and Personality Characteristics." *Journal of Personality and Social Psychology*, 1980, *39*, 352–356.

Billings, J. H., Rosen, D. H., Asirnos, C., and Motto, J. A. "Observations on Long-Term Group Therapy with Suicidal and Depressed Persons." *Life Threatening Behavior*, 1974, *4* (3), 160–170.

Birman, B. F., and Natriello, G. "Perspectives on Absenteeism in High Schools." *Journal of Research in Education*, 1978, *11*, 29–38.

Bittle, R. G. "Recorded Messages: A Technique for Reducing Absenteeism." *Educational Technology*, 1977, *17*, 49–51.

Blechman, E. A., Olson, D. H. L., and Hellman, I. D. "Stimulus Control over Family Problem Solving Behavior: The Family Contract Game." *Behavior Therapy*, 1976, *7*, 686–692.

Blechman, E. A., Taylor, C. J., and Schrader, S. M. "Family Problem Solving vs. Home Notes as Early Intervention with High-Risk Children." *Journal of Consulting and Clinical Psychology*, 1981, *49*, 919–926.

Blizinsky, M. J., and Reid, W. J. "Problem Focus and Change in a Brief-Treatment Model." *Social Work*, 1980, *25*, 89–93.

Blood, L., and D'Angelo, R. "A Progress Research Report on Value Issues in Conflict Between Runaways and Their Parents." *Journal of Marriage and the Family*, 1974, *36*, 486–491.

Bloom, M., and Fischer, J. *Evaluating Practice: Guidelines for the Accountable Profession*. Englewood Cliffs, N.J.: Prentice-Hall, 1982.

Blum, B. "Helping Teenage Mothers." *Public Welfare*, 1984, *42*, 17–21.

Borgman, R. "Antecedents and Consequences of Parental Rights Termination for Abused and Neglected Children." *Child Welfare*, 1981, *60*, 391–403.

Borman, L. D., and Lieberman, M. A. "Conclusion: Contributions, Dilemmas, and Implications for Mental Health Policy." In M. A. Lieberman, L. D. Borman, and Associates, *Self-Help Groups for Coping with Crisis: Origins, Members, Processes, and Impact*. San Francisco: Jossey-Bass, 1979.

Bornstein, M., Bellack, A. S., and Hersen, M. "Social Skills Training for Highly Aggressive Children: Treatment in an Inpatient Psychiatric Setting." *Behavior Modification*, 1980, *4*, 173–186.

Borus, M. E., and Carpenter, S. A. "A Note on the Return of Dropouts to High School." *Youth and Society*, 1983, *14*, 501–507.

Bostock, T., and Williams, C. "Attempted Suicide as an Operant Behavior." *Archives of General Psychiatry*, 1974, *31*, 482–486.

Bracey, D. H. *Baby Pros: Preliminary Profiles of Juvenile Prostitutes*. New York: John Jay Publishers, 1979.

Brager, G., and Holloway, S. *Changing Human Service Organizations: Politics and Practice*. New York: Free Press, 1978.

Braswell, L., Kendall, P. C., Braith, J., Carey, M., and Vye, C. "'Involvement' in Cognitive-Behavioral Therapy with Children: Process and Its Relationship to Outcome." *Cognitive Therapy and Research*, in press.

Breed, W. "The Negro and Fatalistic Suicide." *Pacific Sociology Review*, 1970, *13*, 156–162.

Brehm, J. W. *A Theory of Psychological Reactance*. Orlando, Fla.: Academic Press, 1966.

Brennan, T. "Mapping the Diversity Among Runaways: A Descriptive Multivariate Analysis of Selected Social Psychological Background Conditions." *Journal of Family Issues*, 1980, *1*, 165–189.

Brennan, T., Huizinga, D., and Elliott, D. S. *The Social Psychology of Runaways*. Lexington, Mass.: Heath, 1978.

Brenton, M. *The Runaways: Children, Husbands, Wives, and Parents*. Boston: Little, Brown, 1978.

Brewin, C., and Antaki, C. "The Role of Attributions in Psychological Treatment." In C. Antaki and C. Brewin (eds.), *Attributions and Psychological Change: Applications of Attributional Theories to Clinical and Education Practice*. Orlando, Fla.: Academic Press, 1982.

Brigham, T. A., and Stoerzinger, A. "An Experimental Analysis of Children's Preference for Self-Selected Rewards." In T. A. Brigham, R. Hawkins, J. Scott, and T. F. McLaughlin (eds.), *Behavior Analysis in Education: Self-Control and Reading*. Dubuque, Iowa: Kendall/Hunt, 1976.

Bright, P. B., and Robin, A. L. "Ameliorating Parent-Adolescent Conflict with Problem-Solving Communication Training." *Journal of Behavior Therapy and Experimental Psychology*, 1981, *12*, 275–280.

Brim, O., and Kagan, J. (eds.). *Constancy and Change in Human Development*. Cambridge, Mass.: Harvard University Press, 1980.

Brokinsky, B. *Student Discipline, Problems and Solutions*. AASA Critical Issues Report no. 021-00334. Arlington, Va.: American Association of School Administrators, 1980.

Bronfenbrenner, U. *The Ecology of Human Development: Experiments by Nature and Design*. Cambridge, Mass.: Harvard University Press, 1979.

Brooks, R. B., and Snow, D. L. "Two Case Illustrations of the Use of Behavior Modification Techniques in the School Setting." *Behavior Therapy*, 1972, *3*, 10–103.

Brown, B. J., and Christie, M. *Social Learning Practice in Residential Child Care*. Elmsford, N.Y.: Pergamon Press, 1981.

Brown, G. W., and Harris, T. *Social Origins of Depression: A Study of Psychiatric Disorders of Women*. New York: Free Press, 1978.

Buckner, J. C., and Chesney-Lind, M. "Dramatic Cures for Juvenile Crime: An Evaluation of the Prisoner-Run Delinquency Prevention Program." *Criminal Justice and Behavior*, 1983, *10*, 227–247.

Bush, M., and Gordon, A. C. "The Case for Involving Children in Child Welfare Decisions." *Social Work*, 1982, *27*, 309–314.

Cairns, L. "A Decade of Discipline: The State of the Art of Classroom Management." Paper presented at the Annual Meeting of the American Educational Research Association, Montreal, Canada, 1983.

Cameron, M. I., and Robinson, V. M. J. "Effects of Cognitive Training on Academic and On-Task Behavior of Hyperactive Children." *Journal of Abnormal Child Psychology*, 1980, *8*, 405–419.

Camp, B. W., and Bash, M. A. S. *Think Aloud: Increasing Social and Cognitive Skills—A Problem-Solving Program for Children (Primary Level)*. Champaign, Ill.: Research Press, 1981.

Camp, B. W., and Ray, R. S. "Aggression." In A. W. Meyers and W. E. Craighead (eds.), *Cognitive Behavior Therapy with Children*. New York: Plenum, 1984.

Campbell, M., Anderson, L. T., and Green, W. H. "Behavior-Disordered and Aggressive Children: New Advances in Pharmacotherapy." *Developmental and Behavioral Pediatrics*, 1983, *4*, 265–271.

Campbell, S. B., Scheifer, M., Weiss, G., and Perlman, T. "A Two-Year Follow-up of Hyperactive Preschoolers." *American Journal of Orthopsychiatry*, 1977, *47*, 149–162.

Carbone, V. J. "The Effectiveness of Short Duration Time-Outs in a Juvenile Detention Facility." *Journal of Juvenile and Family Courts*, 1983, *34*, 75–82.

Carlson, G. A., and Cantwell, D. P. "Suicidal Behavior and Depression in Children and Adolescents." *Journal of the American Academy of Child Psychiatry*, 1982, *21*, 361–368.

Carpenter, R., and Casto, G. "A Simple Procedure to Improve a Token Economy." *Journal of Behavior Therapy and Experimental Psychology*, 1982, *13*, 331–332.

Carstens, C. "Application of a Work Penalty Threat in the Treatment of a Case of Juvenile Firesetting." *Journal of Be-*

havior Therapy and Experimental Psychology, 1982, *13*, 159–161.

Cartledge, G., and Milburn, J. F. (eds.). *Teaching Skills to Children: Innovative Approaches*. Elmsford, N.Y.: Pergamon Press, 1980.

Cauce, A. M., Felner, R. D., and Primavera, J. "Social Support in High-Risk Adolescents: Structural Components and Adaptive Impact." *American Journal of Community Psychology*, 1982, *10*, 417–428.

Cautela, J. R. "Covert Sensitization." *Psychological Record*, 1967, *20*, 459–468.

Cautela, J. R. "The Present Status of Covert Modeling." *Behavior Therapy*, 1976, *7*, 323–326.

Cautela, J. R. "Children's Reinforcement Survey Schedule (CRSS)." In J. R. Cautela (ed.), *Behavior Analysis Forms for Clinical Intervention*. Champaign, Ill.: Research Press, 1977.

Cautela, J. R. "Covert Conditioning: Assumptions and Procedures." In D. Upper and J. Cautela (eds.), *Covert Conditioning*. Elmsford, N.Y.: Pergamon Press, 1979.

Cerreto, M. C., and Tuma, J. M. "Distribution of DSM-II Diagnoses in a Child Psychiatric Setting." *Journal of Abnormal Child Psychology*, 1977, *5*, 147–153.

Chamberlain, R. W. "Can We Identify a Group of Children at Age Two Who Are at Risk for the Development of Behavioral or Emotional Problems in Kindergarten or First Grade?" *Pediatrics* (Supplement), 1977, *59*, 971–981.

Chandler, M. J., Greenspan, S., and Barenboim, C. "Assessment and Training of Role-Taking and Preferential Communication Skills in Institutionalized Emotionally-Disturbed Children." *Developmental Psychology*, 1973, *9*, 326–332.

Chatoor, I., Wells, K. C., Conners, C. K., Seidel, W. T., and Shaw, D. "The Effects of Nocturnally Administered Stimulant Medication on EEG Sleep and Behavior in Hyperactive Children." *Journal of the American Academy of Child Psychiatry*, 1983, *22*, 337–342.

Children's Defense Fund. *Children Out of School*. Washington, D.C.: Children's Defense Fund, 1974.

Christensen, A., Johnson, S. M., Phillips, S., and Glasgow, R. E. "Cost Effectiveness in Behavioral Family Therapy." *Behavior Therapy*, 1980, *11*, 208–226.

Christie, D. J., Hiss, M., and Lozanoff, B. "Modification of Inattentive Classroom Behavior: Hyperactive Children's Use of Self-Recording with Teacher Guidance." *Behavior Modification*, 1984, *8*, 391–406.

Christophersen, E. R., Barrish, H. H., Barrish, I. J., and Christophersen, M. R. "Continuing Education for Parents of Infants and Toddlers." In R. F. Dangel and R. A. Polster (eds.), *Parent Training: Foundations of Research and Practice*. New York: Guilford, 1984.

Christy, P. R. "Does Use of Tangible Rewards with Individual Children Affect Peer Observers?" *Journal of Applied Behavior Analysis*, 1975, *8*, 187–196.

Ciminero, A. R., and Drabman, R. S. "Current Developments in the Behavioral Assessment of Children." In B. B. Lahey and A. E. Kazdin (eds.), *Advances in Clinical Child Psychology*. Vol. 1. New York: Plenum, 1977.

Cisneros, F. "Chicano Education Program Starts with Parents' Rights." *Oakland Tribune*, Dec. 20, 1979, p. C-9.

Clarizio, H. F. "In Defense of the IQ Test." *School Psychology Digest*, 1979, *8*, 79–88.

Clarizio, H. F. "Intellectual Assessment of Hispanic Children." *Psychology in the Schools*, 1982, *19*, 61–71.

Clarizio, H. F., and McCoy, G. F. *Behavior Disorders in Children*. New York: Harper & Row, 1983.

Clark, A. M., and Clark, A. B. D. "Problems in Comparing the Effects of Environmental Change at Different Ages." In H. McGurk (ed.), *Ecological Factors in Human Development*. Amsterdam: North-Holland Publishing Co., 1977.

Clark, H. B., and Macrae, J. W. "The Use of Imposed and Self-Selected Training Packages to Establish Classroom Teaching Skills." *Journal of Applied Behavior Analysis*, 1976, *9*, 105.

Clum, G. A., Patsiokas, A. T., and Luscomb, R. L. "Empirically Based Comprehensive Treatment Program for Parasuicide." *Journal of Consulting and Clinical Psychology*, 1979, *47*, 937–945.

Cobb, D. E., and Medway, F. J. "Determinants of Effectiveness in Parent Consultation." *Journal of Community Psychology*, 1978, *6*, 229–240.

Cochran, M. M., and Brassard, J. A. "Child Development

and Personal Social Networks." *Child Development*, 1979, *50*, 601–616.

Cohen, P. A., Kulik, J. A., and Kulik, C. C. "Education Outcomes of Tutoring: A Meta-Analysis of Findings." *American Education Research Journal*, 1982, *19* (2), 237–248.

Cohen, S., Keyworth, M., Kleiner, R., and Libert, L. "The Support of School Behaviors by Home-Based Reinforcement via Parent-Child Contingency Contracts." In E. Ramp and B. Hopkins (eds.), *A New Direction for Education*. Lawrence: Department of Human Development, University of Kansas, 1971.

Cohen-Sandler, R., Berman, A. L., and King, R. A. "A Follow-Up Study of Hospitalized Suicidal Children." *Journal of the American Academy of Child Psychiatry*, 1982, *21*, 398–403.

Coie, J. D., and Krehbiel, G. "Effects of Academic Tutoring on the Social Status of Low-Achieving, Socially Rejected Children." *Child Development*, 1984, *55*, 1465–1478.

Colletta, N. D., and Gregg, C. H. "Adolescent Mothers' Vulnerability to Stress." *Journal of Nervous and Mental Disease*, 1981, *169*, 50–54.

Collins, A. H., and Pancoast, D. L. *Natural Helping Networks*. Washington, D.C.: National Association of Social Workers, 1976.

Coltoff, P., and Luks, A. *Preventing Child Maltreatment: Begin with the Parent*. New York: Children's Aid Society, 1978.

Conger, R. D. "The Assessment of Dysfunctional Family Systems." In B. B. Lahey and A. E. Kazdin (eds.), *Advances in Clinical Child Psychology*. Vol. 4. New York: Plenum, 1981.

Conners, C. K. "Symptom Patterns in Hyperkinetic, Neurotic, and Normal Children." *Child Development*, 1970, *41* (3), 667–682.

Conway, J. B., and Bucher, B. D. "Soap in the Mouth as an Aversive Consequence." *Behavior Therapy*, 1974, *5* (1), 154–156.

Coolidge, J., Willer, M., Tessman, E., and Waldfoger, S. "School Phobia in Adolescence." *American Journal of Orthopsychiatry*, 1960, *30*, 599–607.

Copeland, A. P., and Hammel, R. "Subject Variables in Cognitive Self-Instructional Training." *Cognitive Therapy and Research*, 1981, *5*, 405–420.

Cowen, E. L., Lotyczewski, B. S., and Weissberg, R. P. "Risk and Resource Indicators and Their Relationship to Young Children's School Adjustment." *American Journal of Community Psychology*, 1984, *12*, 353–367.

Cowen, F. L., Pederson, A., Babijian, H., Izzo, L. D., and Trost, M. A. "Longterm Follow-Up of Early Detected Vulnerable Children." *Journal of Consulting and Clinical Psychology*, 1973, *41*, 438–446.

Cretekos, C. J. G. "Some Techniques in Rehabilitating the School Phobic Adolescent." *Adolescence*, 1977, *12*, 237–246.

Crissey, M. S. "Prevention in Retrospect: Adoption Follow-Up." In G. W. Albee and J. M. Joffee (eds.), *The Issues: An Overview of Primary Prevention*. Hanover, N.H.: University of New England, 1977.

Croghan, L. M. "Conceptualizing the Critical Elements in a Rapid Desensitization to School Anxiety: A Case Study." *Journal of Pediatric Psychology*, 1981, *6*, 165–170.

Curtis, M. J., and Zins, J. E. (eds.). *The Theory and Practice of School Consultation*. Springfield, Ill.: Thomas, 1981.

Dangel, R. F., and Polster, R. A. (eds.). *Parent Training: Foundations of Research and Practice*. New York: Guilford, 1984.

Davis, J. M., and Sandoval, J. "Applied Ethics for School-Based Consultants." *Professional Psychology*, 1982, *13*, 543–551.

Delamater, A. M., Conners, C. K., and Wells, K. C. "A Comparison of Staff Training Procedures: Behavioral Applications in the Child Psychiatric Inpatient Setting." *Behavior Modification*, 1984, *8*, 39–58.

DeLong, G. R. "Lithium Carbonate Treatment of Selective Behavior Disorders in Children Suggesting Manic-Depressive Illness." *Journal of Pediatrics*, 1978, *93*, 689–694.

DeMause, L. "Our Forebears Made Childhood a Nightmare." In G. J. Williams and J. Money (eds.), *Traumatic Abuse and Neglect of Children at Home*. Baltimore, Md.: Johns Hopkins University Press, 1980.

DeRisi, W. J., and Butz, G. *Writing Behavioral Contracts: A Case Simulation Practice Manual*. Champaign, Ill.: Research Press, 1975.

DiGiuseppe, R. A. "Therapy with Children." In G. Emery, S. D. Hollon, and R. C. Bedrosian (eds.), *New Directions in Cognitive Therapy: A Casebook.* New York: Guilford, 1981.

DiGiuseppe, R. A. "Rational-Emotive Therapy and Conduct Disorders." In A. Ellis and M. E. Bernard (eds.), *Rational-Emotive Approaches to the Problems of Childhood.* New York: Plenum, 1983.

Dineen, J. P., Clark, H. B., and Risley, T. R. "Peer Tutoring Among Elementary Students: Educational Benefits to the Tutor." *Journal of Applied Behavior Analysis*, 1977, *10*, 231–238.

Doerfler, L. A., and Richards, C. S. "Self-Initiated Attempts to Cope with Depression." *Cognitive Therapy and Research*, 1981, *5*, 367–371.

Doherty, W. J., and Ryder, R. G. "Parent Effectiveness Training: Criticisms and Caveats." *Journal of Marital and Family Therapy*, 1980, *6*, 409–418.

Dohrenwend, B. S., and Dohrenwend, B. P. (eds.). *Stressful Life Events: Their Nature and Effects.* New York: Wiley-Interscience, 1974.

Doleys, D. M. "Enuresis and Encopresis." In T. H. Ollendick and M. Hersen (eds.), *Handbook of Child Psychopathology.* New York: Plenum, 1983.

Doll, E. A. *Vineland Social Maturity Scale.* Circle Pines, Minn.: American Guidance Service, 1965.

Donahue, K. C., and Gullotta, T. P. "The Coping Behavior of Adolescents Following a Move." *Adolescence*, 1983, *18*, 391–401.

Dooley, M. *The Business of Attendance.* West Covina, Calif.: West Covina School District, n.d.

Douglas, V. I., Parry, P., Morton, P., and Garson, C. "Assessment of a Cognitive Training Program for Hyperactive Children." *Journal of Abnormal Child Psychology*, 1976, *4*, 389–410.

Drabman, R. S., and Creedon, D. L. "Marking Timeout: A Procedure for Away from Home Disruptive Behavior." *Child Behavior Therapy*, 1979, *1*, 99–101.

Drabman, R. S., and Lahey, B. B. "Feedback in Classroom Behavior Modification: Effects on the Target and Her Classmates." *Journal of Applied Behavior Analysis*, 1974, *7*, 591–598.

Drew, B. M., Evans, J. H., Bostow, D. E., Geiger, G., and Drash, P. W. "Increasing Assignment Completion and Accuracy Using a Daily Report Card Procedure." *Psychology in the Schools*, 1982, *19*, 540–547.

Drye, R. C., Goulding, R. L., and Goulding, M. E. "No-Suicide Decisions: Patient Monitoring of Suicidal Risk." *American Journal of Psychiatry*, 1973, *130*, 171–174.

Duke, D. L. "Who Misbehaves? A High School Studies Its Discipline Problems." *Educational Administration Quarterly*, 1976, *12*, 65–85.

Dumas, J. E. "Interactional Correlates of Treatment Outcome in Behavioral Parent Training." *Journal of Consulting and Clinical Psychology*, 1984, *52*, 946–954.

Edelbrock, C. "Running Away from Home: Incidence and Correlates Among Children and Youth Referred for Mental Health Services." *Journal of Family Issues*, 1980, *1*, 210–228.

Edelbrock, C., and Achenbach, T. M. "A Typology of Child Behavior Profile Patterns: Distribution and Correlates for Disturbed Children Aged 6–16." *Journal of Applied Behavior Analysis*, 1980, *8*, 441–470.

Edelson, J. L. "Teaching Children to Resolve Conflict: A Group Approach." *Social Work*, 1981, *26*, 488–493.

Edelson, J. L., Ordman, A. M., and Rose, S. "Assessing Children's Social Skills: The Development of and Failure to Validate a Behavioral Role Play Test." *Journal of Social Service Research*, 1982, *6*, 47–61.

Egan, G. *You and Me: The Skills of Communicating and Relating to Others*. Monterey, Calif.: Brooks/Cole, 1977.

Egeland, B., Briefenbacher, M., and Rosenberg, D. "A Prospective Study of the Significance of Life Stress in the Etiology of Child Abuse." *Journal of Consulting and Clinical Psychology*, 1980, *48*, 195–205.

Ehly, S. W., and Larsen, S. C. "Sex, Status, and Liking Tutor and Learner as Predictors of Tutorial Outcomes." *Perceptual and Motor Skills*, 1977, *45*, 335–336.

Elder, J. P., Edelstein, B. A., and Narick, M. M. "Adolescent Psychiatric Patients: Modifying Aggressive Behavior with Social Skills Training." *Behavior Modification*, 1979, *3*, 161–178.

Elliott, D. S., Ageton, S. S., and Canter, R. J. "An Integrated Theoretical Perspective on Delinquent Behaviors." *Journal of Research in Crime and Delinquency*, 1979, *16*, 3–27.

Elliot, T., Smith, R., and Wildman, R. "Suicide and Systematic Desensitization: A Case Study." *Journal of Clinical Psychology*, 1972, *28*, 420–423.

Epps, S., McGue, M., and Ysseldyke, J. "Interjudge Agreement in Clarifying Students as Learning Disabled." *Psychology in the Schools*, 1982, *19*, 209–220.

Epstein, A. *Assessing the Child Development Information Needed by Adolescent Parents with Very Young Children*. Washington, D.C.: Administration for Children, Youth and Families, 1980.

Epstein, J. L., and Becker, H. J. "Teachers' Reported Practices of Parent Involvement: Problems and Possibilities." *The Elementary School Journal*, 1982, *83*, 103–113.

Epstein, L. "The Effects of Intraclass Peer Tutoring on the Vocabulary Development of Learning Disabled Children." *Journal of Learning*, 1978, *11*, 518–521.

Epstein, L. *Helping People: The Task Centered Approach*. St. Louis, Mo.: Mosby, 1980.

Erikson, E. *Childhood and Society*. (2nd ed.) New York: Norton, 1963.

Eron, L. D. "Prescription for Reduction of Aggression." *American Psychologist*, 1980, *35*, 244–252.

Eyberg, S. M., and Johnson, S. M. "Multiple Assessment of Behavior Modification with Families: Effects of Contingency Contracting and Order of Treated Problems." *Journal of Consulting and Clinical Psychology*, 1974, *42*, 594–606.

Eyre, S. L., Rounsaville, B. J., and Kleber, H. D. "History of Childhood Hyperactivity in a Clinic Population of Opiate Addicts." *Journal of Nervous and Mental Disease*, 1982, *170*, 522–529.

Fahlberg, V. *Helping Children When They Must Move: Putting the Pieces Together*. Lansing, Mich.: Department of Social Services, 1979.

Falck, H. S., and Barnes, R. E. "The Change Agent in the Organization." *Administration in Mental Health*, 1975, *3*, 3–11.

Farrington, D. P. "The Family Backgrounds of Aggressive Youths." In L. A. Hersov, M. Berger, and D. Shaffer (eds.), *Aggression and Anti-Social Behavior in Childhood and Adolescence*. Elmsford, N.Y.: Pergamon Press, 1978.

Farrington, D. P. "Longitudinal Analyses of Criminal Violence." In M. E. Wolfgang and N. Weiner (eds.), *Criminal Violence*. Beverly Hills, Calif.: Sage, 1982.

Federal Emergency Management Agency, U.S. Fire Administration. *Interviewing and Counseling Juvenile Firesetters: The Child Under Seven Years of Age*. Washington, D.C.: U.S. Government Printing Office, 1980.

Federal Emergency Management Agency, U.S. Fire Administration National Fire Academy. *Juvenile Firesetting Handbook: Dealing with Children Ages 7–14*. Washington, D.C.: U.S. Government Printing Office, 1984.

Feindler, E. L., Marriott, S. A., and Iwata, M. "Group Anger Control Training for Junior High School Delinquents." *Cognitive Therapy and Research*, 1984, *8*, 299–311.

Feiner, H. A., and Couch, E. H. "I've Got a Secret: The Student in the Agency." *Social Casework*, 1985, *66*, 268–274.

Feldman, H. *Effect of Welfare Women's Working on Their Family*. Ithaca, N.Y.: Cornell University Press, 1972.

Feldman, S. (ed.). *Cognitive Consistency: Motivational Antecedents and Behavioral Consequences*. Orlando, Fla.: Academic Press, 1966.

Felixbrod, J. J., and O'Leary, K. D. "Self-Determination of Academic Standards by Children." *Journal of Educational Psychology*, 1974, *66*, 845–850.

Felner, R. D., Ginter, M., and Primavera, J. "Primary Prevention During School Transitions: Social Support and Environmental Structure." *American Journal of Community Psychology*, 1982, *10*, 277–290.

Ferster, C. B., Culbertson, S., and Boren, M. C. P. *Behavior Principles*. (2nd ed.) Englewood Cliffs, N.J.: Prentice-Hall, 1975.

Feshbach, N. O. "Teaching Styles in Young Children: Implications for Peer Tutoring." In V. L. Allen (ed.), *Children as Teachers*. Orlando, Fla.: Academic Press, 1976.

Feuerstein, R., Miller, R., Hoffman, M. B., Rand, Y., Mintzker, Y., and Jensen, M. R. "Cognitive Modifiability in Adolescence: Cognitive Structure and the Effects of Intervention." *Journal of Special Education*, 1981, *15*, 269–287.

Finch, A. J., and Eastman, E. S. "A Multimethod Approach

to Measuring Anger in Children." *Journal of Psychology*, 1983, *115*, 55–60.

Finckenauer, J. O. "Scared Crooked." *Psychology Today*, 1979, *13*, 6–11.

Fineman, K. R. "Firesetting in Childhood and Adolescence." *Psychiatric Clinics of North America*, 1980, *3*, 483–500.

"Firehawk Children's Program." *Firehawk Dispatch*, Spring 1984, p. 6–7.

Firestone, P. "Factors Associated with Children's Adherence to Stimulant Medication." *American Journal of Orthopsychiatry*, 1982, *52*, 447–457.

Fisch, R., Weakland, J. H., and Segal, L. *The Tactics of Change: Doing Therapy Briefly.* San Francisco: Jossey-Bass, 1982.

Fischer, R., and Ury, W. *Getting to Yes: Negotiating Agreement Without Giving In.* Boston: Houghton Mifflin, 1981.

Fitzharris, T. L. *The Foster Children of California: Profiles of 10,000 Children in Residential Care.* Sacramento, Calif.: Children's Services Foundation, 1985.

Flaherty, M. G. "The National Incidence of Juvenile Suicide in Adult Jails and Juvenile Detention Centers." *Suicide and Life-Threatening Behavior*, 1983, *13*, 85–94.

Flanagan, J., Hindelang, M. J., and Gottfredson, M. R. *Sourcebook of Criminal Justice Statistics—1979.* Washington, D.C.: U.S. Government Printing Office, 1980.

Fleischman, M. J. "Using Parenting Salaries to Control Attrition and Cooperation in Therapy." *Behavior Therapy*, 1979, *10*, 111–116.

Fleischman, M. J., Horne, A. M., and Arthur, J. L. *Troubled Families: A Treatment Approach.* Champaign, Ill.: Research Press, 1983.

Forehand, R. "Training Behavioral Clinicians for a Nonbehavioral World." *The Behavior Therapist*, 1985, *8*, 5–8.

Forehand, R., and Atkeson, B. M. "Generality of Treatment Effects with Parents as Therapists: A Review of Assessment and Implementation Procedures." *Behavior Therapy*, 1977, *8*, 575–593.

Forehand, R., Breiner, J., McMahon, R. J., and Davies, G. "Predictors of Cross Setting Behavior Change in the Treatment of Child Problems." *Journal of Behavior Therapy and Experimental Psychology*, 1981, *12*, 311–313.

Forehand, R., and McMahon, R. J. *"Helping the Noncompliant Child: A Clinician's Guide to Parent Training."* New York: Guilford, 1981.

Forman, S. "A Comparison of Cognitive Training and Response Cost Procedures in Modifying Aggressive Behavior of Elementary School Children." *Behavior Therapy*, 1980, *11*, 594–600.

Foxx, R. M., and Azrin, N. H. "Restitution: A Method of Eliminating Aggressive-Disruptive Behavior of Retarded and Brain Damaged Patients." *Behavior Research and Therapy*, 1972, *10*, 15–27.

Foy, E. W., Eisler, R. M., and Pinkston, S. "Modeling Assertion in a Case of Explosive Rages." *Journal of Behavior Therapy and Experimental Psychology*, 1975, *6*, 135–138.

Frankel, F., Moss, D., Schofield, S., and Simmons, J. Q. "Case Study: Use of Differential Reinforcement to Suppress Self-Injurious and Aggressive Behavior. *Psychological Reports*, 1976, *39*, 843–849.

Frederick, C. J. "Suicide in Young Minority Group Persons." In H. S. Sudak, A. B. Ford, and N. B. Rushforth (eds.), *Suicide in the Young.* Boston: John Wright/PSG, 1984.

Frederick, D. J., and Resnik, H. L. P. "How Suicidal Behaviors Are Learned." *American Journal of Psychotherapy*, 1971, *25*, 37–55.

Frederiksen, L. W., Jenkins, J. O., Foy, D. W., and Eisler, R. M. "Social-Skills Training to Modify Abusive Verbal Outbursts in Adults." *Journal of Applied Behavior Analysis*, 1976, *9*, 117–125.

Freidman, R. C., Corn, R., Arnoff, M. S., Hurt, S. W., and Clarkin, J. F. "The Seriously Suicidal Adolescent: Affective and Character Pathology." In H. S. Sudak, A. B. Ford, and N. B. Rushforth (eds.), *Suicide in the Young.* Boston: John Wright/PSG, 1984.

Frey, D. H., Motto, J. A., and Ritholz, M. D. "Group Therapy for Persons at Risk for Suicide: An Evaluation Using an Intensive Design." *Psychotherapy: Theory, Research, and Practice*, 1983, *20*, 281–292.

Furey, W., and Forehand, R. "The Daily Child Behavior Checklist." *Journal of Behavioral Assessment*, 1983, *5*, 83–95.

Furth, H. G. *The World of Grownups: Children's Conceptions of Society.* New York: Elsevier North Holland, 1980.

Gagne, E. E. "Effects of Immediacy of Feedback and Level of Aspiration Statements on Learning Tasks for Delinquent Youngsters." *Journal of Abnormal Child Psychology*, 1975, *3*, 53–60.

Gambrill, E. *Casework: A Competency-Based Approach.* Englewood Cliffs, N.J.: Prentice-Hall, 1983.

Gambrill, E., and Stein, T. J. *Supervision: A Decision-Making Approach.* Beverly Hills, Calif.: Sage, 1984.

Gammon, G. D., John, K., and Weissman, M. M. "Structured Assessment of Psychiatric Diagnosis and of Psychosocial Function and Supports in Adolescence: A Role in the Secondary Prevention of Suicide." In H. S. Sudak, A. B. Ford, and N. B. Rushforth (eds.), *Suicide in the Young.* Boston: John Wright/PSG, 1984.

Gant, B. L., Barnard, J. D., Kuehn, F. E., Jones, H. H., and Christopherson, E. R. "A Behaviorally Based Approach for Improving Intrafamilial Communication Patterns." *Journal of Clinical Child Psychology*, 1981, *10*, 102–106.

Garbarino, J. "A Preliminary Study of Some Ecological Correlates of Child Abuse: The Impact of Socioeconomic Stress on Mothers." *Child Development*, 1976, *47*, 178–185.

Garbarino, J. *Children and Families in the Social Environment.* Hawthorne, N.Y.: Aldine, 1982.

Garbarino, J., and Sherman, D. "Identifying High-Risk Neighborhoods." In J. Garbarino, S. H. Stocking, and Associates, *Protecting Children from Abuse and Neglect: Developing and Maintaining Effective Support Systems for Families.* San Francisco: Jossey-Bass, 1980.

Gardner, H. *Developmental Psychology: An Introduction.* Boston: Little, Brown, 1978.

Garfield, S. L., and Kurtz, R. "A Survey of Clinical Psychologists: Characteristics, Activities, and Orientations." *The Clinical Psychologist*, 1974, *28*, 7–10.

Garfinkel, B. D., Froese, A., and Hood, J. "Suicide Attempts in Children and Adolescents." *American Journal of Psychiatry*, 1982, *139*, 1257–1261.

Garfinkel, B. D., Wender, P. H., Sloman, L., and O'Neill, I. "Tricyclic Antidepressant and Methylphenidate Treatment of Attention Deficit Disorder in Children." *Journal of the American Academy of Child Psychiatry*, 1983, *22*, 343–348.

Garmezy, N. "The Study of Competence in Children at Risk for Severe Psychopathology." In E. Anthony and C. Koupernick (eds.), *The Child in His Family*. Vol. 3: *Children at Psychiatric Risk*. New York: Wiley, 1974.

Gaudin, J. M., and Kurtz, D. P. "Parenting Skills Training for Child Abusers." *Journal of Group Psychotherapy, Psychodrama, and Sociometry*, 1985, *38*, 35–54.

Gaylin, W., and Macklin, R. (eds.). *Who Speaks for the Child: The Problems of Proxy Consent*. New York: Plenum, 1982.

Gerber, M., and Kauffman, J. M. "Peer Tutoring in Academic Settings." In P. S. Strain (ed.), *The Utilization of Classroom Peers as Behavior Change Agents*. New York: Plenum, 1981.

Germaine, C. B. "Using Social and Physical Environments." In A. Rosenblatt and D. Waldfogel (eds.), *Handbook of Clinical Social Work*. San Francisco: Jossey-Bass, 1983.

Gersten, J. C., Langner, T. S., Eisenberg, J. G., Simcha-Fagan, O., and McCarthy, E. D. "Stability and Change in Types of Behavioral Disturbance of Children and Adolescents." *Journal of Abnormal Child Psychology*, 1976, *4*, 111–127.

Gesten, E. L., Rains, M. H., Rapkin, B. D., Weissberg, R. P., deApocada, R. F., Cowen, E. L., and Bowen, R. "Training Children in Social Problem-Solving Competencies: A First and Second Look." *American Journal of Community Psychology*, 1982, *10*, 95–115.

Gibbons, J. S., Butler, J., Urwin, P., and Gibbons, L. "Evaluation of a Social Work Service for Self-Poisoning Patients." *British Journal of Psychiatry*, 1978, *133*, 111–118.

Gilchrist, L. D., and Schinke, S. P. "Counseling with Adolescents About Their Sexuality." In C. S. Chilman (ed.), *Social and Psychological Aspects of Adolescent Sexuality: A Handbook for Professionals in the Human Services*. New York: Wiley, 1983.

Gilchrist, L. D., Schinke, S. P., and Blythe, B. J. "Primary

Prevention Services for Youth and Children." *Children and Youth Services Review*, 1979, *1*, 379–391.

Gingerich, W. J. "Generalizing Single-Case Evaluation from Classroom to Practice." *Journal of Education for Social Work*, 1984, *20*, 74–82.

Giovannoni, J. M., and Becerra, R. *Defining Child Abuse*. New York: Free Press, 1979.

Gittelman-Klein, R., and Klein, D. F. "School Phobia: Diagnostic Considerations in Light of Imipramine Effects." *Journal of Nervous and Mental Disease*, 1973, *156*, 199–215.

Glasgow, R. E., and Rosen, G. M. "Self-Help Behavior Therapy Manuals: Recent Developments and Clinical Usage." In C. M. Franks (ed.), *New Developments in Behavior Therapy*. New York: Haworth, 1985.

Goff, G. A., and Demetral, D. G. "Mental Health Intervention in the Schools." *Social Work in Education*, 1983, *6*, 15–31.

Goldfried, M. R. (ed.). *Converging Themes in Psychotherapy*. New York: Springer, 1982.

Goldfried, M. R., and Robins, C. "On the Facilitation of Self-Efficacy." *Cognitive Therapy and Research*, 1982, *6*, 361–379.

Goldstein, A. P., Sherman, M., Gershaw, N. J., Sprafkin, R. P., and Glick, B. "Training Aggressive Adolescents in Prosocial Behavior." *Journal of Youth and Adolescence*, 1978, *7*, 73–92.

Gordon, D. A., and Young, R. D. "School Phobia: A Discussion of Etiology, Treatment, and Evaluation." *Psychological Reports*, 1976, *39*, 783–804.

Gorham, K. A., Des Jardins, C., Page, R., Pettis, E., and Scherber, B. "Effect on Parents." In N. Hobbs (ed.), *Issues in the Classification of Children*. San Francisco: Jossey-Bass, 1975.

Gottlieb, D., and Chafetz, J. S. "Dynamics of Familial Generational Conflict and Reconciliation." *Youth and Society*, 1977, *9*, 213–224.

Gould, M. S., Wunsch-Hitzik, R., and Dohrenwend, B. "Estimating the Prevalence of Childhood Psychopathology: A Critical Review." *Journal of the American Academy of Child Psychiatry*, 1981, *20*, 462–476.

Gove, W. R., and Crutchfield, R. D. "The Family and Juvenile Delinquency." *The Sociological Quarterly*, 1982, *23*, 301–319.

Goyette, C. H., Conners, C. K., and Ulrich, R. F. "Normative Data on Revised Conners Parent and Teacher Rating Scales." *Journal of Abnormal Child Psychology*, 1978, *6*, 221–236.

Grala, C., and McCauley, C. "Counseling Truants Back to School: Motivation Combined with a Program for Action." *Journal of Counseling Psychology*, 1976, *23*, 166–169.

Graziano, A. M., DeGiovanni, I. S., and Garcia, K. A. "Behavioral Treatment of Children's Fears." *Psychological Bulletin*, 1979, *86*, 804–830.

Green, J. (ed.). *Cultural Awareness in the Human Services.* Englewood Cliffs, N.J.: Prentice-Hall, 1982.

Greenwood, C. R., Delquadri, J., and Hall, R. V. "Opportunity to Respond and Student Performance." In W. L. Heward, T. E. Heron, J. Trap-Porter, and D. S. Hill (eds.), *Focus on Behavior Analysis in Education.* Westerville, Ohio: Merrill, 1984.

Grieger, T., Kauffman, J. M., and Grieger, R. M. "Effects of Peer Reporting on Cooperative Play and Aggression of Kindergarten Children." *Journal of School Psychology*, 1976, *14*, 307–313.

Griest, D. L., Forehand, R., Rodgers, T., Breiner, J. L., Furey, W., and Williams, C. "Effects of Parent Enhancement Therapy on the Treatment Outcome and Generalization of a Parent Training Program." *Behavior Research and Therapy*, 1982, *20*, 429–436.

Griest, D. L., Forehand, R., and Wells, K. C. "Follow-Up Assessment of Parent Training: An Analysis of Who Will Participate." *Child Study Journal*, 1981, *11*, 2210–2229.

Griest, D. L., and Wells, K. C. "Behavioral Family Therapy with Conduct Disorders in Children." *Behavior Therapy*, 1983, *14*, 37–53.

Groth, A. N. "The Incest Offender." In S. M. Sgroi (ed.), *Handbook of Clinical Intervention in Child Sexual Abuse.* Lexington, Mass.: Lexington Books, 1982.

Gruber, A. R., Heck, E. T., and Mintzer, E. "Children Who Set Fires: Some Background and Behavioral Characteristics." *American Journal of Orthopsychiatry*, 1981, *51*, 484–487.

Guendelman, S. R. "Social Worker and Mexican Journalist Solve Baby Mix-Up." *Bambino*, 1981, *14*, 2–5.

Guidry, L. S. "Use of Covert Punishing Contingency in Compulsive Stealing." *Journal of Behavior Therapy and Experimental Psychology*, 1975, *6*, 169.

Gutkin, T. B., and Ajchenbaum, M. "Teachers' Perceptions of Control and Preferences for Consultative Services." *Professional Psychology: Research and Practice*, 1984, *15*, 565–570.

Haines, A. T., Jackson, M. S., and Davidson, J. "Children's Resistance to the Temptation to Steal in Real and Hypothetical Situations: A Comparison of Two Treatment Programs." *Australian Psychologist*, 1983, *18*, 289–303.

Hall, J. A. "Problem-Solving Training with Parents of Adolescents." Unpublished doctoral dissertation, School of Social Work, University of Wisconsin, 1980.

Hall, R. V., Axlerod, S., Tyler, L., Grief, E., Jones, F. C., and Robertson, R. "Modification of Behavior Problems in the Home with a Parent as Observer and Experimenter." *Journal of Applied Behavior Analysis*, 1972, *5*, 53–64.

Hallahan, D. P., and Kauffman, J. M. "Labels, Categories, and Behaviors: ED, LD, and EMR Reconsidered." *Journal of Special Education*, 1977, *11*, 139–149.

Hallahan, D. P., and Kneedler, R. D. "Attacking the Strategy Deficits of Learning Disabled Children: Research of Self-Monitoring." *Exceptional Education Quarterly*, 1981, *2*, 73–82.

Hallahan, D. P., Lloyd, J. W., Kauffman, J. M., and Loper, A. B. "Academic Problems." In R. J. Morris and T. R. Kratochwill (eds.), *The Practice of Child Therapy*. Elmsford, N.Y.: Pergamon Press, 1983.

Hallahan, D. P., Lloyd, J. W., and Stoller, L. *Improving Attention with Self-Monitoring: A Manual for Teachers*. Charlotte: Learning Disabilities Institute, University of Virginia, 1982.

Hamburg, D. A., and VanLawick-Goodall, J. "Factors Facilitating Development of Aggressive Behavior in Chimpanzees and Humans." In J. deWitt and W. Hartup (eds.), *Determinants and Origins of Aggressive Behavior*. The Hague, Netherlands: Monton, 1974.

Hamilton, S. B., and MacQuiddy, S. L. "Self-Administered Behavioral Parent-Training: Enhancement of Treatment Efficacy Using a Time-Out Signal Seat." *Journal of Clinical Child Psychology*, 1984, *13*, 61–69.

Haney, J. I., and Jones, R. T. "Programming Maintenance as a Major Component of a Community-Centered Prevention Effort: Escape from Fire." *Behavior Therapy*, 1982, *13*, 47–62.

Hanson, J., and Hoeft, D. "Truancy—A Losing Battle—Or Is It?" Unpublished manuscript, James Hanson, Kane County Superintendent of Schools, Kane County, Ill., n.d.

Harbin, H. T., and Madden, D. J. "Assaultive Adolescents: Family Decision-Making Parameters." *Family Process*, 1983, *22*, 109–118.

Harrari, T. "Teenagers Exiting from Foster Family Care: A Retrospective Look." Unpublished doctoral dissertation, School of Social Welfare, University of California, Berkeley, 1980.

Harris, A., and Reid, J. B. "The Consistency of a Class of Coercive Behaviors Across School Settings for Individual Subjects." *Journal of Abnormal Child Psychology*, 1981, *9*, 219–227.

Harris, S. L., and Erner-Hershfield, R. "Behavioral Suppression of Seriously Disruptive Behavior in Psychotic and Retarded Patients: A Review of Punishment and Its Alternatives." *Psychological Bulletin*, 1978, *85*, 1352–1375.

Harris, S. L., and Ferrari, M. "Developmental Factors in Child Behavior Therapy." *Behavior Therapy*, 1983, *14*, 37–53.

Hartmann, A., and Laird, J. *Family-Centered Social Work Practice*. New York: Free Press, 1983.

Hartup, W. W. "Aggression in Childhood: Developmental Perspectives." *American Psychologist*, 1974, *29*, 336–341.

Hartup, W. W. "Peer Relations and the Growth of Social Competence." In M. W. Kent and J. E. Rolf (eds.), *Primary Prevention of Psychopathology*. Vol. 3: *Social Competence in Children*. Hanover, N.H.: University Press of New England, 1979.

Hauser, S. L., DeLong, G. R., and Rosman, N. P. "Pneumographic Findings in the Infantile Autism Syndrome: A Correlation with Temporal Lobe Disease." *Brain*, 1975, *98*, 667–688.

Hawton, K. "Attempted Suicide in Children and Adolescents." *Journal of Child Psychology and Psychiatry*, 1982, *23*, 497–503.

Hawton, K., and Osborn, M. "Suicide and Attempted Suicide in Children and Adolescents." In B. B. Lahey and A. E. Kazdin (eds.), *Advances in Clinical Child Psychology*. Vol. 7. New York: Plenum, 1985.

Hayes, L. M. "And Darkness Closes in . . . A National Study of Jail Suicides." *Criminal Justice and Behavior*, 1983, *10*, 461–484.

Haynes, S. N. *Principles of Behavioral Assessment*. New York: Gardner, 1978.

Heads, T. B. "Ethical and Legal Considerations in Behavior Therapy." In D. Margolin, II (ed.), *Child Behavior Therapy*. New York: Gardner, 1978.

Heath, G. A., Hardesty, V. A., Goldfine, P. E., and Walker, A. M. "Childhood Firesetting: An Empirical Study." *Journal of the American Academy of Child Psychiatry*, 1983, *22*, 370–374.

Hechtman, L., and Weiss, G. "Long-Term Outcomes of Hyperactive Children." *American Journal of Orthopsychiatry*, 1983, *53*, 532–541.

Hechtman, L., Weiss, G., and Perlman, T. "Young Adult Outcome of Hyperactive Children Who Received Long-Term Stimulant Treatment." *Journal of the American Academy of Child Psychiatry*, 1984, *23*, 261–269.

Heiby, E. M. "Toward the Prediction of Mood Change." *Behavior Therapy*, 1983, *14*, 110–115.

Heinstein, G. H. "The Truth about Teenage Shoplifting." *Parents' Magazine*, 1974, *49*, 42–43, 60–61.

Henderson, J. Q. "A Behavioral Approach to Stealing: A Proposal for Treatment Based on Ten Cases." *Journal of Behavior Therapy and Experimental Psychiatry*, 1981, *12*, 231–236.

Henderson, J. Q. *Stealing: Treatment Manual for Combined Treatment*. Dunedin, New Zealand: Psychological Services, 1982.

Hersen, M., Bellack, H. S., and Himmelhoch, J. M. "Skills Training with Unipolar Depressed Women." In J. P. Curran and P. M. Monti (eds.), *Social Skills Training: A Practical Handbook for Assessment and Treatment*. New York: Guilford, 1982.

Hess, P., and Howard, T. "An Ecological Model for Assessing Psychosocial Difficulties in Children." *Child Welfare*, 1981, *60*, 499–518.

Hetherington, E. M. "Divorce: A Child's Perspective." *American Psychologist*, 1979, *34*, 851–858.

Hewison, J., and Tizard, J. "Parental Involvement and Reading Attainment." *British Journal of Educational Psychology*, 1980, *50*, 209–215.

"High Schools Under Fire." *Time*, Nov. 14, 1977, pp. 62–65, 67, 71–72, 75.

Hill, W. C. "Intervention and Postintervention in Schools." In H. S. Sudak, A. B. Ford, and N. B. Rushforth (eds.), *Suicide in the Young*. Boston: John Wright/PSG, 1984.

Hirschi, T. *Causes of Delinquency*. Berkeley and Los Angeles: University of California Press, 1969.

Hobbs, N. "The Role of Insight in Behavior Change: A Commentary." *American Journal of Orthopsychiatry*, 1981, *51*, 632–635.

Hobbs, N. *The Troubled and Troubling Child*. San Francisco: Jossey-Bass, 1982.

Hobbs, N., and Robinson, S. "Adolescent Development and Public Policy." *American Psychologist*, 1982, *37*, 212–223.

Hobbs, S. A., Forehand, R., and Murray, R. G. "Effects of Various Durations of Timeout on the Noncompliant Behavior of Children." *Behavior Therapy*, 1978, *8*, 652–656.

Hogan, W. A., and Johnson, D. P. "Elimination of Response Cost in a Token Economy Program and Improvement in Behavior of Emotionally Disturbed Youth." *Behavior Therapy*, 1985, *16*, 87–98.

Holland, C. J. "Elimination by the Parents of Fire-Setting Behaviour in a 7-Year-Old Boy." *Academic Therapy*, 1969, *7*, 135–137.

Holliday, F. B., and Edwards, C. "Building on Cultural Strengths: A Route to Academic Achievement." *Educational Leadership*, 1978, *36*, 207–210.

Horn, W. F., Chatoor, J., and Conners, C. K. "Additive Effects of Dexedrine and Self-Control Training: A Multiple Assessment." *Behavior Modification*, 1983, *7*, 383–402.

Horne, A. M., and Patterson, G. R. "Working with Parents of Aggressive Children." In R. R. Abidin (ed.), *Parent Education Handbook*. Springfield, Ill.: Thomas, 1979.

Horne, A. M., and Van Dyke, B. "Treatment and Maintenance of Social Learning Family Therapy." *Behavior Therapy*, 1983, *14*, 606–613.

Hsia, H. "Structural and Strategic Approach to School Phobia/School Refusal." *Psychology in the Schools*, 1984, *21*, 360–367.

Huesmann, L. R., and Eron, L. D. "Cognitive Processes and

the Persistence of Aggressive Behavior." *Aggressive Behavior*, 1984, *10*, 243–251.

Hughes, H. M., and Haynes, S. N. "Structured Laboratory Observation in the Behavioral Assessment of Parent-Child Interactions: A Methodological Critique." *Behavior Therapy*, 1978, *9*, 428–447.

Hull, D. B., and Hull, J. H. "Assertiveness and Aggressiveness in Juvenile Offenders." *The Behavior Therapist*, 1983, *6*, 43–44.

Humphrey, L. L., Karoly, P., and Kirschenbaum, D. S. "Self-Management in the Classroom: Self-Imposed Response Cost Versus Self-Reward." *Behavior Therapy*, 1978, *9*, 592–601.

Humphreys, L., Forehand, R., McMahon, R., and Roberts, M. "Parent Behavioral Training to Modify Child Non-Compliance: Effects on Untreated Siblings." *Journal of Behavior Therapy and Experimental Psychology*, 1978, *9*, 235–238.

Humphries, T., Swanson, J., Kinsbourne, M., and Yiu, L. "Stimulant Effects on Persistence of Motor Performance of Hyperactive Children." *Journal of Pediatric Psychology*, 1979, *4*, 55–66.

Ince, L. P. "The Use of Relaxation Training and a Conditioned Stimulus in the Elimination of Epileptic Seizures in a Child: A Case Study." *Journal of Behavior Therapy and Experimental Psychology*, 1977, *8*, 305–307.

Israel, A. C. "Some Thoughts on Correspondence Between Saying and Doing." *Journal of Applied Behavior Analysis*, 1978, *11*, 271–275.

Jackson, A., and Hannon, P. *The Belfield Reading Project*. Rochdale, England: Belfield Community Council, 1981.

Jackson, M. *When a Child Steals: How to Prevent It and What to Do About It*. Hawthorne, Australia: Australian Council for Educational Research, 1984.

Jacobson, N. S., and Margolin, G. *Marital Therapy: Strategies Based on Social Learning and Behavior Exchange Principles*. New York: Brunner/Mazel, 1979.

Janis, J. L. "The Role of Social Support in Adherence to Stressful Decisions." *American Psychologist*, 1983, *38*, 143–160.

Jason, L. A., and Bogat, G. A. "Evaluating a Preventive Orientation Program." *Journal of Social Service Research*, 1983, *7*, 39–50.

Jason, L. A., Ginsburg, E., Rucker, W., Merbitz, C., Taban, D., and Harkness, M. "A Support System for Behavior Analysts in an Urban Area." *The Behavior Therapist*, 1985, *8*, 138–140.

Jastak, J. F., and Wilkinson, G. S. *Wide Range Achievement Test—Revised*. Wilmington, Del.: Jastak Associates, 1984.

Jayaprakash, S., Jung, J., and Panitch, D. "Multi-Factorial Assessment of Hospitalized Children Who Set Fires." *Child Welfare*, 1984, *58*, 74–78.

Jayaratne, S., and Levy, R. L. *Empirical Clinical Practice*. New York: Columbia University Press, 1979.

Jenkins, J., and Jenkins, L. "Peer Tutoring in Elementary and Secondary Programs." *Focus on Exceptional Children*, 1985, *17*, 1–12.

Jessor, R., and Jessor, S. L. *Problem Behavior and Psychosocial Development: A Longitudinal Study of Youth*. Orlando, Fla.: Academic Press, 1977.

Johnson, P. J., and Fried, B. J. "Implementation Dilemmas in North Carolina's Willie M. Program." *Child Welfare*, 1984, *63*, 419–430.

Johnson, S. M., and Eyberg, S. "Evaluating Outcome Data: A Reply to Gordon." *Journal of Consulting and Clinical Psychology*, 1975, *43*, 917–919.

Jones, R. T., and Ollendick, T. H. "Self-Reinforcement: An Assessment of External Influences." *Journal of Behavioral Assessment*, 1980, *1*, 289–303.

Justice, B., and Duncan, D. F. "Running Away: An Epidemic Problem of Adolescence." *Adolescence*, 1976, *11*, 365–371.

Juvenile Justice and Delinquency Prevention Act. Public Law 93-145, 88 Statute 1109. *United States Congressional and Administrative News*. 93rd Cong., 2nd sess., 1974, 1267–1301.

"Juveniles and Fire." *San Francisco Chronicle*, Nov. 1984.

Kadushin, A. *Consultation in Social Work*. New York: Columbia University Press, 1977.

Kaersvang, L. L., and Clark, P. M. *Inter-Agency Staffing Team: Help for Helping Troubled Adolescents*. Ann Arbor: School of Social Work and National Child Welfare Training Center, University of Michigan, 1982.

Kafry, D. *Fire Survival Skills: Who Plays with Matches?* Technical

Report for Pacific Southwest Forest and Range Experiment Station. Washington, D.C.: U.S. Department of Agriculture, 1978.

Kagan, J. *The Growth of the Child: Reflections on Human Development*. New York: Norton, 1978.

Kalfus, G. R. "Peer Mediated Intervention: A Critical Review." *Child and Family Behavior Therapy*, 1984, *6*, 17–43.

Kamerman, S. B., and Hayes, C. D. (eds.). *Families That Work: Children in a Changing Environment of Work, Family, and Community*. Cambridge, Mass.: Harvard University Press, 1979.

Kamerman, S. B., and Kahn, A. J. *Helping America's Families*. Philadelphia: Temple University Press, 1982.

Kandel, D. B., Raveis, V. H., and Kandel, P. I. "Continuity in Discontinuities: Adjustment in Young Adulthood of Former School Absentees." *Youth and Society*, 1984, *15*, 325–352.

Kanfer, F. H., and Grimm, L. G. "Behavioral Analysis: Selecting Target Behaviors in the Interview." *Behavior Modification*, 1977, *1*, 7–28.

Kanfer, F. H., and Grimm, L. G. "Freedom of Choice and Behavior Change." *Journal of Consulting and Clinical Psychology*, 1978, *46*, 873–878.

Kanfer, F. H., and Grimm, L. G. "Managing Clinical Change: A Process Model of Therapy." *Behavior Modification*, 1980, *4*, 419–444.

Kanfer, F. H., Karoly, P., and Newman, A. "Reduction of Children's Fear of the Dark by Competence-Related and Situational Threat-Related Verbal Cues." *Journal of Consulting and Clinical Psychology*, 1975, *43*, 251–258.

Kantor, D., and Lehr, W. *Inside the Family: Toward a Theory of Family Process*. San Francisco: Jossey-Bass, 1975.

Karoly, P. "Behavioral Self-Management in Children: Concepts, Methods, Issues, and Directions." In M. Hersen, R. M. Eisler, and P. Miller (eds.), *Progress in Behavior Modification*. Vol. 5. Orlando, Fla.: Academic Press, 1977.

Karoly, P. "Self-Management Problems in Children." In E. J. Mash and L. G. Terdal (eds.), *Behavioral Assessment of Childhood Disorders*. New York: Guilford, 1981.

Kaufman, A. S. *Intelligence Testing with the WISC-R*. New York: Wiley-Interscience, 1979.

Kaufman, L. M., and Wagner, B. R. "Barb: A Systematic Treatment Technology for Temper Control Disorders." *Behavior Therapy*, 1972, *3*, 84–90.

Kavale, K. A., and Glass, G. V. "The Efficacy of Special Education Interventions and Practices: A Compendium of Meta-Analysis Findings." *Focus on Exceptional Children*, 1982, *15*, 1–16.

Kazdin, A. E. "Response Cost: The Removal of Conditioned Reinforcers for Therapeutic Change." *Behavior Therapy*, 1972, *3*, 533–546.

Kazdin, A. E. "Drawing Valid Inferences from Case Studies." *Journal of Consulting and Clinical Psychology*, 1981, *49*, 183–192.

Kazdin, A. E. *Single-Case Research Designs: Methods for Clinical and Applied Settings*. New York: Oxford University Press, 1982.

Kazdin, A. E. "Psychiatric Diagnosis, Dimensions of Dysfunction, and Child Behavior Therapy." *Behavior Therapy*, 1983a, *14*, 73–99.

Kazdin, A. E. "Single-Case Research Design in Clinical Child Psychiatry." *Journal of the American Academy of Child Psychiatry*, 1983b, *22*, 423–432.

Kazdin, A. E. "Alternative Approaches to the Diagnosis of Childhood Disorders." In P. H. Bornstein and A. E. Kazdin (eds.), *Handbook of Clinical Behavior Therapy with Children*. Homewood, Ill.: Dorsey Press, 1985.

Kazdin, A. E., and Frame, C. "Aggressive Behavior and Conduct Disorder." In R. J. Morris and T. R. Kratochwill (eds.), *The Practice of Child Therapy*. Elmsford, N.Y.: Pergamon Press, 1983.

Keating, D. P. "Thinking Processes in Adolescence." In J. Adelson (ed.), *Handbook of Adolescent Psychology*. New York: Wiley, 1980.

Kellam, S., Adams, R., Brown, H., and Blank, G. "Consequences of Teenage Motherhood for Mother, Child, and Family in a Black Urban Community." Paper presented at the Workshop on Adolescent Pregnancy and Childrearing, National Institute of Child Development, Bethesda, Md., 1979.

Kellam, S. G., Ensminger, M. E., and Turner, R. J. "Family Structure and the Mental Health of Children." *Archives of General Psychiatry*, 1977, *34*, 1012–1022.

Kelly, E. W. "School Phobia: A Review of Theory and Treatment." *Psychology in the Schools*, 1973, *10*, 33–42.

Kendall, P. C. "On the Efficacious Use of Verbal Self-Instructional Procedures with Children." *Cognitive Therapy and Research*, 1977, *1*, 331–341.

Kendall, P. C. "Cognitive-Behavioral Interventions with Children." In B. B. Lahey and A. E. Kazdin (eds.), *Advances in Clinical Child Psychology*. Vol. 4. New York: Plenum, 1981.

Kendall, P. C. "Cognitive-Behavioral Interventions with Children: Further Needs." *The Behavior Therapist*, 1984, *7*, 169–171.

Kendall, P. C., and Braswell, L. "Cognitive-Behavioral Interventions with Children." Workshop presented at the Annual Meeting of the Association for the Advancement of Behavior Therapy, Los Angeles, Nov. 1982.

Kendall, P. C., and Braswell, L. *Cognitive-Behavioral Therapy for Impulsive Children*. New York: Guilford, 1985.

Kendall, P.C., Deardorff, P. A., and Finch, A. J. "Empathy and Socialization in First and Repeated Offenders and Normals." *Journal of Abnormal Child Psychology*, 1977, *5*, 93–97.

Kendall, P. C., and Fischler, G. L. "Behavioral Adjustment Correlates of Problem Solving: Validational Analyses of Interpersonal Cognitive Problem-Solving Measures." *Child Development*, 1984, *55*, 879–892.

Kendall, P. C., and Wilcox, L. E. "A Cognitive-Behavioral Treatment for Impulsivity: Concrete Versus Conceptual Training with Non-Self-Controlled Problem Children." *Journal of Consulting and Clinical Psychology*, 1980, *48*, 80–91.

Kendall, P. C., and Zupan, B. A. "Individual Versus Group Application of Cognitive-Behavioral Self-Control Procedures with Children." *Behavior Therapy*, 1981, *12*, 344–359.

Kennedy, R. E. "Cognitive Behavioral Approaches to the Modification of Aggressive Behavior in Children." *School Psychology Review*, 1982, *11*, 47–55.

Kennedy, W. A. "School Phobia: Rapid Treatment of Fifty Cases." *Journal of Abnormal Psychology*, 1965, *70*, 285–289.

Kent, R. N., and Foster, S. L. "Direct Observational Procedures: Methodological Issues in Naturalistic Settings." In A. R. Adams (ed.), *Handbook of Behavior Assessment*. New York: Wiley, 1977.

Kifer, R. E., Lewis, M. A., Green, D. R., and Phillips, E. L. "Training Predelinquent Youth and Their Parents to Negotiate Conflict Situations." *Journal of Applied Behavior Analysis*, 1974, *7*, 357–364.

King, C., and Young, R. D. "Attentional Deficits With and Without Hyperactivity: Teacher and Peer Perceptions." *Journal of Abnormal Child Psychology*, 1982, *10*, 483–495.

Kirigin, K. A., Braukman, C. J., Atwater, J. D., and Wolf, M. M. "An Evaluation of Teaching-Family (Achievement Place) Group Homes for Juvenile Offenders." *Journal of Applied Behavior Analysis*, 1982, *15*, 1–16.

Kirigan, K. A., Wolf, M. M., Braukman, C. J., Fixsen, D. L., and Phillips, E. L. "Achievement Place: A Preliminary Outcome Evaluation." In J. S. Stumphauzer (ed.), *Progress in Behavior Therapy with Delinquents*. Springfield, Ill.: Thomas, 1979.

Klier, J., Fein, E., and Genero, C. "Are Written or Verbal Contracts More Effective in Family Therapy?" *Social Work*, 1984, *29*, 298–299.

Kneedler, R. D., and Hallahan, D. P. "Self-Monitoring of On-Task Behavior with Learning-Disabled Children: Current Studies and Directions." *Exceptional Education Quarterly*, 1981, *2*, 73–82.

Knitzer, J., Allen, M., and McGowan, B. *Children Without Homes*. Washington, D.C.: Children's Defense Fund, 1978.

Koeppen, A. S. "Relaxation Training for Children." *Elementary School Guidance and Counseling*, 1974, *9*, 14–21.

Kogan, N. "Stylistic Variation in Childhood and Adolescence: Creativity, Metaphor, and Cognitive Styles." In P. H. Mussen (ed.), *Handbook of Child Psychology*. New York: Wiley, 1983.

Koles, M. R., and Jenson, W. R. "Comprehensive Treatment of Chronic Fire Setting in a Severely Disordered Boy." *Journal of Behavior Therapy and Experimental Psychiatry*, 1985, *16*, 81–85.

Kooker, E. "Changes in Grade Distributions Associated with Changes in Class Attendance Policies." *Psychology in the Schools*, 1976, *13*, 57–59.

Kosiewicz, M. M., Hallahan, D. E., Lloyd, J., and Graves, A. "Effects of Self-Instruction and Self-Correction Procedures on Handwriting Performance." *Learning Disability Quarterly*, 1982, *5*, 71–78.

Kosky, R. "Childhood Suicide Behavior." *Journal of Child Psychology and Psychiatry*, 1983, *24*, 457–468.

Kozloff, M. A. *A Program for Families of Children with Learning and Behavior Problems.* New York: Wiley, 1979.

Kraft, T. "Treatment of Compulsive Shoplifting by Altering Social Contingencies." *Behavior Research and Therapy*, 1970, *8*, 393–394.

Kreitman, N. (ed.). *Parasuicide.* New York: Wiley, 1977.

Kreitman, N., and Philip, A. E. "Parasuicide." *British Journal of Psychiatry*, 1969, *115*, 746–747.

Kuhnley, J., Hendren, R. L., and Quinlan, D. M. "Firesetting by Children." *Journal of the American Academy of Child Psychiatry*, 1982, *21*, 560–563.

Kurtz, P. D. "Identifying Handicapped Preschool Children." *Social Work in Education*, 1983, *5*, 221–228.

LaBarbera, J. D., and Lewis, S. "Fathers Who Undermine Children's Treatment: A Challenge for the Clinician." *Journal of Consulting and Clinical Child Psychology*, 1980, *9*, 204–206.

Ladd, G. "Effectiveness of a Social Learning Method for Enhancing Children's Social Interaction and Peer Acceptance." *Child Development*, 1981, *52*, 171–178.

Lahey, B., Gendrich, J., Gendrich, S., Schnelle, L., Gant, D., and McNee, P. "An Evaluation of Daily Report Cards with Minimal Teacher and Parent Contacts as an Efficient Method of Classroom Intervention." *Behavior Modification*, 1977, *1*, 381–394.

Lamb, M. E. "The Role of the Father: An Overview." In M. E. Lamb (ed.), *The Role of the Father in Child Development.* New York: Wiley, 1976.

Lamb, M. E. "Influence of the Child on Marital Quality and Family Interaction During the Prenatal, Perinatal, and Infancy Periods." In R. M. Levine and G. G. Spanier (eds.), *Children's Influences on Marital and Family Interaction: A Life-Span Perspective.* Orlando, Fla.: Academic Press, 1978.

Lambert, N. M. "Children's Problems and Classroom Interventions from the Perspective of Classroom Teachers." *Professional Psychology*, 1976, *7*, 507–517.

Lambert, N. M. "Temperament Profiles of Hyperactive Children." *American Journal of Orthopsychiatry*, 1982, *52*, 458–467.

Lambert, N., and Sandoval, J. "The Prevalence of Learning Disabilities in a Sample of Children Considered Hyperactive." *Journal of Abnormal Child Psychology*, 1980, *8*, 33–50.

Lancaster, J. *Improvements in Education as It Respects the Industrious Classes of the Community.* London: Darton & Harvey, 1803.

Landau, S. F. "Future Time Perspective of Delinquents and Non-Delinquents." *Criminal Justice and Behavior*, 1975, *2*, 22–29.

Lassers, E., Nordan, R., and Bladholm, S. "Steps in the Return to School of Children with School Phobia." *American Journal of Psychiatry*, 1973, *130*, 265–268.

Laub, J. H. "Trends in Serious Juvenile Crime." *Criminal Justice and Behavior*, 1983, *10*, 485–506.

Lavigne, V. V., and Novak, J. "Insights from Behavior Therapy: A Case Study Combining Behavioral and Psychoanalytic Therapies." *Psychotherapy: Theory, Research and Practice*, 1981, *18*, 74–80.

Lawry, J. A., Welsh, M. C., and Jeffrey, W. E. "Cognitive Tempo and Complex Problem Solving." *Child Development*, 1983, *54*, 912–920.

Lazarus, A. A. "The Elimination of Children's Fears by Deconditioning." In H. J. Eysenck (ed.), *Behavior Therapy and the Neuroses.* Elmsford, N. Y.: Pergamon Press, 1960.

Lazarus, A. A., Davison, G. C., and Polefka, D. A. "Classical and Operant Factors in the Treatment of School Phobia." *Journal of Abnormal Psychology*, 1965, *70*, 225–229.

Ledwidge, B. "Cognitive Behavior Modification: A Step in the Wrong Direction?" *Psychological Bulletin*, 1978, *85*, 353–375.

Lee, G. R. "Effects of Social Networks on the Family." In W. Burr, R. Hill, F. E. Nye, and I. L. Russ (eds.), *Contemporary*

Theories of the Family: Research-Based Theories. Vol. 1. New York: Free Press, 1979.

Leighton, D. C. "Community Integration and Mental Health: Documenting Social Change Through Longitudinal Research." In R. F. Muñoz, L. R. Snowden, J. G. Kelley, and Associates, *Social and Psychological Research in Community Settings.* San Francisco: Jossey-Bass, 1979.

Leinhardt, G., and Pallay, A. "Restrictive Educational Settings: Exile or Haven?" *Review of Educational Research*, 1982, *52*, 557–578.

Leon, J. A., and Pepe, H. J. "Self-Instructional Training: Cognitive Behavior Modification for Remediating Arithmetic Deficits." *Exceptional Children*, 1983, *50*, 54–60.

Leton, D. A. "Assessment of School Phobia." *Mental Hygiene*, 1962, *46*, 256–264.

Levine, M., and Levine, A. *A Social History of Helping Settings.* East Norwalk, Conn.: Appleton-Century-Crofts, 1970.

Leviton, L. C., and Cook, T. D. "Evaluation Findings in Education and Social Work Textbooks." *Evaluation Review*, 1983, *7*, 497–518.

Levitt, E. E. "Research on Psychotherapy with Children." In A. E. Bergin and S. L. Garfield (eds.), *Handbook of Psychotherapy and Behavior Change.* New York: Wiley, 1971.

Lewis, N., and Yarnell, H. *Pathological Fire Setting.* Nervous and Mental Disease Monographs, No. 82. New York: Coolidge Foundations, 1951.

Liberman, R. P., and Eckman, T. "Behavior Therapy vs. Insight-Oriented Therapy for Repeated Suicide Attempters. *Archives of General Psychiatry*, 1981, *38*, 1126–1130.

Liem, R., and Rayman, P. "Health and Social Costs of Unemployment." *American Psychologist*, 1982, *37*, 1116–1123.

Lindenbaum, S., and Clark, D. "Toward an Integrative Approach to Psychotherapy with Children." *American Journal of Orthopsychiatry*, 1983, *53*, 449–459.

Lloyd, J., Epstein, M., and Cullinan, D. "Direct Teaching for Learning Disabilities." In J. Gottlieb and S. F. Strickhart (eds.), *Current Theories and Research in Learning Disabilities.* Baltimore, Md.: University Park Press, 1981.

Lloyd, R. *For Money or Love: Boy Prostitution in America.* New York: Vanguard Press, 1976.

Lobitz, G. K., and Johnson, S. M. "Normal Versus Deviant Children: A Multimethod Comparison." *Journal of Abnormal Child Psychology*, 1975, *3*, 353–374.

Lochman, J. E., Nelson, W. M., III, and Sims, J. P. "A Cognitive Behavioral Program for Use with Aggressive Children." *Journal of Child Psychology*, 1981, *10*, 146–148.

Loeber, R. "The Stability of Antisocial and Delinquent Child Behavior: A Review." *Child Development*, 1982, *53*, 1431–1446.

Loeber, R., and Dishion, T. "Early Predictors of Male Delinquency: A Review." *Psychological Bulletin*, 1983, *94*, 68–99.

Loeber, R., Weissman, W., and Reid, J. B. "Family Interactions of Assaultive Adolescents, Stealers, and Nondelinquents." *Journal of Abnormal Child Psychology*, 1983, *11*, 1–14.

Lourie, I. S., Campiglia, P., James, L. R., and DeWitt, J. "Adolescent Abuse and Neglect: The Role of Runaway Programs." *Children Today*, 1979, *8*, 27–40.

Lovaas, O. I. *The Autistic Child: Language Development Through Behavior Modification.* New York: Irvington, 1977.

Lovaas, O. I., Young, D. B., and Newsom, C. D. "Childhood Psychosis: Behavioral Treatment." In B. B. Wolman, J. Egan, and A. O. Ross (eds.), *Handbook of Treatment of Mental Disorders in Childhood and Adolescence.* Englewood Cliffs, N.J.: Prentice-Hall, 1978.

Luiselli, J. K., and Greenidge, A. "Behavioral Treatment of High-Rate Aggression in a Rubella Child." *Journal of Behavior Therapy and Experimental Psychiatry*, 1982, *13*, 152–157.

Lutzker, J. R. "Project 12-Ways: Treating Child Abuse and Neglect from an Ecobehavioral Perspective." In R. F. Dangel and R. A. Polster (eds.), *Parent Training: Foundations of Research and Practice.* New York: Guilford, 1984.

Lutzker, J. R., McGimsey, J. F., McRae, S., and Campbell, R. V. "Behavioral Parent Training: There's So Much to Do." *Behavior Therapy*, 1983, *6*, 110–112.

Lysaght, T. V., and Burchard, J. D. "The Analysis and Modification of a Deviant Parent Youth Communication Pattern."

Journal of Behavior Therapy and Experimental Psychiatry, 1975, *6*, 339–342.

McCord, J. "A 30-Year Follow-Up Study of Treatment Effects." *American Psychologist*, 1978, *33*, 284–289.

McCord, W., McCord, J., and Howard, A. "Familial Correlates of Aggression in Nondelinquent Male Children." *Journal of Abnormal Social Psychology*, 1961, *62*, 79–93.

McCord, W., and Sanchez, J. "The Treatment of Deviant Children: A Twenty-Five Year Follow-Up Study." *Crime and Delinquency*, 1983, *39*, 238–253.

McCulloch, D. "No Excuses Wanted—or Needed." *School Management*, 1974, *18*, 28–29.

McDonald, J. E., and Shepperd, G. "School Phobia: An Overview." *Journal of School Psychology*, 1976, *14*, 291–306.

Macfarlane, J. W., Allen, L., and Honzik, M. P. *Developmental Study of the Behavior Problems of Normal Children Between Twenty-One Months and Fourteen Years.* Berkeley and Los Angeles: University of California Press, 1954.

McGrath, P., Marshall, P. G., and Prior, K. "A Comprehensive Treatment Program for a Firesetting Child." *Behavior Therapy and Experimental Psychiatry*, 1979, *10*, 69–72.

McHenry, S. "Sister-to-Sister: 'We're About Navigation Systems.'" *Ms.*, 1980, *9*, 63.

Macht, L. B., and Mack, J. E. "The Firesetter Syndrome." *Psychiatry*, 1968, *31*, 277.

McIntire, M. S., and Angle, C. R. "Psychological 'Biopsy' in Self-Poisoning of Children and Adolescents." *American Journal of Diseases of Children*, 1972, *126*, 42–46.

McIntire, M. S., Angle, C. R., Wikoff, R. L., and Schlict, M. L. "Recurrent Adolescent Suicidal Behavior." *Pediatrics*, 1977, *60*, 605–608.

McLean, P. "Parental Depression: Incompatible with Effective Parenting." In E. J. Mash, L. C. Handy, and L. A. Hamerlynck (eds.), *Behavior Modification Approaches to Parenting.* New York: Brunner/Mazel, 1976.

McMahon, R. J., and Forehand, R. L. "Consumer Satisfaction in Behavioral Treatment of Children: Types, Issues, and Recommendations." *Behavior Therapy*, 1983, *14*, 209–225.

McMahon, R. J., and Forehand, R. "Parenting Training for the Noncompliant Child: Treatment Outcome, Generalization, and Adjunctive Therapy Procedures." In R. F. Dangel and R. A. Polster (eds.), *Parent Training: Foundations of Research and Practice*. New York: Guilford, 1984.

MacMillan, D. *Mental Retardation in School and Society*. Boston: Little, Brown, 1982.

McMullin, R., and Casey, B. *Talk Sense to Yourself: A Guide to Cognitive Restructuring Therapy*. Lakewood, Colo.: Counseling Research Institute, 1975.

McNees, M. P., Kennon, M., Schnelle, J. F., Kirchner, R. E., and Thomas, M. M. "An Experimental Analysis of a Program to Reduce Retail Theft." *American Journal of Community Psychology*, 1980, *8*, 379–385.

Madden, N. A., and Slavin, R. E. "Mainstreaming Students with Mild Handicaps: Academic and Social Outcomes." *Review of Educational Research*, 1983, *53*, 519–569.

Maher, C. A., and Barbrack, C. R. "Preventing High School Maladjustment: Effectiveness of Professional and Cross-Age Behavioral Group Counseling." *Behavior Therapy*, 1982, *13*, 259–270.

Mahoney, M. J. "Psychotherapy and the Structure of Personal Revolutions." In M. J. Mahoney (ed.), *Psychotherapy Process*. New York: Plenum, 1980.

Mahoney, M. J., and Arnkoff, D. "Cognitive and Self-Control Therapies." In S. L. Garfield and A. E. Bergin (eds.), *Handbook of Psychotherapy and Behavior Change: An Empirical Analysis*. (2nd ed.) New York: Wiley, 1978.

Malbon, L. C., and Nuttall, R. L. "A Promising Approach to Absenteeism in the Secondary School." *Phi Delta Kappan*, 1982, *64*, 66–67.

Maloney, D. M., Surber, R. R., Fixsen, D. L., and Phillips, E. L. "The Teaching-Family Model: Working with Runaways." *Journal of Family Issues*, 1980, *1*, 304–307.

Mann, L., and Sabatino, D. A. *Foundations of Cognitive Process in Remedial and Special Education*. Rockville, Md.: Aspen Systems Corporation, 1985.

Marlatt, G. A., and Gordon, J. R. "Determinants of Relapse:

Implications for the Maintenance of Behavior Change." In P. O. Davidson and S. M. Davidson (eds.), *Behavioral Medicine: Changing Health Lifestyles*. New York: Brunner/Mazel, 1980.

Mash, E. J., and Johnston, C. "Parental Perceptions of Child Behavior Problems, Parenting Self-Esteem, and Mother's Reported Stress in Younger and Older Hyperactive and Normal Children." *Journal of Consulting and Clinical Psychology*, 1983, *51*, 86–99.

Mash, E. J., and Terdal, L. G. "Behavioral Assessment of Childhood Disturbance." In E. J. Mash and L. G. Terdal (eds.), *Behavioral Assessment of Childhood Disorders*. New York: Guilford, 1981.

Masters, J. C., and Santrock, J. W. "Studies in the Self-Regulation of Behavior: Effects of Contingent Cognitive and Affective Events." *Developmental Psychology*, 1976, *12*, 234–348.

Matson, J. L., Coleman, D., DiLorenzo, T. M., and Vucelic, I. "Eliminating Stealing in Developmentally Disabled Children." *Child Behavior Therapy*, 1981, *2/3*, 57–66.

Matson, J. L., and Ollendick, T. H. "Elimination of Low Frequency Biting." *Behavior Therapy*, 1976, *7* (3), 410–412.

Mayer, G. R., Butterworth, T., Nafpaktitis, M., and Sulzer-Azaroff, B. "Preventing School Vandalism and Improving Discipline: A Three-Year Study." *Journal of Applied Behavior Analysis*, 1983, *16*, 355–369.

Mayer, J. E., and Timms, N. *The Client Speaks: Working Class Impressions of Casework*. New York: Atherton, 1970.

Meador, A. E., and Ollendick, T. H. "Cognitive Behavior Therapy with Children: An Evaluation of Its Efficacy and Clinical Utility." *Child and Family Behavior Therapy*, 1984, *6*, 25–44.

Medical World News. Apr. 19, 1984.

Medway, F. J., and Forman, S. G. "Psychologists' and Teachers' Reactions to Mental Health and Behavioral School Consultation." *Journal of School Psychology*, 1980, *18*, 338–348.

Mehren, E. "Firehawks Curb Juvenile Arson." *Daily Californian*, May 3, 1984, pp. 3, 7, 10.

Meichenbaum, D. *Cognitive Behavior Modification*. New York: Plenum, 1977.

Meichenbaum, D. "Teaching Children Self-Control." In B. B. Lahey and A. E. Kazdin (eds.), *Advances in Clinical Child Psychology*. Vol. 2. New York: Plenum, 1979.

Meichenbaum, D. H., and Goodman, J. "Training Impulsive Children to Talk to Themselves: A Means of Developing Self-Control." *Journal of Abnormal Psychology*, 1971, *77*, 115–126.

Mercer, J. "In Defense of Racially and Culturally Nondiscriminatory Assessment." *School Psychology Digest*, 1979, *8*, 89–115.

Mercer, J. R. "What Is a Racially and Culturally Nondiscriminatory Test? A Sociological and Pluralistic Perspective." In C. R. Reynolds and R. T. Brown (eds.), *Perspectives on Bias in Mental Testing*. New York: Plenum, 1984.

Michelson, L., Foster, S. L., and Ritchey, W. L. "Social Skills Assessment of Children." In B. B. Lahey and A. E. Kazdin (eds.), *Advances in Clinical Child Psychology*. Vol. 4. New York: Plenum, 1981.

Mickler, M. J. "Self-Management Skill Training for Educable Mentally Retarded Persons." *Journal of Special Education*, 1984, *18*, 143–149.

Milburn, M. A. "Theories of Aggression: A Critique and Possible Reformulation." *Human Relations*, 1980, *33*, 353–368.

Minuchin, M. D. "Reflections on Boundaries." *American Journal of Orthopsychiatry*, 1982, *52*, 655–663.

Minuchin, S., and Fischman, H. C. *Family Therapy Techniques*. Cambridge, Mass.: Harvard University Press, 1981.

Mischel, W. "Delay of Gratification as Process and as Person Variable in Development." In D. Magnussen and V. P. Allen (eds.), *Human Development: An Interactional Perspective*. Orlando, Fla.: Academic Press, 1983.

Mischel, W., and Peake, P. K. "Beyond Déjà Vu in the Search for Cross-Situational Consistency." *Psychological Review*, 1982, *89*, 730–755.

Mitchell, S., and Rosa, P. "Boyhood Behavior Problems as Precursors of Criminality: A Fifteen-Year Follow-Up Study." *Journal of Child Psychology and Psychiatry*, 1981, *22*, 19–33.

Moffitt, T. E. "The Learning Theory Model of Punishment: Implications for Delinquency Deterrence." *Criminal Justice and Behavior*, 1983, *10*, 131–158.

Moler, H. J. "Psychopathology of Stealing Acts Without Substantial Personal Enrichment." *Archives of Psychiatry and Neurological Science*, 1977, *223*, 323-336.

Moon, J. R., and Eisler, R. M. "Anger Control: An Experimental Comparison of Three Behavioral Treatments." *Behavior Therapy*, 1983, *14*, 493-505.

Moore, D., Chamberlain, P., and Mukai, L. "Children at Risk for Delinquency: A Follow-Up Comparison of Aggressive Children and Children Who Steal." *Journal of Abnormal Child Psychology*, 1979, *7*, 345-355.

Moore-Kirkland, J., and Irey, K. V. "A Reappraisal of Confidentiality." *Social Work*, 1981, *26*, 319-322.

Morgan, H. G. *Death Wishes? The Understanding and Management of Deliberate Self-Harm*. New York: Wiley, 1979.

Morgan, R. R. "An Exploratory Study of Three Procedures to Encourage School Attendance." *Psychology in the Schools*, 1975, *12*, 209-215.

Morris, G. T. "The Truant." *Today's Education*, 1979, *47*, 41-42.

Morris, R. J., and Kratochwill, T. R. *Treating Children's Fears and Phobias: A Behavioral Approach*. Elmsford, N.Y.: Pergamon Press, 1983.

Morris, W. (ed.). *The American Heritage Dicitonary of the English Language*. Boston: American Heritage, 1969.

Morton, T. D., and Kurtz, P. D. "Educational Supervision: A Learning Theory Approach." *Social Casework*, 1980, *61*, 240-246.

Motto, J. A. "Treatment Concerns in Preventing Youth Suicide." In M. L. Peck, N. L. Farberow, and R. E. Litman (eds.), *Youth Suicide*. New York: Springer, 1985.

Mulvey, E. P., and Hicks, A. "The Paradoxical Effect of a Juvenile Code Change in Virginia." *American Journal of Community Psychology*, 1982, *10*, 705-721.

National Association of Social Workers. "Code of Ethics." In *1983-84 Supplement to the Encyclopedia of Social Work*. (17th ed.) Silver Spring, Md.: National Association of Social Workers, 1983.

National Center for Health Statistics. "Advance Report of Final Natality Statistics." *Monthly Vital Statistics Report*, 1981, *31*, 1-27.

National Indian Child Welfare Act. Public Law 95-608, 25 U.S.C. Sec. 1901. Washington, D.C.: U.S. Government Printing Office, 1978.

Neale, J. M., and Weintraub, S. "Children Vulnerable to Psychopathology: The Stony Brook High-Risk Project." *Journal of Abnormal Child Psychology*, 1975, *3*, 95–113.

Neilans, T. H., and Israel, A. C. "Towards Maintenance and Generalization of Behavior Change: Teaching Children Self-Regulation and Self-Instructional Skills." *Cognitive Therapy and Research*, 1981, *5*, 189–196.

Nelsen, J. C. "Intermediate Treatment Goals as Variables in Single-Case Research." *Social Work Research and Abstracts*, 1984, *20*, 3–10.

Nelson, W., and Birkimer, J. S. "Role of Self-Instruction and Self-Reinforcement in the Modification of Impulsivity." *Journal of Consulting and Clinical Psychology*, 1978, *46*, 183.

Neuhring, R. E. E. "Convicted Auto Theft Offenders: An Investigation of a Behaviorally Defined Offender Group." *Dissertation Abstracts International*, Part B: *Sciences*, 1976, *37*, 3622–3623.

Nidiffer, F. D. "Combining Cognitive and Behavioral Approaches to Suicidal Depression: A 42-Month Follow-Up." *Psychological Reports*, 1980, *47*, 539–542.

Norcross, J. S., and Prochaska, J. O. "A National Survey of Clinical Psychologists: Affiliations and Orientations." *The Clinical Psychologist*, 1982, *35*, 1, 4–6.

Novaco, R. W. *Anger Control: The Development and Evaluation of an Experimental Treatment.* Lexington, Mass.: Heath, 1975.

Oden, M. H. "The Fulfillment of Promise: 40-Year Follow-Up of the Terman Gifted Group." *Genetic Psychology Monographs*, 1968, *77*, 3–95.

O'Leary, K. D., and Turkewitz, H. "Methodological Errors in Marital and Child Treatment Research." *Journal of Consulting and Clinical Psychology*, 1978, *46*, 747–758.

O'Leary, S. G., and Dubey, D. R. "Applications of Self-Control Procedures by Children: A Review." *Journal of Applied Behavior Analysis*, 1979, *12*, 449–465.

Ollendick, T. H. "Behavioral Treatment of Anorexia Nervosa:

A Five-Year Study." *Behavior Modification*, 1981, *5*, 75–84.

Ollendick, T. H., and Cerny, J. A. *Clinical Behavior Therapy with Children*. New York: Plenum, 1981.

Ollendick, T. H., Elliott, W., and Matson, J. L. "Locus of Control as Related to Effectiveness in a Behavior Modification Program for Juvenile Delinquents." *Journal of Behavior Therapy and Experimental Psychology*, 1980, *11*, 259–262.

Ollendick, T. H., and Hersen, M. (eds.). *Child Behavioral Assessment: Principles and Procedures*. Elmsford, N.Y.: Pergamon Press, 1984.

Ollendick, T. H., and Matson, J. L. "Overcorrection: An Overview." *Behavior Therapy*, 1978, *9*, 830–842.

Olson, L., Leibow, E., Mannino, F. V., and Shore, M. F. "Runaway Children Twelve Years Later: A Follow-Up." *Journal of Family Issues*, 1980, *1*, 165–188.

Olweus, D. "Stability of Aggressive Reaction Patterns in Males: A Review." *Psychological Bulletin*, 1979, *86*, 852–875.

Olweus, D. "Familial and Temperamental Determinants of Aggressive Behavior in Adolescent Boys: A Causal Analysis." *Developmental Psychology*, 1980, *16*, 644–660.

Opinion Research Corporation. *National Statistical Survey of Runaway Youth*. Princeton, N.J.: Opinion Research Corp., 1976.

Oppel, W. C., Harper, P. A., and Ryder, R. V. "The Age of Obtaining Bladder Control." *Pediatrics*, 1968, *42*, 614–626.

Orbach, I., Gross, Y., and Glaubman, H. "Some Common Characteristics of Latency-Aged Suicidal Children: A Tentative Model Based on Case Study Analyses." *Suicide and Life Threatening Behavior*, 1981, *11*, 180–190.

Orten, J. D., and Soll, S. K. "Runaway Children and Their Families: A Treatment Typology." *Journal of Family Issues*, 1980, *1*, 249–261.

Ostensen, K. W. "The Runaway Crisis: Is Family Therapy the Answer?" *American Journal of Family Therapy*, 1981, *9*, 3–12.

Palmer, J. O. *The Psychological Assessment of Children*. (2nd ed.) New York: Wiley, 1983.

Pany, D., and Jenkins, J. R. "Learning Word Meanings: A Comparison of Instructional Procedures." *Learning Disability Quarterly*, 1978, *1*, 21–32.

Parke, R. D. "Rules, Roles, and Resistance to Deviation: Recent Advances in Punishment, Discipline, and Self-Control." In A. D. Pick (ed.), *Minnesota Symposia on Child Psychology.* Vol. 8. Minneapolis: University of Minnesota Press, 1975.

Parker, F. C., and McCoy, J. F. "School-Based Intervention for the Modification of Excessive Absenteeism." *Psychology in the Schools,* 1977, *14,* 84–88.

Parloff, M. B. "Who Will Be Satisfied by 'Consumer Satisfaction' Evidence?" *Behavior Therapy,* 1983, *14,* 242–246.

Parsons, L. R., and Heward, W. L. "Training Peers to Tutor: Evaluation of a Tutor Training Package for Primary Learning Disabled Students." *Journal of Applied Behavior Analysis,* 1979, *12,* 309–310.

Patterson, G. R. *Families.* Champaign, Ill.: Research Press, 1975.

Patterson, G. R. "The Aggressive Child: Victim and Architect of a Coercive System." In E. J. Mash, L. C. Handy, and L. A. Hamerlynck (eds.), *Behavior Modification and Families: Theory and Research.* Vol. 1. New York: Brunner/Mazel, 1976a.

Patterson, G. R. *Living with Children: New Methods for Parents and Teachers.* (3rd ed.) Champaign, Ill.: Research Press, 1976b.

Patterson, G. R. "Mothers: The Unacknowledged Victims." *Monographs of the Society for Research in Child Development,* 1980, *45* (Serial no. 186), 1–64.

Patterson, G. R. *A Social Learning Approach.* Vol. 3: *Coercive Family Process.* Eugene, Ore.: Castalia, 1982.

Patterson, G. R., and Reid, J. B. "Intervention for Families of Aggressive Boys: A Replication Study." *Behavior Research and Therapy,* 1973, *11,* 383–394.

Patterson, G. R., Reid, J. B., Jones, R. R., and Conger, R. E. *Families with Aggressive Children: A Social Learning Approach to Family Intervention.* Vol. 1. Eugene, Ore.: Castalia, 1975.

Patti, R. J., and Resnick, H. "Changing the Agency from Within." *Social Work,* 1972, *17,* 48–57.

Pearlin, L. I., and Schooler, C. "The Structure of Coping." *Journal of Health and Social Behavior,* 1978, *19,* 2–21.

Pearson, R. E. "Personal Support System Survey (Adult IA)." Unpublished manuscript, Department of Psychology, Syracuse University, 1981.

Peck, M. L. "Crisis Intervention Treatment with Chronically and Acutely Suicidal Adolescents." In M. L. Peck, N. L. Farberow, and R. E. Litman (eds.), *Youth Suicide*. New York: Springer, 1985.

Peck, M. L., Farberow, N. L., and Litman, R. E. (eds.). *Youth Suicide*. New York: Springer, 1985.

Peirce, N. "Houston: Urban School Districts Can Succeed." *San Francisco Chronicle*, Oct. 2, 1983, p. B9.

Pelton, L. H. (ed.). *The Social Context of Child Abuse and Neglect*. New York: Human Sciences Press, 1981.

Pennekamp, M., and Sarvis, M. A. *Collaboration in School Guidance: A Creative Approach to Pupil Personnel Work*. New York: Brunner/Mazel, 1974.

Perlman, H. H. *Relationship: The Heart of Helping People*. Chicago: University of Chicago Press, 1979.

Petti, T. A. "Depression and Withdrawal in Children." In T. H. Ollendick and M. Hersen (eds.), *Handbook of Child Psychopathology*. New York: Plenum, 1983.

Pfeffer, C. R. "Suicidal Behavior of Children: A Review with Implications for Research and Practice." *American Journal of Psychiatry*, 1981, *138*, 154–159.

Pfeffer, C. R., Conte, H. R., Plutchik, R., and Jarrett, I. "Suicide Behavior in Latecy-Age Children: An Outpatient Population." *Journal of the American Academy of Child Psychiatry*, 1980, *19*, 703–710.

Pfeffer, C. R., Plutchik, R., and Mizruchi, M. "Predictions of Assaultiveness in Latency Age Children." *American Journal of Psychiatry*, 1983, *140*, 31–35.

Pfeiffer, S. I. "A School Psychologist's Use of Behavior Therapy in a High School Setting." *Psychology in the Schools*, 1977, *14*, 40–44.

Phillips, D., and Wolpe, S. "Multiple Behavioral Techniques in Severe Separation Anxiety of a Twelve-Year-Old." *Journal of Behavior Therapy and Experimental Psychiatry*, 1981, *12*, 329–332.

Phillips, E. L., Fixsen, D. L., Phillips, E. A., and Wolf, M. M. "The Teaching Family Model: A Comprehensive Approach to Residential Treatment of Youth." In D. Cullinan and M. H. Epstein (eds.), *Special Education for Adolescents: Issues and Perspectives*. Westerville, Ohio: Merrill, 1979.

Phillips, E. L., Phillips, E. A., Fixsen, D. L., and Wolf, M. M. *The Teaching-Family Handbook*. (Rev. ed.) Lawrence: University of Kansas, 1974.

Phillips, R. H. "Increasing Positive Self-Referent Statements to Improve Self-Esteem in Low Income Elementary School Children." *Journal of School Psychology*, 1984, *22*, 155–163.

Piaget, J. *The Moral Judgement of the Child*. New York: Free Press, 1954.

Piccione, P. M., and Barth, R. P. "Sleep: An Expanding Area of Practice and Research." *Social Work*, 1983, *28*, 228–233.

Piersel, W. C., and Gutkin, T. B. "Resistance to School-Based Consultation: A Behavioral Analysis of the Problem." *Psychology in the Schools*, 1983, *20*, 311–320.

Pilgrim, C. W. "Pyromania-So-Called." *American Journal of Insanity*, 1884–1885, *41*, 457.

Pincus, A., and Minahan, A. *Social Work Practice: Model and Method*. Itasca, Ill.: Peacock, 1973.

Pines, M. "Aggression: The Violence Within." *Science Digest*, 1985, *93* (7), 36–39, 68.

Platt, J. E., Campbell, M., Green, W. H., and Grega, D. M. "Cognitive Effects of Lithium Carbonate and Holoperidol in Treatment-Resistant Aggressive Children." *Archives of General Psychiatry*, 1984, *120*, 657–662.

Platt, J. E., Campbell, M., Green, W. H., Perry, R., and Cohen, I. L. "Effects of Lithium Carbonate and Haloperidol on Cognition in Aggressive Hospitalized School-Aged Children." *Journal of Clinical Psychopharmacology*, 1981, *1*, 8–13.

Polster, R. A., Lynch, M. A., and Pinkston, E. M. "Reaching Underachievers." In S. P. Schinke (ed.), *Behavioral Methods in Social Welfare*. Hawthorne, N.Y.: Aldine, 1981.

Powell, D. R. "Social Network and Demographic Predictors of Length of Participation in a Parent Education Program." *Journal of Community Psychology*, 1984, *12*, 13–20.

Prater, J. S., Wolter, C. F., and Clement, P. W. "Setting Generalization During Self-Reinforcement with Educationally Handicapped Children." *Child and Family Behavior Therapy*, 1982, *4*, 25–40.

Presser, H. B. "Sally's Corner: Coping with Unmarried Motherhood." *Journal of Social Issues*, 1980, *36*, 107–129.

Pressley, M. "Increasing Children's Self Control Through Cognitive Interventions." *Review of Educational Research*, 1979, *49*, 319–370.

Prinz, R. J. "The Assessment of Parent-Adolescent Relations: Discriminating Distressed and Non-Distressed Dyads." Unpublished doctoral dissertation, Department of Psychology, State University of New York at Stony Brook, 1976.

Prinz, R. J., Foster, S., Kent, R. N., and O'Leary, K. D. "Multivariate Assessment of Conflict in Distressed and Non-Distressed Mother-Adolescent Dyads." *Journal of Applied Behavior Analysis*, 1979, *4*, 691–700.

Puig-Antich, J., Perel, J. M., Lupatkin, W., Chambers, W. J., Shea, C., Tabrazi, M. A., and Stiller, R. L. "Plasma Levels of Imipramine (IMI) and Desmethylimipramine (DMI) in Clinical Response to Prepubertal Major Depressive Disorder: A Preliminary Report." *Journal of the American Academy of Child Psychiatry*, 1979, *18*, 616–627.

Quay, H. C., and Peterson, D. R. *Manual for the Behavior Problem Checklist*. Highland Park, N.J.: H. C. Quay and D. R. Peterson, 1979.

Rapoport, J. L., Bushbaum, M. S., Weingartner, H., Zahn, T. P., Ludlow, C., and Mikkelsen, E. J. "Dextroamphetamine: Its Cognitive and Behavioral Effect in Normal and Hyperactive Boys and Normal Men." *Archives of General Psychiatry*, 1980, *37*, 933–943.

Rapoport, J. L., and Ismond, D. R. *DSM-III Training Guide for Diagnosis of Childhood Disorders*. New York: Brunner/Mazel, 1984.

Rappaport, J., Seidman, F., and Davidson, W. S., II. "Demonstration Research and Manifest Versus True Adoption: The Natural History of a Research Project to Divert Adolescents from the Legal System." In R. F. Muñoz, L. R. Snowden, J. G. Kelly, and Associates, *Social and Psychological Research in Community Settings*. San Francisco: Jossey-Bass, 1979.

Rapport, M. D. "Hyperactivity and Stimulant Treatment: Abusus Non Tollit Usum." *Behavior Therapy*, 1984, *7*, 133–134.

Rehm, L. P., Fuchs, C. Z., Roth, D. M., Kornblith, S. J., and Romano, J. M. "A Comparison of Self-Control and Assertion Skills Treatment of Depression." *Behavior Therapy*, 1979, *10*, 429–442.

Reid, J. B. "Behavioral Approaches to Intervention and Assessment with Child-Abusive Families." In P H. Bornstein and A. E. Kazdin (eds.), *Handbook of Clinical Behavior Therapy with Children*. Homewood, Ill.: Dorsey Press, 1985.

Reid, J. B., and Hendriks, A. F. C. J. "Preliminary Analysis of the Effectiveness of Direct Home Intervention for the Treatment of Predelinquent Boys Who Steal." In L. A. Hamerlynck, L. C. Handy, and E. J. Mash (eds.), *Behavior Change*. Champaign, Ill.: Research Press, 1973.

Reid, J. B., and Patterson, G. R. "The Modification of Aggression and Stealing Behavior of Boys in the Home Settings." In A. Bandura and E. Ribes (eds.), *Behavioral Modification: Experimental Analyses of Aggression and Delinquency*. Hillsdale, N.J.: Erlbaum, 1976.

Reid, W. J. *The Task Centered System*. New York: Columbia University Press, 1978.

Reid, W. J. "Family Treatment Within a Task-Centered Framework." In E. R. Tolson and W. J. Reid (eds.), *Models of Family Treatment*. New York: Columbia University Press, 1981.

Reid, W. J., and Epstein, L. *Task-Centered Casework*. New York: Columbia University Press, 1972.

Renshaw, D. C. "Stealing and School." *The Pointer*, 1977, *21*, 9–13.

Repp, A. C., and Deitz, D. "On the Selective Use of Punishment: Suggested Guidelines for Administrators." *Mental Retardation*, 1978, *16*, 250–254.

Repucci, N. D. "Implementation Issues for the Behavior Modifier as Institutional Change Agent." *Behavior Therapy*, 1977, *8*, 594–605.

Reschly, D. J., and Lamprecht, M. J. "Expectancy Effects of Labels: Fact or Artifact?" *Exceptional Children*, 1979, *46*, 55–58.

Reynolds, C. R. "Issues of Cultural Bias in the Assessment of Minority Handicapped Children." In C. R. Reynolds and J. H. Clark (eds.), *Assessment and Programming for Young Children with Low-Incidence Handicaps*. New York: Plenum, 1983.

Richard, B. A., and Dodge, K. A. "Social Maladjustment and Problem Solving in School-Aged Children." *Journal of Consulting and Clinical Psychology*, 1982, *2*, 226–233.

Richman, J. "The Family Therapy of Attempted Suicide." *Family Process*, 1979, *18*, 131–142.

Richter, N. C. "The Efficacy of Relaxation Training with Children." *Journal of Abnormal Child Psychology*, 1984, *12*, 319–344.

Rinn, R. C., and Markle, A. "Parent Effectiveness Training: A Review." *Psychological Report*, 1977, *41*, 95–109.

Ritvo, E., Shanok, S. S., and Lewis, D. O. "Firesetting and Nonfiresetting Delinquents: A Comparison of Neuropsychiatric, Psychoeducational, Experiential, and Behavioral Characteristics." *Child Psychiatry and Human Development*, 1983, *13*, 259–267.

Roberts, A. R. *Runaways and Non-Runaways in an American Suburb: An Exploratory Study of Adolescent and Parental Coping.* New York: John Jay Press, 1981.

Roberts, M. W. "The Effects of Warned Versus Unwarned Time Out Procedures on Child Noncompliance." *Child and Family Behavior Therapy*, 1984, *4*, 37–54.

Roberts, M. W., Hatzenbuehler, L. C., and Bean, A. W. "The Effects of Differential Attention and Time Out on Child Noncompliance." *Behavior Therapy*, 1981, *12*, 93–99.

Robertson, S. J., Simon, S. J., Pachman, J. S., and Drabman, R. S. "Self-Control and Generalization Procedures in a Classroom of Disruptive Retarded Children." *Child Behavior Therapy*, 1979, *1*, 347–362.

Robin, A. L. "Problem-Solving Communication Training: A Behavioral Approach to the Treatment of Parent-Adolescent Conflict." *American Journal of Family Therapy*, 1979, *7*, 69–82.

Robin, A. L. "Parent-Adolescent Conflict: A Skill-Training Approach." In D. P. Rathjen and J. P. Foreyt (eds.), *Developing Social Competence: Interventions for Children and Adults.* Elmsford, N.Y.: Pergamon Press, 1980.

Robin, A. L. "A Controlled Evaluation of Problem-Solving Communication Training with Parent-Adolescent Conflict." *Behavior Therapy*, 1982, *12*, 593–609.

Robin, A. L., Kent, R., O'Leary, K. D., Foster, S., and Prinz, R. "An Approach to Teaching Parents and Adolescents Problem-Solving Communication Skills: A Preliminary Report." *Behavior Therapy*, 1977, *8*, 639–643.

Robins, L. N. "Epidemiological Approaches to Natural History Research: Antisocial Disorders in Children." *Journal of the American Academy of Child Psychiatry*, 1981, *20*, 556–580.

Robinson, B. E., and Fields, N. H. "Casework with Invulnerable Children." *Social Work*, 1983, *28*, 63–65.

Robinson, R. *Attendance and Absenteeism in California Schools.* Sacramento, Calif.: State Joint Legislative Audit Committee, 1979.

Roff, M., Sells, S. B., and Golden, M. M. *Social Adjustment and Personality Development in Children.* Minneapolis: University of Minnesota Press, 1972.

Romanczyk, R. G., and Goren, E. "Severe Self-Injurious Behavior: The Problem of Clinical Control." *Journal of Consulting and Clinical Psychology*, 1975, *43*, 730–739.

Rosen, H. S., and Rosen, L. A. "Eliminating Stealing: Use of Stimulus Control with an Elementary Student." *Behavior Modification*, 1983, *7*, 56–63.

Rosen, L. W., and Thomas, M. A. "Treatment Technique for Chronic Wrist Cutters." *Journal of Behavior Therapy and Experimental Psychiatry*, 1984, *15*, 33–36.

Rosenbaum, A., and O'Leary, K. D. "Children: The Unintended Victims of Marital Violence." *American Journal of Orthopsychiatry*, 1981a, *51*, 692–699.

Rosenbaum, A., and O'Leary, K. D. "Marital Violence: Characteristics of Abusive Couples." *Journal of Consulting and Clinical Psychology*, 1981b, *49*, 63–71.

Rosenbaum, M., and Baker, E. "Self-Control Behaviors in Hyperactive and Nonhyperactive Children." *Journal of Abnormal Child Psychology*, 1984, *12*, 110–119.

Rosenbaum, P. S. *Peer-Mediated Instruction.* New York: Teachers College Press, 1973.

Rosenheim, M. K. "Some Reflections on Runaways." Unpublished paper, School of Social Service Administration, University of Chicago, 1977.

Ross, A. O. *Child Behavior Therapy: Principles, Procedures, and Empirical Basis.* New York: Wiley, 1981.

Ross, C. "Mobilizing Schools for Suicide Prevention." *Suicide and Life-Threatening Behavior*, 1980, *10*, 239–243.

Ross, C. P. *Suicide in Youth and What You Can Do About It.* Burlingame, Calif.: Suicide Prevention and Crisis Center of San Mateo County, n.d.

Ross, C. P., and Motto, J. A. "Group Counseling for Suicidal

Adolescents." In H. S. Sudak, A. B. Ford, and N. B. Rush-forth (eds.), *Suicide in the Young.* Boston: John Wright/PSG, 1984.

Rowe, J., Cain, H., Hundleby, M., and Keane, A. *Long-Term Foster Care.* New York: St. Martin's Press, 1984.

Ruby, T., and Law, R. "School Dropouts—They Are Not What They Seem to Be." *Children and Youth Services Review,* 1982, *4,* 279–291.

Rueveni, U. *Networking Families in Crises.* New York: Human Science Press, 1979.

Runyan, W. M. *Life Histories and Psychobiography: Explorations in Theory and Method.* New York: Oxford University Press, 1982.

Russell, M. L. "Behavioral Consultation: Theory and Process." *Personnel and Guidance Journal,* 1978, *56,* 346–350.

Russo, E. M., and Shyne, A. W. *Coping with Disruptive Behavior in Group Care.* New York: Child Welfare League of America, 1980.

Rutter, M. "Family, Area, and School Influences in the Genesis of Conduct Disorders." In L. A. Hersov, M. Berger, and D. Shaffer (eds.), *Aggression and Antisocial Behavior in Childhood and Adolescence.* Elmsford, N.Y.: Pergamon Press, 1978.

Rutter, M. "Protective Factors on Children's Responses to Stress and Disadvantage." In M. W. Kent and J. E. Rolf (eds.), *Primary Prevention of Psychopathology.* Vol. 3: *Competence in Children.* Hanover, N.H.: University Press of New England, 1979.

Rutter, M., and Giller, H. *Juvenile Delinquency: Trends and Perspectives.* New York: Guilford, 1984.

Rutter, M., Maugham, B., Mortimore, P., and Ouston, P. *Fifteen Thousand Hours.* Cambridge, Mass.: Harvard University Press, 1979.

Rutter, M., and Schaffer, D. "DSM-III: A Step Forward or Back in Terms of the Classification of Child Psychiatric Disorders?" *Journal of the American Academy of Child Psychiatry,* 1980, *19,* 371–394.

Rutter, M., Tizard, J., and Whitmore, K. (eds.). *Education, Health and Behavior.* Green, N.Y.: Longmans, 1970.

Sadler, O. W., Seyden, T., Howe, B., and Kaminsky, T. "An Evaluation of 'Groups for Parents': A Standardized Format Encompassing Both Behavior Modification and Humanistic Methods." *Journal of Community Psychology*, 1976, *4*, 157–163.

Sagotsky, G., Patterson, C. J., and Lepper, M. R. "Training Children's Self-Control: A Field Experiment in Self-Monitoring and Goal-Setting in the Classroom." *Journal of Experimental Child Psychology*, 1978, *25*, 242–253.

Sajwaj, T., Libet, J., and Agras, S. "Lemon-Juice Therapy: The Control of Life-Threatening Rumination in a Six-Month-Old Infant." *Journal of Applied Behavior Analysis*, 1974, *7*, 557–563.

Salend, S. J., and Allen, E. M. "Comparative Rates of Externally Managed and Self-Managed Response-Cost Systems in Inappropriate Classroom Behavior." *Journal of School Psychology*, 1985, *23*, 59–67.

Salkind, N. J., and Nelson, C. F. "A Note on the Developmental Nature of Reflection-Impulsivity." *Developmental Psychology*, 1980, *3*, 237–238.

Sanders, M. R. "The Generalization of Parents Responding to Community Settings: The Effects of Instructions, Plus Feedback, and Self-Management Training." *Behavioral Psychotherapy*, 1982, *10*, 273–287.

Sanders, M. R., and Glynn, T. "Training Parents in Behavioral Self-Management: An Analysis of Generalization and Maintenance." *Journal of Applied Behavior Analysis*, 1981, *14*, 223–237.

Sandler, I. N. "Social Support Resources, Stress, and Maladjustment of Poor Children." *American Journal of Community Psychology*, 1979, *7*, 425–440.

Sarri, R. "Juvenile Justice." In A. D. Kadushin (ed.), *Child Welfare Strategy in the Coming Years*. Washington, D.C.: Department of Health and Human Services, 1980.

Satir, V. *Conjoint Family Therapy*. (Rev. ed.) Palo Alto, Calif.: Science and Behavior Books, 1967.

Sawin, D. B., and Parke, R. D. "Inconsistent Discipline of Aggression in Young Boys." *Journal of Experimental Child Psychology*, 1979, *28*, 525–538.

Saylor, C. F., Benson, B., and Einhaus, L. "Evaluation of an

Anger Management Program for Aggressive Boys in Inpatient Treatment." *Journal of Child and Adolescent Psychotherapy*, 1985, *2*, 5–15.

Schiller, M. "On the Licensure of Behavioral Health Psychologists." *The Behavior Therapist*, 1985, *8*, 127–128.

Schilling, R. F., Gilchrist, L. D., and Schinke, S. P. "Coping and Social Support in Families of Developmentally Disabled Children." *Family Relations*, 1984, *33*, 47–54.

Schinke, S. P. (ed.). *Behavioral Methods in Social Welfare: Helping Children, Adults, and Families in Community Settings*. Hawthorne, N.Y.: Aldine, 1981.

Schinke, S. P., Gilchrist, L. D., and Snow, W. H. "Skills Intervention to Prevent Cigarette Smoking Among Adolescents." *American Journal of Public Health*, 1985, *75*, 665–667.

Schlichter, K. J., and Horan, J. J. "Effects of Stress Inoculation on the Anger and Aggression Management Skills of Institutionalized Juvenile Delinquents." *Cognitive Therapy and Research*, 1981, *5*, 359–365.

Schmitt, B. D. "School Phobia—The Great Imitator: A Pediatrician's Viewpoint." *Pediatrics*, 1971, *48*, 433–471.

Schnelle, J. F. "A Brief Report on the Invalidity of Parent Evaluation of Behavior Change." *Journal of Applied Behavior Analysis*, 1974, *7*, 341–343.

Schopler, E. "Discussion." *Journal of Autism and Childhood Schizophrenia*, 1978, *8*, 167–169.

Schrader, C., Long, J., Panzer, C., Gillet, D., and Kornblath, R. "An Anger Control Package for Adolescent Drug Abusers." Paper presented at the Annual Meeting of the Association for the Advancement of Behavior Therapy, Atlanta, Ga., Dec. 1977.

Schreibman, L. "Are We Forgetting the Parent in Parent Training?" *The Behavior Therapist*, 1983, *6*, 107–109.

Schumaker, J. B., Hovell, M. F., and Sherman, J. A. *Managing Behavior: A Home-Based School Achievement System*. Lawrence, Kans.: H & H Enterprises, 1977.

Schunk, D. H. "Reward Contingencies and the Development of Children's Skills and Self-Efficacy." *Journal of Educational Psychology*, 1983, *75*, 511–518.

Sewell, T. E., Chandler, M. E., and Smith, R. "Self-Regulation and External Reinforcement in Problem-Solving Strategies of Black Adolescents." *Journal of Clinical Psychology*, 1983, *39*, 39–45.

Seymour, F. W., and Stokes, T. F. "Self-Recording in Training Girls to Increase Work and Evoke Staff Praise in Institution for Offenders." *Journal of Applied Behavior Analysis*, 1976, *9*, 41–54.

Sgroi, S. M. "An Approach to Case Management." In S. M. Sgroi (ed.), *Handbook of Clinical Intervention in Child Sexual Abuse.* Lexington, Mass.: Lexington Books, 1982.

Sgroi, S. M., Blick, L. C., and Porter, F. S. "A Conceptual Framework for Child Sexual Abuse." In S. M. Sgroi (ed.), *Handbook of Clinical Intervention in Child Abuse.* Lexington, Mass.: Lexington Books, 1982.

Shaffer, D., and Fischer, P. "The Epidemiology of Suicide in Children and Young Adolescents." *Journal of the American Academy of Child Psychiatry*, 1981, *20*, 545–565.

Shafii, M., Carrigan, S., Wittinghill, J. R., and Derrick, A. "Psychological Autopsy of Completed Suicide in Children and Adolescents." *American Journal of Psychiatry*, 1985, *142*, 1061–1064.

Shapiro, E. S., McGonigle, J. J., and Ollendick, T. H. "An Analysis of Self-Assessment and Self-Reinforcement in a Self-Managed Token Economy with Mentally Retarded Children." *Journal of Applied Research in Mental Retardation*, 1980, *1*, 227–240.

Shelton, J. L., and Levy, R. L. *Behavioral Assignments and Treatment Compliance.* Champaign, Ill.: Research Press, 1981.

Signell, K. A. "Kindergarten Entry: A Preventative Approach to Community Mental Health." *Community Mental Health Journal*, 1972, *11*, 645–674.

Simonitch, B., and Anderson, J. L. "On Their Own: An Oregon Experiment." *Children Today*, 1979, *8*, 28–31.

Skinner, B. F. *Beyond Freedom and Dignity.* New York: Knopf, 1971.

Skodak, M., and Skeels, H. M. "A Final Follow-Up Study of One Hundred Adopted Children." *Journal of Genetic Psychology*, 1949, *75*, 82–125.

Slavin, R. E. "A Case Study of Psychological Research Affecting Classroom Practice: Student Team Learning." *Elementary School Journal*, 1981, *82*, 5–17.

Sloane, R. B., Staples, F. R., Cristol, A. H., Yorkston, N. J., and Whipple, K. *Psychotherapy Versus Behavior Therapy*. Cambridge, Mass: Harvard University Press, 1975.

Smith, L. K. C., and Fowler, S. A. "Positive Peer Pressure: The Effects of Peer Monitoring on Children's Disruptive Behavior." *Journal of Applied Behavior Analysis*, 1984, *17*, 213–227.

Smith, R. E., and Sharpe, T. M. "Treatment of a School Phobia with Implosive Therapy." *Journal of Consulting and Clinical Psychology*, 1970, *35*, 239–243.

Snowden, L. R. (ed.). *Reaching the Underserved: Mental Health Needs of Neglected Populations*. Beverly Hills, Calif.: Sage, 1982.

Snyder, J. "The Identification of Socially-Skilled Behavior in Children." Paper presented at the Annual Convention of the Association for the Advancement of Behavior Therapy, Los Angeles, Nov. 1982.

Snyder, J. J., and White, M. J. "The Use of Cognitive Self-Instruction in the Treatment of Behaviorally Disturbed Adolescents." *Behavior Therapy*, 1979, *10*, 227–235.

Solomon, M. I., and Murphy, G. E. "Cohort Studies of Suicide." In H. S. Sudak, A. B. Ford, and N. B. Rushforth (eds.), *Suicide in the Young*. Boston: John Wright/PSG, 1984.

Spakes, P. "Mandatory Work Registration for Welfare Parents: A Family Impact Analysis." *Journal of Marriage and the Family*, 1982, *44*, 685–699.

Sparrow, S. S., Balla, D. A., and Chicchetti, D. V. *This Is Your Sampler of the Vineland Adaptive Behavior Scales*. Circle Pines, Minn.: American Guidance Service, 1984.

Speck, R., and Attneave, C. L. *Family Networks*. New York: Random House, 1973.

Spirito, A., Finch, A. J., Jr., Smith, T. L., and Cooley, W. H. "Stress Inoculation for Anger and Anxiety Control: A Case Study with an Emotionally Disturbed Boy." *Journal of Clinical Child Psychology*, 1981, *10*, 67–70.

Spitzer, R. L., and Cantwell, D. P. "The DSM-III Classification of the Psychiatric Disorders of Infancy, Childhood, and

Adolescence." *Journal of the American Academy of Child Psychiatry*, 1980, *19*, 356–370.

Spitzer, R. L., and Endicott, J. *Schedule for Affective Disorders and Schizophrenia (SADS)*. New York: State Psychiatric Institute, 1978.

Spitzer, R. L., Endicott, J., and Robbins, E. "Research Diagnostic Criteria: Rationale and Reliability." *Archives of General Psychiatry*, 1978, *35*, 773–782.

Spivack, G., and Shure, M. B. *Social Adjustment of Young Children*. San Francisco: Jossey-Bass, 1974.

Standards Relating to Noncriminal Misbehavior. Institute of Judicial Administration and American Bar Association, Juvenile Justice Standards Project. Cambridge, Mass.: Ballinger, 1982.

Stanton, M. D., and Todd, T. C. "Engaging 'Resistant' Families in Treatment." *Family Process*, 1981, *20*, 261–293.

Stawar, T. L. "Fable Mod: Operantly Structured Fantasies as an Adjunct in the Modification of Firesetting Behavior." *Journal of Behavior Therapy and Experimental Psychiatry*, 1976, *7*, 285–287.

Steele, M. "Enrolling Community Support." *Journal of Research and Development in Education*, 1978, *11*, 84–94.

Stein, T. J. "Some Ethical Considerations of Short-Term Workshops in the Principles and Methods of Behavior Modification." *Journal of Applied Behavior Analysis*, 1975, *8*, 113–115.

Stein, T. J. *Social Work Practice in Child Welfare*. Englewood Cliffs, N.J.: Prentice-Hall, 1981.

Stein, T. J. "Permanency Planning: A Dialogue." *Social Work*, 1982, *27*, 457–458.

Steinberg, L., Blinde, P. L., and Chan, K. S. "Dropping Out Among Language Minority Youth." *Review of Educational Research*, 1984, *54*, 113–132.

Stewart, M. A., and Culver, K. W. "Children Who Set Fires: The Clinical Picture and a Follow-Up." *American Journal of Psychiatry*, 1982, *140*, 357–363.

Stewart, M. J., and Ray, R. E. "Truants and the Court: A Diversionary Program." *Social Work in Education*, 1984, *6*, 179–192.

Stierlin, H. *Separating Parents and Adolescents: A Perspective on Run-*

ning Away, Schizophrenia, and Waywardness. New York: Quadrangle, 1974.

Stipek, D. J., and Weisz, J. R. "Perceived Personal Control and Academic Achievement." *Review of Educational Research*, 1981, *51*, 101–137.

Stolz, S. B. "Adoption of Innovations from Applied Behavioral Research: 'Does Anybody Care?'" *Journal of Applied Behavior Analysis*, 1981, *14*, 491–505.

Stroebel, C. F., Stroebel, E. L., and Holland, M. *Kiddie QR.* Weathersfield, Conn.: QR Institute, 1980.

Stromer, R. "Remediating Academic Deficiencies in Learning Disabled Children." *Exceptional Children*, 1977, *43*, 432–440.

Strother, D. B. "Homework: Too Much, Just Right, or Not Enough?" *Phi Delta Kappan*, 1984, *65*, 423–426.

Stuart, R. B. "Behavioral Contracting Within the Families of Delinquents." *Journal of Behavior Therapy and Experimental Psychology*, 1971, *2*, 1–11.

Stumphauzer, J. S. "Elimination of Stealing by Self-Reinforcement of Alternative Behavior and Family Contracting." *Journal of Behavioral Therapy and Experimental Psychiatry*, 1976, *7*, 265–268.

Sudak, H. S., Ford, A. B., and Rushforth, N. B. (eds.). *Suicide in the Young.* Boston: John Wright/PSG, 1984.

Sudak, H. S., Sterin, G., and Hauser, H. "Suicide Rate of Callers to a Poison Information Service." *American Journal of Psychiatry*, 1975, *132*, 1212–1214.

Swan, G. E., and MacDonald, M. L. "Behavior Therapy in Practice: A National Survey of Behavior Therapists." *Behavior Therapy*, 1978, *9*, 799–807.

Swanson, L. "Modification of Comprehension Deficits in Learning Disabled Children." *Learning Disability Quarterly*, 1981, *4*, 189–202.

Sweeney-Rader, J., Snyder, G. L., Goldstein, H., and Rosenwald, P. "School Supervision: An In-House Prevention Model." *Children Today*, 1980, *9*, 19–21.

Swenson, C. R. "Using Natural Helping Networks to Promote Competence." In A. N. Maluccio (ed.), *Promoting Competence in Clients: A Newfold Approach to Social Work Practice.* New York: Free Press, 1981.

Switzer, E. B., Deal, T. E., and Bailey, I. S. "The Reduction of Stealing in Second Graders Using a Group Contingency." *Journal of Applied Behavior Analysis*, 1977, *10*, 267–272.

Szykula, S. A., Fleischman, M. J., and Shilton, P. E. "Implementing a Family Therapy Program in a Community: Relevant Issues on One Promising Program for Families in Conflict." *Behavioral Counseling Quarterly*, 1982, *2*, 67–79.

"Teen Suicide: Alarming Trend on the Rise." *National Association of Social Work News*, Apr. 1985, pp. 7–8.

Ten Broeck, E., and Barth, R. P. "Lessons from Implementing a Pilot Permanency Planning Program." *Child Welfare*, in press.

Tharp, R. G., and Wetzel, R. J. *Behavior Modification in the Natural Environment*. Orlando, Fla.: Academic Press, 1969.

Thomas, J., Presland, I., Grant, M., and Glynn, T. "Natural Rates of Teacher Approval and Disapproval in Grade 7 Classrooms." *Journal of Applied Behavior Analysis*, 1978, *11*, 91–94.

Thomlison, R. J. "Implications of Parent Training Research for Behavioral Family Systems Therapy." Paper presented to the Special Interest Group on Social Work at the Annual Meeting of the Association for the Advancement of Behavior Therapy, Los Angeles, Nov. 1982.

Thoresen, K., Thoresen, C., Klein, S., Wilbur, C., Becker-Haven, J., and Haven, W. "Learning House: Helping Troubled Children and the Parents Change Themselves." In J. S. Stumphauzer (ed.), *Progress in Behavior Therapy with Delinquents*. Springfield, Ill.: Thomas, 1979.

Tishler, C. L. "Adolescent Suicides Following Elective Abortion: A Special Anniversary Reaction." *Pediatrics*, 1981, *68*, 670–671.

Tishler, C. L., and McKenry, P. C. "Parental Negative Self and Adolescent Suicide Attempts." *Journal of the American Academy of Child Psychiatry*, 1982, *21*, 404–408.

Tizard, J., Schofield, W. N., and Hewison, J. "Collaboration Between Teachers and Parents in Assisting Children's Reading." *British Journal of Educational Psychology*, 1982, *52*, 1–15.

Torrey, E. F. *Surviving Schizophrenia: A Family Manual*. New York: Harper & Row, 1983.

Trautman, P. D., and Shaffer, D. "Treatment of Child and

Adolescent Suicide Attempters." In H. S. Sudak, A. B. Ford, and N. B. Rushforth (eds.), *Suicide in the Young.* Boston: John Wright/PSG, 1984.

Tuma, J. M., and Pratt, J. M. "Clinical Child Psychology Practice and Training: A Survey." *Journal of Clinical Child Psychology*, 1982, *11*, 27–34.

Tyrer, P., and Tyrer, S. "School Refusal and Adult Neurotic Illness." *Psychological Medicine*, 1974, *4*, 416–421.

Unikel, I. P., and Blanchard, E. B. "Psychopathy, Race, and Delay of Gratification by Adolescent Delinquents." *Journal of Nervous and Mental Disease*, 1973, *156*, 57–60.

U.S. Department of Transportation. *On the Run.* Washington, D.C.: U.S. Department of Transportation, 1980.

University of Wisconsin. *Permanency Planning with an Adolescent* (Film). Madison: School of Social Work, University of Wisconsin, 1980.

Upper, D., and Cautela, J. (eds.). *Covert Conditioning.* Elmsford, N.Y.: Pergamon Press, 1979.

Urbain, E. S., and Kendall, P. C. "Reviews of Social-Cognitive Problem-Solving Interventions with Children." *Psychlogical Bulletin*, 1980, *88*, 109–143.

Valente, S. H. M., and Hatton, C. L. "Bereavement Group for Parents Who Suffered a Suicidal Loss of an Adolescent or Youth." In J. P. Soubrier and J. Vedrinne (eds.), *Depression and Suicide.* Elmsford, N.Y.: Pergamon Press, 1981.

Van Hasselt, V. B., Hersen,, M., Bellack, A. S., Rosenblum, N. D., and Lamparski, D. "Assessment of the Effects of Systematic Desensitization in a Multi-Phobic Child: An Experimental Analysis." *Journal of Behavior Therapy and Experimental Psychiatry*, 1979, *10*, 51–55.

Van Houten, R. *How to Use Reprimands.* Lawrence, Kans.: H & H Enterprises, 1980.

Van Houten, R., Nau, P. A., MacKenzie-Keating, S. E., Sameoto, D., and Colavecchia, B. "An Analysis of Some Variables Influencing the Effectiveness of Reprimands." *Journal of Applied Behavior Analysis*, 1982, *15*, 65–83.

Varley, C. K. "Effects of Methylphenidate in Adolescents with Attention Deficit Disorders." *Journal of the American Academy of Child Psychiatry*, 1983, *22*, 351–354.

Vasta, R., and Brockner, J. "Self-Esteem and Self-Evaluative Covert Statements." *Journal of Consulting and Clinical Psychology*, 1979, *47*, 766–777.

Wachtel, P. L. *Psychoanalysis and Behavior Therapy*. New York: Basic Books, 1977.

Waddell, K. J. "The Self-Concept and Social Adaptation of Hyperactive Children in Adolescence." *Journal of Clinical Child Psychology*, 1984, *13*, 50–55.

Wade, T., Baker, T., and Hartmann, D. "Behavior Therapists' Self-Reported Views and Practices." *Behavior Therapist*, 1979, *2*, 3–6.

Wadsworth, M. *Roots of Delinquency: Infancy, Adolescence, and Crime*. New York: Barnes & Noble, 1979.

Wahler, R. G. "The Insular Mother: Her Problems in Parent-Child Treatment." *Journal of Applied Behavior Analysis*, 1980, *13*, 207–221.

Wahler, R. G., and Dumas, J. E. "Changing the Observational Coding Styles of Insular and Noninsular Mothers: A Step Toward Maintenance of Parent Training Effects." In R. F. Dangel and R. A. Polster (eds.), *Parent Training: Foundations of Research and Practice*. New York: Guilford, 1984.

Wahler, R. G., and Fox, J. J. "Setting Events in Applied Behavioral Analysis: Toward a Conceptual and Methodological Expansion." *Journal of Applied Behavior Analysis*, 1981, *14*, 327–338.

Wahler, R. G., and Graves, M. G. "Setting Events in Social Networks: Ally or Enemy in Child Behavior Therapy?" *Behavior Therapy*, 1983, *14*, 19–36.

Walberg, H. J. "Families as Partners in Educational Productivity." *Phi Delta Kappan*, 1984, *65*, 397–400.

Walker, H. M. *Problem Behavior Identification Checklist*. Los Angeles: Western Psychological Services, 1976.

Walter, H. I., and Gilmore, S. K. "Placebo Versus Social Learning Effects in Parent Training Procedures Designed to Alter the Behavior of Aggressive Boys." *Behavior Therapy*, 1973, *4*, 361–377.

Warner, M. M., Schumaker, J. B., Alley, G. R., and Deshler, D. D. "Learning Disabled Adolescents in the Public Schools: Are They Different from Other Low Achievers?" *Exceptional Education Quarterly*, 1980, *1*, 27–36.

Weathers, L., and Liberman, R. P. "The Family Contracting Exercise." *Journal of Behavior Therapy and Experimental Psychiatry*, 1975, *6*, 208–214.

Webb, E. J., Campbell, D. T., Schwartz, R. D., Sechrest, L., and Grove, J. B. *Nonreactive Measures in the Social Sciences*. (Rev. ed.) Boston: Houghton Mifflin, 1981.

Wechsler, D. *Manual for the Wechsler Intelligence Scale for Children— Revised*. New York: Psychological Corporation, 1974.

Weil, M., Karls, J. M., and Associates. *Case Management in Human Service Practice*. San Francisco: Jossey-Bass, 1985.

Weinrott, M. R., Corson, J. A., and Wilchesky, M. "Teacher-Mediated Treatment of Social Isolation." *Behavior Therapy*, 1979, *10*, 281–294.

Weintraub, S., Prinz, R. J., and Neale, J. M. "Peer Evaluations of the Competence of Children Vulnerable to Psychopathology." *Journal of Abnormal Child Psychology*, 1978, *6*, 461–473.

Weisner, S., and Silver, M. "Community Work and Social Learning Theory." *Social Work*, 1981, *26*, 146–150.

Weissman, A. "Industrial Social Services: Linkage Technology." *Social Casework*, 1976, *57*, 50–54.

Welch, G. J. "Will Graduates Use Single Subject Designs to Evaluate Their Casework Practice?" *Journal of Education for Social Work*, 1983, *19*, 42–47.

Wells, C. F., and Stuart, I. R. (eds.). *Self-Destructive Behavior in Children and Adolescents*. New York: Van Nostrand Reinhold, 1981.

Wells, K. C., Conners, C. K., Imber, L., and Delamater, A. "Use of Single-Subject Methodology in Clinical Decision-Making with Hyperactive Children on the Psychiatric Inpatient Unit." *Behavioral Assessment*, 1981, *3*, 359–369.

Wells, K. C., Griest, D. L., and Forehand, R. "The Use of a Self-Control Package to Enhance Temporal Generality of a Parent Training Program." *Behavior Research and Therapy*, 1980, *18*, 347–358.

Wells, R. A. "The Empirical Base of Family Therapy: Practice Implications." In E. R. Tolson and W. J. Reid (eds.), *Models of Family Treatment*. New York: Columbia University Press, 1981.

Welsh, R. S. "The Use of Stimulus Satiation in the Elimination of Juvenile Firesetting Behavior." In A. M. Graziano (ed.), *Behavior Therapy with Children*. Hawthorne, N.Y.: Aldine, 1971.

Werry, J. S., and Aman, M. G. "Methylphenidate and Haloperidol in Children: Effects on Attention, Memory, and Activity." *Archives of General Psychiatry*, 1975, *32*, 790–795.

West, D. J., and Farrington, D. P. *The Delinquent Way of Life*. London: Heinemann Educational Publishers, 1977.

Wetzel, R. "Use of Behavioral Techniques in a Case of Compulsive Stealing." In A. M. Graziano (ed.), *Behavior Therapy with Children*. Hawthorne, N. Y.: Aldine, 1971.

Whalen, C. K. "Hyperactivity, Learning Problems, and the Attention Deficit Disorders." In T. H. Ollendick and M. Hersen (eds.), *Handbook of Child Psychopathology*. New York: Plenum, 1983.

Whan, M. "Tricks of the Trade: Questionable Theory and Practice in Family Therapy." *British Journal of Social Work*, 1983, *13*, 321–337.

White, R. W. "Competence as an Aspect of Personal Growth." In M. W. Kent and J. E. Rolf (eds.), *Primary Prevention of Psychopathology*. Vol. 3: *Competence in Children*. Hanover, N.H.: University Press of New England, 1979.

Whitman, T., Burgio, L., and Johnston, M. B. "Cognitive Behavioral Interventions with Mentally Retarded Children." In A. W. Meyers and W. E. Craighead (eds.), *Cognitive Behavior Therapy with Children*. New York: Plenum, 1984.

Whitman, T. L., Scibak, J. W., Butler, K. M., Richter, R., and Johnson, M. R. "Improving Classroom Behavior in Mentally Retarded Children Through Correspondence Training." *Journal of Applied Behavior Analysis*, 1982, *15*, 545–564.

Whittaker, J. K. "Causes of Childhood Disorders." *Social Work*, 1976, *21*, 91–96.

Whittaker, J. K. "Mutual Helping in Human Service Practice." In J. K. Whittaker, J. Garbarino, and Associates, *Social Support Networks: Informal Helping in the Human Services*. Hawthorne, N.Y.: Aldine, 1983.

Whittaker, J. K., Garbarino, J., and Associates. *Social Support*

Networks: Informal Helping in the Human Services. Hawthorne, N.Y.: Aldine, 1983.

Wicks, R. J. "Suicidal Manipulators in the Penal Setting." *Chitty's Law Journal*, 1974, *22*, 249–250.

Williams, C. A., and Forehand, R. "An Examination of Predictor Variables for Child Compliance and Noncompliance." *Journal of Abnormal Child Psychology*, 1984, *12*, 491–504.

Wilson, D. R., and Lyman, R. D. "Time Out in the Treatment of Childhood Behavior." *Child and Family Behavior Therapy*, 1982, *4*, 5–20.

Wiltse, K. T., and Remy, L. L. *Conceptual Statement on Case Management for Family and Children's Services.* Mill Valley, Calif.: Loring Associates, 1982.

Wispe, L. (ed.). *Altruism, Sympathy, and Helping: Psychological and Sociological Principles.* Orlando, Fla.: Academic Press, 1978.

Witt, J. C., and Elliott, S. N. "The Response Cost Lottery: A Time Effective and Efficient Classroom Intervention." *Journal of School Psychology*, 1982, *20*, 155–161.

Witt, J. C., and Elliott, S. N. "Acceptability of Classroom Management Strategies." In T. R. Kratochwill (ed.), *Advances in School Psychology.* Hillsdale, N.J.: Erlbaum, 1985.

Witt, J. C., Elliott, S. N., and Marstens, B. K. "Acceptability of Behavioral Interventions Used in Classrooms: The Influence of Teacher Time, Severity of Behavior Problem, and Type of Intervention." *Behavioral Disorders*, 1984, *10*, 95–104.

Wodarski, J. S. "Group Reward Structures in the Classroom." *Social Work in Education*, 1981, *3*, 45–61.

Wolf, M. M. "Social Validity: The Case for Subjective Measurement or How Applied Behavior Analysis Is Finding Its Heart." *Journal of Applied Behavior Analysis*, 1978, *11*, 203–214.

Wolfe, D., Kaufman, K., Aragona, J., and Sandler, J. *The Child Management Program for Abusive Parents: Procedures for Developing a Child Abuse Intervention Program.* Winter Park, Fla.: Anna Publishing, 1981.

Wolfe, D. A., St. Lawrence, J., Graves, K., Brehony, K., Bradlyn, D., and Kelly, J. A. "Intensive Behavioral Parent Training for a Child Abusive Mother." *Behavior Therapy*, 1982, *13*, 438–451.

Wolff, R. "Satiation in the Treatment of Inappropriate Fire-Setting." *Journal of Behavior Therapy and Experimental Psychiatry*, 1984, *15*, 337–340.

Wolins, M., and Wozner, Y. *Revitalizing Residential Settings*. San Francisco: Jossey-Bass, 1982.

Wolk, S., and Brandon, J. "Runaway Adolescents' Perceptions of Parents and Self." *Adolescence*, 1977, *12*, 175–188.

Wood, R., and Flynn, J. M. "A Self-Evaluation Token System vs. an External Evaluation Token System Alone in a Residential Setting with Predelinquent Youth." *Journal of Applied Behavior Analysis*, 1978, *11*, 503–512.

Wooden, W. S. "Arson Is Epidemic—And Spreading like Wildfire." *Psychology Today*, 1985, *19*, 23–28.

Wooden, W. S., and Berkey, M. L. *How to Deal with Children and Arson*. New York: Plenum, 1984.

Woolfolk, A., Woolfolk, R., and Wilson, G. T. "A Rose by Any Other Name . . . : Labeling Bias and Attitude Toward Behavior Modification." *Journal of Consulting and Clinical Psychology*, 1977, *45*, 184–191.

Yates, B. T. "Therapy for Human Service Systems: Five Basic Steps for Measuring and Improving Cost-Effectiveness." In A. J. McSweeney, W. J. Fremouw, and R. P. Hawkins (eds.), *Practical Program Evaluation in Youth Treatment*. Springfield, Ill.: Thomas, 1982.

York, P., and York, D. *Toughlove: A Self-Help Manual for Parents Troubled by Teenage Behavior*. Sellersville, Pa.: Community Service Foundations, 1980.

Yudin, L. W., Ring, S. I., Nowakiwska, M., and Heinemann, S. H. "School Dropout or College Bound: Study in Contrast." *Journal of Educational Research*, 1973, *67*, 87–93.

Zich, J. M. "A Reciprocal Control Approach to the Treatment of Repeated Parasuicide." *Suicide and Life-Threatening Behavior*, 1984, *14*, 36–51.

Ziesemer, C. "Student and Staff Perceptions of Truancy and Court Referrals." *Social Work in Education*, 1984, *6* (3), 167–178.

Zimmerman, B. J., and Ringle, J. "Effects of Model Persistence and Statements of Confidence on Children's Self-Efficacy and Problem Solving." *Journal of Educational Psychology*, 1981, *73*, 485–493.

Name Index

510

Subject Index

A

AA. *See* Alcoholics Anonymous (AA)
Achievement Place, 25, 369
ADD. *See* Attention Deficit Disorder (ADD)
Adolescence: correction potential in, 28
AFDC. *See* Aid to Families with Dependent Children (AFDC)
Age: and use of contracts, 172–173
Aggression: assessment of, 193–197; case study of, 192–193, 197–198, 219–222; cognitive interventions with, 212–218; development of, 189–192; family and child background of, 188–189; how a caregiver and child teach (table), 191; personalized checklist for (exhibit), 197; physical interventions with, 218–219; prediction of, in adults, 187–188; social interventions with, 199–212; and social support, 222
Aid to Families with Dependent Children (AFDC), 25
Al-anon, 25
Ala-teen, 112
Alcoholics Anonymous (AA), 25
American Psychiatric Association, 70, 187, 444
American Psychological Association, 432, 444

Anger: control of, 213–216; expression of, 218–219
Anger Inventory, 214
Arousal management, 20
Association of Retarded Citizens, 25
Attention Deficit Disorder (ADD), 259–260
Autism, 29

B

Barb technique: with aggression, 207–208
Beck Depression Inventory (BDI), 414
Bed-wetting, 27; choosing intervention strategy for, 73
Behavior: decreasing undesirable, 156–171; increasing desirable, 149–156
Behavior, aggressive. *See* Aggression
Behavior, suicidal. *See* Suicide Beliefs: and choice of intervention strategy, 74; culturally shaped (table), 24
Berkeley Planning Associates, 362, 372, 449

C

Caregiver(s): as child helpers, 114–121; collaboration with, with underachievement in school, 285–289; handout to help, define stealing, 310;

525